Stand Out
Lesson
Planner

Staci Lyn Sabbagh

Rob Jenkins

THOMSON

HEINLE

Australia • Canada • Mexico • Singapore • Spain • United Kingdom • United States

THOMSON

HEINLE

Stand Out 4

Lesson Planner

Staci Lyn Sabbagh and Rob Jenkins

Acquisitions Editor
Sherrise Roehr

Managing Editor
James W. Brown

Senior Developmental Editor
Ingrid Wisniewska

Developmental Editor
Sarah Barnicle

Editorial Assistant
Audra Longert

Contributing Editor
Alfred Meyer

Marketing Manager
Eric Bredenberg

Director, Global ESL Training & Development
Evelyn Nelson

Production Editor
Jeff Freeland

Senior Manufacturing Coordinator
Mary Beth Hennebury

Photo Researcher
Sheri Blaney

Compositor
TSI Graphics

Text Printer/Binder
Banta

Cover Printer
Phoenix Color Corporation

Designers
Elise Kaiser
Julia Gecha

Cover Designer
Gina Petti

Illustrators
James Edwards represented by Sheryl Beranbaum
Vilma Ortiz-Dillon
Michael DiGiorgio

Cover Art
Diana Ong/SuperStock

CREDITS

PHOTO CREDITS

Page v: Courtney Sabbagh

Unit 1:
Page 1: left: Dion Ogust/The Image Works; right: David Young-Wolff/Photo Edit
Page 3: top: Dean Berry/Index Stock Imagery; bottom: Grantpix/Index Stock Imagery
Page 6: Bill Lai/Index Stock Imagery
Page 9: top left: Bill Lai/Index Stock Imagery; center: Myrleen Cate/Index Stock Imagery; bottom left: Benelux Press/Index Stock Imagery; bottom right: David Young-Wolff/Photo Edit
Page 12: left: Jeff Greenberg/Photo Edit; center: Jeff Dunn/Index Stock Imagery; right: Comstock RF
Page 13 Myrleen Cate/Photo Edit

Unit 2:
Page 24: top: Comstock RF; 2nd from top: Jean Coughlin; 3rd from top: Comstock RF; bottom: Jean Coughlin
Page 26: Michael Keller/Index Stock Imagery

Unit 3:
Page 41: left: Gay Bumgarner/Index Stock Imagery; center: Carl/Joan Vanderschuit/Index Stock Imagery; right: Omni Photo Communications/Index Stock Imagery
Page 43: top: Carl/Joan Vanderschuit/Index Stock Imagery; bottom: Omni Photo Communications/Index Stock Imagery
Page 47: left: John Connell/Index Stock Imagery; center left: Wendell Metzen/Index Stock Imagery; center right: John Connell/Index Stock Imagery; right: Gay Bumgarner/Index Stock Imagery
Page 57: top left: Wendell Metzen/Index Stock Imagery; center: John Connell/Index Stock Imagery; bottom left: Gay Bumgarner/Index Stock Imagery

Unit 4:
Page 63: Bill Aron/Photo Edit
Page 75: top: Robert Ginn/Index Stock Imagery; 2nd from top: Thomas Craig/Index Stock Imagery; 3rd from top: Diaphor/Index Stock Imagery; bottom: Jeff Greenberg/Photo Edit

Unit 5:
Page 81: left: Myrleen Cate/Index Stock Imagery; center left: Steve Dunwell/Index Stock Imagery; center right: Chip Henderson/Index Stock Imagery; right: David Young-Wolff/Photo Edit

Unit 6:
Page 102: top: Digital Vision RF/Picture Quest; 2nd from top: Jeff Greenberg/Photo Edit; 3rd from top: Scott Witte/Index Stock Imagery; bottom: Diaphor Agency/Index Stock Imagery
Page 105: Richard Lord/The Image Works
Page 107: Spencer Grant/Photo Edit
Page 114: Spencer Grant/Photo Edit

Unit 7:
Page 122: left: Michelle D. Bridwell/Photo Edit; right: Myrleen Ferguson Cate/Photo Edit
Page 125: Dana White/Photo Edit
Page 135: Michael Newman/Photo Edit
Page 145: John Neubauer/Photo Edit

Unit 8:
Page 152: top left: Asami Haseqawa/Index Stock Imagery; top right: Jose Azel/AURORA; bottom left: David Rosenberg/Index Stock Imagery; bottom right: Spencer Ainsley/The Image Works
Page 154: top: Rob Bartee/Index Stock Imagery; center: Larry George/Index Stock Imagery; bottom: Peter Walton/Index Stock Imagery
Page 155: Peter Walton/Index Stock Imagery

TEXT CREDITS

Pages 17, 58, and 96: Special thanks to Kate Kinsella of San Francisco State University for permission to use her ideas on vocabulary cards and tips for writing summaries.
Page 23: Information on how to be a smart consumer adapted from www.ftc.gov, web site of the Federal Trade Commission.
Page 28: Article on how to choose a credit card adapted with permission from www.creditcardmenu.com, a service of Gromco Inc.
Pages 53 and 54: Statistics on Homeownership in the United States from U.S. Census Bureau, Current Population Survey.
Page 68: Information on public library services adapted with permission from Coronado Public Library, Coronado CA.
Page 88: Medical insurance application adapted with permission from Allen Insurance, http://www.allenins.com
Page 91: Text on reading nutrition labels adapted with permission from Physicians Wellness Network Ltd. (PWNLTD.com).
Page 94: Article on the common cold adapted from information prepared by The National Institute of Allergy and Infectious Diseases, National Institute of Health, U.S. Department of Health and Human Services, www.niaid.nih.gov/factsheets/cold.htm
Page 132: Article on 'How to Ask for a Raise' adapted with permission from Business and Professional Women/USA, http://www.bpwusa.org.
Page 146: Jury summons adapted with permission from Metropolitan Government of Nashville & Davidson County, www.nashville.gov
Pages 147 and 148: Income tax forms from The Internal Revenue Service, Department of the Treasury
Lesson Planner page 178, Suggestions for Computer Use adapted with permission from Susan Gaer and "The Web Rangers." (unpublished work)

The authors and publisher would like to thank the following reviewers, consultants, and participants in focus groups:

Elizabeth Aderman
New York City Board of Education, New York, NY

Sharon Baker
Roseville Adult School, Roseville, CA

Shannon Bailey
Austin Community College, Austin, TX

Lillian Barredo
Stockton School for Adults, Stockton, CA

Linda Boice
Elk Grove Adult Education, Elk Grove, CA

Rose Cantu
John Jay High School Adult Education, San Antonio, TX

Toni Chapralis
Fremont School for Adults, Sacramento, CA

Melanie Chitwood
Miami-Dade Community College, Miami, FL

Geri Creamer
Stockton School for Adults, Stockton, CA

Irene Dennis
San Antonio College, San Antonio, TX

Eileen Duffell
P.S. 64, New York, NY

Nancy Dunlap
Northside Independent School District, San Antonio, TX

Gloria Eriksson
Old Marshall Adult Education Center, Sacramento, CA

Marti Estrin
Santa Rosa Junior College, Santa Rosa, CA

Judith Finkelstein
Reseda Community Adult School, Reseda, CA

Lawrence Fish
Shorefront YM-YWHA English Language Program, Brooklyn, NY

Victoria Florit
Miami-Dade Community College, Miami, FL

Kathleen Flynn
Glendale Community College, Glendale, CA

Rhoda Gilbert
New York City Board of Education, New York, NY

Kathleen Jimenez
Miami-Dade Community College, Miami, FL

Nancy Jordan
John Jay High School Adult Education, San Antonio, TX

Renee Klosz
Lindsey Hopkins Technical Education Center, Miami, FL

David Lauter
Stockton School for Adults, Stockton, CA

Patricia Long
Old Marshall Adult Education Center, Sacramento, CA

Maria Miranda
Lindsey Hopkins Technical Education Center, Miami, FL

Karen Moore
Stockton School for Adults, Stockton, CA

Erin Nyhan
Triton College, Chicago, IL

Marta Pitt
Lindsey Hopkins Technical Education Center, Miami, FL

Sylvia Rambach
Stockton School for Adults, Stockton, CA

Myra Redman
Miami-Dade Community College, Miami, FL

Charleen Richardson
San Antonio College, San Antonio, TX

Eric Rosenbaum
Bronx Community College, New York, NY

Laura Rowley
Old Marshall Adult Education Center, Sacramento, CA

Sr. M. B. Theresa Spittle
Stockton School for Adults, Stockton, CA

Andre Sutton
Belmont Adult School, Belmont, CA

Jennifer Swoyer
Northside Independent School District, San Antonio, TX

Claire Valier
Palm Beach County School District, West Palm Beach, FL

The authors would like to thank Joel and Rosanne for believing in us, Eric for seeing our vision, Nancy and Sherrise for going to bat for us, and Jim, Ingrid, and Sarah for making the book a reality.

Rob Jenkins

Staci Lyn Sabbagh

I love teaching. I love to see the expressions on my students' faces when the light goes on and their eyes show such sincere joy of learning. I knew the first time I stepped into an ESL classroom that this was where I needed to be and I have never questioned that resolution. I have worked in business, sales, and publishing, and I've found challenge in all, but nothing can compare to the satisfaction of reaching people in such a personal way.

Thanks to my family who have put up with late hours and early mornings, my friends at church who support me, and everyone at Santa Ana College, School of Continuing Education who believe in me and are a source of tremendous inspiration.

Ever since I can remember, I've been fascinated with other cultures and languages. I love to travel and every place I go, the first thing I want to do is meet the people, learn their language, and understand their culture. Becoming an ESL teacher was a perfect way to turn what I love to do into my profession. There's nothing more incredible than the exchange of teaching and learning from one another that goes on in an ESL classroom. And there's nothing more rewarding than helping a student succeed.

I would especially like to thank Mom, Dad, CJ, Tete, Eric, my close friends and my Santa Ana College, School of Continuing Education family. Your love and support inspired me to do something I never imagined I could. And Rob, thank you for trusting me to be part of such an amazing project.

We are lesson plan enthusiasts! We have learned that good lesson planning makes for effective teaching and, more importantly, good learning. We also believe that learning is stimulated by task-oriented activities in which students find themselves critically laboring over decisions and negotiating meaning from their own personal perspectives.

The need to write **Stand Out** came to us as we were leading a series of teacher workshops on project-based simulations designed to help students apply what they have learned. We began to teach lesson planning within our workshops in order to help teachers see how they could incorporate the activities more effectively. Even though teachers showed great interest in both the projects and planning, they often complained that lesson planning took too much time that they simply didn't have. Another obstacle was that the books available to the instructors were not conducive to planning lessons.

We decided to write our own materials by first writing lesson plans that met specific student-performance objectives. Then we developed the student pages that were needed to make the lesson plans work in the classroom. The student book only came together after the plans! Writing over 300 lesson plans has been a tremendous challenge and has helped us evaluate our own teaching and approach. It is our hope that others will discover the benefits of always following a plan in the classroom and incorporating the strategies we have included in these materials.

ABOUT THE SERIES

The *STAND OUT* series is designed to facilitate *active* learning while challenging students to build a nurturing and effective learning community.

Stand Out Book 4 is divided into eight distinct units mirroring competency areas most useful to newcomers. These areas are outlined in CASAS assessment programs and different state model standards for adults. Each unit is then divided into eight lessons and a team project activity. Lessons are driven by performance objectives and are filled with challenging activities that progress from teacher-presented to student-centered tasks.

USER QUESTIONS ABOUT *STAND OUT*

• **What are SCANS and EFF and how are they integrated into the book?**
SCANS is the **S**ecretary's **C**ommission on **A**cquiring **N**ecessary **S**kills. **SCANS** was developed to encourage students to prepare for the workplace. The standards developed through **SCANS** have been incorporated throughout the *STAND OUT* student books and their components.

STAND OUT addresses **SCANS** a little differently than other books. **SCANS** standards elicit effective teaching strategies by incorporating essential skills such as critical thinking and group work. We have incorporated **SCANS** standards in every lesson, not isolating these standards to the work unit as is typically found.

EFF, or **E**quipped **f**or the **F**uture, is another set of standards established to address students' roles as parents, workers, and citizens with a vision of student literacy and lifelong learning. *STAND OUT* addresses these standards and integrates them into the materials similarly to **SCANS**.

• **What about CASAS?**
The federal government has mandated that states show student outcomes as a prerequisite to funding. Some states have incorporated the **C**omprehensive **A**dult **S**tudent **A**ssessment **S**ystem (**CASAS**) testing to standardize agency reporting. Unfortunately, many of our students are unfamiliar with standardized testing and struggle with it, so adult schools need to develop lesson plans to address specific concerns. *STAND OUT* was developed with careful attention to **CASAS** skill areas in most lessons and performance objectives.

• **Are the tasks too challenging for my students?**
Students learn by doing and learn more when challenged. *STAND OUT* provides tasks that encourage critical thinking in a variety of ways. The tasks in each lesson move from teacher-directed to student-centered so the learner clearly understands what's expected and is willing to "take a risk." The lessons are expected to be challenging; when students work together as a learning community, anything becomes possible. The satisfaction of accomplishing something both as an individual and as a member of a team results in greater confidence and effective learning.

• **Do I need to understand lesson planning to teach from the student book?**
If you don't understand lesson planning when you start, you will when you finish! Teaching from *STAND OUT* is like a course on lesson planning, especially if you use the *Stand Out Lesson Planner* on a daily basis.

STAND OUT does *stand out* from other series because, in the writing of this text, performance objectives were first established for each lesson. Then lesson plans were designed, followed by the student book pages. The introduction to each lesson varies because different objectives demand different approaches. *STAND OUT's* variety of tasks makes learning more interesting for the students.

• **What are team project activities?**

The final lesson of each unit is a **team project.** The project is often a team simulation that incorporates the objectives of the unit and provides an additional opportunity for students to actively apply what they have learned. The project allows students to produce something that represents their progress in learning. These end-of-unit projects were created with a variety of learning styles and individual skills in mind. While the projects can be skipped or simplified, we encourage instructors to implement them as presented, enriching the overall student experience.

• **Is this a grammar-based or a competency-based series?**

This is a competency-based series with grammar identified more clearly and more boldly than in other similar series. We believe that grammar instruction in context is extremely important. In *Stand Out Book 4,* different structures are identified as principle objectives in 16 lessons. Students are first given a context incorporating the grammar, followed by an explanation and practice. In level four, we expect students to acquire the language structure after hearing and reading grammar in useful contexts. For teachers who want to enhance grammar instruction, the *Activity Bank 4 CD-ROM* and/or the *Stand Out Grammar Challenge 4* workbook will provide ample opportunities.

The six competencies that drive ***STAND OUT*** are basic communication, consumer economics, community resources, health, occupational knowledge, and lifelong learning. (The unit on government and law replaces lifelong learning in Books 3 and 4.)

• **Are there enough activities so I don't have to supplement?**

STAND OUT stands alone in providing 231 hours of instruction and activities, even without the additional suggestions of the *Lesson Planner.* The *Lesson Planner* also shows you how to streamline lessons to provide 115 hours of class work and still have thorough lessons if you meet less often. When supplementing with the *Activity Bank 4 CD-ROM,* the *Stand Out* ExamView® Pro *Test Bank,* and the *Stand Out Grammar Challenge 4* workbook, you gain unlimited opportunities to extend class hours and continue to provide activities related directly to each lesson objective. Calculate how many hours your class meets in a semester and look to ***STAND OUT*** to address the full class experience.

THE *LESSON PLANNER*

The *Stand Out Lesson Planner* replicates the student book in full color with 77 complete lesson plans, taking the instructor through each stage of a lesson, from warm-up and review through application. The *Lesson Planner* is a new and innovative approach. As many seasoned teachers know, good lesson planning can make a substantial difference in the classroom. Students continue coming to class, understanding, applying, and remembering more of what they learn. They are more confident in their learning when good lesson planning techniques are incorporated.

Each lesson is written in the following lesson plan format. All of the lessons have three practices that help extend the lesson for longer class periods and for students who may need more practice with the same objective(s).

1. Warm-up and review

Use previously learned content and materials that are familiar to students from previous lessons to begin a lesson.

2. Introduction

Begin focusing the students' attention on the lesson by asking questions, showing visuals, telling a story, etc. State the objective of the lesson and tell students what they will be doing. The objective should address what you expect students to be able to do by the end of the lesson.

3. Presentation

Introduce new information to the students through visuals, realia, description, explanation, or written text. Check on students' comprehension.

4. Practice

Have students practice what they have just learned through different activities. These activities can be done as a class, in small groups, pairs, or individually. The practice is guided through materials. Model each activity, monitor progress, and provide feedback.

5. Evaluation

Evaluate students on attainment of the objective. This can be oral, written, or by demonstrated performance.

6. Application

Students apply new knowledge to their own lives or new situations.

HOW TO USE THE *LESSON PLANNER*

Each lesson plan page is placed next to the *Stand Out 4 Student Book* page for easy reference. In your *Lesson Planner,* the answers to the *Student Book* exercises are filled in on the student pages.

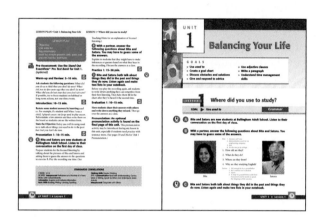

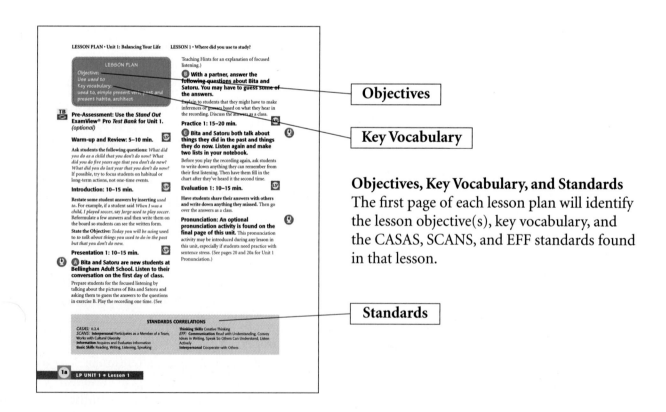

Objectives

Key Vocabulary

Objectives, Key Vocabulary, and Standards
The first page of each lesson plan will identify the lesson objective(s), key vocabulary, and the CASAS, SCANS, and EFF standards found in that lesson.

Standards

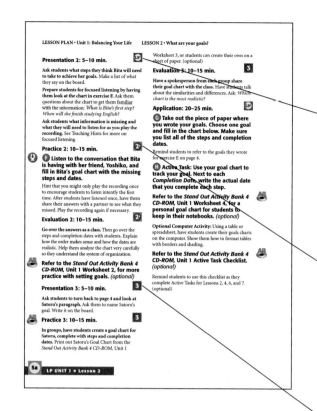

Class Length

The lesson planner includes lessons for classes that are from one and a half hours in length up to three hours in length.

Instructors who teach one and one half hour classes should follow the steps of the lesson plan next to these icons. There may be additional exercises in the *Stand Out Student Book* or activities on the *Activity Bank CD-ROM* that you don't have time for in class, but those exercises can be assigned for homework.

Instructors who teach two-hour classes should follow the steps of the lesson plan next to these icons. Again, there may be some additional exercises in the *Student Book* or activities on the *Activity Bank CD-ROM* that you don't have time for in class, but these exercises can be assigned for homework.

Instructors who teach three-hour classes should follow the steps of the lesson plan next to these icons. Sufficient activities are available for homework.

SUPPLEMENTAL MATERIALS

- **The *Stand Out Activity Bank CD-ROM*** contains supplemental listening, grammar, reading, and writing activities, as well as project sheets. These activities are all presented in Word format and can be downloaded and modified to meet the needs of your class. If you see this icon in a lesson plan, it indicates that there is an additional activity worksheet or template that you can print out to use with your students.

- **How do I use the *Activity Bank CD-ROM*?**
To use the *Stand Out Activity Bank,* put the CD-ROM into your computer and open it. Find the folder for the unit you are working on and open it. Inside you will see all of the worksheets for that unit. (There is a Table of Contents that gives you a brief description of each activity.) Open the file you want and customize it for your class. Save the file on your computer's hard drive or on a disk or CD and print it out. All the worksheets are reproducible and modifiable, so make as many copies as you want!

- **What are some ways I can modify the activities and worksheets in the *Activity Bank*?**

-Change items in supplemental vocabulary, grammar, and life skills activities;
-Personalize activities with student names and popular locations in your area;
-Extend every lesson with additional practice where you feel it is most needed.

- **Listening Components:** The main listening scripts are found in the back of the *Stand Out Student Book.* Teachers will find all listening scripts in the *Lesson Planner.* Cassette tapes and audio CD-ROMs are available for all main listening activities described in the *Stand Out Student Book.* The recordings for the supplemental listenings can only be found on the *Activity Bank CD-ROM.*

- ***Stand Out Grammar Challenge 4*** is a workbook that offers further grammar explanation and challenging practice. While incorporating the same contexts and vocabulary studied in the *Stand Out 4 Student Book,* the *Grammar Challenge 4* workbook complements all the grammar objectives taught. Additional grammar challenges reinforce structures passively introduced throughout the *Student Book.*

- ***Stand Out* ExamView® Pro *Test Bank CD-ROM*** allows teachers to customize pre-tests and post-tests for each unit as well as a pre-tests and post-tests for the whole book. The *ExamView®Pro* is an easy-to-use, innovative test bank system. Each unit has a set of test questions from which unit quizzes can be generated.

- **How can teachers create tests using the *Stand Out* ExamView® Pro *Test Bank CD-ROM?*** In order to compose a test, teachers indicate the number of questions that they want. They either can have questions randomly selected or they can select the questions themselves. Teachers can further customize quizzes by combining questions from the *Test Bank* with original, teacher-generated questions. They can then simply print out the pre-formatted quiz for the students to take a traditional paper and pencil test. The *Stand Out* ExamView® Pro *Test Bank CD-ROM* also allows the test to be administered by computer. It can even be administered on-line with automatic scoring. When the test is given on-line, the test results can be automatically e-mailed to the instructor!

- **What types of questions appear in the ExamView® Pro *Test Bank?*** The tests and quizzes give students practice with a number of different question types including multiple choice, true/false, completion, yes/no, numeric response, and matching. For students who need more practice with CASAS testing, the first group of questions in each test bank are CASAS-style questions, and there is a CASAS-style answer sheet on the *Activity Bank 4 CD-ROM.*

STAND OUT **is a comprehensive approach to adult language learning, meeting needs of students and instructors completely and effectively.**

LESSON PLANNER CONTENTS

STUDENT BOOK CONTENTS

EFF	SCANS (Workplace)	Academic/Math	CASAS
Most EFF skills are incorporated into this unit, with an emphasis on: • Taking responsibility for learning • Reflecting and evaluating • Conveying ideas in writing (Technology is optional.)	Most SCANS are incorporated into this unit, with an emphasis on: • Monitoring and correcting performance • Sociability • Speaking (Technology is optional.)	ACADEMIC • Discuss learning strategies • Edit a paragraph • Identify parts of a paragraph • Write a paragraph • Plan educational goals	**1:** 0.1.4, 0.2.1, 0.2.2, 0.2.4, 7.1.1, 7.2.1 **2:** 0.1.2, 4.8.1, 6.1.1, 6.7.2, 7.4.1, 7.4.9 **3:** 7.1.1 **4:** 7.2.4, 7.4.1, 7.4.3, 7.4.5
Most EFF skills are incorporated into this unit, with an emphasis on: • Taking responsibility for learning • Reflecting and evaluating • Solving problems and making decisions • Planning (Technology is optional.)	Most SCANS are incorporated into this unit, with an emphasis on: • Responsibility • Self-Management • Decision making • Problem solving • Seeing things in the mind's eye (Technology is optional.)	ACADEMIC • Use context to work out meaning of new words • Create a goal chart and estimate time needed for different goals • Write a paragraph • Identify main ideas in an article • Make vocabulary cards MATH • Create a cluster diagram	**1:** 0.2.4 **2:** 7.1.1, 7.1.2, 7.1.3, 7.1.4, 7.2.4 **3:** 7.2.7, 7.3.2 **4:** 7.2.5, 7.2.7 **5:** 7.2.1, 7.2.2 **6:** 7.2.6 **7:** 7.1.2, 7.2.1, 7.2.4 **R:** 7.1.4, 7.2.1, 7.4.1, 7.4.2 **TP:** 4.8.1, 4.8.5, 4.8.6
Most EFF skills are incorporated into this unit, with an emphasis on: • Learning through research • Using mathematics in problem solving and communication • Planning (Technology is optional.)	Most SCANS are incorporated into this unit, with an emphasis on: • Allocating money • Understanding systems • Acquiring and evaluating information • Decision making (Technology is optional.)	ACADEMIC • Understand main ideas in an article • Organize information in a chart • Write a business letter MATH • Use addition and subtraction to calculate monthly budgeted and actual expenses • Make a budget • Compare prices, fees, and other numerical data	**1:** 1.5.1, 6.1.1, 6.1.2 **2:** 1.2.5 **3:** 7.2.2, 7.2.7 **4:** 1.2.5, 1.3.1, 1.3.2, 1.3.3 **5:** 1.3.1, 1.4.6, 1.5.2 **6:** 1.2.1, 1.2.2 **7:** 1.6.3 **R:** 7.1.4, 7.2.1, 7.4.1, 7.4.2 **TP:** 1.5.2, 4.8.1, 4.8.5, 4.8.6
Most EFF skills are incorporated into this unit, with an emphasis on: • Learning through research • Listening actively • Reading with understanding • Solving problems and making decisions • Planning (Technology is optional.)	Most SCANS are incorporated into this unit, with an emphasis on: • Self-management • Acquiring and evaluating information • Decision making • Writing • Reasoning (Technology is optional.)	ACADEMIC • Make inferences from reading a text • Understand steps in a process • Make notes and use them to write a formal letter MATH • Interpret a bar chart • Create a bar chart • Compare numerical and other data	**1:** 1.4.1, 1.4.2 **2:** 1.4.2 **3:** 1.4.2 **4:** 7.2.4 **5:** 7.2.6, 7.2.7 **6:** 6.7.2 **7:** 1.4.6 **R:** 7.1.4, 7.2.1, 7.4.1, 7.4.2 **TP:** 4.8.1, 4.8.5, 4.8.6
Most EFF skills are incorporated into this unit, with an emphasis on: • Learning through research • Speaking so others can understand • Listening actively • Guiding others • Cooperating with others (Technology is optional.)	Most SCANS are incorporated into this unit, with an emphasis on: • Sociability • Teaching others • Exercising leadership • Interpreting and communicating information • Listening • Speaking • Decision making (Technology is optional.)	ACADEMIC • Make inferences from reading a text MATH • Measure distances on a map and use a scale to calculate real distances • Use addition and multiplication to calculate journey times by road	**1:** 2.1.1 **2:** 0.1.2 **3:** 2.5.4, 2.5.5 **4:** 2.5.4, 2.5.6 **5:** 1.9.1, 1.9.3, 1.9.4 **6:** 2.1.1, 7.5.1 **7:** 2.1.1, 2.6.1 **R:** 7.1.4, 7.2.1, 7.4.1, 7.4.2 **TP:** 4.8.1, 4.8.5, 4.8.6

CASAS: Numbers in bold indicate lesson numbers; **R** indicates Review lesson; **TP** indicates Team Project.

CONTENTS

EFF	SCANS (Workplace)	Academic/Math	CASAS
Most EFF skills are incorporated into this unit, with an emphasis on: • Learning through research • Reading with understanding • Using mathematics in problem solving and communication • Advocating and influencing (Technology is optional.)	Most SCANS are incorporated into this unit, with an emphasis on: • Understanding systems • Acquiring and evaluating information • Interpreting and communicating information • Reading • Decision making • Reasoning (Technology is optional.)	ACADEMIC • Read for detail • Identify main ideas of a paragraph • Write a summary MATH • Interpret a bar graph • Create a bar graph • Calculate percentages • Interpret amounts in grams and percentages on a food label	**1:** 3.5.8, 3.5.9, 6.4.3, 6.7.2 **2:** 3.1.1 **3:** 3.1.1 **4:** 3.2.3 **5:** 3.5.1 **6:** 3.3.1, 3.3.2, 3.3.3 **7:** 7.2.1, 7.4.2 **R:** 7.1.4, 7.2.1, 7.4.1, 7.4.2 **TP:** 4.8.1, 4.8.5, 4.8.6
Most EFF skills are incorporated into this unit, with an emphasis on: • Taking responsibility for learning • Conveying ideas in writing • Speaking so others can understand • Observing critically • Planning • Cooperating with others (Technology is optional.)	Most SCANS are incorporated into this unit, with an emphasis on: • Responsibility • Self-esteem • Organizing and maintaining information • Writing • Speaking • Reasoning (Technology is optional.)	ACADEMIC • Discuss research strategies • Write a formal letter • Set goals based on self-evaluation MATH • Organize information in chronological order • Rank skills on a numerical scale	**1:** 4.1.9, 4.4.2 **2:** 4.1.8 **3:** 4.1.3 **4:** 4.6.5 **5:** 4.1.2 **6:** 4.1.2 **7:** 4.1.5, 4.1.7 **R:** 7.1.4, 7.2.1, 7.4.1, 7.4.2 **TP:** 4.8.1, 4.8.5, 4.8.6
Most EFF skills are incorporated into this unit, with an emphasis on: • Speaking so others can understand • Listening actively • Observing critically • Solving problems and making decisions • Resolving conflict and negotiating • Cooperating with others (Technology is optional.)	Most SCANS are incorporated into this unit, with an emphasis on: • Monitoring and correcting performance • Responsibility • Self-management • Integrity/honesty • Participating as a member of a team • Listening • Speaking • Problem solving (Technology is optional.)	ACADEMIC • Work out meanings from context • Use critical thinking to analyze problems and solve them MATH • Create a Venn diagram • Interpret a flow chart	**1:** 4.4.1 **2:** 0.1.2, 0.1.6 **3:** 4.4.1, 4.8.1, 4.8.5, 7.3.2, 7.4.8 **4:** 0.1.2, 0.1.6 **5:** 4.8.1, 4.8.5, 4.8.6, 7.2.2, 7.2.5, 7.2.7, 7.3.2, 7.3.4 **6:** 4.1.6, 4.4.2, 7.2.1, 7.2.4 **7:** 4.4.1, 4.4.2 **R:** 7.1.4, 7.2.1, 7.4.1, 7.4.2 **TP:** 4.8.1, 4.8.5, 4.8.6
Most EFF skills are incorporated into this unit, with an emphasis on: • Taking responsibility for learning • Learning through research • Solving problems and making decisions (Technology is optional.)	Most SCANS are incorporated into this unit, with an emphasis on: • Understanding systems • Responsibility • Self-esteem • Exercising leadership • Listening • Speaking • Problem solving • Seeing things in the mind's eye (Technology is optional.)	ACADEMIC • Use transition words in writing • Write a paragraph describing a process • Understand a speech • Write a speech MATH • Interpret a flow chart • Interpret numerical information • Calculate taxes and tax exemptions	**1:** 5.6.3 **2:** 1.9.2 **3:** 5.3.3, 5.6.3 **4:** 5.4.1, 5.4.3 **5:** 5.1.4 **6:** 5.6.1 **7:** 5.1.4, 5.1.6 **R:** 7.1.4, 7.2.1, 7.4.1, 7.4.2 **TP:** 4.8.1, 4.8.5, 4.8.6

CASAS: Numbers in bold indicate lesson numbers; **R** indicates Review lesson; **TP** indicates Team Project.

Getting to Know You

GOALS

- Fill out an admission application
- Discuss learning strategies
- Edit a paragraph
- Recognize word families

College admission application

GOAL ▶ Fill out an admission application

Life skill

A Imagine that you have decided to take some classes at a college. Fill out the section of the admission application below.

CANYON COUNTY COLLEGE
Admission Application

1. _____ (Answers will vary.) _____ _____
   Last Name   First Name   Middle Name

2. Date of Birth ___/___/___ 3. (___)-___-_____ 4. ___ __**XXX–XX–XXXX**___
       Mo Day Year   Area Code Telephone Number Student ID Number

5. Sex: Male 6. Place of Birth _____ _____
     Female   City   State or Foreign Country

7. Citizen of what country _____

8. What is the highest level of education you have achieved? _____
_____

9. What is your educational goal? _____

B Talk to three students. Find out their first names, where they are from, and one other piece of interesting information (tidbit) about them. Then introduce your new friends to another group of students.

LESSON PLAN

Objectives: Fill out a college admissions application, Meet your classmates
Key vocabulary: register, admission, citizen, goal, strategies, level of education, achieved, greet, introduce, tidbit

Warm-up and Review: 5–10 min.

As students enter your class for the first time, introduce yourself by saying, *Nice to meet you* and shaking hands.

Introduction: 10–15 min.

Introduce yourself and give students any practical class or schedule information they need for the rest of the semester.

State the Objectives: *This week, you will meet your classmates and we will discuss learning strategies that will help you this semester. Today you will practice filling out a college admission application.*

Presentation 1: 10–15 min.

Ask students how they registered for school. Lead them to the idea of filling out an application. Ask them what information goes on a college admission application.

Practice 1: 15–20 min.

A Imagine that you have decided to take some classes at a college. Fill out the section of the admission application below. Do this as a class.

Evaluation 1: 10–15 min.

Have students share their application with others. Go over the application as a class, helping students when necessary.

Presentation 2: 5–10 min.

Ask a few students the following: *What is your name? What country are you from? Tell me something interesting about yourself.* Write these questions on the board and ask a volunteer to ask you the questions.

Practice 2: 10–15 min.

B Talk to three students. Find out their first names, where they are from, and one other piece of interesting information (tidbit) about them. Then introduce your new friends to another group of students. Shorter classes can do this activity instead of the Application activity.

Evaluation 2: 10–15 min.

Observe the activity. Call on students to introduce their new friends to the class.

Presentation 3: 5–10 min.

Ask a few students questions about what they wrote on the admission application.

Practice 3: 10–15 min.

Refer to the *Stand Out Activity Bank 4 CD-ROM,* Pre-Unit Worksheet 1, for an expanded interview activity. Have students form new groups and create questions together. Students should interview up to four students they don't yet know.

Evaluation 3: 10–15 min.

Ask volunteers to share what they learned about their classmates.

Application: 20–25 min.

Refer to the *Stand Out Activity Bank 4 CD-ROM,* Pre-Unit Worksheet 2 (two pages), for a longer college admission application. Have all students fill out and share the information with another student. Discuss any new vocabulary as a class.

STANDARDS CORRELATIONS

CASAS: 0.1.4, 0.2.1, 0.2.2, 0.2.4, 7.1.1, 7.2.1
SCANS: **Interpersonal** Participates as a Member of a Team, Teaches Others New Skills, Exercises Leadership, Works with Cultural Diversity; **Information** Acquires and Evaluates Information, Organizes and Maintains Information, Interprets and Communicates Information; **Basic Skills** Reading, Writing, Listening, Speaking; **Thinking Skills** Decision Making; **Personal Qualities** Responsibility, Self-Esteem, Sociability, Integrity/Honesty
EFF: **Communication** Read with Understanding, Convey Ideas in Writing, Speak So Others Can Understand, Listen Actively; **Interpersonal** Cooperate with Others; **Lifelong Learning** Learn through Research

LESSON PLAN

Objective:
Discuss and identify learning strategies
Key vocabulary:
native speakers, strategy

Warm-up and Review: 5–10 min. *(1.5+)*
Have students take out their admission applications from the previous lesson and share them with a new partner.

Introduction: 5–10 min. *(1.5+)*
Ask students how they learn and study English. Accept any answers they offer.

State the Objective: *Today we will discuss different strategies that you can use to learn English.*

Presentation 1: 10–15 min. *(1.5+)*
A Learning a new language takes place inside and outside the classroom. Below is a list of some strategies you can use to learn a new language. Read them with your teacher. Go through each strategy with students and ask them to raise their hands if they already use that strategy.

Practice 1: 10–15 min. *(1.5+)*
B Think of some other strategies that are not listed above and add them to the list. Have students do this in pairs or groups.

Evaluation 1: 10–15 min. *(1.5+)*
Make a list on the board of all the strategies that students named.

Presentation 2: 5–10 min. *(1.5+)*
Go over the questions in exercise C with students, giving examples where necessary. Don't allow too much discussion, so students can come up with their own ideas later.

Practice 2: 10–15 min. *(1.5+)*
C Answer the following questions about your personal studying strategies.

Evaluation 2: 10–15 min. *(2+)*
D Share your answers with another student. Observe students.

Presentation 3: 5–10 min. *(3)*
Prepare students to make a bar graph. Make a bar graph on the board or a transparency that lists each learning strategy from exercise A on the horizontal axis and the number of students on the vertical axis. Tell students they will take a class poll to see who uses which learning strategy.

Refer to the *Stand Out Activity Bank 4 CD-ROM,* Pre-Unit Worksheet 3, for a learning strategies bar graph. *(optional)*

Practice 3: 10–15 min. *(3)*
Divide the class into groups. Assign each group one of the learning strategies listed in exercise A. Tell each group to take a poll of the class and then record their information on the board (or on the transparency).

Evaluation 3: 10–15 min. *(3)*
Discuss the results of the poll.

Application: 20–25 min. *(1.5+)*
Divide students into four groups and assign each group one question from exercise C. Have each group break up and ask the other students the assigned question. Have the groups reassemble, compile their results, and present them to the class.

STANDARDS CORRELATIONS

CASAS: 0.1.2, 4.8.1, 6.1.1, 6.7.2, 7.4.1, 7.4.9
SCANS: **Resources** Allocates Human Resources; **Interpersonal** Participates as a Member of a Team, Works with Diversity; **Information** Acquires and Evaluates Information, Organizes and Maintains Information, Interprets and Communicates Information, Uses Computers to Process Information; **Systems** Understands Systems; **Technology** Applies Technology to Task (optional); **Basic Skills** Reading, Writing, Arithmetic, Listening, Speaking; **Thinking Skills** Knowing How to Learn, Reasoning; **Personal Qualities** Responsibility, Self-Esteem, Sociability, Integrity/Honesty
EFF: **Communication** Read with Understanding, Speak So Others Can Understand, Listen Actively; **Decision Making** Use Math to Solve Problems and Communicate, Plan; **Interpersonal** Cooperate with Others; **Lifelong Learning** Take Responsibility for Learning, Reflect and Evaluate, Learn through Research, Use Information and Communications Technology (optional)

LESSON 2 Learning strategies

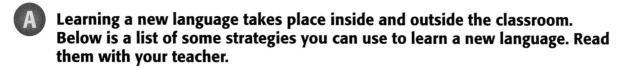

GOAL ▶ Discuss learning strategies   *Academic skill*

A Learning a new language takes place inside and outside the classroom. Below is a list of some strategies you can use to learn a new language. Read them with your teacher.

Learning Strategies

Learn grammar rules

Listen to the radio in English

Read English language books, magazines, and newspapers

Talk to native speakers

Watch TV in English

Write in English

B Think of some other strategies that are not listed above and add them to the list. *(Answers will vary.)*

C Answer the following questions about your personal studying strategies.

1. Where do you usually study? *(Answers will vary.)* _____

2. What strategies do you use inside the classroom? _____
   _____

3. What strategies do you use outside the classroom? _____
   _____

4. Choose two strategies that you don't use now, but that you would like to use in the future. _____
   _____

D Share your answers with another student.

| GOAL ▶ Edit a paragraph | *Academic skill* |

 A **Look at the first draft of Takuji's paragraph. There are eight more errors. Can you find and correct them?**

> ### My Goals
>
>   Ever since I came to the United State, I have had three goal. First I
> need to improve my English by going at school every day and studying at
> night. Once my English are better, I will look for a job that pays more
> money. Finally, when I have saved up enough money, I will buy a house new
> for my family. This are the three goals that I made when I first come to the
> united states.

B **Write each of the errors in the chart below. Write the correct form and identify the type of error using the words in the box.**

punctuation	capitalization	spelling	word order
singular/plural	verb tense	word choice	subject/verb agreement

Error	Correction	Type of error
goal	goals	singular/plural
at	to	word choice
are	is	subject/verb agreement
money.	money,	punctuation
house new	new house	word order
This	These	singular/plural
come	came	verb tense
united states	United States	capitalization

LESSON PLAN

Objectives:
Edit a paragraph, Write a paragraph about your goals
Key vocabulary:
first draft, paragraph, topic, topic sentence, support sentence, conclusion, brainstorm

Warm-up and Review: 5–10 min.

Review learning strategies with students. Ask students what learning strategies they used the previous day or before class. Ask students what strategies they plan to use over the coming weekend.

Introduction: 5–10 min.

Ask students what a *paragraph* is. Come up with a definition as a class. Remind them that a paragraph has *a beginning (topic sentence), a middle (support sentences),* and *an end (a conclusion sentence).*

State the Objectives: *Today you will look at a paragraph written by another student and learn how to edit another student's work. Then you will write your own paragraph and help another classmate edit his or her paragraph.*

Presentation 1: 10–15 min.

Ask students to name three of their goals. You might get them started by telling them what your own goals are. Have a few students share their goals.

Have students open their books and look at Takuji's paragraph in exercise A. Tell them that they will be looking for mistakes in his paragraph. Focus their attention on the vocabulary box in exercise B. Go through each word and explain to students that these are the errors they should be looking for. You may have to give them an example of each error type.

Practice 1: 15–20 min.

A **Look at the first draft of Takuji's paragraph. There are eight more errors. Can you find and correct them?**

B **Write each of the errors in the chart below. Write the correct form and identify the type of error using the words in the box.**

Evaluation 1: 10–15 min.

Go over the answers as a class.

Presentation 2: 5–10 min.

C What is a paragraph? Discuss the words in italics with your teacher.

Practice 2: 10–15 min.

D Look at Takuji's final version of his paragraph. Can you find each of the sentence types?

Evaluation 2: 5 min.

Go over the answers as a class.

Note: There is no Presentation 3, Practice 3, or Evaluation 3. Have students in longer classes begin the Application Activity.

Application: 20–25 min.

Help students brainstorm what they will write in their paragraphs before they begin.

 Refer to the *Stand Out Activity Bank 4 CD-ROM*, Pre-Unit Worksheet 4, for a brainstorming template. *(optional)*

E What are your goals? On a separate sheet of paper, write a paragraph about your goals. Make sure your first sentence is a topic sentence. Follow your topic sentence with support sentences and finish with a conclusion sentence.

 Refer to the *Stand Out Activity Bank 4 CD-ROM*, Pre-Unit Worksheet 5, for a paragraph-writing template. *(optional)*

F Exchange paragraphs with a partner. Check your partner's work for errors using the error types on the previous page.

 Refer to the *Stand Out Activity Bank 4 CD-ROM*, Pre-Unit Worksheet 6, for an editing chart. *(optional)*

If you decide to use this editing chart, have students record and review their errors with a partner.

Optional Computer Activity: Have students enter their paragraphs on the computer using word processing. If students have e-mail accounts, show them how to send their paragraphs to another student. In addition, show students how to operate the permanent pen setting to peer edit or make remarks in colored font.

Instructor's Notes for Lesson 3

_____

_____

_____

_____

_____

_____

_____

_____

_____

_____

_____

_____

_____

_____

_____

_____

_____

_____

C **What is a paragraph? Discuss the words in italics with your teacher.**

    A paragraph is a group of sentences (usually 5–7 sentences) about the *same topic*. A *topic sentence* is usually the first sentence. It introduces the *topic* or *main idea*. *Support sentences* are the sentences that follow the topic sentence. They give *details* about the topic. A *conclusion sentence* is the last sentence of the paragraph and it summarizes what has been written.

D **Look at Takuji's final version of his paragraph. Can you find each of the sentence types?**

My Goals

    Ever since I came to the United States, I have had three goals. First, I need to improve my English by going to school every day and studying at night. Once my English is better, I will look for a job that pays more money. Finally, when I have saved up enough money, I will buy a new house for my family. These are the three goals that I made when I first came to the United States.

(sentence 1, topic sentence; sentences 2–4, support sentences; sentence 5, conclusion sentence)

E **What are your goals? On a separate sheet of paper, write a paragraph about your goals. Make sure your first sentence is a topic sentence. Follow your topic sentence with support sentences and finish with a conclusion sentence.** *(Answers will vary.)*

F **Exchange paragraphs with a partner. Check your partner's work for errors using the error types on the previous page.**

Word families

GOAL ▶ Recognize word families

A In this book, you will be learning many new strategies to help you learn and remember vocabulary. The first strategy involves word families. What do you think a word family is? Look at the example below.

Noun	Verb	Adjective	Adverb
creation	create	creative	creatively

B Read the following paragraph. There are five words that belong to the same word family. Can you find and underline them?

Learning new vocabulary is very important for second language learners. To be successful, you need to be <u>organized</u>. Good <u>organization</u> requires writing down the new words you learn and finding out their meanings. You should <u>organize</u> the words so you can easily find them. Once you learn how to keep a <u>well-organized</u> vocabulary list, you can say, "I have good <u>organizational</u> skills!"

C Complete the following chart with words in the same word family. You may need to use a dictionary or ask another student for help.

Noun	Verb	Adjective	Adverb
education	*educate*	educational	*educationally*
success	*succeed*	*successful*	*successfully*
decision	decide	*decisive*	*decisively*
activity	*activate*	*active*	actively

LESSON PLAN

Objective: Recognize word families
Key vocabulary: word family

Warm-up and Review: 5–10 min. `1.5+`

Have students take out their paragraphs from the previous lesson and share with a partner. Ask volunteers to share with the class.

Introduction: 5–10 min. `1.5+`

Write _word family_ on the board. Ask if students know what the term means. Help them understand by providing an example.

State the Objectives: _Today you will learn how to find word families and understand the meaning of different words in a word family._

Presentation 1: 10–15 min. `1.5+`

A In this book, you will be learning many new strategies to help you learn and remember vocabulary. The first strategy involves word families. What do you think a word family is? Look at the example below. Have students put it in their own words. Go over the examples.

Practice 1: 10–15 min. `1.5+`

B Read the following paragraph. There are five words that belong to the same word family. Can you find and underline them? Ask students to find the words on their own before asking a volunteer to write them on the board.

Evaluation 1: 10–15 min. `1.5+`

As a class, go through the meaning of each word as it appears in the sentence. Review parts of speech and explain how each word fits into the example sentences.

Presentation 2: 5–10 min. `1.5+`

Preview exercise C. Students may use English-English dictionaries if need be.

Practice 2: 10–15 min. `2+`

C Complete the following chart with words in the same word family. You may need to use a dictionary or ask another student for help. Have students work in small groups.

Evaluation 2: 10–15 min. `2+`

Go over the answers as a class.

Presentation 3: 5–10 min. `3`

Look again at the words in exercise A and have students help you come up with sentences for each word. Now go back through the paragraph in exercise B and show students how these sentences are all related to each other.

Practice 3: 15–20 min. `3`

Put students in groups and assign each group one of the word families from exercise C. Have each group write a paragraph of related sentences using all four words from the word family.

Evaluation 3: 10–15 min. `3`

Ask group representatives to share their paragraphs.

Application: 20–25 min. `1.5+`

Refer to the _Stand Out Activity Bank 4 CD-ROM,_ **Pre-Unit Worksheet 7 (two-pages), for practice with word families.** Students will complete another word family chart like in exercise C and additional practice exercises. If there's time, have students write a sentence with each word in one of the word families.

STANDARDS CORRELATIONS

CASAS: 7.2.4, 7.4.1, 7.4.3, 7.4.5
SCANS: **Interpersonal** Participates as a Member of a Team, Works with Cultural Diversity; **Information** Acquires and Evaluates Information, Organizes and Maintains Information; **Systems** Understands Systems; **Basic Skills** Reading, Writing; **Thinking Skills** Creative Thinking, Knowing How to Learn,

Reasoning
EFF: **Communication** Read with Understanding, Convey Ideas in Writing; **Interpersonal** Cooperate with Others; **Lifelong Learning** Take Responsibility for Learning, Learn through Research

> **LESSON PLAN**
>
> Objective:
> Use used to
> Key vocabulary:
> used to, simple present verb, past and present habits, architect

Pre-Assessment: Use the *Stand Out* ExamView® Pro *Test Bank* for Unit 1. (optional)

Warm-up and Review: 5–10 min.

Ask students the following questions: *What did you do as a child that you don't do now? What did you do five years ago that you don't do now? What did you do last year that you don't do now?* If possible, try to focus students on habitual or long-term actions, not one-time events.

Introduction: 10–15 min.

Restate some student answers by inserting *used to.* For example, if a student said *When I was a child, I played soccer,* say *Jorge used to play soccer.* Reformulate a few answers and then write them on the board so students can see the written form.

State the Objective: *Today you will be using* used to *to talk about things you used to do in the past but that you don't do now.*

Presentation 1: 10–15 min.

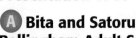 **Bita and Satoru are new students at Bellingham Adult School. Listen to their conversation on the first day of class.**

Prepare students for the focused listening by talking about the pictures of Bita and Satoru and asking them to guess the answers to the questions in exercise B. Play the recording one time. (See

Teaching Hints for an explanation of focused listening.)

ⓑ With a partner, answer the following questions about Bita and Satoru. You may have to guess some of the answers.

Explain to students that they might have to make inferences or guesses based on what they hear in the recording. Discuss the answers as a class.

Practice 1: 15–20 min.

ⓒ Bita and Satoru both talk about things they did in the past and things they do now. Listen again and make two lists in your notebook.

Before you play the recording again, ask students to write down anything they can remember from their first listening. Then have them fill in the chart after they've heard it the second time.

Evaluation 1: 10–15 min.

Have students share their answers with others and write down anything they missed. Then go over the answers as a class.

Pronunciation: An optional pronunciation activity is found on the final page of this unit.

This pronunciation activity may be introduced during any lesson in this unit, especially if students need practice with sentence stress. (See pages 20 and 20a for Unit 1 Pronunciation.)

STANDARDS CORRELATIONS

CASAS: 0.2.4
SCANS: **Interpersonal** Participates as a Member of a Team, Works with Cultural Diversity
Information Acquires and Evaluates Information
Basic Skills Reading, Writing, Listening, Speaking

Thinking Skills Creative Thinking
EFF: **Communication** Read with Understanding, Convey Ideas in Writing, Speak So Others Can Understand, Listen Actively
Interpersonal Cooperate with Others

UNIT 1 — Balancing Your Life

GOALS

- Use *used to*
- Create a goal chart
- Discuss obstacles and solutions
- Give and respond to advice
- Use adjective clauses
- Write a paragraph
- Understand time management skills

LESSON 1

Where did you use to study?

GOAL ▶ Use *used to*   **Grammar**

A Bita and Satoru are new students at Bellingham Adult School. Listen to their conversation on the first day of class.

B With a partner, answer the following questions about Bita and Satoru. You may have to guess some of the answers.

Bita:
1. *Answers will vary.*
2. *Administrative work for an engineering company.*
3. *Iran*
4. *So she can go to college.*

Bita

1. How old are they?

2. What do they do?

3. Where are they from?

4. Why are they studying English?

Satoru:
1. *Old enough to be a grandfather.*
2. *He is retired and a student.*
3. *Japan*
4. *To help his grandchildren with their homework and he wants to speak the language of the country.*

Satoru

C Bita and Satoru both talk about things they did in the past and things they do now. Listen again and make two lists in your notebook.

D Study the chart with your teacher.

Used to	
Example sentence	**Rule**
Satoru *used to* <u>attend</u> this school five years ago. Bita *used to* <u>be</u> an architect in Iran.	Affirmative: *used to* + base verb
Bita *did not use to* <u>go</u> to school at night. Satoru *didn't use to* <u>take</u> care of his grandchildren.	Negative: *did* + *not* (*didn't*) + *use to* + base verb. Incorrect: ~~I didn't used to go to school.~~
Did Satoru *use to* <u>work</u>? *Did* Bita *use to* <u>study</u> English?	Yes/no question: *did* + subject + *use to* + base verb. Incorrect: ~~Did Bita used to live in Iran?~~
Where *did* Satoru *use to* <u>work</u>? What *did* Bita *use to* <u>study</u>?	Wh- question: wh- word + *did* + subject + *use to* + base verb

Used to + *base verb* expresses a past habit or state that is now different.

E Look at the examples that you wrote in exercise C on the previous page. With a partner, make sentences and questions about what Bita and Satoru *used to* do.

EXAMPLE:
Bita used to go to another school in the daytime.

F Think about things you used to do. Write three sentences below and share them with your class.

1. *(Answers will vary.)* _____
2. _____
3. _____

G Write three *Wh-* questions using *used to.* Then ask your partner.

EXAMPLE:
Where did you use to work?

1. *(Answers will vary.)* _____
2. _____
3. _____

Presentation 2: 5–10 min.

D Study the chart with your teacher.

In addition to the examples in the chart, remind students of some things they said in the warm-up and go over those examples again as well.

Practice 2: 10–15 min.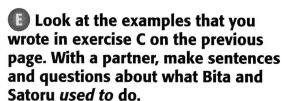

E Look at the examples that you wrote in exercise C on the previous page. With a partner, make sentences and questions about what Bita and Satoru *used to* do.

Encourage students to talk, not write, for this exercise.

F Think about things you used to do. Write three sentences below and share them with your class.

After students have had time to complete this exercise, ask for volunteers to read their sentences aloud.

G Write three *Wh-* questions using *used to*. Then ask your partner.

Ask volunteers to write their questions on the board. Focus on the difference between *used to* in a sentence (I used to . . .) and *use to* in a question (Did you use to . . . ?).

Evaluation 2:

Observe the activities.

 Refer to the *Stand Out Activity Bank 4 CD-ROM,* Unit 1 Worksheet 1, for additional practice with *used to.* (optional)

Presentation 3: 5–10 min. `3`

Go over the example in exercise H with students, asking them when they should use *used to* and when they should use the simple present.

Practice 3: 15–25 min. `3`

H **Complete the following sentences with *used to* or the simple present verb.**

For extra practice, have students rewrite the sentences in question form on a separate piece of paper. For example, *When did Bita use to attend school?* Students can then practice asking and answering the questions they wrote with a partner.

I **Look at the pictures below. Write sentences comparing the past to the present.**

Evaluation 3: 10–15 min. `3`

Go over the answers as a class.

GC **Refer to *Stand Out Grammar Challenge 4*, Unit 1 pages 5, 6, and 7 for more practice with *used to*. (optional)**

Application: 20–25 min. `15+`

J **Write two sentences comparing your past and present habits.**

Call on individual students to write their sentences on the board. If you have time, erase the sentences and ask questions about what was written on the board to see what the class remembers. For example, if *I used to run in the mornings, but now I walk in the evenings* was written on the board, ask *Who used to run in the mornings?* or *What did Lisa use to do in the mornings?*

Instructor's Notes for Lesson 1

H **Complete the following sentences with *used to* or the simple present verb.**

EXAMPLE:

__Bita used to live with her family, but now she lives alone.__

1. Bita _____*used to go*_____ (go) to school in the daytime, but now she

_____*goes*_____ (go) at night.

2. She _____*is*_____ (be) an administrative assistant now, but she

_____*used to be*_____ (be) an architect in Iran.

3. Satoru _____*used to attend*_____ (attend) class during the day, but now he

_____*attends*_____ (attend) at night.

4. He just _____*goes*_____ (go) to school and _____*helps*_____ (help) his

grandchildren now, but he _____*used to assemble*_____ (assemble) computers.

I **Look at the pictures below. Write sentences comparing the past to the present.**

Subject / verb	Past	Present
1. Suzanne/play piano		
2. Eli and Rosa/live in New York		

EXAMPLE:

__Bita used to live with her family, but now she doesn't.__

1. *Suzanne used to play the piano, but now she doesn't.*

2. *Eli and Rosa used to live in New York, but now they don't.*

J **Write two sentences comparing your past and present habits.**

1. *(Answers will vary.)*

2. _____

GOAL ▶ Create a goal chart

Academic skill

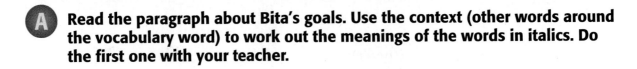

A Read the paragraph about Bita's goals. Use the context (other words around the vocabulary word) to work out the meanings of the words in italics. Do the first one with your teacher.

My name is Bita and I'm from Iran. I've been in the United States for six years. In my country I was an *architect* and I designed schools and hospitals, but in the United States, I don't have the right *qualifications* to be an architect. I have a plan. I'm going to learn English, go to school for architecture, and become an architect in the United States. Here is my dream. In eight years, I will be an architect working for a *firm* with three other partners. We will design and build homes in *suburban* neighborhoods. I will live in a nice home that I designed and I will look for the man of my dreams to share my life with me. How does that sound to you?

B Read the paragraph about Satoru. Use the context to work out the meanings of the words in italics.

I'm Satoru and I've been in the United States since 1975. I came here as an *immigrant* from Japan. I used to work for a computer company, but now I'm *retired*. I help take care of my grandchildren while their parents are working. But I also do something else on the side. I make jewelry to sell to local jewelers. My father was a jeweler in Japan and he taught me his art. My goal is to help send my grandchildren to college, so I've saved every penny I make from the jewelry. This is my dream. In five years, my oldest grandchild will teach elementary school in the community where she lives and she will *raise* her own family. My other grandchild will study medicine at one of the best schools in the country because he wants to be a *surgeon*. I hope that all of their dreams come true.

C Answer the questions with a partner.

1. What are Bita's and Satoru's goals?

2. What are they doing to make their goals a reality?

3. What are their dreams?

(See answers above.)

D What are some examples of different goals? Discuss your ideas with your teacher.

E What are your future goals? Write them down on a separate piece of paper.

LESSON PLAN

Objectives:
Create a goal chart, Use context clues to work out meaning
Key vocabulary:
goals, dreams, reality, qualifications, firm, suburban, refugee, retired, raise, jewelry, medicine, surgeon, intern, partner, context

Warm-up and Review: 5–10 min.

Ask volunteers to read the sentences they wrote with *used to* from the previous Application activity.

Introduction: 10–15 min.

Write *dream* and *goal* on the board. Ask students to help you define these two words. *Do they have the same meaning? How are their meanings different?*

State the Objectives: *Today you will read about Bita's and Minh's goals and help Bita fill in her goal chart. Then you will create your own chart for a goal you'd like to achieve.*

Presentation 1: 10–15 min.

Prepare students for the readings in exercises A and B by asking them what Bita's and Satoru's goals might be. Go over exercise A with students and show them how to use context to find the meaning of new vocabulary words. The first italicized word is *architect*. Ask students the

following questions: *What does this word mean? What words near this word might help you find its meaning? Is it a noun or a verb?* Suggest strategies to find the meanings of unfamiliar words.

Practice 1: 15–20 min.

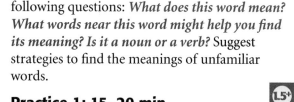

A **Read the paragraph about Bita's goals. Use the context (other words around the vocabulary word) to work out the meanings of the words in italics. Do the first one with your teacher.**

B **Read the paragraph about Satoru. Use the context to work out the meanings of the words in italics.**

C **Answer the questions with a partner.**

Evaluation 1: 10–15 min.

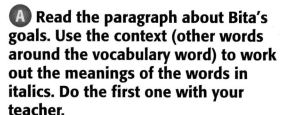

As a class, go over the new vocabulary. Go over the answers to exercise C together.

D **What are some examples of different goals? Discuss your ideas with your teacher.**

Help students come up with examples of different types of goals: *personal*, *educational*, *vocational*, and *professional*.

E **What are your future goals? Write them down on a separate piece of paper.**

Ask students to list at least three goals. They will use these goals in the Application activity.

STANDARDS CORRELATIONS

CASAS: 7.1.1, 7.1.2, 7.1.3, 7.1.4, 7.2.4
SCANS: **Interpersonal** Participates as a Member of a Team, Works with Cultural Diversity
Information Acquires and Evaluates Information, Organizes and Maintains Information
Systems Understands Systems, Monitors and Corrects Performance, Improves and Designs Systems
Basic Skills Reading, Writing, Listening, Speaking

Thinking Skills Decision Making, Seeing Things in the Mind's Eye, Reasoning
Personal Qualities Responsibility, Self-Esteem, Sociability, Self-Management
EFF: **Communication** Read with Understanding, Listen Actively
Decision Making Solve Problems and Make Decisions, Plan

Presentation 2: 5–10 min.

Ask students what steps they think Bita will need to take to achieve her goals. Make a list of what they say on the board.

Prepare students for focused listening by having them look at the chart in exercise F. Ask them questions about the chart to get them familiar with the information: *What is Bita's first step? When will she finish studying English?*

Ask students what information is missing and what they will need to listen for as you play the recording. See Teaching Hints for more on focused listening.

Practice 2: 10–15 min.

 F Listen to the conversation that Bita is having with her friend, Yoshiko, and fill in Bita's goal chart with the missing steps and dates.

Hint that you might only play the recording once to encourage students to listen intently the first time. After students have listened once, have them share their answers with a partner to see what they missed. Play the recording again if necessary.

Evaluation 2: 10–15 min.

Go over the answers as a class. Then go over the steps and completion dates with students. Explain how the order makes sense and how the dates are realistic. Help them analyze the chart very carefully so they understand the system of organization.

 Refer to the *Stand Out Activity Bank 4 CD-ROM,* Unit 1 Worksheet 2, for more practice with setting goals. *(optional)*

Presentation 3: 5–10 min.

Ask students to turn back to page 4 and look at Satoru's paragraph. Ask them to name Satoru's goal. Write it on the board.

 ## Practice 3: 10–15 min.

In groups, have students create a goal chart for Satoru, complete with steps and completion dates. Print out Satoru's Goal Chart from the *Stand Out Activity Bank 4 CD-ROM,* Unit 1

Worksheet 3, or students can create their own on a sheet of paper. (optional)

Evaluation 3: 10–15 min.

Have a spokesperson from each group share their goal chart with the class. Have students talk about the similarities and differences. Ask: *Which chart is the most realistic?*

Application: 20–25 min.

G Take out the piece of paper where you wrote your goals. Choose one goal and fill in the chart below. Make sure you list all of the steps and completion dates.

Remind students to refer to the goals they wrote for exercise E on page 4.

H Active Task: Use your goal chart to track your goal. Next to each *Completion Date,* write the actual date that you complete each step.

Refer to the *Stand Out Activity Bank 4 CD-ROM,* Unit 1 Worksheet 4, for a personal goal chart for students to keep in their notebooks. *(optional)*

Optional Computer Activity: Using a table or spreadsheet, have students create their goals charts on the computer. Show them how to format tables with borders and shading.

Refer to the *Stand Out Activity Bank 4 CD-ROM,* Unit 1 Active Task Checklist. *(optional)*

Remind students to use this checklist as they complete Active Tasks for Lessons 2, 4, 6, and 7. (optional)

F Listen to the conversation that Bita is having with her friend, Yoshiko, and fill in Bita's goal chart with the missing steps and dates.

Goal: To become an architect and become a partner in a firm	
Steps	Completion Date
Step 1: Study English.	Spring 2004
Step 2: *Register for college.*	Fall 2004
Step 3: *get degree.*	*Spring 2008*
Step 4: Become an intern.	Summer 2008
Step 5: *get license.*	Winter 2009
Step 6: Become a partner in a firm.	*2010*

G Take out the piece of paper where you wrote your goals. Choose one goal and fill in the chart below. Make sure you list all of the steps and completion dates.

Goal:	
Steps	Completion Date
Step 1: *(Answers will vary.)*	
Step 2:	
Step 3:	
Step 4:	
Step 5:	
Step 6:	

H **Active Task:** Use your goal chart to track your goal. Next to each *Completion Date*, write the actual date that you complete each step.

Obstacles and solutions

GOAL ▶ **Discuss obstacles and solutions** *Life skill*

A **Sometimes, we have problems achieving our goals. These problems are called *obstacles.* In order to overcome these obstacles, it can be a good idea to brainstorm a number of different possible solutions. Look at the example below.**

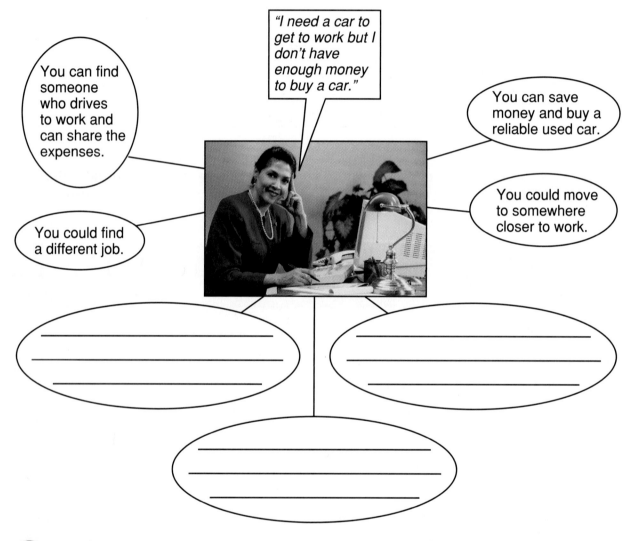

B **Can you think of any other solutions? Add them to the blank circles in the cluster diagram above.** *(Answers will vary.)*

LESSON PLAN

Objectives:
Identify obstacles to personal goals and identify possible solutions
Key vocabulary:
obstacle, solution, brainstorm, overcome, reliable, cluster diagram

Warm-up and Review: 5–10 min.

Have students take out their goal charts from the previous lesson and share them with another student in the class.

Introduction: 10–15 min.

Ask students the following questions: *Are goals easy to achieve? Why or why not? What are some problems that you might have achieving your goals? What can you do about those problems?*

State the Objectives: *Today we will discuss obstacles (problems) that might get in the way of your achieving your goals and how to come up with solutions to remove those obstacles. Then you will take one of your own goals and come up with obstacles and possible solutions.*

Presentation 1: 10–15 min.

Write the words *obstacle* **and** *solution* **on the board.** Help students understand the meaning by talking about Bita and her goal. *What problems or obstacles might Bita have? How can she solve those obstacles?*

Practice 1: 15–20 min.

A **Sometimes, we have problems achieving our goals. These problems are called** *obstacles.* **In order to overcome these obstacles, it can be a good idea to brainstorm a number of different possible solutions. Look at the example below.**

Ask students what the woman's obstacle is. Ask them for some possible solutions.

B **Can you think of any other solutions? Add them to the blank circles in the cluster diagram above.**

Have students work with a partner or a small group to complete the cluster diagram.

Evaluation 1: 10–15 min.

Have the partners or groups share their ideas with the class.

STANDARDS CORRELATIONS

CASAS: 7.2.7, 7.3.2
SCANS: **Interpersonal** Participates as a Member of a Team, Works with Cultural Diversity
Information Acquires and Evaluates Information, Organizes and Maintains Information
Systems Understands Systems
Basic Skills Reading, Writing, Listening, Speaking
Thinking Skills Creative Thinking, Decision Making, Problem Solving, Seeing Things in the Mind's Eye, Reasoning

Personal Qualities Sociability, Self-Management, Integrity/Honesty
EFF: **Communication** Read with Understanding, Convey Ideas in Writing, Speak So Others Can Understand, Listen Actively, Observe Critically
Decision Making Solve Problems and Make Decisions, Plan
Interpersonal Resolve Conflict and Negotiate, Advocate and Influence, Cooperate with Others

Presentation 2: 5–10 min.

Go over the instructions and first example in exercise C.

Practice 2: 10–15 min.

C Read each of the situations below and try to come up with two possible solutions for each. Use *can* or *could* when writing your solutions.

Have students do this exercise in small groups.

Evaluation 2: 10–15 min.

Have students share their answers with the class.

Presentation 3: 5–10 min.

Remind students about the goal charts that they worked on in the previous lesson. Ask them what two items are essential for a goal chart.

Practice 3: 10–15 min.

Have students form small groups. Ask each group to choose one of the people listed in Exercise C and create a goal chart for the person, complete with steps and completion dates. Each group will need to choose a solution to the problem listed and incorporate that solution into the goal chart.

Evaluation 3: 10–15 min.

Have each group share their chart with the class.

Application: 20–25 min.

D Now take one of your goals that you wrote for exercise E on page 4 and think of an obstacle that might get in your way. Make a cluster diagram like the one on page 6 and brainstorm different solutions with a partner.

 Refer to the *Stand Out Activity Bank 4 CD-ROM,* Unit 1 Worksheet 5, for more practice with obstacles and solutions. *(optional)*

Instructor's Notes for Lesson 3

_____

_____

_____

_____

_____

_____

_____

_____

_____

_____

_____

_____

_____

_____

_____

_____

_____

_____

_____

_____

_____

_____

_____

_____

C **Read each of the situations below and try to come up with two possible solutions for each. Use *can* or *could* when writing your solutions.**

1. Magda wants to go back to school but she has two children that she has to take care of. One of her children is in fourth grade and goes to school from 7:30 A.M.–2 P.M., but her other child is a toddler who isn't in school yet. *(Answers will vary. Possible answers below.)*

    EXAMPLE: Solution 1: **_She could ask a family member to take care of her toddler so she can go to school during the day._**

    Solution 2: *She could wait until both children are in school during the day and then return to school.*

    Solution 3: *She can go to night school and have a babysitter care for her children when she is in class.*

2. Frank wants to open up a restaurant in his neighborhood. He can get a loan to buy the property, but he won't have enough money to pay his employees until the restaurant starts making money.

    Solution 1: *He could try to find a partner to help him finance the restaurant.*

    Solution 2: *He could wait to open the restaurant until he has saved more money.*

    Solution 3: *He can apply for a small business loan.*

3. Sergei works for a computer software company and wants to move up to be a project manager. The problem is he needs to get more training before he can move up, but he doesn't have time to do training during the day.

    Solution 1: *He could take classes at night.*

    Solution 2: *He could talk to his supervisor about ways to make time for training in his schedule.*

    Solution 3: *He could come in early and stay late to make time for training during the day.*

D **Now take one of your goals that you wrote for exercise E on page 4 and think of an obstacle that might get in your way. Make a cluster diagram like the one on page 6 and brainstorm different solutions with a partner.**

What should I do?

GOAL ▶ Give and respond to advice

Life skill

 A **Read the following ways of giving and responding to advice.**

Problem	Give advice
Magda wants to go back to school but she has two children that she has to take care of. One of them is a toddler who isn't in school yet.	*Why don't you* ask your mother to take care of him?
	How about going to night school?
	You should take some courses at home on the Internet.
	You could find a school with a daycare facility.

Respond to advice (positive)	Respond to advice (negative)
That's a great idea.	I don't think I can do that because . . .
Why didn't I think of that?	That doesn't sound possible because . . .
That's what I'll do.	That won't work because . . .

 B **Look back at the problems on page 7. Imagine that you have these problems. With a partner, make conversations like the one below. Use different ways of giving and responding to advice from the chart above.**

EXAMPLE:

Student A: I want to go back to school, but I have a young child to take care of.

Student B: Why don't you ask your mother to take care of him?

Student A: That won't work because she lives too far away.

Student B: Then how about taking some courses on the Internet?

Student A: That's a great idea!

LESSON PLAN

Objective:
Give and respond to advice
Key vocabulary:
advice, responding, toddler, daycare
facility, counseling

Warm-up and Review: 5–10 min. 15+

Write this problem on the board: *Miyoko wants to go to college, but she doesn't have enough money to pay for it.* Put a circle around the statement and ask students to come up to the board and write possible solutions for Miyoko's problem, making a cluster diagram as on page 6.

Introduction: 10–15 min. 15+

Write *advice* on the board and help students define it.

State the Objective: *Today, you will practice giving and responding to advice.*

Presentation 1: 10–15 min. 15+

A **Read the following ways of giving and responding to advice.**

Go over the chart with students.

Practice 1: 15–20 min. 15+

Ask two volunteers to perform the conversation in the example below exercise B. Ask the class for different ways that Student B could respond to the advice, using examples from the chart above. Remind students that more than one response is possible.

B **Look back at the problems on page 7. Imagine that you have these problems. With a partner, make conversations like the one below. Use different ways of giving and responding to advice from the chart above.**

Have students work in pairs and practice the three conversations.

Evaluation 1: 10–15 min. 15+

Call on students to present the conversations for the class.

STANDARDS CORRELATIONS

CASAS: 7.2.5, 7.2.7
SCANS: **Interpersonal** Participates as a Member of a Team, Works with Cultural Diversity
Information Interprets and Communicates Information
Basic Skills Reading, Writing, Listening, Speaking
Thinking Skills Creative Thinking, Decision Making, Problem Solving, Reasoning

Personal Qualities Sociability
EFF: **Communication** Read with Understanding, Speak So Others Can Understand, Listen Actively
Decision Making Solve Problems and Make Decisions
Interpersonal Advocate and Influence, Cooperate with Others

Presentation 2: 5–10 min.

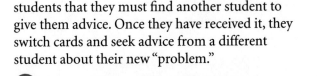

Go over the instructions for exercise C. Ask students to look at the chart and tell you what they will be listening for.

Practice 2: 10–15 min.

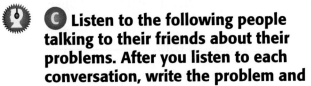

C **Listen to the following people talking to their friends about their problems. After you listen to each conversation, write the problem and two pieces of advice that each person receives.**

Evaluation 2: 10–15 min.

Go over the answers as a class.

Presentation 3: 5–10 min.

Ask for a volunteer. Tell this student that he or she is Miyuki in exercise C. Ask the student to tell you his or her problem and ask for advice. Role-play this situation with the student, offering advice from the chart. Ask for another volunteer to listen to you play Miyuki and offer you advice. Now ask for two student volunteers to role-play the conversation for the class.

Practice 3: 10–15 min.

Have each student find a new partner and practice giving and responding to advice as if they were the people in exercise C.

Evaluation 3: 10–15 min.

Ask volunteers to role-play for the class.

Application: 20–25 min.

Pass out note cards and ask students to write down a problem. Ask them to write it in the first person, such as: *I'm going on vacation next week and I don't have anyone to watch my dog.* As you walk around to collect each card, check and make sure it is a real problem that can be plausibly solved. Once you've collected all the cards, ask for a volunteer to role-play with you. He or she should read the problem and ask for advice. This would be a good time to introduce the phrase *What should I do?* for use after the problem is

stated. Role-play with one more volunteer before calling up two students to role-play for the class. Then, pass out the "problem" cards and explain to students that they must find another student to give them advice. Once they have received it, they switch cards and seek advice from a different student about their new "problem."

D **Active Task: Where can you go to get advice if you have a problem? Make a list of agencies or centers that can offer advice or counseling for different types of problems. Go to the public library or look up counseling agencies on the Internet to find more information.**

If you have phone books or Internet access in the classroom, have students do this exercise in groups. If not, ask students to do some research at home and bring their list in for the next class period.

Remind students to use the Active Task Checklist.

Refer to the *Stand Out Activity Bank 4 CD-ROM*, Unit 1 Worksheet 6, for a supplemental listening exercise about advice. *(optional)*

Refer to *Stand Out Activity Bank 4 CD-ROM*, Unit 1 Worksheet 7, for practice writing a letter of advice. *(optional)*

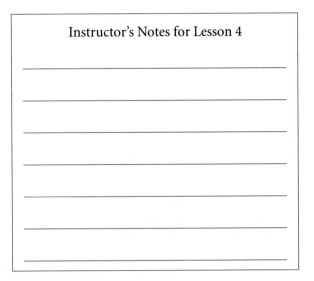

Instructor's Notes for Lesson 4

C Listen to the following people talking to their friends about their problems. After you listen to each conversation, write the problem and two pieces of advice that each person receives.

Miyuki	Problem	Advice 1	Advice 2
	Her son is always angry and fights with other students.	*talk to the guidance counselor*	*observe some classes and get to know the teachers*
Ron			
	His landlord wants him to get rid of his dog.	*let the landlord meet his dog*	*look for another apartment*
Patty			
	She needs an operation but doesn't have health insurance.	*save up money*	*find a job that gives health insurance*

D **Active Task:** Where can you go to get advice if you have a problem? Make a list of agencies or centers that can offer advice or counseling for different types of problems. Go to the public library or look up counseling agencies on the Internet to find more information.

What is most important to me?

| GOAL ▶ | Use adjective clauses | *Grammar* |

A **Look at the pictures and listen to Eliana talking about what is important to her. Then read the paragraphs below.**

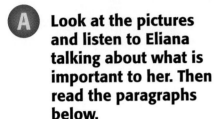

This is a picture of the house <u>where</u> I grew up in Argentina. It's very important to me because it holds a lot of memories. This is the garden <u>where</u> I played with my brothers and sisters, and the veranda <u>where</u> I often sat with my parents in the evenings, listening to their stories and watching the stars and dreaming about my future.

This is the person <u>who</u> influenced me the most when I was young. She was my teacher in first grade, and we stayed friends until I left home. She was always so calm and gave me good advice. She was the kind of person <u>who</u> is able to give you another perspective on a problem and makes you feel hopeful, no matter how troubled you are.

This is my daily journal. I use it to write about my feelings and hopes and it helps me to understand them better. Sometimes I just write about things <u>that</u> happened to me during the day. My journal is something <u>which</u> helps me to focus on the important things in my life.

B **Read the paragraphs again and underline the words *who, which, that,* and *where*.**

C **Choose the correct answer below.**

1. We use *which* or *that* for ○ places ○ people ● things.

2. We use *who* for ○ places ● people ○ things.

3. We use *where* for ● places ○ people ○ things.

LESSON PLAN

Objective:
Use adjective clauses
Key vocabulary:
veranda, calm, influence, perspective,
hopeful, troubled, daily journal, focus,
adjective clause

Warm-up and Review: 5–10 min.

Ask students to take out the list they wrote for the
Active Task, either from the previous lesson in class
or the research they did at home. Ask students to
share the information they found.

Introduction: 10–15 min.

**Ask students to tell what is the most important
thing in the world to them.** Then ask them to tell
you why. Write what they say on the board in note
form. (Do not erase this information because you
will use it in Presentation 2.)

State the Objective: *Today we will talk about
what is important to you and use adjective
clauses to describe those things.*

Presentation 1: 10–15 min.

**Have students open their books and look at
Eliana's pictures.** Ask them what they think is
important to her and why.

**A Look at the pictures and listen to
Eliana talking about what is important
to her. Then read the paragraphs
below.**

Play the recording and then call on individuals to
read the paragraphs aloud. Ask students some basic
comprehension questions about the reading.

Practice 1: 15–20 min.

**B Read the paragraphs again and
underline the words *who, which, that,*
and *where.***

C Choose the correct answer below.

Evaluation 1: 10–15 min.

Go over the answers as a class.

Refer to *Stand Out Grammar Challenge 4,* Unit 1 pages 1–3 for more practice with adjective clauses. *(optional)*

STANDARDS CORRELATIONS

CASAS: 7.2.1, 7.2.2
SCANS: **Interpersonal** Participates as a Member of a
Team, Works with Cultural Diversity
Information Acquires and Evaluates Information
Systems Monitors and Corrects Performance
Basic Skills Reading, Writing, Listening, Speaking

Personal Qualities Sociability
EFF: **Communication** Read with Understanding, Convey
Ideas in Writing, Speak So Others Can Understand, Listen
Actively
Interpersonal Cooperate with Others
Lifelong Learning Reflect and Evaluate

Presentation 2: 5–10 min.

D **Study the chart with your teacher.**

Have students go back to the reading and underline examples of adjective clauses. Go over them as a class. Now go back to the information that you wrote on the board during the introduction and help students make adjective clauses about what they regard as important.

Practice 2: 10–15 min.

E **Combine the following sentences using adjective clauses. In which sentences can you leave out the relative pronoun?**

Go over the example and do the first one with students to make sure they understand. Have students complete this exercise on their own and then share their answers with a partner.

Evaluation 2: 10–15 min.

Go over the answers as a class.

 Refer to the *Stand Out Activity Bank 4 CD-ROM,* Unit 1 Worksheet 8, for additional practice with adjective clauses. *(optional)*

Study the chart with your teacher.

Adjective clauses		
Main clause	**Relative pronoun**	**Adjective clause**
This is the place	*where*	I grew up.
She is the person	*who*	influenced me the most.
A journal is something	*that (which)*	can help you focus on important things.

Adjective clauses describe a preceding noun. They can describe a subject noun or an object noun. If the noun is an object, you can leave out the relative pronoun.

 Combine the following sentences using adjective clauses. In which sentences can you leave out the relative pronoun?

EXAMPLE: This is the house. I grew up there. **_This is the house where I grew up._**

1. That is the city. I was born there.

 That is the city where I was born.

2. I have a friend. She helps me when I am sick.

 I have a friend who helps me when I am sick.

3. Do you know a school? I can learn about computers.

 Do you know a school where I can learn about computers?

4. She has many problems. They are making her sad.

 She has many problems that (which) are making her sad.

5. This is a good dictionary. It can help you improve your vocabulary.

 This is a good dictionary that (which) can help you improve your vocabulary.

6. My son has a new teacher. He gives him a lot of homework.

 I am trying to find the teacher whom (who) I met yesterday.

7. We have some neighbors. They are very friendly.

 We have some neighbors who are very friendly.

8. This is a gold ring. It reminds me of my mother.

 This is a gold ring that (which) my mother bought for me.

(The relative pronoun may be left out in sentences 6 and 8.)

F **Look at the pictures below and make sentences about them using adjective clauses.**

This is a place where _____ *(Answers will vary.)* _____ .

This is a person who _____ .

This is a thing that _____ .

G **Work in pairs. Make sentences about these nouns using adjective clauses (but don't say the noun in your sentence). Your partner will guess which place, person, or thing you are talking about.**

EXAMPLE:
Student A: It's a thing that opens doors.
Student B: A key.

Places	People	Things
supermarket	firefighter	key
library	senator	paintbrush
hospital	counselor	diary
hotel	friend	stamp
airport	guide	newspaper
school	lawyer	car

H **Choose a place, a person, and a thing. Tell your partner why they are important to you. On a separate sheet of paper, write a description for each one. Use adjective clauses in your description.** *(Answers will vary.)*

Presentation 3: 5–10 min.

F Look at the pictures below and make sentences about them using adjective clauses.

Practice 3: 10–15 min.

G Work in pairs. Make sentences about these nouns using adjective clauses (but don't say the noun in your sentence). Your partner will guess which place, person, or thing you are talking about.

To make sure students understand that this is a verbal exercise, demonstrate a few times with a student volunteer. Ask partners to switch roles after three sentences.

Evaluation 3:

Observe students.

 Refer to *Stand Out Grammar Challenge 4*, Unit 1 pages 1–4 for more practice with adjective clauses. *(optional)*

Application 20–25 min.

H Choose a place, a person, and a thing. Tell your partner why they are important to you. On a separate sheet of paper, write a description for each one. Use adjective clauses in your description.

Walk around and help students with their writing. If there's time, ask for volunteers to share one of their three descriptions with the class.

Instructor's Notes for Lesson 5

> ### LESSON PLAN
>
> Objective:
> Write a paragraph about the most important person in your life
> Key vocabulary:
> patience, determination, positive influence

Warm-up and Review: 5–10 min.

Ask students to take out their descriptions from the previous lesson and share them with the class. Ask if students have any questions about adjective clauses. Review if necessary.

Introduction: 5 min.

Ask students to think of someone who has influenced them. Now ask them to think about why this person is important to them. Give them a few seconds to think about this. Don't ask them to tell you, just ask them to keep it in mind.

State the Objective: *Today you will write a paragraph about someone who has influenced you in life.*

Presentation 1: 10–15 min.

A **Bita wrote a paragraph about her brother. Read the paragraph, then discuss the questions below with your partner.**

Ask students to read the paragraph to themselves.

Practice 1: 15–20 min.

Discuss the questions. Then ask students to help you define what a paragraph is. Remind students about the parts of a paragraph. Have them turn back to page P5 if they need help. Make a list on the board of parts of a paragraph: *topic sentence, support sentences, conclusion sentence.* Have students read Bita's paragraph again and look for each part you listed. Ask them to label the sentences in their books accordingly.

Evaluation 1: 10–15 min.

Point out the transitions used to connect different paragraph parts.

Presentation 2: 5–10 min.

Ask students to think about someone who has influenced their lives (the person that came to mind during the introduction). Tell them to begin thinking of what they will write about that person in their paragraph.

Practice 2: 10–15 min.

B **Now it's your turn to write about a person who has influenced you. Complete the following pre-writing activities before you begin writing.**

Evaluation 2:

Observe the activity.

STANDARDS CORRELATIONS

CASAS: 7.2.6
SCANS: **Interpersonal** Participates as a Member of a Team, Teaches Others New Skills, Works with Cultural Diversity **Information** Uses Computers to Process Information (optional)
Systems Monitors and Corrects Performance
Technology Applies Technology to Task (optional)
Basic Skills Reading, Writing, Listening, Speaking
Thinking Skills Creative Thinking, Decision Making, Problem Solving, Seeing Things in the Mind's Eye, Knowing How to Learn

Personal Qualities Responsibility, Sociability, Self-Management
EFF: **Communication** Read with Understanding, Convey Ideas in Writing, Speak So Others Can Understand, Listen Actively, Observe Critically
Decision Making Solve Problems and Make Decisions, Plan
Interpersonal Guide Others, Resolve Conflict and Negotiate, Advocate and Influence, Cooperate with Others
Lifelong Learning Take Responsibility for Learning, Reflect and Evaluate, Use Information and Communications Technology (optional)

My favorite person

GOAL ▶ **Write a paragraph**

Academic skill

 A **Bita wrote a paragraph about her brother. Read the paragraph, then discuss the questions below with your partner.**

Someone Who Has Influenced Me

The person who has influenced me the most in my life is my brother, Karim. I admire my brother for three reasons. First, he has patience and determination. Second, he does a fantastic job helping the community. Third, he is the type of person who always has time for his friends and family, no matter how busy he is. He has had a very positive influence on my life.

1. What type of person is Bita's brother?

2. Why does Bita admire him? *(See answers above.)*

3. How has he influenced Bita?

B **Now it's your turn to write about a person who has influenced you. Complete the following pre-writing activities before you begin writing.**

- *Brainstorm* (Think about your ideas before you write.)

  Who has influenced you the most in your life? *(Answers will vary.)* _____

  Why is this person so important to you? List three reasons.

  1. _____

  2. _____

  3. _____

- *Introduce* (Tell your readers what you are writing about.) Write your topic sentence(s) below.

  _____

- *Conclude* (Remind your reader of the main idea but don't restate your topic sentence.) Write your conclusion sentence below.

  _____

C Write a paragraph about the most important person in your life. Start with your topic sentence, put your reasons (support sentences) in the middle, and finish with your conclusion sentence. Remember to write a title.

_____

(Answers will vary.)

_____

_____

_____

_____

_____

_____

_____

D Remember the editing techniques you learned in the pre-unit? Reread your paragraph and make any necessary corrections.

E Now share your paragraph with two other students and have them use the questions below to make suggestions for you.

Content	Punctuation and grammar
1. Is there a clear topic sentence that states the main idea? 2. Are there three support sentences that support the main idea? 3. Are the three ideas connected using *first, second,* and *third?* 4. Is there a conclusion sentence that restates the main idea in different words?	1. Is the beginning of every sentence capitalized? 2. Is every sentence punctuated correctly? 3. Are all the words spelled correctly? 4. Do the subjects agree with the verbs? 5. Are the verb forms correct? 6. Are the verb tenses correct?

F Take out a clean sheet of paper and rewrite your paragraph.

G **Active Task:** Read your paragraph to the person you wrote about or to someone who knows that person.

Note: There is no Presentation, Practice, or Evaluation 3. Have students work on the Application Activity. Shorter classes may complete portions of the Application for homework.

 Refer to the *Stand Out Activity Bank 4 CD-ROM,* Unit 1 Worksheet 9, for more practice with parts of a paragraph, sentence order, and transitional words. *(optional)*

Application: 30–45 min.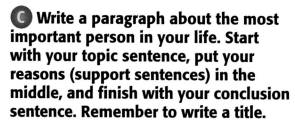

C Write a paragraph about the most important person in your life. Start with your topic sentence, put your reasons (support sentences) in the middle, and finish with your conclusion sentence. Remember to write a title.

D Remember the editing techniques you learned in the pre-unit? Reread your paragraph and make any necessary corrections.

Review page P4 for editing ideas.

E Now share your paragraph with two other students and have them use the questions below to make suggestions for you.

F Take out a clean sheet of paper and rewrite your paragraph.

Optional Computer Activity: Have students type their paragraph on the computer. Also suggest they bring in pictures of their topic person to scan into the computer.

 G Active Task: Read your paragraph to the person you wrote about or to someone who knows that person.

Remind students to use the Active Task Checklist.

Instructor's Notes for Lesson 6

LESSON PLAN

Objective:
Understand and apply time management skills

Key vocabulary:
organized, time management, last-minute changes, in advance, to the last minute, accomplish, sacrifice, allocate, realistic, prioritize, simultaneously, deadlines

Warm-up and Review: 5–10 min.

Have students take out the paragraphs they wrote in the previous lesson and share them with a partner.

Introduction: 10–15 min.

Write *time management* **on the board.** Ask students to help you define the term.

State the Objectives: *Today you will read about time management and think about your own time management strategies. In this unit, you will find some new strategies to incorporate into your life.*

Presentation 1: 10–15 min.

A Are you an organized person? Do you . . .

Have students read these sentence endings to themselves and put a check next to each one that describes them. Take an informal poll of the class for each item.

B What do you know about time management strategies? Make a list of any time management strategies that you use.

You may have to get students started with an example or two.

Practice 1: 15–20 min.

C Read the following paragraphs about time management. Write the number of each paragraph next to the correct topic below.

Tell students not to worry about the meaning of every single word, just enough to get the general idea and so that they can complete the exercise.

Evaluation 1: 10–15 min.

Go over the answers as a class. Ask students to tell you how they came up with their decisions.

STANDARDS CORRELATIONS

CASAS: 7.1.2, 7.2.1, 7.2.4
SCANS: **Resources** Allocates Time
Information Acquires and Evaluates Information, Organizes and Maintains Information, Interprets and Communicates Information

Systems Understands Systems
Basic Skills Reading, Writing
Thinking Skills Reasoning
Personal Qualities Self-Management
EFF: **Communication** Read with Understanding

LESSON 7 Time management

GOAL ▶ **Understand time management skills**　　*Academic skill*

A **Are you an organized person? Do you . . .**

❑ try to do everything but run out of time?

❑ always plan everything far in advance?

❑ dislike planning things too far ahead?

❑ tend to leave things to the last minute?

❑ get upset by last-minute changes to your schedule?

❑ only plan for important tasks like exams and job interviews?

Important	Very Important	Urgent

B **What do you know about time management strategies? Make a list of any time management strategies that you use.**

_____ *(Answers will vary.)*　　_____

_____　　_____

_____　　_____

C **Read the following paragraphs about time management. Write the number of each paragraph next to the correct topic below.**

__4__ How can I use my time more efficiently?

__5__ Why is good health important to time management?

__2__ How can I be organized?

__1__ What is time management? Why is it important?

__3__ How can I get important tasks done first?

Time Management Skills

(1) Finding enough time to study is very important for all students. There are a number of time management strategies that can help you to manage your time wisely. You can use them to *accomplish* the goals you have set for yourself without *sacrificing* the time you spend with your family and friends.

(2) One of the best ways to stay organized is to keep a schedule. Write down everything you need to do in a week. This includes work, study, children, shopping, and other tasks. Then *allocate* a time slot to each of these tasks. Be *realistic* about the time you will need for each task. Then check off each task when you have completed it.

(3) It is a good idea to *prioritize* your tasks in order of importance. Make a "To Do" list of all your tasks. Divide your list into A, B, and C. The A list is for tasks you need to do today. The B list is for tasks you need to do tomorrow. The C list is for tasks you need to do this month. This will help you to get your most important tasks done first. You can also list tasks according to urgency: tasks you have to do, tasks you should do, and tasks you'd like to do if you have time.

(4) Another time management strategy is to combine two or more tasks and do them *simultaneously.* You can listen to audio study tapes while you are on the bus, for example. Or, you can review verb tenses while you are eating lunch.

(5) Remember that good health is also important for managing your time effectively. If you are burned out or overtired, you cannot do your best. You need to allow time for rest and for exercise. You also need to have time to spend with family, friends, and other people who are important to you. Set realistic *deadlines* and mark them on your schedule. Don't get upset if you cannot accomplish all your goals. Be positive about your *achievements* and reward yourself for the goals that you have accomplished.

D **Use the diagram below to record the main points of the reading.**

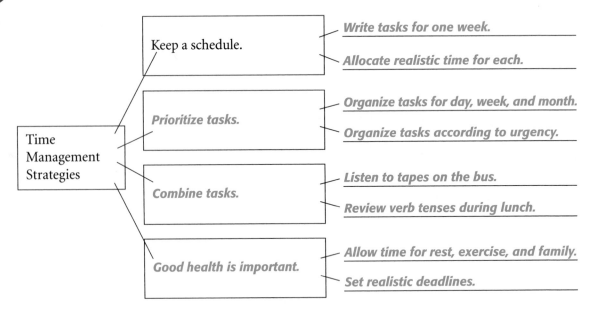

E **Find the following words in the reading and use the context to work out their meaning: *accomplish, sacrificing, allocate, realistic, prioritize, simultaneously, deadlines, achievements.***

 F **Active Task:** Go to the library or use the Internet to find tips on time management. Find one tip and tell your classmates.

Presentation 2: 5–10 min.

Explain the diagram in exercise D. Show students how it goes from the main topic to more specific topics to smaller details. Help them find the details for "Keep a schedule."

Practice 2: 10–15 min.

D **Use the diagram below to record the main points of the reading.**

Have students complete this task by themselves.

Evaluation 2: 10–15 min.

Go over the answers as a class.

Presentation 3: 5–10 min.

Review making inferences about vocabulary with students. Remind them to look for clues in the sentences around the word to uncover its meaning. Look back at the reading and uncover the meaning of the first italicized word (*accomplish*) together.

Practice 3: 10–15 min.

E **Find the following words in the reading and use the context to work out their meaning:** *accomplish, sacrificing, allocate, realistic, prioritize, simultaneously, deadlines, achievements.*

Have students do this exercise by themselves.

Evaluation 3: 10–15 min.

Go over the meanings as a class. If you have extra time, ask students to write a sentence or two using a few of the words. Have them share their sentences with a partner and then the class.

Application: 20–25 min.

Write the following chart on the board (or make a transparency using the chart from the *Activity Bank 4 CD-ROM*) and ask students to complete it with some example time management strategies.

Time Management	
Strategies I Use	New Strategies I Will Start Using

Refer to the *Stand Out Activity Bank 4 CD-ROM*, Unit 1 Worksheet 11, for a copy of the time management chart. *(optional)*

Have students fill in the chart individually and share responses with a small group.

Optional Computer Activity: Students can recreate this chart on the computer and print out a copy to post somewhere in the classroom or at home.

Refer to the *Stand Out Activity Bank 4 CD-ROM*, Unit 1 Worksheet 10, for an outlining and discussion activity about time management. *(optional)*

F **Active Task: Go to the library or use the Internet to finds tips on time management. Find one tip and tell your classmates.**

Remind students to use the Active Task Checklist.

Instructor's Notes for Lesson 7
_____
_____
_____
_____
_____
_____
_____

LESSON PLAN

Objective:
Review all previous unit objectives
Key vocabulary:
Review all previous unit vocabulary

Warm-up and Review: 5–10 min.

Ask students to take out the filled-in time management charts from the previous lesson. Ask them if they have used any of the new strategies yet.

Introduction: 5–10 min.

Write the words *Evaluation* **and** *Review* **on the board.** Ask students what these words mean and what their purpose is.

State the Objective: *Today you will review everything you have learned in this unit and prepare for your team project.*

Ask students as a class to recall all the goals of this unit without looking at their books. Then remind them which goals they omitted, if any.

Unit goals: *Use used to, Use context clues to work out meaning, Discuss obstacles and solutions, Give and respond to advice, Use adjective clauses, Write a paragraph, Understand time management skills.*

Presentation, Practice, and Evaluation 1:

Do the Learner Log on page 20. Notes are next to the page.

Presentation 2: 5–10 min.

 It is useful to make vocabulary cards to practice new vocabulary words and phrases. Look at the sample card below.

Go over the idea of vocabulary cards with your students. Make sure they understand each part of the card.

Practice 2: 20–25 min.

 Choose five new words you learned in this unit and make vocabulary cards using note cards. If you don't have cards, use pieces of paper.

 Use the words from this unit to complete these sentences.

Evaluation 2: 5–10 min.

Go over the answers as a class.

STANDARDS CORRELATIONS

CASAS: 7.1.4, 7.2.1, 7.4.1, 7.4.2
SCANS: **Interpersonal** Participates as a Member of a Team, Teaches Others New Skills, Works with Cultrual Diversity
Information Acquires and Evaluates Information, Organizes and Maintains Information
Systems Understands Systems, Monitors and Corrects Performance
Basic Skills Reading, Writing, Listening, Speaking
Thinking Skills Creative Thinking, Decision Making, Seeing

Things in the Mind's Eye, Knowing How to Learn, Reasoning
Personal Qualities Responsibility, Self-Esteem, Sociability, Self-Management, Integrity/Honesty
EFF: **Communication** Convey Ideas in Writing, Speak So Others Can Understand, Listen Actively
Decision Making Solve Problems and Make Decisions
Interpersonal Guide Others, Cooperate with Others
Lifelong Learning Take Responsibility for Learning, Reflect and Evaluate, Learn Through Research

Review

A It is useful to make vocabulary cards to practice new words and phrases. Look at the sample card below.

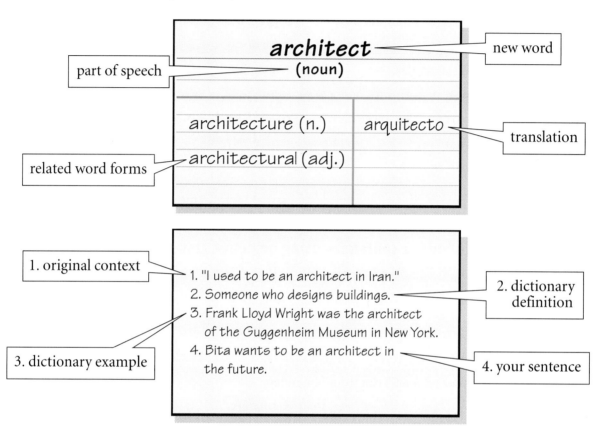

part of speech

architect — new word

(noun)

architecture (n.)	arquitecto — translation
architectural (adj.)	

related word forms

1. original context

2. dictionary definition

3. dictionary example

4. your sentence

1. "I used to be an architect in Iran."
2. Someone who designs buildings.
3. Frank Lloyd Wright was the architect of the Guggenheim Museum in New York.
4. Bita wants to be an architect in the future.

B Choose five new words you learned in this unit and make vocabulary cards using note cards. If you don't have cards, use pieces of paper.

C Use the words from this unit to complete these sentences.

1. Someone who stops work because he or she is old is _____ *retired* _____ .

2. Someone who moves to another country to live is an _____ *immigrant* _____ .

3. If you are taking care of your children, you are _____ *raising* _____ a family.

4. If you are doing two things at the same time, you are doing them _____ *simultaneously* _____ .

5. If you have to complete a task by a certain time, that is your _____ *deadline* _____ .

6. When you put things in order of importance, you _____ *prioritize* _____ them.

Review

D **Make sentences to contrast past and present habits.**

EXAMPLE:
Past: I ate meat.   Present: I don't eat meat now.
I used to eat meat, but now I don't.

1. Past: Paolo didn't have a computer.   Present: He has a computer.

   Paolo didn't use to have a computer, but now he does.

2. Past: Maria swam every day.   Present: She doesn't swim now.

   Maria used to swim every day, but now she doesn't.

3. Past: My children didn't like vegetables.   Present: They like vegetables now.

   My children didn't use to like vegetables, but now they do.

4. Past: I didn't study full-time.   Present: Now I study full-time.

   I didn't use to study full-time, but now I do.

E **Combine the following sentences using adjective clauses.**

1. Esra has many brothers and sisters. They live in Argentina.

   Esra has many brothers and sisters who live in Argentina.

2. This is a good grammar book. It could help you improve your writing.

   This is a good grammar book that could help you improve your writing.

3. I am trying to find a school. I can study computers.

   I am trying to find a school where I can study computers.

4. E-mail is a type of communication. It is fast and easy to use.

   E-mail is a type of communication that we use at home and at work.

F **Your friend wants to study at college, but he needs a full-time job at the same time. Make a conversation with your partner. Suggest two or three different solutions to his problem. Use expressions from this unit for giving and responding to advice. Then write the conversation below.**

You: _____ *(Answers will vary.)* _____

Your friend: _____

You: _____

Your friend: _____

You: _____

Your friend: _____

Presentation 3: 5–10 min.

Review *used to,* adjective clauses, and modals with students.

 Refer to *Stand Out Grammar Challenge 4,* Unit 1 pages 1–8 for review practice. *(optional)*

Practice 3: 10–15 min.

D Make sentences to contrast past and present habits.

E Combine the following sentences using adjective clauses.

F Your friend wants to study at college, but he needs a full-time job at the same time. Make a conversation with your partner. Suggest two or three different solutions to his problem. Use expressions from this unit for giving and responding to advice. Then write the conversation below.

Evaluation 3: 10–15 min.

Ask a few volunteers to read their conversations to the class.

Application: 1–2 days

The Team Project Activity on the following page is the Application Activity to be done on the next day.

 Post-Assessment: Use the *Stand Out* ExamView® Pro *Test Bank* for Unit 1. *(optional)*

Note: On *Stand Out* ExamView® Pro *Test Bank* for Unit 1 you can design a post-assessment that focuses on what students have learned. It is designed to serve three purposes:

- To help students practice taking a test similar to current standardized tests available.

- To help the teacher evaluate how much students have learned, retained, and acquired.

- To help students see their progress when they compare their scores to the pre-test they took earlier.

Instructor's Notes for Unit 1 Review

Unit 1 Application Activity

> **TEAM PROJECT**
> **CREATE A GOAL CHART**
> Objective: Project designed to apply all the objectives of this unit.
> Product: A chart with team goals and time management techniques

Introduction: 1–5 min. `L5+`

State the objective: *With a team, you will create a goal chart for goals you want to accomplish in this class.*

Together, students will think of obstacles and solutions for each goal and also incorporate time management techniques to help other members achieve their individual goals. Shorter classes can do this project over two periods.

Refer to the *Stand Out Activity Bank 4 CD-ROM,* Unit 1 Worksheet 12 (six pages), for three goal charts. *(optional)*
You can use this template and give it to students if you want to eliminate Stage 3.

Stage 1: 5 min. `L5+`

Form a team with four or five students. Choose positions for each member of your team.

Explain that this project requires both individual and collaborative effort. Provide well-defined directions for how teams should proceed. Explain that members rotate so that each one does every job. Teams don't go to the next stage until the previous one is complete.

Stage 2: 20–30 min. `L5+`

Write down three goals that your team would like to accomplish by the end of this class. Write down the steps it will take to reach each goal. Write down a completion date for each step.

Stage 3: 20–25 min. `L5+`

Design a goal chart template. Make sure your chart has room for Steps, Completion Dates, Actual Completion Dates, Obstacles, Solutions, and Time Management Techniques.

Have students enter all the information gathered for Stage 2 onto their charts.

Stage 4: 15–20 min. `L5+`

Write down obstacles that might get in the way of your goals and solutions for each. Add these to your chart.

Stage 5: 10–15 min. `L5+`

Make a list of five time management techniques that will help you reach your goals and add them to your chart.

Stage 6: 10–15 min. `L5+`

Have team representatives present their charts to the class.

Stage 7: 10–15 min. `L5+`

Ask the class to vote on which team will achieve its goals the soonest.

STANDARDS CORRELATIONS

CASAS: 4.8.1, 4.8.5, 4.8.6
SCANS: **Resources** Allocates Materials and Facility Resources, Allocates Human Resources
Interpersonal Participates as a Member of a Team, Teaches Others New Skills, Exercises Leadership, Works with Cultural Diversity
Information Acquires and Evaluates Information, Organizes and Maintains Information, Interprets and Communicates Information, Uses Computers to Process Information (optional)
Systems Understands Systems, Monitors and Corrects Performance, Improves and Designs Systems
Technology Applies Technology to Task (optional)
Basic Skills Reading, Writing, Listening, Speaking

Thinking Skills Creative Thinking, Decision Making, Problem Solving, Seeing Things in the Mind's Eye, Knowing How to Learn, Reasoning
Personal Qualities Responsibility, Self-Esteem, Sociability, Self-Management, Integrity/Honesty
EFF: **Communication** Read with Understanding, Convey Ideas in Writing, Speak So Others Can Understand, Listen Actively, Observe Critically
Decision Making Solve Problems and Make Decisions, Plan
Interpersonal Guide Others, Resolve Conflict and Negotiate, Advocate and Influence, Cooperate with Others
Lifelong Learning Take Responsibility for Learning, Reflect and Evaluate, Learn through Research, Use Information and Communications Technology (optional)

Create a Goal Chart

With a team, you will create a goal chart for goals you want to accomplish in this class.

1. Form a team with four or five students. Choose positions for each member of your team.

Position	Job Description	Student Name
Student 1 Leader	See that everyone speaks English. See that everyone participates.	
Student 2 Secretary	Take notes and fill out the goal chart.	
Student 3 Designer	Design the goal chart layout.	
Students 4/5 Member(s)	Help the secretary and the designer with their work.	

2. Write down three goals that your team would like to accomplish by the end of this class. Write down the steps it will take to reach each goal. Write down a completion date for each step.

3. Design a goal chart template. Make sure your chart has room for Steps, Completion Dates, Actual Completion Dates, Obstacles, Solutions, and Time Management Techniques.

4. Write down obstacles that might get in the way of your goals and solutions for each. Add these to your chart.

5. Make a list of five time management techniques that will help you reach your goals and add them to your chart.

PRONUNCIATION

Sentence stress. We can use stress to emphasize words that we want to contrast and to make the meaning clearer. Listen and repeat the first sentence. Then listen to sentences 2, 3, and 4. Underline the stressed words.

•   •   •   •

1. Last year she studied computers, but this year she wants to study accounting.

2. They used to like skiing, but now they prefer yoga.

3. Cooking is my job, but jewelry-making is my hobby.

4. We weren't able to attend college, so we want our children to graduate.

LEARNER LOG

In this unit, you learned many things about balancing your life. How comfortable do you feel doing each of the skills listed below? Rate your comfort level on a scale of 1 to 4.
1 = Not so comfortable **2** = Need more practice **3** = Comfortable **4** = Very comfortable
If you circle 1 or 2, write down the page number where you can review this skill.

Life Skill	Comfort Level	Page(s)
Identify and discuss future goals.	1 2 3 4	4, 5
Create a goal chart.	1 2 3 4	5, 18
Discuss obstacles and solutions.	1 2 3 4	6, 7, 9, 18
Identify important relationships.	1 2 3 4	10, 13
Analyze your personal time management techniques.	1 2 3 4	15

Grammar		
Use *used to* for habits in the past.	1 2 3 4	2, 3
Contrast past and present habits.	1 2 3 4	1, 3, 18
Give and respond to advice.	1 2 3 4	8, 9
Use adjective clauses.	1 2 3 4	10, 11, 12, 18

Academic Skill		
Use context clues to discover word meaning.	1 2 3 4	4, 16
Write a paragraph.	1 2 3 4	13, 14
Read about time management.	1 2 3 4	15
Analyze a reading on time management.	1 2 3 4	16

Reflection
Complete the following statements about this unit.

I learned _____ *(Answers will vary.)* _____

I would like to find out more about _____

I am still confused about _____

Unit 1 Pronunciation and Learner Log

Pronunciation: 10–15 min. (optional)

Sentence Stress

We can use stress to emphasize words that we want to contrast and to make the meaning clearer. Listen and repeat the first sentence. Then listen to sentences 2, 3, and 4. Underline the stressed words.

Play the recording, pausing after each part of the sentence. Ask students to repeat. Then ask them to underline the stressed words. Write the answers on the board or on a transparency.

For additional pronunciation practice: Practice creating new sentences by giving students the sentence starters below and asking them to complete the sentences. Then have students dictate their sentence endings to each other in pairs, underlining the stressed words. Example sentence completions are in parentheses.

Examples:

1. *Last weekend we went skiing, (but this weekend we want to go climbing.)*

2. *She used to read a lot of science fiction, (but now she likes detective stories.)*

3. *Santa Clara is my hometown, (but Portland is where I live now.)*

4. *I never use computers, (but my children use them every day.)*

Learner Log

Presentation 1: 5–10 min.

If needed, review the purpose of the Learner Log. Make sure students understand how to rate the comfort level they feel in reaching the individual goals listed under *Life Skill, Grammar,* and *Academic Skill.* They should rate their comfort level on a scale of 1 to 4:

1. Not so comfortable
2. Need more practice
3. Comfortable
4. Very comfortable

Practice 1: 5–10 min.

If a student circles 1 or 2, he or she should enter the page number on which the skill is featured. The student can then more easily revisit that page and study the material again.

Evaluation 1: 5–10 min.

Finally, emphasize to students the importance of answering the two questions posed in *Reflection.* They are designed to help students assign real-life value to their classwork.

Instructor's Notes for Unit 1 Team Project, Pronunciation, and Learner Log

_____

_____

_____

_____

_____

_____

_____

_____

_____

_____

_____

_____

_____

_____

LESSON PLAN

Objective:
Calculate monthly expenses
Key vocabulary:
personal expenses, monthly expenses,
budgeted amount, budget

 Pre-Assessment: Use the *Stand Out* ExamView® Pro *Test Bank* for Unit 2. *(optional)*

Warm-up and Review: 5–10 min.

Write *budget* on the board. Find out if anyone knows its meaning. Ask the class: *How many of you budget your money? What are the benefits of budgeting your money?*

Introduction: 10–15 min.

 Think about your personal finances. What do you spend money on every month?

Give students about five minutes to make a list. Then ask them to call out individual items. Make a list on the board of what students spend money on. Ask students to suggest general categories for monthly expenses.

State the Objective: *Today we will look at a budget and see how one family spends its money. Then you will make your own personal budget.*

Presentation 1: 10–15 min.

Have students look at the Masons' monthly expenses in exercise B. Ask them to guess how much money the family spends in each category. Prepare students for focused listening by telling them they will be listening for how much the Masons have decided to budget in each category. (See Teaching Hints for more on focused listening.)

Practice 1: 10–15 min.

 Listen to Sara and Todd Mason talk about their finances. Fill in the amounts.

Evaluation 1: 10–15 min.

Go over the answers as a class.

 **Compare your list of categories to the Masons' list. What are the similarities? What are the differences?**

Have students add any missing categories to the lists they made in exercise A.

Pronunciation: An optional pronunciation activity is found on the final page of this unit. This pronunciation activity may be introduced during any lesson in this unit, especially if students need practice with word linking. (See pages 40 and 40a for Unit 2 Pronunciation.)

STANDARDS CORRELATIONS

CASAS: 1.5.1, 6.1.1, 6.1.2
SCANS: **Resources** Allocates Money
Information Acquires and Evaluates Information, Organizes and Maintains Information, Uses Computers to Process Information (optional)
Systems Understands Systems, Improves and Designs Systems
Technology Applies Technology to Task (optional)
Basic Skills Reading, Writing, Arithmetic, Listening, Speaking

Thinking Skills Decision Making, Problem Solving, Reasoning
Personal Qualities Responsibility, Self-Management
EFF: **Communication** Read with Understanding, Speak So Others Can Understand, Listen Actively
Decision Making Use Math to Solve Problems and Communicate, Solve Problems and Make Decisions, Plan
Lifelong Learning Use Information and Communications Technology (optional)

UNIT 2

Personal Finance

GOALS

- Calculate monthly expenses
- Understand main ideas in a text
- Use contrary-to-fact conditionals
- Interpret credit card information
- Interpret loan information
- Analyze advertising techniques
- Express complaints

LESSON 1

Money in, money out

| GOAL ▶ | Calculate monthly expenses | *Life skill* |

A Think about your personal finances. What do you spend money on every month?

B Listen to Sara and Todd Mason talk about their finances. Fill in the amounts.

Monthly expenses	
Auto	$450
Rent	*$1,500*
Utilities	$ 160
Cable/Phone/Internet	$ 160
Food	$ 600
School supplies	$ 60
Clothing	$ 200
Medical	$ 50
Entertainment	$ 150

C Compare your list of categories to the Masons' list. What are the similarities? What are the differences?

(Answers will vary.)

D Look at the chart below. The first column, Monthly expenses, lists everything Todd and Sara spend money on. The second column, Budgeted amount, is how much they think they will spend this month. Look at the numbers you wrote on the previous page and transfer them to this column.

E Listen to Sara and Todd talk about what they actually spent in the month of May. Write down their actual expenses in the third column.

Monthly expenses	Budgeted amount	Actual amount spent in May	Difference
Auto	$450	$362.43	$-87.57
Rent	$1,500	$1,500	$0
Utilities	$ 160	$ 208.12	$ 48.12
Cable/Phone/Internet	$ 160	$ 235.72	$ 75.72
Food	$ 600	$ 659.81	$ 59.81
School	$ 60	$ 30	$-30
Clothing	$ 200	$ 200	$ 0
Medical	$ 50	$ 45.28	$ -4.72
Entertainment	$ 150	$ 132.96	$-17.04
TOTAL	$3,330	$3,374.32	$ 44.32

F Find the difference between the amount they budgeted and the amount they actually spent and write the amounts in the chart. What is the total amount they budgeted? What is the total amount they spent? What is the difference?

Example:

$212.43
– $200.00
_____
$ 12.43

G **Active Task:** Make a budget like the Masons' budget. Keep track of how much money you spend over the next month. Then adjust your budget if you need to.

Presentation 2: 5–10 min.

Have students look at the Masons' budget in exercise E. Explain each column. Ask why it is important to keep track of such information.

D **Look at the chart below. The first column, Monthly expenses, lists everything Todd and Sara spend money on. The second column, Budgeted amount, is how much they think they will spend this month. Look at the numbers you wrote on the previous page and transfer them to this column.**

Prepare students for focused listening by asking the following: *Did the Masons spend more or less than they thought they would on auto expenses? Why was their Budgeted Amount for rent and their Actual Amount exactly the same?* This is a good time to explain the difference between *fixed* and *variable expenses.*

Practice 2: 10–15 min.

E **Listen to Sara and Todd talk about what they actually spent in the month of May. Write down their actual expenses in the third column.**

Evaluation 2: 10–15 min.

Go over the answers as a class.

Presentation 3: 5–10 min.

Show students how to find the difference between the Budgeted amount and the Actual amount by doing simple subtraction. Ask for a volunteer to come to the board and do an example.

Practice 3: 10–15 min.

F **Find the difference between the amount they budgeted and the amount they actually spent and write the amounts in the chart. What is the total amount they budgeted? What is the total amount they spent? What is the difference?**

Evaluation 3: 10–15 min.

Go over the answers as a class. If there's time, lead a class discussion on what the Masons should do with their extra money or how they should handle spending more money than they thought they would.

Refer to the *Stand Out Activity Bank 4 CD-ROM,* Unit 2 Worksheet 1, for more budget practice. *(optional)*

Application: 20–25 min.

G **Active Task: Make a budget like the Masons' budget. Keep track of how much money you spend over the next month. Then adjust your budget if you need to.**

Have students make and fill in their own budget sheets, or refer to the *Stand Out Activity Bank 4 CD-ROM,* Unit 2 Worksheet 2, for a blank budget sheet that you can copy and distribute. (optional)

Optional Computer Activity: Have students make a spreadsheet for their budget. Show them how the computer can calculate the numbers and also make graphs of their budgets. (See Teaching Hints for suggestions on how to use computers in the classroom.)

Instructor's Notes for Lesson 1

_____

_____

_____

_____

_____

_____

_____

_____

LESSON PLAN

Objective:
Read consumer purchasing information

Key vocabulary:
savvy, shop around, price matching, shipping costs, delivery time, bargain, warranty

Warm-up and Review: 5–10 min.

Have students take out their budgets from the previous lesson. Review by asking some questions about categories, budgeted amount, and actual amount.

Introduction: 10–15 min.

Ask students to think of something expensive they've bought within the last year. Make a list on the board. Ask them what they did before they bought the expensive item (researched, saved money, etc.). Make a list of these activities.

State the Objective: *Today we will read a web page that gives information about what you should do before you make a large purchase.*

Presentation 1: 10–15 min.

A **The Masons have decided to buy a new couch for their family. They want a good-quality piece of furniture that will last a long time. What do you think they will do before buying the couch? Discuss ideas with your teacher.**

Have students get into small groups and discuss this question. Give them about 5–10 minutes and then ask the groups to report to the class. Make a list of everything that is said.

Have students look at the web page in their books. Ask them what sort of information they think they will read about.

Practice 1: 15–20 min.

B **Sara did some research on the Internet. Read the web page below to see what information she found.**

(Practice 1 continues on page 24a.)

STANDARDS CORRELATIONS

CASAS: 1.2.5
SCANS: **Interpersonal** Participates as a Member of a Team, Works with Cultural Diversity
Information Acquires and Evaluates Information, Organizes and Maintains Information, Interprets and Communicates Information
Technology Applies Technology to Task (optional)
Basic Skills Reading, Writing, Listening, Speaking
Thinking Skills Creative Thinking, Decision Making, Problem Solving, Reasoning

Personal Qualities Sociability
EFF: **Communication** Read with Understanding, Convey Ideas in Writing, Speak So Others Can Understand, Listen Actively
Decision Making Solve Problems and Make Decisions, Plan
Interpersonal Resolve Conflict and Negotiate, Cooperate with Others
Lifelong Learning Learn through Research, Use Information and Communications Technology (optional)

LESSON 2 Savvy Shopper

GOAL ▶ **Understand main ideas in a text** | *Academic skill*

A The Masons have decided to buy a new couch for their family. They want a good-quality piece of furniture that will last a long time. What do you think they will do before buying the couch? Discuss ideas with your teacher.

B Sara did some research on the Internet. Read the web page below to see what information she found.

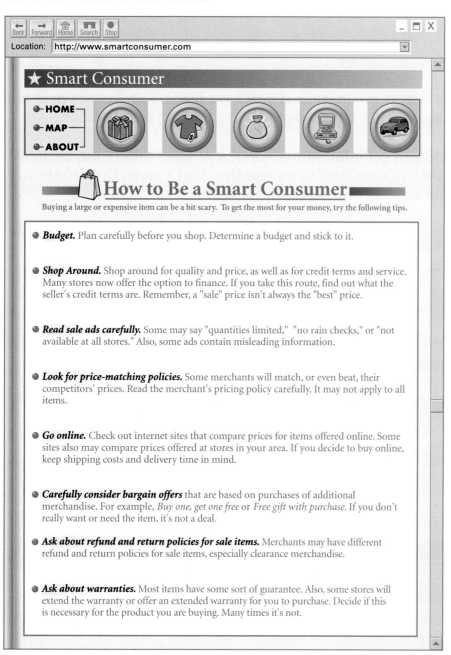

Back | Forward | Home | Search | Stop | _ □ X

Location: http://www.smartconsumer.com ▼

★ Smart Consumer

● HOME
● MAP
● ABOUT

How to Be a Smart Consumer
Buying a large or expensive item can be a bit scary. To get the most for your money, try the following tips.

● **Budget.** Plan carefully before you shop. Determine a budget and stick to it.

● **Shop Around.** Shop around for quality and price, as well as for credit terms and service. Many stores now offer the option to finance. If you take this route, find out what the seller's credit terms are. Remember, a "sale" price isn't always the "best" price.

● **Read sale ads carefully.** Some may say "quantities limited," "no rain checks," or "not available at all stores." Also, some ads contain misleading information.

● **Look for price-matching policies.** Some merchants will match, or even beat, their competitors' prices. Read the merchant's pricing policy carefully. It may not apply to all items.

● **Go online.** Check out internet sites that compare prices for items offered online. Some sites also may compare prices offered at stores in your area. If you decide to buy online, keep shipping costs and delivery time in mind.

● **Carefully consider bargain offers** that are based on purchases of additional merchandise. For example, *Buy one, get one free* or *Free gift with purchase.* If you don't really want or need the item, it's not a deal.

● **Ask about refund and return policies for sale items.** Merchants may have different refund and return policies for sale items, especially clearance merchandise.

● **Ask about warranties.** Most items have some sort of guarantee. Also, some stores will extend the warranty or offer an extended warranty for you to purchase. Decide if this is necessary for the product you are buying. Many times it's not.

C Based on the reading, make a list of eight things you should do before you make a large purchase. *(Answers may vary. Possible answers below.)*

1. *Plan your budget.*
2. *Compare prices and terms at different stores.*
3. *Read ads carefully for misleading information.*
4. *Look for price-matching policies.*
5. *Shop Internet sites.*
6. *Don't buy more than you want.*
7. *Find out about return and refund policies.*
8. *Ask about warranty policies.*

D Think about a large purchase that you have made. Put a check next to each of the tips in exercise C that you used before making that purchase.

E Where would you get information about a product before buying it? What factors would you consider? Complete the chart below. Then share your answers with a group and explain your reasons.

(Answers may vary. Possible answers below.)

Product	Where I would get information	What I would consider
	TV/audio store	Good picture and sound
	Newspaper ads	Size of screen
	Internet	Warranty
	Newspaper ads	Gas mileage
	Internet	Size/comfort
	Consumer Reports	Reliability
	Newspaper ads	Price
	Internet	Quality
		Comfort
	Computer store	Size of memory
	Internet	Software
		Functions
		Warranty

F **Active Task:** Go to the library for a book or magazine or use the Internet to find a web site that gives advice to consumers before they buy.

(Practice 1 continued from page 23a)

C **Based on the reading, make a list of eight things you should do before you make a large purchase.**

Evaluation 1: 10–15 min.

Have students share their lists with each other. Then ask volunteers to write their lists on the board. Go back to the reading and ask students if they have any questions about what they read.

Refer to the *Stand Out Activity Bank 4 CD-ROM,* Unit 2 Worksheet 3 (two pages), for more practice with consumer vocabulary. *(optional)*

Presentation 2: 5–10 min.

Review what the students mentioned during the Introduction activity. Ask the class to recall what some students purchased.

Practice 2: 10–15 min.

D **Think about a large purchase that you have made. Put a check next to each of the tips in exercise C that you used before making that purchase.**

Evaluation 2: 10–15 min.

Take a class poll to see the strategies students use before making an expensive purchase.

Presentation 3: 5–10 min.

Ask students the following questions: *Where would you get information if you wanted to purchase a television set? What things would you consider?* Write what students say on the board.

Practice 3: 10–15 min.

E **Where would you get information about a product before buying it? What factors would you consider? Complete the chart below. Then share your answers with a group and explain your reasons.**

Evaluation 3:

Observe group discussions.

Application: 20–25 min.

Have students in groups create a list of important points for consumers to consider. They can use information that they read in the web site on page 23, but tell them they must use different language. They can add some of their own ideas and exclude ideas that they think are not important.

Optional Computer Activity: Have students type their lists on the computer and add art, if possible. Show students how to create numbered or bulleted lists. (See Teaching Hints for more suggestions on how to use computers in the classroom.)

F **Active Task: Go to the library for a book or magazine or use the Internet to find a web site that gives advice to consumers before they buy.**

Refer to the *Stand Out Activity Bank 4 CD-ROM,* Unit 2 Active Task Checklist. *(optional)*

Remind students to use this checklist as they complete Active Tasks for Lessons 2, 4, and 6.

Instructor's Notes for Lesson 2

_____

_____

_____

_____

_____

_____

_____

_____

LESSON PLAN

Objective:
Use contrary-to-fact conditionals
Key vocabulary:
lottery

Warm-up and Review: 5–10 min. **1.5⁺**

Ask students who completed the Active Task in the previous lesson to share the information they gathered with the class. Also ask students to share the lists they created for exercise C in that lesson.

Introduction: 10–15 min. **1.5⁺**

Ask students the following questions:

What would you do if you had a million dollars?

What would you do if you won the lottery?

What would you do if you could speak English perfectly?

Don't expect grammatically correct answers. The point is get students thinking about the use of *if*.

State the Objective: *Today you will use contrary-to-fact conditionals and write statements about what you would do if your financial situation were different.*

Presentation 1: 10–15 min. **1.5⁺**

A **Contrary-to-fact conditionals express a condition and a result that are not true at this point in time. Study the examples below. Can you find the condition and the result in each of the statements?**

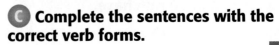 **B** **Study the chart below with your teacher.**

Practice 1: 15–20 min. **1.5⁺**

C **Complete the sentences with the correct verb forms.**

Evaluation 1: 10–15 min. **1.5⁺**

Go over the answers as a class.

Refer to *Stand Out Grammar Challenge 4,* Unit 2 page 9 for more practice with contrary-to-fact conditionals. *(optional)*

STANDARDS CORRELATIONS

CASAS: 7.2.2, 7.2.7
SCANS: **Interpersonal** Participates as a Member of a Team, Works with Cultural Diversity
Information Acquires and Evaluates Information, Interprets and Communicates Information
Systems Understands Systems, Monitors and Corrects Performance, Improves and Designs Systems
Basic Skills Reading, Writing, Speaking

Thinking Skills Creative Thinking, Decision Making, Reasoning
Personal Qualities Sociability
EFF: **Communication** Read with Understanding, Convey Ideas in Writing, Speak So Others Can Understand
Decision Making Solve Problems and Make Decisions
Interpersonal Cooperate with Others

LESSON 3 **What if?**

| GOAL ▶ Use contrary-to-fact conditionals | *Grammar* |

A Contrary-to-fact conditionals express a condition and a result that are not true at this point in time. Study the examples below. Can you find the condition and the result in each of the statements?

EXAMPLES:

If I were rich, I would buy a new car. (*I'm not really rich, so I can't buy a new car.*)
If they had a million dollars, they would move to Beverly Hills. (*They don't have a million dollars, so they can't move to Beverly Hills.*)

B Study the chart below with your teacher.

Contrary-to-fact conditionals	
Condition (*if* + past tense verb)	**Result (*would* + base verb)**
If she *got* a raise,	she *would buy* a new house.
If they *didn't spend* so much money on rent,	they *would have* more money for entertainment.
If I *were* a millionaire,	I'*d give* all my money to charity.
If John *weren*'t so busy at work,	he *would spend* more time with his children.

Contrary-to-fact (or unreal) conditional statements are sentences that are not true. The *if* clause can come in the first or second part of the sentence. In written English, use *were* (instead of *was*) for *if* clauses with first- and third-person singular forms of *be.* Notice how commas are used in the examples below.

C Complete the sentences with the correct verb forms.

1. If Bita _____*were*_____ (be) an architect in the United States, she _____*would design*_____ (design) beautiful homes.

2. If the Petersons both _____*retired*_____ (retire), they _____*would travel*_____ (travel) around the world.

3. Van _____*would buy*_____ (buy) a new computer if she _____*had*_____ (have) some extra money.

4. If my husband _____*were*_____ (be) rich, he _____*would buy*_____ (buy) me an expensive diamond ring.

5. George _____*would save*_____ (save) more money if he _____*didn't spend*_____ (not spend) so much on eating out.

6. You _____*wouldn't be*_____ (not be) so tired if you _____*had*_____ (have) more time to relax.

D   **Study the chart with your teacher.**

Wh- question	Yes/no question
what + *would* + subject + base verb + *if* + subject + past tense	*would* + subject + base verb + *if* + subject + past tense
What would you do if you won the lottery?	Would you give up your job if you won the lottery?

E   **Work in groups. Take turns asking your group the questions below. Each person must answer with a conditional statement.**

EXAMPLE:
Student A: What would you do if you won the lottery?
Student B: If I won the lottery, I'd give up my job.
Student C: If I won the lottery, I'd buy a house.
Student D: If I won the lottery, I'd travel round the world.

What would you do if . . .

1. _____ you had a million dollars?

2. _____ you lived in a mansion?

3. _____ you had your own airplane?

4. _____ you were the boss of a huge company?

5. _____ you owned an island in the Pacific?

6. _____ (your own idea)

F   **Write three personal statements about what you would do if your financial situation were different.**

1. _____ *(Answers will vary.)* _____

2. _____

3. _____

Presentation 2: 5–10 min.

D Study the chart with your teacher.

Review the chart at the top of the page with students. Create similar questions with the class by starting the questions and have students suggest the *if*-clause.

Shorter classes: Complete the following exercises for homework.

Practice 2: 15–20 min.

E Work in groups. Take turns asking your group the questions below. Each person must answer with a conditional statement.

Evaluation 2: 10–15 min.

Call on different group members to complete the sentences aloud. If a student makes a mistake, write what he or she said on the board and ask the class to help you correct it.

Refer to *Stand Out Grammar Challenge,* Unit 2 pages 10–12 for additional practice with contrary-to-fact conditionals. (optional)

Presentation 3: 5–10 min.

Go over the instructions for exercise F. Give students an example personal statement.

Practice 3: 10–15 min.

F Write three personal statements about what you would do if your financial situation were different.

Ask students to stay with their groups but write the statements individually.

Evaluation 3: 10–15 min.

Ask students to share answers with their groups. Observe the activity.

Application: 20–25 min.

Have each group choose and then share its three best statements from exercise F with the class. If you have time, have each group also write its three best statements on the board or on poster paper to place around the classroom.

Refer to the *Stand Out Activity Bank 4 CD-ROM,* Unit 2 Worksheet 4, for more practice with contrary-to-fact conditionals. (optional)

Instructor's Notes for Lesson 3

_____
_____
_____
_____
_____
_____
_____
_____
_____
_____
_____
_____
_____
_____
_____
_____
_____
_____
_____
_____
_____
_____

> ## LESSON PLAN
>
> Objective:
> Interpret and evaluate credit card information
> Key vocabulary:
> private, credit card, debit card, annual fee, APR, introductory rate, grace period, late fee, creditworthiness, credit limit, capacity, character, collateral

Warm-up and Review: 10–15 min.

A Fill out the credit card application below with all of your basic information. If you don't want to use your real information in your book, you can make it up.

Discuss why it's important to keep some personal information private, especially a social security number. Assist students in filling out the application.

Introduction: 10–15 min.

B Do you have a credit card? What kind of card is it? What is the interest rate? What do you use it for? Discuss these questions with your group.

Have students work in small groups. If time allows, have students report group answers without using student names.

State the Objective: *Today you will read about credit cards and evaluate different types of cards. Then you will weigh the advantages and disadvantages of using a credit card.*

STANDARDS CORRELATIONS

CASAS: 1.2.5, 1.3.1, 1.3.2, 1.3.3
SCANS: **Interpersonal** Participates as a Member of a Team, Works with Cultural Diversity
Information Acquires and Evaluates Information, Organizes and Maintains Information, Interprets and Communicates Information
Systems Understands Systems
Basic Skills Reading, Writing, Listening, Speaking

Thinking Skills Creative Thinking, Decision Making, Problem Solving, Reasoning
Personal Qualities Sociability, Self-Management
EFF: **Communication** Read with Understanding, Convey Ideas in Writing, Speak So Others Can Understand, Listen Actively, Observe Critically
Decision Making Solve Problems and Make Decisions
Interpersonal Cooperate with Others
Lifelong Learning Learn through Research

Charge it!

GOAL ▶ Interpret credit card information

 Fill out the credit card application below with all of your basic information. If you don't want to use your real information in your book, you can make it up.

(Answers will vary.)

Credit Card Application

Title (Optional): Mr. ☐ Mrs. ☐ Ms. ☐

First Name: ☐☐☐☐☐☐☐☐☐☐☐☐☐☐☐ MI: ☐

Last Name: ☐☐☐☐☐☐☐☐☐☐☐☐☐☐

Date of Birth: ☐☐/☐☐/☐☐ mm/dd/19yy

Social Security Number: ☐☐☐-☐☐-☐☐☐☐

Home Address: ☐☐☐☐☐☐☐☐☐☐☐☐☐☐☐☐☐☐☐☐☐ Apt./Suite #: ☐☐☐☐☐

City: ☐☐☐☐☐☐☐☐☐☐☐☐ State: ☐☐ Zip Code: ☐☐☐☐☐-☐☐☐☐

Home Phone: (☐☐☐)-☐☐☐-☐☐☐☐ Time at Home Address: ☐☐years, ☐☐months

Do you: Own? ☐ Rent? ☐ Monthly Rent or Mortgage Amount: $☐☐☐☐.00

- - -

Company Name: ☐☐☐☐☐☐☐☐☐☐☐☐☐☐☐☐☐☐☐☐☐☐☐☐☐☐☐☐

Street Address: ☐☐☐☐☐☐☐☐☐☐☐☐☐☐☐☐☐☐☐☐ Floor/Suite #: ☐☐☐☐☐

City: ☐☐☐☐☐☐☐☐☐☐☐☐☐☐ State: ☐☐ Zip Code: ☐☐☐☐☐-☐☐☐☐

Business Phone: (☐☐☐)-☐☐☐-☐☐☐☐

Time at This Company: ☐☐years, ☐☐months

- - -

Household Income: $☐☐☐☐☐☐☐☐

Do you have a (check all that apply) Checking Account? ☐ Money Market/Savings Account? ☐

B **Do you have a credit card? What kind of card is it? What is the interest rate? What do you use it for? Discuss these questions with your group.**

Read the following information about credit cards. Do you agree with this advice? Which parts do you disagree with?

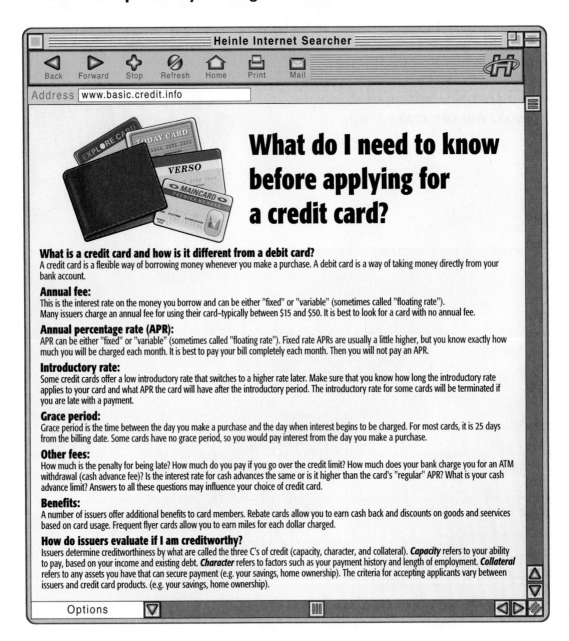

Heinle Internet Searcher

◁ Back   ▷ Forward   ✛ Stop   ⊘ Refresh   ⌂ Home   🖨 Print   ✉ Mail

Address www.basic.credit.info

What do I need to know before applying for a credit card?

What is a credit card and how is it different from a debit card?
A credit card is a flexible way of borrowing money whenever you make a purchase. A debit card is a way of taking money directly from your bank account.

Annual fee:
This is the interest rate on the money you borrow and can be either "fixed" or "variable" (sometimes called "floating rate").
Many issuers charge an annual fee for using their card–typically between $15 and $50. It is best to look for a card with no annual fee.

Annual percentage rate (APR):
APR can be either "fixed" or "variable" (sometimes called "floating rate"). Fixed rate APRs are usually a little higher, but you know exactly how much you will be charged each month. It is best to pay your bill completely each month. Then you will not pay an APR.

Introductory rate:
Some credit cards offer a low introductory rate that switches to a higher rate later. Make sure that you know how long the introductory rate applies to your card and what APR the card will have after the introductory period. The introductory rate for some cards will be terminated if you are late with a payment.

Grace period:
Grace period is the time between the day you make a purchase and the day when interest begins to be charged. For most cards, it is 25 days from the billing date. Some cards have no grace period, so you would pay interest from the day you make a purchase.

Other fees:
How much is the penalty for being late? How much do you pay if you go over the credit limit? How much does your bank charge you for an ATM withdrawal (cash advance fee)? Is the interest rate for cash advances the same or is it higher than the card's "regular" APR? What is your cash advance limit? Answers to all these questions may influence your choice of credit card.

Benefits:
A number of issuers offer additional benefits to card members. Rebate cards allow you to earn cash back and discounts on goods and seervices based on card usage. Frequent flyer cards allow you to earn miles for each dollar charged.

How do issuers evaluate if I am creditworthy?
Issuers determine creditworthiness by what are called the three C's of credit (capacity, character, and collateral). *Capacity* refers to your ability to pay, based on your income and existing debt. *Character* refers to factors such as your payment history and length of employment. *Collateral* refers to any assets you have that can secure payment (e.g. your savings, home ownership). The criteria for accepting applicants vary between issuers and credit card products. (e.g. your savings, home ownership).

Options ▽

Presentation 1: 5 min.

Have students first look only at the title and the bold headings in the article on this page. Ask them what kind of information they think they will be reading about.

Practice 1: 15–20 min.

C Read the following information about credit cards. Do you agree with this advice? Which parts do you disagree with?

Ask volunteers to read one paragraph aloud. Go over any vocabulary questions students might raise. Then ask them to reread the entire article by themselves.

Optional Internet Activity: Have students go to a consumer advice web site to see if they can find similar information on line.

Evaluation 1:

As you go through the reading, answer any questions that come up about the article's content and vocabulary.

Presentation 2: 5–10 min.

Ask students to look back in the reading and find the word *debit card*. Ask them if they know what the word means. Ask them if the article explains its meaning.

Practice 2: 10–15 min.

D What did you learn from the article about the following words? Discuss them with your class.

Ask students to go back to the article and find each of the words listed in the box. Have them make notes of what each word means or what they think it means based on the reading.

Evaluation 2: 10–15 min.

Discuss the boxed words with the class.

Presentation 3: 5–10 min.

Have students look at the chart in exercise E. Ask them what sort of information it contains. Ask them such basic comprehension questions as *What is Verso's annual fee? Does Maincard charge a late fee? What is it?*

Practice 3: 10–15 min.

E Read the chart and decide which credit card is the best deal.

Guide students in comparing cards. For example, point out that Today card requires no annual fee but charges a high APR. Also, explain how the Explore Card differs from the others. (It extends credit only for a maximum of thirty days, after which a stiff late fee applies.)

Evaluation 3: 10–15 min.

F Which card did you choose? Why?

Have students share their choices and reasons for making them with the class.

Application: 20–25 min.

G What are the advantages and disadvantages of having a credit card? Discuss with your group.

Have students work in small groups to complete this exercise. Then make a list on the board and have each group share what they came up with.

H Active Task: Find a real credit card application and fill it out. (Don't send it in unless you really want the card!)

Remind students to use the Active Task Checklist for Lesson 4.

Refer to the *Stand Out Activity Bank 4 CD-ROM,* Unit 2 Worksheet 5, for an extended credit card application form and Worksheet 6 (two pages), for a credit card team project. *(optional)*

Instructor's Notes for Lesson 4

D What did you learn from the article about the following words? Discuss them with your class.

annual fee	late fee	credit limit	introductory rate
grace period	annual percentage rate (APR)	creditworthiness	

E Read the chart and decide which credit card is the best deal.

	Verso	Maincard	Explore Card (must pay in full each month)	Todaycard
Annual Fee	$20	$15	$55	$0
APR	15%	14.9%	NA	21%
Introductory Rate (6 months)	2.9%	0%	3.8%	9.9%
Late Fee	$20	$10	$50	$25
Benefits	none	airline miles (1 for each dollar you spend)	none	cash back (1% of purchases)

F Which card did you choose? Why?

(Answers will vary.)

_____

_____

G What are the advantages and disadvantages of having a credit card? Discuss with your group.

 H **Active Task:** Find a real credit card application and fill it out. (Don't send it in unless you really want the card!)

LESSON 5 Apply for a loan

A Todd and Sara are thinking of buying a house. Todd is worried about money, so he made an appointment with a financial planner to talk about a mortgage. Look at the expressions below and discuss them with your teacher. Then listen to Todd talking with the financial planner.

mortgage	down payment	price range	credit check	deposit
afford	get approved for a loan	financial commitment		purchase price

B Listen to the first part of the conversation again. What are the three questions Todd must ask himself? Write them below.

1. *Do we have money set aside for a down payment?*

2. *Do we have enough money each month to make a loan payment?*

3. *Are we ready to make a long-term financial commitment?*

C What are the next steps Todd must take? Listen to what the financial planner says and write the four steps below.

1. *Determine how much he can afford to spend.*

2. *Get approved for a loan for that amount.*

3. *Start looking for a home in his price range.*

4. *Make an offer on the house he wants.*

D Todd will need to give the financial planner six things. Do you remember what they are? Write them below. If you can't remember, listen again.

1. *social security number*

2. *tax statements from the past two years*

3. *two most recent pay stubs*

4. *most recent statements from all bank accounts*

5. *most recent credit card statements*

6. *statements from any other loans*

E Imagine you are trying to get a mortgage and you have to gather all of the items listed above. Put a check next to each one that you have at home right now.

LESSON PLAN

Objective:
Interpret loan information
Key vocabulary:
down payment, determine, make an offer, long-term financial commitment, afford, credit check, get approved for a loan, recent pay stubs, put down a deposit, price range, purchase price, mortgage

the entire recording once and ask students to listen only.

Practice 1: 15–20 min. `1.5+`

Before you play the recordings for each exercise below, see how many blanks students can fill in based on what they heard in the first listening.

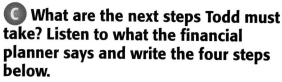

B Listen to the first part of the conversation again. What are the three questions Todd must ask himself? Write them below.

C What are the next steps Todd must take? Listen to what the financial planner says and write the four steps below.

D Todd will need to give the financial planner six things. Do you remember what they are? Write them below. If you can't remember, listen again.

Warm-up and Review: 5–10 min. `1.5+`

Review the *advantages* and *disadvantages* of using credit cards. Ask volunteers to write their ideas on the board under each of the two categories.

Introduction: 10–15 min. `1.5+`

Ask students, *What if an item you want to buy costs more than the cash you have or than your credit card limit?* If their answers don't include *borrowing*, bring it up. Then define *credit* so students can distinguish between a credit card and a bank loan (a different form of credit).

State the Objective: *In this lesson we will interpret loan information by listening to Todd talk with a financial planner and then compare getting a loan to using a credit card.*

Evaluation 1: 10–15 min. `1.5+`

Review each exercise as students finish.

E Imagine you are trying to get a mortgage and you have to gather all of the items listed above. Put a check next to each one that you have at home right now.

Presentation 1: 10–15 min. `1.5+`

A Todd and Sara are thinking of buying a house. Todd is worried about money, so he made an appointment with a financial planner to talk about a mortgage. Look at the expressions below and discuss them with your teacher. Then listen to Todd talking with a financial planner.

Go over the words in the box as a class. Then play

Presentation 2: 5–10 min. `1.5+`

Ask students to close their books. Then dictate the boxed words at the top of the page. Ask volunteers to write them on the board.

Practice 2: 10–15 min. `2+`

Ask students to write a brief definition for each word to share with their group.

Evaluation 2: 10–15 min. `2+`

Write the definitions on the board.

STANDARDS CORRELATIONS

CASAS: 1.3.1, 1.4.6, 1.5.2
SCANS: **Interpersonal** Participates as a Member of a Team
Information Acquires and Evaluates Information, Organizes and Maintains Information, Interprets and Communicates Information
Basic Skills Reading, Writing, Listening, Speaking
Thinking Skills Creative Thinking, Decision Making,

Problem Solving, Reasoning
Personal Qualities Sociability
EFF: **Communication** Read with Understanding, Convey Ideas in Writing, Speak So Others Can Understand, Listen Actively, Observe Critically
Decision Making Solve Problems and Make Decisions
Interpersonal Cooperate with Others

Presentation 3: 5–10 min.   `3`

F Read the information about loans.

Read this information aloud to your students. Have the class ask questions and help you make a list on the board with information about loans.

Practice 3: 10–15 min.   `3`

G With a partner, discuss the differences between these purchasing options. Make notes in the chart below.

Evaluation 3: 10–15 min.   `3`

Ask students to share their answers with the class. Make a two-column list on the board.

Application: 20–25 min.   `1.5+`

H Look across the list of items below. Decide if you should get a loan or use a credit card to pay for each item. Compare your answers with a group and explain why.

When students are finished, take a class poll to see if there is a consensus on how to pay for each item.

AB **Refer to the *Stand Out Activity Bank 4 CD-ROM,* Unit 2 Worksheet 7, for more vocabulary and writing practice around the theme of buying a home.** *(optional)*

Instructor's Notes for Lesson 5

Read the information about loans.

When you decide to purchase something that costs more than you can pay for right now, you can put it on your credit card, or you can get a loan. A loan from a bank or lending institution is something you have to apply for directly. You usually have to specify the amount and what kind of purchase you want to make. For large purchases, you usually need collateral, such as your house, your business, or a down payment. The interest rate will vary according to the amount you borrow, where you borrow the money from, and your creditworthiness.

With a partner, discuss the differences between these purchasing options. Make notes in the chart below.
(Answers may vary. Possible answers below.)

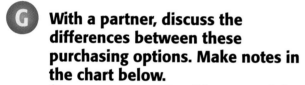

Loan	Credit card
must apply for	*may charge up to limit without approval*
need collateral	*no collateral needed*
interest rates vary	*interest rates vary*
may or may not be approved	

Look across the list of items below. Decide if you should get a loan or use a credit card to pay for each item. Compare your answers with a group and explain why. *(Answers will vary.)*

	Car	College course	Computer	TV	Airline ticket	Small business
loan						
credit card						

 **LESSON** **How they pull you in**

GOAL ▶ Analyze advertising techniques | **Life skill**

 A **Look at the following ads for cameras.**

> pixels – tiny squares that make up a digital image
>
> megapixel – one million pixels
>
> zoom – a zoom lens makes an image appear close up

B **Discuss these questions with your group.**

1. Which ad is most attractive? Why? *(Answers will vary.)*

2. What kind of information do the ads give?

3. What information is not included?

4. How do the ads try to persuade you to buy?

LESSON PLAN

Objective:
Analyze and interpret ads
Key vocabulary:
best buy, on impulse, pixels, zoom lens,
battery, charger, connectivity, coupon,
rebate

Warm-up and Review: 5–10 min.

Write *car*, *computer*, *TV*, **and** *airline ticket* **on the board.** Ask students if they would pay for these items by taking out a loan or using a credit card. (Also, ask if they would buy on impulse or do some research beforehand. How would they do such research?)

Introduction: 10–15 min.

Ask students the following questions:

How do advertisements serve the purpose of both the buyer and the seller?

Do you look at advertisements?

For what products? Why?

State the Objective: *Today you will look at advertisements for cameras and interpret the information you see in the ads. Then you will make a decision about the best buy.*

Presentation 1: 10–15 min.

A Look at the following ads for cameras.

Have students read the ads. If they don't know very much about cameras, you may have to briefly explain the features of each of the four.

Practice 1: 15–20 min.

B Discuss these questions with your group.

(Practice 1 continues on page 33a.)

STANDARDS CORRELATIONS

CASAS: 1.2.1, 1.2.2
SCANS: **Interpersonal** Participates as a Member of a Team, Exercises Leadership, Works with Cultural Diversity
Information Acquires and Evaluates Information, Organizes and Maintains Information, Interprets and Communicates Information, Uses Computers to Process Information (optional)
Systems Understands Systems, Monitors and Corrects Performance
Technology Applies Technology to Task (optional)
Basic Skills Reading, Writing, Listening, Speaking
Thinking Skills Creative Thinking, Decision Making,

Knowing How to Learn, Reasoning
Personal Qualities Responsibility, Self-Esteem, Sociability
EFF: **Communication** Read with Understanding, Convey Ideas in Writing, Speak So Others Can Understand, Listen Actively, Observe Critically
Decision Making Solve Problems and Make Decisions, Plan
Interpersonal Guide Others, Advocate and Influence, Cooperate with Others
Lifelong Learning Take Responsibility for Learning, Reflect and Evaluate, Learn through Research, Use Information and Communications Technology (optional)

(Practice 1 continued from page 32a)

C Look at the ads on the previous pages to complete the table below.

Evaluation 1: 10–15 min.

Display a transparency of the chart on an overhead projector and have students come up to write the answers in the blanks, or duplicate the chart on the board.

Presentation 2: 5–10 min.

Ask, *Do advertisers always include all of the necessary information in their ads?* Ask students if any needed information is missing in ads they usually see.

Practice 2: 10–15 min.

D Is there more information you'd like to know about the cameras? Write three questions below that you might ask a salesperson.

Evaluation 2: 10–15 min.

Ask volunteers to share their questions with the class.

Optional Internet Activity: Have students find web sites that sell cameras and e-mail the site questions about particular cameras. (Note: Students will need a return e-mail address to do this.) Ask students to check their e-mail in a few days for a response and report the results to the class.

Presentation 3: 5–10 min.

Have students get into groups of four or five. Tell them that they are consumer advocates. Explain that consumer advocates help protect the rights of consumers by promoting such practices as safe products, clear labeling, honesty in advertising, and fair pricing.

Practice 3: 15–20 min.

E Discuss these questions with your group.

F Based on the advertisements, which camera would you buy? Why?

Help each group prepare a five–minute class presentation based on the questions. Remind them that they are acting as *advocates* and are therefore interested in *influencing* public opinion.

Evaluation 3: 10–15 min.

Have each group give its presentation to the class.

Refer to the *Stand Out Activity Bank 4 CD-ROM,* Unit 2 Worksheet 8, for an additional exercise analyzing ads for information. *(optional)*

Application: 20–25 min.

G Active Task: Look at some digital camera ads in the newspaper or on the Internet. How do they compare to the ads in your book?

Based on the advertisements, which camera would students buy? Why? Have them brainstorm and write a paragraph explaining their choice. Have students peer correct and rewrite their paragraphs accordingly.

Remind students to use the Active Task Checklist for Lesson 6.

Instructor's Notes for Lesson 6

_____

C **Look at the ads on the previous pages to complete the table below.**

	Olympic	Canyon	Minertia	Niken
Price	$249	*$359*	*$699*	*$599*
Coupon or rebate needed?	*yes*	no	*yes*	*no*
Zoom	*4.4x*	*2x*	10x	*3x*
Pixels	*2.1 million*	*2 million*	*3.34 million*	2.6 million
Features	offers movie clips with audio	*stainless steel body*	*direct prints using a Minertia printer*	*movie recording and playback with sound*
Special Offers	*includes extra battery*	none	free camera bag	*50 free prints*

D **Is there more information you'd like to know about the cameras? Write three questions below that you might ask a salesperson.**

1. *Are batteries included?*

2. *Is the picture quality good?*

3. *How does the digital camera differ from the others?*

   (Answers may vary. Possible answers above.)

E **Discuss these questions with your group.**

1. What do advertisers do to get you interested in their products?

2. Can you always trust advertisements?

3. What's the best way to find out the truth about a product?

F **Based on the advertisements, which camera would you buy? Why?**

  G **Active Task:** Look at some digital camera ads in the newspaper or on the Internet. How do they compare to the ads in your book?

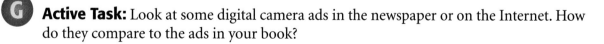

A   **Tell the class about a time when you complained about a product or service.**

B   **Look at each of the situations below. With a partner, decide who you would talk to and what you would say, and what you would like to see happen.**

1. You got home from the grocery store and realized the milk is bad.

   Who would you talk to? _____ *grocery store manager* _____

   What would you say? _____ ***I just got home and realized this milk is bad.***

   What would you like to see happen? _____ ***I would like a new carton of milk.***

2. You took a suit to the cleaners and it came back with a stain on it.

   Who would you talk to?

   manager

   What would you say?

   This suit has a stain on it.

   What would you like to see happen?

   I would like the stain removed or a refund.

3. You paid cash for your meal in a restaurant, but the server did not bring back your change.

   Who would you talk to? *the server*

   What would you say? *You have not brought me my change.*

   What would you like to see happen? *Please bring me my change.*

4. There is something on your credit card bill that you didn't purchase.

   Who would you talk to?

   customer service representative

   What would you say?

   I did not purchase this item.

   What would you like to see happen?

   I would like the item removed from my bill.

MAINCARD	Account Summary	
	Closing Date	08/25/02
	Account Number	0000
	Payment Due Date	09/20/02

Transactions			
Sale Date	Post Date	Description	Amount
08/01/02	08/01/02	VIDEO BUYS	21.19
08/06/02	08/07/02	DISCOUNT STORE	27.50
08/09/02	08/09/02	SPORTS	13.90
08/11/02	08/11/02	CARD STORE	50.19
08/14/02	08/16/02	BOOK MART	
08/15/02	08/17/02	PET STOP	52.98
08/19/02	08/20/02	SHOE EXPRESS	89.90
08/24/02	08/24/02	DAVE'S CLUB	15.75

Extra item

(Answers may vary. Possible answers above.)

C   **With your partner, choose one of the topics above and write a conversation between the two people. Practice your conversation and present it to the class.**

> **LESSON PLAN**
>
> Objective:
> Express complaints
> Key vocabulary:
> complain, complaint, return address, inside address, greeting, salutation, body, closing, signature

Warm-up and Review: 5–10 min.

A Tell the class about a time when you complained about a product or service.

As an example, tell the students about a product complaint you've had. If they need ideas, ask what they do if food from the supermarket is bad or if clothes from a department store don't fit.

Introduction: 1 min.

State the Objective: *Today you will practice complaining about something you bought or a service you received. Then you will write a business letter complaining.*

Presentation 1: 10–15 min.

Go over the instructions and first example for exercise B.

Practice 1: 15–20 min.

B Look at each of the situations below. With a partner, decide whom you would talk to and what you would say, and what you would like to see happen.

C With your partner, choose one of the topics above and write a conversation between the two people. Practice your conversation and present it to the class.

Evaluation 1: 10–15 min.

Have each pair present their conversation.

Refer to the *Stand Out Activity Bank 4 CD-ROM,* Unit 2 Worksheet 9, for a supplemental listening activity and additional conversation writing activity. *(optional)*

STANDARDS CORRELATIONS

CASAS: 1.6.3
SCANS: **Interpersonal** Participates as a Member of a Team, Exercises Leadership, Works with Cultural Diversity
Information Acquires and Evaluates Information, Interprets and Communicates Information
Systems Monitors and Corrects Performance
Technology Applies Technology to Task (optional)
Basic Skills Reading, Writing, Listening, Speaking
Thinking Skills Creative Thinking, Decision Making,

Problem Solving
Personal Qualities Responsibility, Sociability, Self-Management, Integrity/Honesty
EFF: **Communication** Read with Understanding, Convey Ideas in Writing, Speak So Others Can Understand, Listen Actively
Decision Making Solve Problems and Make Decisions
Interpersonal Resolve Conflict and Negotiate, Advocate and Influence, Cooperate with Others

Presentation 2: 5–10 min.

Have students look at the letter on page 35. Ask them some basic questions such as, *Who wrote the letter? Whom did she write it to? Where is the restaurant located? Why would you write a letter to a restaurant?*

Practice 2: 10–15 min.

D One of the most effective ways to complain is to write a business letter. Read the letter below.

E Answer the questions about the letter.

Evaluation 2: 5–10 min.

Go over the answers as a class.

D **One of the most effective ways to complain is to write a business letter. Read the letter below.**

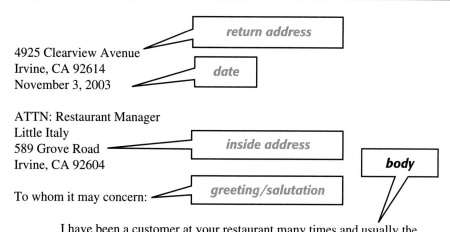

4925 Clearview Avenue
Irvine, CA 92614
November 3, 2003

ATTN: Restaurant Manager
Little Italy
589 Grove Road
Irvine, CA 92604

To whom it may concern:

return address

date

inside address

body

greeting/salutation

     I have been a customer at your restaurant many times and usually the food and service are wonderful. However, last night I was there having dinner with my husband, and we had a terrible experience. First of all, our server, Kimberly, greeted us, took our order, and then never returned. When we finally tracked her down, forty minutes later, she was bringing our food, which was cold because it had been sitting in the kitchen too long. We never did get our drinks. When we were finished, we had to find another food server to get our check. We spent two hours at your restaurant and had bad service and a bad meal.

     We have really enjoyed eating at your restaurant in the past, so I hope you will take this letter seriously and do more training with your staff.

Sincerely,   *closing*

Sara Mason   *signature*
Sara Mason

typed/printed name

E **Answer the questions about the letter.**

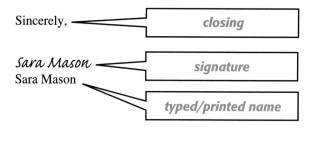

1. Who is Sara complaining to? _the restaurant manager_

2. What is she complaining about? _bad service_

3. What do you think will happen? _The manager may offer a complimentary meal, and the server may be reprimanded._

F **Use the words below to label the parts of the business letter on the previous page.**

- return address
- date
- inside address
- greeting/salutation

- ~~body~~
- closing
- typed/printed name
- signature

G **A business letter should contain the following information. Look at Sara's letter again. Did she mention all of these in her letter?**

- who you are
- why you are writing
- an explanation of the problem or situation
- a resolution

H **Choose one of the situations below and write a business letter to make a complaint. Remember to format the letter correctly and include all of the necessary information.**

Company	Reason for letter
1. Lane's Accessories 8695 Tiguk Ave. Sioux Falls, SD 57104	The purse you bought is falling apart after one month.
2. Media Vision 4679 Lolly Lane Long Beach, CA 90745	You were charged for two months of cable instead of one.
3. Riverview Bank 47986 Washington Ave Grand Rapids, MI 49503	There is a charge on your credit card statement that doesn't belong to you.
4. Produce World 875 7th Ave New York, NY 10011	You were treated poorly by an employee.
5. Your own idea	Your own idea

Presentation 3: 5–10 min.   **3**

Prepare students for Practice 3 by going over the directions to exercises F and G.

Practice 3: 10–15 min.   **3**

F **Use the words below to label the parts of the business letter on the previous page.**

G **A business letter should contain the following information. Look at Sara's letter again. Did she mention all of these in her letter?**

Evaluation 3: 10–15 min.   **3**

Go over the answers as a class.

Application: 20–25 min.   **L5⁺**

H **Choose one of the situations below and write a business letter to make a complaint. Remember to format the letter correctly and include all of the necessary information.**

Optional Computer Activity: Have students enter their business letters onto the computer. This would be a good time to show them how to use the Business Letter Wizard or templates available on the computer. (See Teaching Hints for suggestions on how to use computers in the classroom.)

Instructor's Notes for Lesson 7

LESSON PLAN

Objective:
Review all previous unit objectives
Key vocabulary:
Review all previous unit vocabulary

Warm-up and Review: 5–10 min.

Ask volunteers to share the letters that they wrote in the previous lesson.

Introduction: 5–10 min.

Write *evaluation* and *review* **on the board.** Ask students what these words mean and their purpose.

State the Objective: *Today we will review all that we have done in the past unit in preparation for the application project to follow.*

Ask students as a class to recall all the goals of this unit without looking at their books. Then remind them of the goals they haven't mentioned.

Unit goals: *Calculate monthly expenses, Understand main ideas in a text, Use contrary-to-fact conditionals, Interpret credit card information, Interpret loan information, Organize information, Express complaints.*

Presentation, Practice, and Evaluation 1:

Do the Learner Log on page 40. Notes are next to the page.

Presentation 2: 5–10 min.

 A **Look back at page 17 and review how to make vocabulary cards. Choose four new words that you learned in this unit and write them below. Make a vocabulary card for each word or expression.**

Practice 2: 10–15 min.

B **You have just inherited $100,000 from a relative who passed away. What would you do with it? Write three conditional statements about the possibilities. Then share your answers with the class.**

C **Complete each of the following questions.**

D **Now ask three people in your class each of these questions and write their answers below. Share their answers with the class.**

Evaluation 2: 10–15 min.

Ask students to share their answers.

STANDARDS CORRELATIONS

CASAS: 7.1.4, 7.2.1, 7.4.1, 7.4.2
SCANS: **Interpersonal** Participates as a Member of a Team, Teaches Others New Skills, Works with Cultural Diversity
Information Acquires and Evaluates Information, Organizes and Maintains Information
Systems Understands Systems, Monitors and Corrects Performance
Basic Skills Reading, Writing, Listening, Speaking
Thinking Skills Creative Thinking, Decision Making, Seeing

Things in the Mind's Eye, Knowing How to Learn, Reasoning
Personal Qualities Responsibility, Self-Esteem, Sociability, Self-Management, Integrity/Honesty
EFF: **Communication** Convey Ideas in Writing, Speak So Others Can Understand, Listen Actively
Decision Making Solve Problems and Make Decisions
Interpersonal Guide Others, Cooperate with Others
Lifelong Learning Take Responsibility for Learning, Reflect and Evaluate, Learn through Research

A Look back at page 17 and review how to make vocabulary cards. Choose four new words that you learned in this unit and write them below. Make a vocabulary card for each word or expression.

1. _____*(Answers will vary.)*_____   3. _____

2. _____   4. _____

B You have just inherited $100,000 from a relative who passed away. What would you do with it? Write three conditional statements about the possibilities. Then share your answers with the class.

1. ___*If I inherited $100,000, I would buy a house.*_____

2. ___*If I inherited $100,000, I would take a trip around the world.*_____

3. ___*If I inherited $100,000, I would save it for my children's college education.*_____

(Answers may vary. Possible answers above.)

C Complete each of the following questions. *(Answers may vary. Possible answers below.)*

1. What would you do if ___*your car broke down?*_____

2. What would you buy if ___*you won the lottery?*_____

3. What would you take with you if ___*you went on a picnic?*_____

D Now ask three people in your class each of these questions and write their answers below. Share their answers with the class. *(Answers will vary.)*

Question	Student 1	Student 2	Student 3
No. 1			
No. 2			
No. 3			

Review

E **Decide if each statement below is true or false based on what you learned in this unit. On a separate piece of paper, take each false statement and make it a true statement.**

_T_ 1. A smart consumer asks a lot of questions about a product before buying it.

               don't
_F_ 2. Advertisements always tell you everything about the product.
                ^

_F_ 3. Budgets are ~~only for people with a lot of money.~~ *helpful for everyone.*

_F_ 4. Getting a loan isn't a long-term financial commitment.

_T_ 5. It is better to pay your credit card balance every month.

_T_ 6. Sometimes, credit cards carry high interest rates.

_T_ 7. Writing a business letter is a good way to express a complaint.

          could use
_F_ 8. You ~~must have~~ a credit card to buy an expensive item.
           ^

F **Imagine that your family of four has $3,000 to live on per month. Realistically, how would you budget your money? Fill in the chart below.**
(Answers may vary. Possible answers below.)

Expense	Budgeted amount
Rent/Mortgage payment	*$1,200*
Utilities: Gas/Electricity	*$ 150*
Auto: Car payment/Gas/Insurance	*$ 400*
Food	*$ 400*
Medical	*$ 100*
Clothing	*$ 200*
Cable/Phone/Internet	*$ 150*
Entertainment	*$ 200*
Savings	*$ 200*
TOTAL	$3,000

G **With a group, make a list of the things you need to think about and do before you purchase an expensive item. Compare your list with another group and add any new ideas to your list.**

H **Imagine you are writing an advertisement for a product. What information should be included in your ad? Make a list and share it with the class.**
(Answers will vary.)

Presentation 3: 5–10 min.

Go over the instructions for each of the exercises. Shorter classes may complete exercises for homework and review the next day.

Practice 3: 10–15 min.

E **Decide if each statement below is true or false based on what you learned in this unit. On a separate piece of paper, take each false statement and make it a true statement.**

F **Imagine that your family of four has $3,000 to live on per month. Realistically, how would you budget your money? Fill in the chart below.**

G **With a group, make a list of the things you need to think about and do before you purchase an expensive item. Compare your list with another group and add any new ideas to your list.**

H **Imagine you are writing an advertisement for a product. What information should be included in your ad? Make a list and share it with the class.**

Evaluation 3: 10–15 min.

Ask students to share their answers.

Application: 1–2 days

The Team Project Activity on the following page is the Application Activity to be done during the next class period.

Post-Assessment: Use the *Stand Out* ExamView® Pro *Test Bank* for Unit 2. *(optional)*

Note: With the *Stand Out* ExamView® Pro *Test Bank* you can design a post-assessment that focuses on what students have learned. It is designed for three purposes:

- To help students practice taking a test similar to current standardized tests.
- To help the teacher evaluate how much the students have learned, retained, and acquired.
- To help students see their progress when they compare their scores to the pre-test they took earlier.

Instructor's Notes for Unit 2 Review

_____

_____

_____

_____

_____

_____

_____

_____

_____

_____

_____

_____

_____

_____

_____

_____

_____

_____

_____

_____

_____

_____

_____

_____

Unit 2 Application Activity

> **TEAM PROJECT**
> **CREATE A PURCHASING PLAN**
> Objective:
> Project designed to apply all the
> objectives of this unit.
> Product:
> A purchase plan and an advertisement

Introduction: 1 min. `1.5+`

In teams, students will think of a large item they would like to buy, create a print ad for it, and design a plan outlining the steps they will need to take to purchase this item.

Note: Shorter classes can extend this project over two periods.

State the Objective: *With a team you will create a purchase plan for a large and expensive item.*

Stage 1: 5 min. `1.5+`

Form a team with four or five students. Choose positions for each member of your team.

Have students decide who will take which position as described on the student page. Provide well-defined directions on the board for how teams should proceed. Explain to the students that all the students do every task. The students don't go to the next stage until the previous one is complete.

Stage 2: 5 min. `1.5+`

Think of a large item that you would like to purchase.

Teams report their choice to the class.

Stage 3: 15–20 min. `1.5+`

Create an advertisement for this product.

As a class, brainstorm what needs to be included in the advertisement. Then let each team create its own ad.

Stage 4: 10–15 min. `1.5+`

Write down all the steps you will need to take to purchase this item. (Hint: budget, comparison shopping, ads, loan information)

Stage 5: 15–20 min. `1.5+`

Write a brief description of how you will do each step.

Stage 6: 20–25 min. `1.5+`

Design a purchase plan document that has a space for the ad, each step in your purchase plan, and artwork.

Stage 7: 15–20 min. `1.5+`

Present what you've created to the class.

Help each team prepare its five-minute presentation to the class. Consider videotaping these presentations or have students videotape themselves to polish their presentations.

STANDARDS CORRELATIONS

CASAS: 1.5.2, 4.8.1, 4.8.5, 4.8.6
SCANS: **Resources** Allocates Materials and Facility Resources, Allocates Human Resources
Interpersonal Participates as a Member of a Team, Teaches Others New Skills, Exercises Leadership, Works with Cultural Diversity
Information Acquires and Evaluates Information, Organizes and Maintains Information, Interprets and Communicates Information, Uses Computers to Process Information (optional)
Systems Understands Systems, Monitors and Corrects Performance, Improves and Designs Systems
Technology Applies Technology to Task (optional)
Basic Skills Reading, Writing, Listening, Speaking

Thinking Skills Creative Thinking, Decision Making, Problem Solving, Seeing Things in the Mind's Eye, Knowing How to Learn, Reasoning
Personal Qualities Responsibility, Self-Esteem, Sociability, Self-Management, Integrity/Honesty
EFF: **Communication** Read with Understanding, Convey Ideas in Writing, Speak So Others Can Understand, Listen Actively, Observe Critically
Decision Making Solve Problems and Make Decisions, Plan
Interpersonal Guide Others, Resolve Conflict and Negotiate, Advocate and Influence, Cooperate with Others
Lifelong Learning Take Responsibility for Learning, Reflect and Evaluate, Learn through Research, Use Information and Communications Technology (optional)

Create a purchasing plan

With a team, you will create a purchase plan for a large item.

1. Form a team with four or five students. Choose positions for each member of your team.

Position	Job Description	Student Name
Student 1 Leader	See that everyone speaks English. See that everyone participates.	
Student 2 Secretary	Take notes and write purchase plan.	
Student 3 Designer	Design ad for product and purchase plan layout.	
Students 4/5 Member (s)	Help secretary and designer with their work.	

2. Think of a large item that you would like to purchase.

3. Create an advertisement for this product.

4. Write down all the steps you will need to take to purchase this item. (Hint: budget, comparison shopping, ads, loan information)

5. Write a brief description of how you will do each step.

6. Design a purchase plan document that has a space for the ad, each step in your purchase plan, and artwork.

7. Present what you've created to the class.

PRONUNCIATION

Word Linking. Listen to sentences 1–3 and notice how the word ending in /w/ is linked to the following word in each sentence. Then listen to sentences 4–6. Listen to how the /w/ sound is introduced to link words. Listen again and repeat. Make new sentences using this type of word linking.

1. How often do you make large purchases?

2. What do you know about personal finance?

3. Now is the time to check out our special offers.

4. I want to apply for a credit card.

5. It is so easy to borrow money.

6. Go online to check our prices.

LEARNER LOG

In this unit, you learned many things about personal finance. How comfortable do you feel doing each of the skills listed below? Rate your comfort level on a scale of 1 to 4.

1 = Not so comfortable **2** = Need more practice **3** = Comfortable **4** = Very comfortable

If you circle 1 or 2, write down the page number where you can review this skill.

Life Skill	Comfort Level				Page(s)
I can calculate monthly expenses.	1	2	3	4	22
I can plan a monthly budget.	1	2	3	4	21, 22
I know how to be a smart consumer.	1	2	3	4	23, 24
I can fill out a credit card application.	1	2	3	4	27
I can listen to information about loans.	1	2	3	4	30
I can discuss purchasing options.	1	2	3	4	31
I can analyze advertising techniques.	1	2	3	4	32, 33
I can express consumer complaints.	1	2	3	4	34

Grammar					
I can use contrary-to-fact conditionals.	1	2	3	4	25, 26

Academic Skill					
I can read consumer purchasing information.	1	2	3	4	23
I can read and evaluate credit card information.	1	2	3	4	28, 29
I can compare numerical data and organize information.	1	2	3	4	29, 33
I can write a business letter.	1	2	3	4	35, 36

Reflection

Complete the following statements with your thoughts from this unit. *(Answers will vary.)*

I learned _____

I would like to find out more about _____

I am still confused about _____

Unit 2 Pronunciation and Learner Log

Pronunciation: 10–15 min.
(optional)

Word linking

Listen to sentences 1–3 and notice how the word ending in /w/ is linked to the following word in each sentence. Then listen to sentences 4–6. Listen to how the /w/ sound is introduced to link words. Listen again and repeat. Make new sentences using this type of word linking.

Play the recording and pause after each sentence. Ask students to repeat. Then ask them to make their own examples.

For additional pronunciation practice: You may wish to extend this practice by introducing another type of word linking using the sound /y/. Write the following sentences on the board or on a transparency. Ask students to copy the questions and then read them to a partner. Have them mark the words that are linked with a /y/ sound. Review answers with the class.

1. *Why aren't we saving more money?*
2. *They are at home today, aren't they?*
3. *Why is he on the phone all day?*
4. *Do we agree with them?*
5. *He is retired, isn't he?*
6. *Does she often go to the library?*

Learner Log:

Presentation 1: 5–10 min.

If needed, review the purpose of the Learner Log. Make sure students understand how to rate the comfort level they feel in reaching the individual goals listed under *Life Skill, Grammar,* and *Academic Skill.* They should rate their comfort level on a scale of 1 to 4:

1. Not so comfortable
2. Need more practice
3. Comfortable
4. Very comfortable

Practice 1: 5–10 min.

If a student circles 1 or 2, he or she should enter the page number on which the skill is featured. The student can then more easily revisit that page and study the material again.

Evaluation 1: 5–10 min.

Finally, emphasize to students the importance of finishing the three statements in *Reflection.* They are designed to help students assign real-life value to their classwork.

Instructor's Notes for Unit 2 Team Project, Pronunciation, and Learner Log

_____

_____

_____

_____

_____

_____

_____

_____

_____

_____

_____

_____

_____

_____

_____

_____

_____

LESSON PLAN

Objective:
Interpret housing advertisements
Key vocabulary:
asking price, offer, closing, detached, market, negotiate, cozy, nightlife, secluded, needs loving care, seasonal views, working fireplace, single-family, built-in, master suite, amenities

Pre-Assessment: Use the *Stand Out* ExamView® Pro *Test Bank* for Unit 3. *(optional)*

Warm-up and Review: 5–10 min.

Write the following words on the board and ask students the difference between these types of housing: *house, condominium, apartment, mobile home.*

Introduction: 10–15 min.

Ask students to raise their hands based on the type of housing they live in.

State the Objective: *In this unit we will learn about housing and what you need to know about buying a home. Today you will read advertisements and learn vocabulary that you need in order to understand ads for homes.*

Presentation 1: 5–10 min.

Have students look at the three homes pictured in their books. Ask them where they think each one is located.

Practice 1: 15–20 min.

A Read the following advertisements from *Homes for Sale*. Write the names from the box with the correct description.

Evaluation 1: 5 min.

Go over the answers as a class. Ask students what information is given in an ad. Make a list on the board.

Pronunciation: An optional pronunciation activity is found on the final page of this unit. This pronunciation activity may be introduced during any lesson in this unit, especially if students need practice with rising and falling intonation in questions. (See pages 60 and 60a for Unit 3 Pronunciation.)

STANDARDS CORRELATIONS

CASAS: 1.4.1, 1.4.2
SCANS: **Interpersonal** Participates as a Member of a Team, Works with Cultural Diversity
Information Acquires and Evaluates Information, Organizes and Maintains Information, Interprets and Communicates Information, Uses Computers to Process Information (optional)
Systems Monitors and Corrects Performance
Technology Selects Technology, Applies Technology to Task, Maintains and Troubleshoots Equipment (optional)
Basic Skills Reading, Writing, Listening, Speaking

Thinking Skills Creative Thinking, Decision Making, Reasoning
Personal Qualities Sociability
EFF: **Communication** Read with Understanding, Convey Ideas in Writing, Speak So Others Can Understand, Listen Actively
Decision Making Solve Problems and Make Decisions, Plan
Interpersonal Advocate and Influence, Cooperate with Others
Lifelong Learning Use Information and Communications Technology (optional)

Buying a Home

GOALS

- Interpret housing advertisements
- Use comparative and superlative adjectives
- Use comparative and superlative questions
- Use *yes/no* and information questions
- Write a letter to a real estate agent
- Interpret a bar graph
- Understand steps in a process

LESSON 1

The American dream

GOAL ▶ Interpret housing advertisements   *Vocabulary*

A Read the following advertisements from *Homes for Sale.* Write the names from the box with the correct description.

HOMES FOR SALE

Country Cottage	*Suburban Dream*	*Downtown Condo*
Cozy two-bedroom, two-bath single family home. Located in a secluded neighborhood, far from city life.  *You won't believe this price for a house in this area.* Working fireplace. Big yard. Excellent seasonal views. Must sell. Come see and make an offer now! $120,000 ★★★★★★★★★	Single-family 4-bedroom, 3-bath, 1500 sq. ft. home with an added family room. **Location is great!** Near jobs, bus, and schools. You must see this home and area. Amenities: pool, fire-place, central a/c, master suite and big yard! **Let's negotiate!** **Asking price $225,000** RENTAL SALES	You'd think this 1000-square-foot condo was brand new! **Located in the heart** of Los Angeles, near all the nightlife you could imagine. Seller just added new carpet, paint, new faucets and sinks, and beautiful ceramic tile flooring. Two master suites, laundry room, underground parking, balcony with spectacular views. This condo will not last long on the market, *so hurry!* **$200,000**

Downtown Condo

Country Cottage

Suburban Dream

B **What do you think the following words from the ads could mean? Is there more than one meaning?** *(Answers may vary. Possible answers below.)*

cozy _____ *small* _____   secluded _____ *far from stores, services* _____

near nightlife _____ *noisy, on a busy street* _____   seasonal views *lots of trees, not close to other houses*

C **Find each of the vocabulary words in the ads and try to work out the meaning using the context.**

| asking price | offer | amenities | market | negotiate |

D **Complete the following chart by looking at the *Homes for Sale* ads.**

	Type of property	Size	Asking price	Number of bedrooms	Number of bathrooms	Location	Amenities
Country Cottage	*single family home*	*cozy (small)*	$120,000	2	2	*country*	big yard, *fireplace*
Suburban Dream	single family home	1500 sq. ft.	$225,000	4	3	*suburb*	*pool, fireplace, a/c, big yard*
Downtown Condominium	*condo*	1000 sq.ft.	*$200,000*	2	*not given*	*city*	*new carpet, new bathroom fixtures, balcony, parking*

E **Using the ads on the previous page as examples, write an advertisement for the place you live on a separate piece of paper.**

F **Active Task:** Read some housing ads in the newspaper or on the Internet. Make a list of any words or abbreviations you don't understand and try to work out the meanings.

Presentation 2: 5–10 min.

B What do you think the following words from the ads could mean? Is there more than one meaning?

Do this exercise with students to prepare them for Practice 2. Have them go back to the ads and find the words. Then help them figure out their meaning from the context.

Practice 2: 10–15 min.

C Find each of the vocabulary words in the ads and try to work out the meaning using the context.

Optional Internet Activity: Have students go to the Internet and look for housing ads. Have them identify some new vocabulary.

Evaluation 2: 10–15 min.

Walk around and help students. Also ask students to help others. Then go over the answers as a class.

 Refer to the *Stand Out Activity Bank 4, Unit 3 Worksheet 1* (two pages), for more housing ad exercises. *(optional)*

Presentation 3: 5–10 min.

Ask students questions about the already filled-in blanks in the chart for exercise D: *What type of property is the Suburban Dream? What is the size of the Downtown Condominium? Does the Country Cottage have any amenities?*

Practice 3: 10–15 min.

D Complete the following chart by looking at the *Homes for Sale* ads.

Evaluation 3: 10–15 min.

Put up a transparency of the chart or copy the chart on the board and have students come up to fill it in.

Application: 20–25 min.

E Using the ads on the previous page as examples, write an advertisement for the place you live on a separate piece of paper.

Optional Computer Activity: Have students enter their ads onto the computer. Suggest that they find a picture of a house on the Internet to insert in their ad or bring in a picture of where they actually live to scan it in or attach it to the printed ad. Show them how to use the Format Picture features in the computer program to make their picture bigger, smaller, behind text, beside text, and so on.

F Active Task: Read some housing ads in the newspaper or on the Internet. Make a list of any words or abbreviations you don't understand and try to work out the meanings.

Refer to the *Stand Out Activity Bank 4 CD-ROM,* Unit 3 Active Task Checklist. *(optional)*

Remind students to use this checklist as they complete Active Tasks for Lessons 1 and 5.

Instructor's Notes for Lesson 1

_____

_____

_____

_____

_____

_____

_____

_____

_____

_____

_____

LESSON PLAN

Objective:
Use comparative and superlative adjectives
Key vocabulary:
properties, advantages, disadvantages, comparative, superlative, noisy, spacious

Warm-up and Review: 5–10 min. `1.5+`

Ask volunteers to share the ads they wrote in the previous lesson. Encourage the rest of the class to ask questions about the ads.

Introduction: 10–15 min. `1.5+`

Describe two dwellings to students, one very nice and one not as nice. Ask students which one they would rather live in and why.

State the Objective: *Today you will review comparative and superlative adjectives to compare housing. By the end of the lesson, you will compare the place you live in now to the place you used to live.*

Presentation 1: 10–15 min. `1.5+`

Prepare students for focused listening by having them look at the two pictures in the book. Ask them what they think the differences are.

Practice 1: 15–20 min. `1.5+`

A Listen to Joey and Courtney discuss two properties that Courtney looked at. As you listen, take notes about the *advantages* and *disadvantages* of each place.

(See Teaching Hints for suggestions on focused listening.)

B With a partner, compare the house and the condominium.

Evaluation 1: 10–15 min. `1.5+`

C Which one would you rather live in? Why? Write a paragraph.

Have students write their answers, and then discuss them as a class.

STANDARDS CORRELATIONS

CASAS: 1.4.2
SCANS: **Interpersonal** Participates as a Member of a Team, Works with Cultural Diversity
Information Acquires and Evaluates Information, Organizes and Maintains Information, Interprets and Communicates Information
Systems Monitors and Corrects Performance

Basic Skills Reading, Writing, Listening, Speaking
Thinking Skills Creative Thinking, Decision Making
Personal Qualities Sociability
EFF: **Communication** Convey Ideas in Writing, Speak So Others Can Understand, Listen Actively
Interpersonal Cooperate with Others

LESSON 2 Bigger? Better?

GOAL ▶ Use comparative and superlative adjectives   *Grammar*

A Listen to Joey and Courtney discuss two properties that Courtney looked at. As you listen, take notes about the *advantages* and *disadvantages* of each place.

House	Advantages	Disadvantages
	closer to job no association fees bigger	higher price not as nice a neighborhood
Condominium	nicer neighborhood less expensive friendly neighbors safer because of gate	association fees

B With a partner, compare the house and the condominium.

EXAMPLE:
Student A: What is the advantage of living in the house?
Student B: The house is quieter than the condo and you have more space.

C Which one would you rather live in? Why? Write a paragraph.

(Answers will vary.)

_____

_____

_____

_____

_____

_____

_____

_____

_____

D Review comparative and superlative adjectives by completing the chart below.

Adjective	Comparative	Superlative
beautiful	more beautiful	most beautiful
noisy	noisier	noisiest
safe	safer	safest
comfortable	more comfortable	most comfortable
far	farther	farthest
hot	hotter	hottest
friendly	friendlier/more friendly	friendliest/most friendly
bad	worse	worst
cheap	cheaper	cheapest
dark	darker	darkest
spacious	more spacious	most spacious
flat	flatter	flattest

* Note: Some two-syllable adjectives have two forms: e.g., *quieter* or *more quiet.*

E Which of the adjectives above correspond to the rules below? *(Suggested answers below.)*

1. Add -*er* or -*est* to a one-syllable adjective. _____ *cheap, dark* _____

2. Use *more* or *most* before adjectives of two or more syllables. _____ *spacious* _____

3. Add –*r* to one-syllable adjectives that end in *e.* _____ *safe* _____

4. Change *y* to *i* and add -*er* or -*est.* _____ *noisy, friendly* _____

5. These adjectives have irregular forms. _____ *bad, far* _____

6. Double the final consonant of adjectives ending in consonant-vowel-consonant and add -*er* or -*est.*

_____ *hot, flat* _____

F Find opposites for each adjective in the chart above. Write the comparative and superlative form of each new adjective on a separate piece of paper.

G With a partner, describe the place you are living in now and compare it to the place you used to live, using the adjectives above.

EXAMPLE: I used to live in a small one-bedroom apartment with uncomfortable furniture. But now I live in a bigger apartment with the most comfortable couch!

Presentation 2: 5–10 min.

Write *beautiful* **on the board.** Ask students to give you the comparative and superlative forms. You might need to remind them how to form comparative and superlative adjectives.

Practice 2: 10–15 min.

D **Review comparative and superlative adjectives by completing the chart below.**

 Refer to *Stand Out Grammar Challenge 4,* **Unit 3 pages 18, 19, and 21 for more practice.** *(optional)*

Evaluation 2: 10–15 min.

Go over the answers as a class.

 Refer to the *Stand Out Activity Bank 4 CD-ROM,* **Unit 3 Worksheet 2 (two pages), for additional exercises with comparative and superlative adjectives.** *(optional)*

Presentation 3: 5–10 min.

Review *syllables* **with students.** Help them figure out how many syllables are in each adjective in exercise D. Then go over questions one and two in exercise E and help students find the answers.

Practice 3: 10–15 min.

E **Which of the adjectives above correspond to the rules below?**

F **Find opposites for each adjective in the chart above. Write the comparative and superlative form of each new adjective on a separate piece of paper.**

Evaluation 3: 10–15 min.

Go over the answers as a class.

Application: 20–25 min.

G **With a partner, describe the place you are living in now and compare it to** the place you used to live, using the adjectives above.

Expansion activity or homework: Have students write a paragraph comparing the place they live in now to the place where they used to live.

Refer to the *Stand Out Activity Bank 4 CD-ROM,* **Unit 3 Worksheet 3 (two pages), for a fun activity working with comparative and superlative adjectives.** *(optional)*

Instructor's Notes for Lesson 2

_____

_____

_____

_____

_____

_____

_____

_____

_____

_____

_____

_____

_____

_____

_____

_____

_____

_____

_____

_____

_____

_____

LESSON PLAN

Objective:
Use questions with comparative and superlative adjectives
Key vocabulary:
floor plan, expensive taste

Warm-up and Review: 5–10 min.

Ask some students to compare the home they are living in now to the one where they used to live. Begin with your own example.

Introduction: 10–15 min.

As students describe their former and current homes, ask them such questions as, *Which one is bigger? Which one is more comfortable? Which one is cheaper?*

State the Objective: *In the last lesson you practiced using comparative and superlative adjectives to describe housing. Today you will practice asking questions with comparative and superlative adjectives to get more information about housing.*

Presentation 1: 10–15 min.

Have students look at the picture in the book and study the people. Ask students what they think Sara and Courtney might be talking about.

Practice 1: 15–20 min.

A Sara and Courtney have been comparing notes on houses they've looked at. Listen to their conversation.

Ask students to close their books. Play the recording of Sara and Courtney talking.

Ask students comprehension questions about what they heard, such as, *Which place sounds more comfortable to Courtney?* Now have the students open their books and read the conversation while you play the recording again.

B What questions does Courtney ask? How does Sara answer her? Discuss as a class.

Have students underline the questions and answers they find in the conversation.

Evaluation 1: 10–15 min.

Ask a volunteer to write the conversation questions on the board. Then ask another volunteer to come up and write short forms of the answers. (You will need this information for Presentation 2.)

C Practice the conversation with a partner.

STANDARDS CORRELATIONS

CASAS: 1.4.2
SCANS: **Interpersonal** Participates as a Member of a Team, Works with Cultural Diversity
Information Acquires and Evaluates Information, Organizes and Maintains Information, Interprets and Communicates Information
Systems Monitors and Corrects Performance,
Basic Skills Reading, Writing, Listening, Speaking

Thinking Skills Creative Thinking, Decision Making, Reasoning
Personal Qualities Sociability
EFF: **Communication** Read with Understanding, Convey Ideas in Writing, Speak So Others Can Understand, Listen Actively
Decision Making Solve Problems and Make Decisions
Interpersonal Cooperate with Others

LESSON 3 Which one is safer?

| GOAL ▶ | Use comparative and superlative questions | *Grammar* |

What are Sara and Courtney discussing? What do you think they are saying?

A **Sara and Courtney have been comparing notes on houses they've looked at. Listen to their conversation.**

Courtney: Have you looked at any new houses this week?

Sara: Yes, I saw three places the other day. Look at this brochure!

Courtney: The Country Cottage, the Suburban Dream, and the Downtown Condo. I like the sound of the Country Cottage best. It sounds more comfortable than the others.

Sara: Yeah, and it's the closest to where we live now.

Courtney: Oh really? Which place is the safest?

Sara: Actually, I think the Suburban Dream is the safest.

Courtney: Which one has the biggest floor plan?

Sara: The Suburban Dream. That would be ideal for our family.

Courtney: Is it the most expensive?

Sara: Of course! I have expensive taste.

B **What questions does Courtney ask? How does Sara answer her? Discuss as a class.**

C **Practice the conversation with a partner.**

D Study the charts with your teacher.

Questions using comparative and superlative adjectives				
Question word	**Subject**	**Verb**	**Adjective or noun**	**Rule**
Which	one place house	is	*bigger?* *closer* to work? the *safest?*	Use *be* when following with an adjective.
		has	*more* rooms? *the biggest* floor plan?	Use *have* before a noun.

Answers			
Question	**Short answer**	**Long answer**	**Rule**
Which one is *bigger,* the condominium or the house?	The condominium.	The condominium *is bigger.* The condominium *is bigger than* the house.	When talking about two things, and mentioning both of them, use *than.*
Which place has *more rooms?*	The house.	The house *has more rooms.* The house *has more rooms than* the condominium.	When talking about two things, but only mentioning one of them, **do not** use *than.*

E What are some adjectives used to describe homes? What are some nouns used to describe homes? Make two lists on a separate sheet of paper.
(Answers may vary. Possible answers below.)

Adjectives	Nouns
safe, new, elegant, cozy, charming	**great location**, fireplace, porch
spacious, sunny, open, big	**big yard**, garage, family room

F Using the information about the three properties on page 41, practice this conversation with different students in the class. Use the adjectives and nouns from your lists. *(Answers will vary.)*

Student A: Have you looked at any new houses this week?

Student B: Actually, I looked at three places the other day.

Student A: Oh really? Which place is/has _____?

Student B: The _____ is/has _____.

Presentation 2: 5–10 min.

 Study the charts with your teacher.

After explaining the charts, review the questions and answers already written on the board and show the students how these follow the same rules.

Practice 2: 10–15 min.

E What are some adjectives used to describe homes? What are some nouns used to describe homes? Make two lists on a separate sheet of paper.

F Using the information about the three properties on page 41, practice this conversation with different students in the class. Use the adjectives and nouns from your lists.

(See Teaching Hints on how to present dialogs.)

Evaluation 2: 10–15 min.

Observe, and then ask volunteers to perform the dialog.

 Refer to the *Stand Out Grammar Challenge 4,* Unit 3 page 22 for more practice forming questions using comparative and superlative adjectives. *(optional)*

Note: In order to do the Application activity, all class lengths must do Practice 3.

Presentation 3: 5–10 min.

Prepare students for focused listening by asking them to look at the photos and think about what they will be listening for. Ask them which property they think will be the most expensive, cheapest, biggest, smallest, etc.

Practice 3:10–15 min.

 G Listen to the four advertisements for *Homes for Sale* and fill in the information you hear.

Evaluation 3: 10–15 min.

Go over the answers as a class.

Application: 20–25 min.

H Write four comparative and superlative questions about the homes above.

I With a partner, practice asking and answering the questions in exercise H.

J Which home would you like to live in? Why? Tell your group.

After students have had a chance to discuss, take a class poll.

Refer to the *Stand Out Activity Bank 4 CD-ROM,* Unit 3 Worksheet 4, for additional exercises with comparative and superlative questions. *(optional)*

Instructor's Notes for Lesson 3

G Listen to the four advertisements for *Homes for Sale* and fill in the information you hear.

Prince's Palace	**Fixer-Upper**	**City High-Rise**	**Rural Residence**
Price: *$1.2 million*	Price: *$150,000*	Price: *$2,000/mo.*	Price: *$125,000*
Size: *15,000 sq. ft.*	Size: *2,000 sq. ft.*	Size: *1,000 sq. ft.*	Size: *3,500 sq. ft.*
Neighborhood: *far from other houses*	Neighborhood: *busy*	Neighborhood: *city*	Neighborhood: *rural*
Amenities: *hardwood floors, appliances*	Amenities: *near other families*	Amenities: *24-hr. security, washer and dryer in basement*	Amenities: *huge yard, pool*

H Write four comparative and superlative questions about the homes above.
(Answers may vary. Posible answers below.)
EXAMPLE:

Which place has the best amenities?

1.   *Which place is the most affordable?*
2.   *Which home is the largest? OR Which home is larger than the Fixer-Upper?*
3.   *Which place is in the quietest location?*
4.   *Which home is the closest to downtown? OR Which home is closer to families?*

I With a partner, practice asking and answering the questions in exercise H.

J Which home would you like to live in? Why? Tell your group.

GOAL ▶ Use *yes/no* and information questions   *Grammar*

A **Think about the following questions as you listen to the story about the Bwarie family.**

1. Why is the Bwarie family looking for a new home?

2. What are they looking for in a new home?

> The Bwarie family has outgrown their apartment. They have three children and a baby on the way and they are now renting a two-bedroom house. They've been putting away money every month from their paychecks and finally have enough money for a 10% down payment on a house. Every Sunday, the whole family piles into the car and they go look at properties for sale in the $100,000 to $120,000 price range. Until now, they have been doing this on their own. But now it's time to find a real estate agent.
>
> However, before they meet with a real estate agent, they need to decide exactly what they want. Courtney and Joey Bwarie have thought long and hard about what they want to purchase. First of all, they want a house in a safe neighborhood that is within walking distance to their children's school. Second of all, they want four bedrooms, one for Courtney and Joey, one for the two boys, and another for their daughter and the baby girl who will be born next month. The fourth room will be used as an office for Courtney, who works from home. As far as bathrooms, four would be ideal, but they could survive with three if they had to. Some other things they would like are a big backyard for the children to play in and an attached two-car garage. Other amenities, such as air conditioning or a pool, are not important to them.
>
> Now they know what they are looking for in a new home. That was the easy part. Finding a real estate agent, that's a different story!

B **Read the story again and try to work out the meanings of the following words using the context.**

survive	on the way	outgrown
pile into	ideal	putting away
real estate agent	within walking distance	down payment
thought long and hard	works from home	

C **Go over the meanings with your teacher. Choose three words or expressions and write sentences.** *(Answers will vary.)*

> **LESSON PLAN**
>
> Objective:
> Use yes/no and information questions
> Key vocabulary:
> preferences, down payment, on the way, outgrown, pile into, putting away, realtor, within walking distance, attached garage, works out of the home, ideal, survive, thought long and hard, property, location, price range

Warm-up and Review: 5–10 min.

Go over any questions students have about the previous lesson.

Introduction: 10–15 min.

Have students open their books and look at Mr. Bwarie and the picture of the Bwarie family. Ask them the two questions in exercise A.

State the Objective: *Today you will ask about housing preferences using* yes/no *and information questions.*

Presentation 1: 10–15 min.

A Think about the following questions as you listen to the story about the Bwarie family.

Write the two questions from exercise A on the board. Ask students to close their books while they listen to the recording. Ask them the questions on the board after they listen. Next let them read the story while they listen to the recording a second time.

Practice 1: 15–20 min.

B Read the story again and try to work out the meanings of the following words using the context.

Go over the first word with the students and show them how to use the context clues to discover a word's meaning.

Evaluation 1: 15–20 min.

C Go over the meanings with your teacher. Choose three words or expressions and write sentences.

Ask a few volunteers to write their sentences on the board. Evaluate as a class.

(Evaluation 1 continues on page 49a.)

STANDARDS CORRELATIONS

CASAS: 7.2.4
SCANS: **Interpersonal** Participates as a Member of a Team, Works with Cultural Diversity
Information Acquires and Evaluates Information, Organizes and Maintains Information, Interprets and Communicates Information
Systems Monitors and Corrects Performance
Basic Skills Reading, Writing, Listening, Speaking

Thinking Skills Creative Thinking, Decision Making, Reasoning
Personal Qualities Sociability
EFF: **Communication** Read with Understanding, Speak So Others Can Understand, Listen Actively
Decision Making Solve Problems and Make Decisions
Interpersonal Guide Others, Cooperate with Others
Lifelong Learning Take Responsibility for Learning

(Evaluation 1 continued from page 48a)

D What are the Bwaries looking for in a home? Complete the checklist, based on the reading in exercise A.

Use this exercise to check that students understood what they read. Then go over the answers with them.

E What information did the Bwaries not talk about? What do you think their preferences might be?

Presentation 2: 5–10 min.

F When asking someone about their preferences, you can use *yes/no* questions. Study the chart below.

 Refer to *Stand Out Grammar Challenge 4,* Unit 3 page 23 for more practice with *yes/no* questions. *(optional)*

Practice 2: 10–15 min.

G Practice asking *yes/no* questions with a partner based on the information in exercise D.

Go over the example with the students.

Evaluation 2:

Observe the student pairs.

 Refer to the *Stand Out Activity Bank 4 CD-ROM,* Unit 3 Worksheet 5 (two pages), for additional exercises with *yes/no* questions. *(optional)*

D What are the Bwaries looking for in a home? Complete the checklist, based on the reading in exercise A.

Housing preferences checklist				
Features	Yes	No	Features	Preference
air conditioning	☐	☒	type of property	*house*
backyard	☒	☐	number of bathrooms	*four*
balcony	☐	☒	number of bedrooms	*four*
garage	☒	☐	location	*in a safe neighborhood, close to their children's school*
elevator	☐	☒	price range	*none*
pool	☐	☒	down payment (%)	*none*

E What information did the Bwaries not talk about? What do you think their preferences might be? *(Answers may vary. Possible answer below.)*

They did not talk about price range, kitchen amenities, style of house.

F When asking someone about their preferences, you can use *yes/no* questions. Study the chart below.

Yes/no questions and short answers		
Do you want	air conditioning? a backyard?	Yes, I do. No, I don't.
Do they need	a balcony? a garage?	Yes, they do. No, they don't.
Does the house have	heating? a pool?	Yes, it does. No, it doesn't.

G Practice asking *yes/no* questions with a partner based on the information in exercise D.

EXAMPLE:
Student A: Do they want air conditioning?
Student B: No, they don't.

H Information questions start with *who, what, where, when, why,* or *how.* Study the chart below.

Information questions			
Information	**Example questions**		
type of property	What type	of property	do you want? is it?
number of bathrooms	How many	bedrooms	do you want?
number of bedrooms		bathrooms	does it have?
location	Where		is it?
price range	What		is your price range?
down payment (percentage)	How much		can you put down?

I Practice asking information questions to a partner based on the information in exercise D.

EXAMPLE:
Student A: What type of property does the Bwarie family want?
Student B: They want a house.

J Complete your own checklist based on things you would want in a new home. Add some extra things that are not on the list.

(Answers will vary.)

Housing preferences checklist				
Features	**Yes**	**No**	**Features**	**Preference**
air conditioning	❏	❏	type of property	
backyard	❏	❏	number of bathrooms	
balcony	❏	❏	number of bedrooms	
garage	❏	❏	location	
elevator	❏	❏	type of heating	
pool	❏	❏	price range	
	❏	❏	down payment (%)	
	❏	❏		

Presentation 3: 5–10 min. (1.5+)

H **Information questions start with** *who, what, where, when, why,* **or** *how.* **Study the chart below.**

Practice 3: 10–15 min. (3)

I **Practice asking information questions to a partner based on the information in exercise D.**

Go over the example with the students.

Evaluation 3:

Observe and listen to question forms.

GC **Again, refer to** *Stand Out Grammar Challenge 4,* **Unit 3 page 23 for more practice with information questions.** *(optional)*

Application: 20–25 min. (1.5+)

J **Complete your own checklist based on things you would want in a new home. Add some extra things that are not on the list.**

After students have completed their lists, have them interview a partner using *yes/no* and information questions. Ask some students to report to the class what they learned from their partners.

AB **Refer to the** *Stand Out Activity Bank 4 CD-ROM,* **Unit 3 Worksheet 6, for additional information question exercises.** *(optional)*

Instructor's Notes for Lesson 4

LESSON PLAN

Objective:
Write a letter to a real estate agent
Key vocabulary:
enclosed, priority, central heating,
built-in closet space, real estate agent

Warm-up and Review: 5–10 min.

Have students find a partner and ask each other questions about the Housing Preferences Checklists they completed in the previous lesson.

Introduction: 10–15 min.

 A What are some ways you can think of to look for a house? Make a list of ideas with a group.

State the Objective: *Today we will try one way to look for a home by writing a letter to a real estate agent. By the end of the lesson, you will have written your own letter to an agent asking for help in finding properties.*

Presentation 1: 10–15 min.

Have the students look at the letter and review the parts of a business letter that they learned in the previous unit. (This may be easier if you put up a transparency of this book page.) Ask students such letter-format questions as, *What is the greeting? What is the first word of the body? What is the closing?*

Practice 1: 10–15 min.

B Read the letter that Joey wrote to Paradise Realty.

Evaluation 1: 10–15 min.

Ask the students basic comprehension questions about the letter to make sure they understood what they read.

STANDARDS CORRELATIONS

CASAS: 7.2.6, 7.2.7
SCANS: **Information** Acquires and Evaluates Information, Organizes and Maintains Information, Interprets and Communicates Information, Uses Computers to Process Information (optional)
Systems Monitors and Corrects Performance
Technology Applies Technology to Task (optional)
Basic Skills Reading, Writing, Listening, Speaking
Thinking Skills Creative Thinking, Decision Making, Reasoning

Personal Qualities Responsibility, Self-Esteem, Sociability, Self-Management, Integrity/Honesty
EFF: **Communication** Read with Understanding, Convey Ideas in Writing, Speak So Others Can Understand, Listen Actively
Decision Making Solve Problems and Make Decisions, Plan
Interpersonal Guide Others, Advocate and Influence, Cooperate with Others
Lifelong Learning Take Responsibility for Learning, Reflect and Evaluate, Use Information and Communications Technology (optional)

LESSON 5 A business letter

A What are some ways you can think of to look for a house? Make a list of ideas with a group.

B Read the letter that Joey wrote to Paradise Realty.

15236 Dahlia Avenue
Costa Mesa, CA 92627
February 13, 2003

Paradise Realty
9875 Timber Lane
Costa Mesa, CA 92627

Dear Paradise Realty,

(3) My family has decided to purchase a new home and we would appreciate any information you can send us about homes for sale.

(1) We are looking for a four-bedroom home. We would like to live in a safe neighborhood, close to our children's school. We would prefer a home with a big enclosed yard that our children can play in. We might want to build a pool in the future, but right now it is not a priority. Other amenities, such as air conditioning, central heating, and built-in closet space would be nice, but they are not essential. Our price range is between $100,000 and $120,000 and we are prepared to put down 10%.

Please contact me at the address above, or you may call me or my wife Courtney at (949) 555-2408. Thank you for your time.

Sincerely,

(2)

Joseph Bwarie
Joseph Bwarie

(Circled numbers are for exercise D, page 52.)

C If you were looking for a house, what things would you tell your real estate agent? (Hint: Remember your preferences checklist.) Make a list.

Things to tell the real estate agent

(Answers will vary.)

D In the last unit you learned about parts of a business letter. Look at the list below. Find each piece of information in the letter on the previous page and write the correct number next to the paragraph where you find the information.

1. Describe what you want.

2. Thank the person for their time.

3. Explain why you are writing the letter.

E Now it's your turn. Imagine you are going to buy a new house and you are writing a letter to a real estate agent. Use the letter on the previous page as an example and the list you made in exercise D. Write your letter on a separate sheet of paper. *(Answers will vary.)*

F **Active Task:** Use the Internet or the newspaper to find out about real estate agents in your area. What kind of services do they offer? What kind of fees do they charge?

Presentation 2: 5–10 min.

Ask students if they've ever dealt with a real estate agent before. Ask students, *What does a real estate agent need to know to help you look for a house?*

Practice 2: 10–15 min.

C **If you were looking for a house, what things would you tell your real estate agent? (Hint: Remember your preferences checklist.) Make a list.**

Evaluation 2: 10–15 min.

Observe. Have students share their lists with other students and add things that they may have forgotten.

Presentation 3: 5–10 min.

D **In the last unit you learned about parts of a business letter. Look at the list below. Find each piece of information in the letter on the previous page and write the correct number next to the paragraph where you find the information.**

Practice 3: 10–15 min.

Think about what you should write in the letter. Discuss each numbered sentence in exercise D with your teacher.

Evaluation 3: 10–15 min.

Go over the answers as a class. Ask students if they would add any additional information.

 Refer to the *Stand Out Activity Bank 4 CD-ROM*, Unit 3 Worksheet 7, for an additional exercise on working with parts of a business letter. *(optional)*

Application: 20–25 min.

E **Now it's your turn. Imagine you are going to buy a new house and you are writing a letter to a real estate agent. Use the letter on the previous page as** an example and the list you made in exercise D. Write your letter on a separate sheet of paper.

Have students peer edit, focusing on correct business letter format and the content elements they reviewed in exercise D. Then have them rewrite their letters.

Optional Computer Activity: Have students write their letters on the computer. Show them how to use spell check and different formatting options such as font style and size.

F **Active Task: Use the Internet or the newspaper to find out about real estate agents in your area. What kind of services do they offer? What kind of fees do they charge?**

Remind students to use the Active Task Checklist for Lesson 5.

Instructor's Notes for Lesson 5

_____

_____

_____

_____

_____

_____

_____

_____

_____

_____

_____

_____

_____

LESSON PLAN

Objective:
Interpret a bar graph
Key vocabulary:
bar graph, regions, homeownership,
householder, citizenship status,
legend, age categories

Warm-up and Review: 5–10 min.

Call on some students to read to the class the
letters to real estate agents they wrote in the
previous lesson.

Introduction: 10–15 min.

Write *bar graph* **on the board.** Ask students if
they know how to read bar graphs.

State the Objective: *Today you will interpret a
bar graph about homeowners in the United
States from different regions and then create your
own bar graph using information about the age
of homeowners in the United States.*

Presentation 1: 10–15 min.

**A Study the bar graph. What
vocabulary do you need to understand
the information? Make a list and
discuss it with your class.**

Check student comprehension by asking questions
about the graph.

Practice 1: 15–20 min.

**B Ask and answer questions about
the bar graph with your partner.**

Demonstrate an example with a student.

Evaluation 1:

Observe and help students.

Presentation 2: 5–10 min.

Write the following statements on the board:

*In the West, more citizens born outside the
United States own their own homes than do
citizens born in the United States.*

*There are more noncitizens who own homes in
the Northeast than in the South.*

Ask students to look at the bar graph and decide
which statement is true and which one is false.

Practice 2: 10–15 min.

**C Write two false statements and two
true statements about the bar graph on
a separate sheet of paper. Then ask
your partner which are true and which
are false. (Your partner cannot look at
the graph.)**

Evaluation 2: 10–15 min.

**Have students share their statements with the
class.** Ask the entire class to decide whether the
statements are true or false.

STANDARDS CORRELATIONS

CASAS: 6.7.2
SCANS: **Interpersonal** Participates as a Member of a
Team, Works with Cultural Diversity
Information Acquires and Evaluates Information,
Organizes and Maintains Information, Interprets and
Communicates Information, Uses Computers to Process
Information (optional)
Systems Understands Systems, Monitors and Corrects
Performance
Technology Applies Technology to Task (optional)

Basic Skills Reading, Writing, Listening, Speaking
Thinking Skills Creative Thinking, Decision Making,
Reasoning
Personal Qualities Sociability
EFF: **Communication** Read with Understanding, Convey
Ideas in Writing, Speak So Others Can Understand, Listen
Actively
Interpersonal Cooperate with Others
Lifelong Learning Use Information and Communications
Technology (optional)

 A Study the bar graph. What vocabulary do you need to understand the information? Make a list and discuss it with your class.

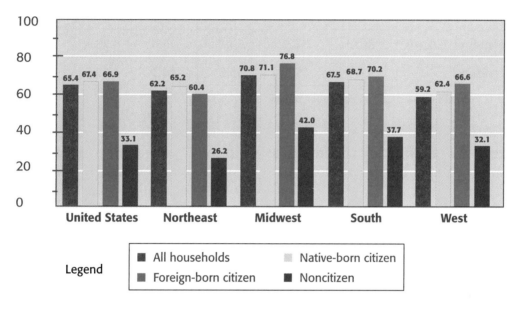

Homeownership Rates by Citizenship Status of Householder for the United States and Regions

Source: U.S. Census Bureau, Current Population Survey

 B Ask and answer questions about the bar graph with your partner.

EXAMPLES:
Student A: What percentage of households in the United States own their own homes?
Student B: 65.4% of households in the United States own their own homes.

Student B: What percentage of foreign-born citizens own their own homes in the United States?
Student A: 66.9% of foreign-born citizens own their own homes.

 C Write two false statements and two true statements about the bar graph on a separate sheet of paper. Then ask your partner which are true and which are false. (Your partner cannot look at the graph.)

EXAMPLE:
Student A: In the West, more foreign-born citizens own their own homes than native-born citizens.
Student B: I think that's true.
Student A: Yes, it is true.

D Read the information in the chart below. What does it mean? Discuss it with your class.

Homeownership Rates by Citizenship Status and Age of Householder for the United States						
	United States	Under 35 years	35–44	45–54	55–64	65+
All households	65.4	39.1	65.5	75.6	80	78.9
Native-born citizens	67.4	41.1	67.9	77.1	81.5	80.2
Foreign-born citizens	66.9	38.5	64.1	75.4	78.5	72.3
Noncitizens	33.1	19.8	35.6	48.3	49.3	43.5

Source: U.S. Census Bureau, Current Population Survey

E Make a bar graph using the information above. Make sure you create a legend for the citizenship status.

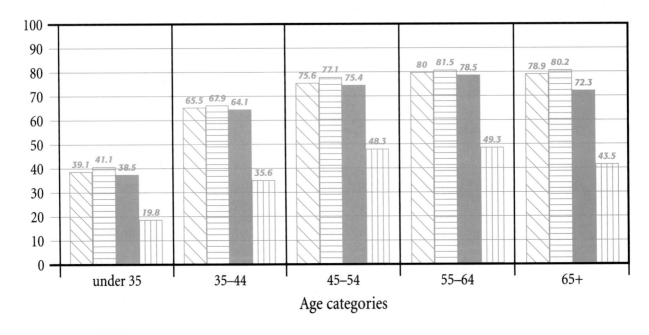

Age categories

All households

Native-born citizens

Foreign-born citizens

Non citizens

(Style of legend may vary.)

Presentation 3: 5–10 min.

D Read the information in the chart below. What does it mean? Discuss it with your class.

Practice 3: 20–25 min.

Have students repeat exercises B and C using the information from the chart in exercise D.

Evaluation 3: 10–15 min.

Observe and ask volunteers to share their statements with the class while the class again guesses true or false.

Application: 20–25 min.

E Make a bar graph using the information above. Make sure you create a legend for the citizenship status.

Optional Computer Activity: Have students recreate the graph on the computer using a word processing or spreadsheet program. (See Teaching Hints for suggestions on how to use computers in the classroom.)

Refer to the *Stand Out Activity Bank 4 CD-ROM*, Unit 3 Worksheet 8 (two pages), for more housing exercises with bar graphs. *(optional)*

Instructor's Notes for Lesson 6

LESSON PLAN

Objective:
Understand steps in a process
Key vocabulary:
apply, inspection, negotiate, comparable, motivate, cost comparison, afford, contract, closing, lender, listing price, offer, drawbacks, open houses, motivation, recorders, assessor, low-ball, counter-offer, contingency clause

Warm-up and Review: 5–10 min. `1.5+`

Ask how many students own homes. Ask how many students *would like* to own homes.

Introduction: 10–15 min. `1.5+`

Ask students if they or anyone they know has ever bought a home. Ask them to share their experiences.

State the Objective: *Today you will read about the steps involved in buying a home and write a paragraph putting the steps in the correct order.*

Presentation 1: 10–15 min. `1.5+`

Go through each step in exercise A and make sure students understand what each one means.

Practice 1: 15–20 min. `1.5+`

A **What do you know about the steps involved in buying a home? Read the steps for buying a home and put them in the correct order. Write a number next to each sentence.**

Evaluation 1: 10–15 min. `1.5+`

Put up a transparency of the home-buying steps or have a student write them on the board. Have the class put the steps in the correct order. At this point, don't tell the students if this order is correct.

Presentation 2: 5–10 min. `1.5+`

Ask students what they think the article will be about. What specific information do they think they might find?

Practice 2: 10–15 min. `2+`

B **Now read the article about home buying and check your answers.**

Evaluation 2: 10–15 min. `2+`

Have students compare the steps they numbered in the article to those the class numbered. Go over the article with the students and help them with any ideas they don't understand.

STANDARDS CORRELATIONS

CASAS: 1.4.6
SCANS: **Interpersonal** Participates as a Member of a Team, Works with Cultural Diversity
Information Acquires and Evaluates Information, Organizes and Maintains Information, Interprets and Communicates Information
Systems Monitors and Corrects Performance
Basic Skills Reading, Writing, Listening, Speaking

Thinking Skills Decision Making, Reasoning
Personal Qualities Sociability
EFF: **Communication** Read with Understanding, Convey Ideas in Writing, Speak So Others Can Understand, Observe Critically
Decision Making Solve Problems and Make Decisions, Plan
Interpersonal Advocate and Influence, Cooperate with Others

Step by step

GOAL ▶ **Understand steps in a process**   *Academic skill*

 A **What do you know about the steps involved in buying a home? Read the steps for buying a home and put them in the correct order. Write a number next to each sentence.**

   3   Find out how much money you can borrow.

   5   Choose a home you'd like to buy.

   2   Decide how much money you can spend.

   1   Decide what you are looking for.

   7   Have the home inspected.

   6   Make an offer on a home.

   9   Move in.

   8   Negotiate until both parties come to an agreement.

   4   Start looking for homes in a neighborhood you'd like to live in.

 B **Now read the article about home buying and check your answers.**

Buying a Home

Homebuyers can spend up to three months, and possibly more, looking for and purchasing a home. Their search begins by looking at housing ads, driving through neighborhoods they are interested in, and walking through open houses. Many first-time buyers will meet with a real estate agent to get help finding and buying a home.

Homebuyers should know how much they can afford. It isn't worth your time to look for a new home if you can't really afford to buy one. So it's a good idea to look at your financial situation first. You might be surprised at how much you can borrow, especially if the interest rates are good. Also, if you have some money saved for a down payment, your monthly payments may be lower than you think.

You should never make an offer on a home without looking at other houses in the same neighborhood. Just as you would comparison shop for a car or a computer, you should do a cost comparison on different homes for sale. You can do this by asking about the recent sales of similar properties. This information is available at local recorder's or assessor's offices, as well as through private companies or on the Internet. Also, if you can do some research on the seller, and his or her motivation for selling, it will put you in a better position. For instance, maybe the seller needs to sell quickly and would accept a low offer.

Once you have found the property that you want and can afford, you are ready to make an offer. A low-ball offer is an offer on a house that is a great deal less than the asking price. Unless the house is really overpriced, the seller will probably not accept a low-ball offer. Once you make an offer that is reasonable to the seller, he or she will either accept it or make a counter-offer. In this case, the negotiating process has begun. You may have to go back and forth three or four times before an agreement is reached.

Being a good negotiator can be tricky. Take your time when making your decision. This is a very important decision and you don't want to be rushed. Sometimes you can negotiate for repairs to the home before you move in, or you can ask the seller to pay for some of your closing costs. As soon as a written offer is made and accepted by both parties, the document becomes a legally binding contract.

Then the loan is processed by the lender (usually a bank) and the home is inspected. You should always have the home inspected. This will give you a chance to find out if anything is wrong that the seller didn't notify you of. After that, the final papers for the transfer of the title are prepared and any other last-minute business is taken care of. Finally, the closing takes place on a date agreed upon in the offer. On that date the title comes to you and soon you can enjoy your new home!

C **Find each of the following words in the article and match each vocabulary word/phrase with its correct meaning.**

_i_ 1. afford   a. a legal document

_a_ 2. contract   b. amount of money that the buyer is willing to pay for a house

_e_ 3. cost comparison   c. amount of money that the seller wants for the house

_j_ 4. negotiate   d. to look something over for problems or defects

_d_ 5. inspect   e. looking at different prices of homes

_f_ 6. lender   f. person or company that loans money

_c_ 7. asking price   g. the desire to do something

_g_ 8. motivation   h. date when the title to the house becomes yours

_b_ 9. offer   i. to have enough money to purchase something

_h_ 10. closing   j. discuss until you reach an agreement

D **What are the benefits of owning your own home? What are the drawbacks? Tell your partner.**

Presentation 3: 5 min.

Go over the instructions and one example in exercise C with students.

Practice 3: 10–15 min.

C **Find each of the following words in the article and match each vocabulary word/phrase with its correct meaning.**

Evaluation 3: 10–15 min.

Go over the answers as a class.

Refer to the *Stand Out Activity Bank 4 CD-ROM,* Unit 3 Worksheet 9 (two pages), for more practice with reading comprehension and vocabulary. *(optional)*

Application: 20–25 min.

Have students write a paragraph about the steps involved in buying a home. Encourage them to look back at the steps from exercise A and connect the ideas with sequencing transitions.

D **What are the benefits of owning your own home? What are the drawbacks? Tell your partner.**

Optional Activity: If time allows, have students write a list with their partner of the benefits and drawbacks they discussed. Using the list students in longer classes should write a paragraph recommending or not recommending the purchase of a home.

Instructor's Notes for Lesson 7

LESSON PLAN

Objective:
Review all previous unit objectives
Key vocabulary:
Review all previous unit vocabulary

Warm-up and Review: 5–10 min.

Review the benefits and drawbacks of owning your own home. Ask students if they think the benefits outweigh the drawbacks or vice versa.

Introduction: 1 min.

Write *evaluation* and *review* **on the board.** Ask students what these words mean and what their purpose is.

State the Objective: *Today we will review all that we have done in the past unit in preparation for the application project to follow.*

Ask students as a class to recall all the goals of this unit without looking at their books. Then remind them of the goals they haven't mentioned.

Unit goals: *Interpret housing advertisements, Use comparative and superlative adjectives, Use questions with comparative and superlative adjectives, Use yes/no and information questions, Write a letter to a real estate agent, Interpret a bar graph, Understand steps in a process.*

Presentation, Practice, and Evaluation 1:

Do the Learner Log on page 60. Notes are next to the page.

Presentation 2: 5–10 min.

Go over the instructions for exercise A with the students. Pair the students up.

Practice 2: 20–25 min.

A **Read the housing advertisements and do the following activities with a partner.**

Evaluation 2: 10–15 min.

Review each individual task as a class. Have students volunteer to read their work or to ask the class questions about the housing ads.

Refer to *Grammar Challenge* 4 Unit 3, pages 17 to 23 to review comparative and superlative adjectives, and *yes/no* and information questions. *(optional)*

STANDARDS CORRELATIONS

CASAS: 7.1.4, 7.2.1, 7.4.1, 7.4.2
SCANS: **Interpersonal** Participates as a Member of a Team, Teaches Others New Skills, Works with Cultural Diversity
Information Acquires and Evaluates Information, Organizes and Maintains Information
Systems Understands Systems, Monitors and Corrects Performance
Basic Skills Reading, Writing, Listening, Speaking
Thinking Skills Creative Thinking, Decision Making, Seeing

Things in the Mind's Eye, Knowing How to Learn, Reasoning
Personal Qualities Responsibility, Self-Esteem, Sociability, Self-Management, Integrity/Honesty
EFF: **Communication** Convey Ideas in Writing, Speak So Others Can Understand, Listen Actively
Decision Making Solve Problems and Make Decisions
Interpersonal Guide Others, Cooperate with Others
Lifelong Learning Take Responsibility for Learning, Reflect and Evaluate, Learn through Research

Review

A **Read the housing advertisements and do the following activities with a partner.**

1. Always wanted to take a house and make it your own? Here's your chance! Settle into this 4-bedroom, 3.5 ba, 2,000 square foot fixer-upper. $150,000. Located in a busy neighborhood with lots of other families, this place is perfect for a young family.

2. Move out of the slow life and into the fast lane! A beautifully spacious 1,000 square foot studio apartment at the top of one of the city's newest high-rises is just what you're looking for. The building has 24-hour security. Utility room with washers and dryers is in the basement. The owner wants to lease it for $2000 a month but is willing to sell. Hurry! This one will go fast!

3. You've finally decided it's time to move out of the city and into the country. Well, we've got just the place for you. This three-bedroom rural residence is just what you need. It's a spacious 1,500 square foot ranch-style home with a huge backyard and a pool. It's located at the end of cul-de-sac where there are only five other homes. It is now being offered at $125,000.

1. Compare the three properties using comparative and superlative adjectives. Take turns making statements.

2. Ask each other *yes/no* and information questions based on the advertisements. Take turns asking questions.

3. Choose one of the ads and rewrite it to fit the description of a house you'd like to buy. Be prepared to read your ad to the class.

4. Describe the process of buying a home, using new words from this unit.

B **Make a list of ten new vocabulary words that you learned in this unit.**

1. _____*(Answers will vary.)*_____   6. _____

2. _____   7. _____

3. _____   8. _____

4. _____   9. _____

5. _____   10. _____

C **Choose three words and make vocabulary cards for them.**

EXAMPLE:

negotiate	
(verb)	
negotiation (noun)	negociar
negotiator (person)	(translation)

1. "Buyers commonly negotiate for better amenities."
2. To reach an agreement through discussion.
3. Negotiate until you reach an agreement.
4. We negotiated an agreement.

D **Complete the sentences below. Then read your answers to the rest of the class. The class will decide on the best answer.**

1. We need to write a business letter when ___*we want to make a complaint about a product or*___ *service.*

2. We need to understand a bar graph when ___*we want to evaluate the different categories of*___ *information presented.*

3. It is important to understand advertisements because ___*it helps you to chose the best product.*___

4. We can use a preferences checklist when ___*deciding what features we want in a house.*___

5. We use comparative adjectives when ___*we are comparing two or more things.*___

6. We use superlative adjectives when ___*we are describing the most extreme degree of*___ *comparison.*

(Answers may vary. Possible answers above.)

Presentation 3: 5–10 min.

Go over the instructions for exercises B and C. You may have to do an example of a word family for exercise C.

Practice 3: 15–20 min.

B **Make a list of ten new vocabulary words that you learned in this unit.**

C **Choose three words and make vocabulary cards for them.**

D **Complete the sentences below. Then read your answers to the rest of the class. The class will decide on the best answer.**

Evaluation 3: 10–15 min.

Have the class vote on the best answer(s) for exercise D.

Application: 1–2 days

The Team Project Activity on the following page is the Application Activity to be done on the next day.

Post-Assessment: Use the *Stand Out* ExamView® Pro *Test Bank* for Unit 3. *(optional)*

Note: With the *Stand Out* ExamView® Pro *Test Bank* you can design a post-assessment that focuses on what students have learned. It is designed for three purposes:

- To help students practice taking a test similar to current standardized tests.
- To help the teacher evaluate how much the students have learned, retained, and acquired.
- To help students see their progress when they compare their scores to the pre-test they took earlier.

Instructor's Notes for Unit 3 Review

Unit 3 Application Activity

> **TEAM PROJECT:**
> **BUY YOUR DREAM HOME**
> Objective: Project designed to apply all the objectives of this unit.
> Products: Create a real estate agency and a real estate brochure

Introduction: 1 min.

State the Objective: *With a team you will create a real estate brochure, choose properties that you are interested in, meet with a real estate agent, and decide which property to purchase.*

Note: Shorter classes can do this project over two periods.

Stage 1: 5 min.

Form a team with four or five students. Choose positions for each member of your team.

Have students decide who will take which position as described on the student page. Provide well-defined directions on the board for how teams should proceed. Explain to the students that all the students do every task. The students don't go to the next stage until the previous one is complete.

Stage 2: 5 min.

Create an imaginary real estate agency. What is the name of your agency? What type(s) of properties do you sell? Have each team report its agency name and the types of properties it sells.

Stage 3: 20–30 min.

Choose three properties that your agency is trying to sell. Make up a brochure for these properties, including pictures and brief advertisements. Display your brochures around the room.

Stage 4: 5–10 min.

Now you are a family who wants to move to a new house. Decide what your housing preferences are and make a list.

Stage 5: 10–15 min.

From the brochures posted around the room, choose two properties that you are interested in, each one from a different agency.

Stage 6: 10–15 min.

Prepare a list of questions that you'd like to ask about each property.

Stage 7: 10–15 min.

In teams of two or three, set up appointments with the real estate agencies and meet with them about the properties you are interested in purchasing. This will take some planning because each team will need to split into two, half talking to the real estate agencies as family members, and the other half responding as the real estate agencies to families.

Stage 8: 10–15 min.

Report back to your group and make a decision about which property you'd like to make an offer on, comparing the information to your checklist.

Stage 9: 10–15 min.

Report your decision to the class.

STANDARDS CORRELATIONS

CASAS: 4.8.1, 4.8.5, 4.8.6
SCANS: **Resources** Allocates Materials and Facility Resources, Allocates Human Resources
Interpersonal Participates as a Member of a Team, Teaches Others New Skills, Exercises Leadership, Works with Cultural Diversity
Information Acquires and Evaluates Information, Organizes and Maintains Information, Interprets and Communicates Information, Uses Computers to Process Information (optional)
Systems Understands Systems, Monitors and Corrects Performance, Improves and Designs Systems
Technology Applies Technology to Task (optional)
Basic Skills Reading, Writing, Listening, Speaking

Thinking Skills Creative Thinking, Decision Making, Problem Solving, Seeing Things in the Mind's Eye, Knowing How to Learn, Reasoning
Personal Qualities Responsibility, Self-Esteem, Sociability, Self-Management Integrity/Honesty
EFF: **Communication** Read with Understanding, Convey Ideas in Writing, Speak So Others Can Understand, Listen Actively, Observe Critically
Decision Making Solve Problems and Make Decisions, Plan
Interpersonal Guide others, Resolve Conflict and Negotiate, Advocate and Influence, Cooperate with Others
Lifelong Learning Take Responsibility for Learning, Reflect and Evaluate, Learn through Research, Use Information and Communications Technology (optional)

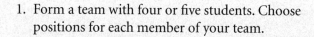

TEAM PROJECT

Buy your dream home

With a team, you will create a real estate brochure, choose properties that you are interested in, meet with a real estate agent, and decide which property to purchase.

1. Form a team with four or five students. Choose positions for each member of your team.

Position	Job Description	Student Name
Student 1 Leader	See that everyone speaks English. See that everyone participates.	
Student 2 Real Estate Agent	Take notes and write advertisements.	
Student 3 Graphic Designer	Design a brochure.	
Students 4/5 Member (s)	Help the real estate agent and the designer with their work.	

2. Create an imaginary real estate agency. What is the name of your agency? What type(s) of properties do you sell?

3. Choose three properties that your agency is trying to sell. Make up a brochure for these properties, including pictures and brief advertisements. Display your brochures around the room.

4. Now you are a family who wants to move to a new house. Decide what your housing preferences are and make a list.

5. From the brochures posted around the room, choose two properties that you are interested in, each one from a different agency.

6. Prepare a list of questions that you'd like to ask about each property.

7. In teams of two or three, set up appointments with the real estate agencies and meet with them about the properties you are interested in purchasing.

8. Report back to your group and make a decision about which property you'd like to make an offer on, comparing the information to your checklist.

9. Report your decision to the class.

PRONUNCIATION

Intonation Yes/no questions usually have a rising intonation. Information questions usually have a falling intonation. Listen to these examples. Underline the stressed words and draw arrows to show the intonation pattern that you hear.

1. Do you want a garage?

2. Do they need air conditioning?

3. Does it have a backyard?

4. What type of property do you want?

5. How many rooms does it have?

6. Where is it located?

LEARNER LOG

In this unit, you learned many things about buying a home. How comfortable do you feel doing each of the skills listed below? Rate your comfort level on a scale of 1 to 4.
1 = Not so comfortable **2** = Need more practice **3** = Comfortable **4** = Very comfortable
If you circle 1 or 2, write down the page number where you can review this skill.

	Comfort Level	Page(s)
Vocabulary		
I can interpret housing advertisements.	1 2 3 4	*41, 42, 47, 57*
I can use context clues to understand vocabulary.	1 2 3 4	*42, 48, 56*
Life Skill		
I can write an advertisement.	1 2 3 4	*42, 57*
I can complete a housing preferences checklist.	1 2 3 4	*49, 50*
I can write a letter to a real estate agent.	1 2 3 4	*52*
Grammar		
I can use comparative and superlative questions.	1 2 3 4	*45, 46, 47*
I can use yes/no and information questions.	1 2 3 4	*49, 57*
Academic Skill		
I can organize information.	1 2 3 4	*42, 43, 47*
I can interpret a bar graph.	1 2 3 4	*53*
I can create a bar graph.	1 2 3 4	*54*

Reflection
Complete the following statements with your thoughts from this unit. *(Answers will vary.)*

I learned _____

I would like to find out more about _____

I am still confused about _____

Unit 3 Pronunciation and Learner Log

Pronunciation: 10–15 min.
(optional)

Intonation

Yes/no questions usually have a rising intonation. Information questions usually have a falling intonation. Listen to these examples. Underline the stressed words and draw arrows to show the intonation pattern that you hear.

Play the recording and pause after each question. Ask students to repeat. Then ask them to underline the stressed words and mark the intonation using arrows. Write the answers on the board or on a transparency. Have students find other examples of *wh-* questions and *yes/no* questions in the unit.

For additional pronunciation practice: You may want to extend this practice by having students identify which words are stressed in the new questions. Have students practice saying the words in each question clearly and distinctly. Then contrast this by saying them rapidly and smoothly, with all the words running together as in normal speech.

Learner Log

Presentation 1: 5–10 min.

If needed, review the purpose of the Learner Log. Make sure students understand how to rate the comfort level they feel in reaching the individual goals listed under *Life Skill, Grammar,* and *Academic Skill.* They should rate their comfort level on a scale of 1 to 4:

1. Not so comfortable
2. Need more practice
3. Comfortable
4. Very comfortable

Practice 1: 5–10 min.

If a student circles 1 or 2, he or she should enter the page number on which the skill is featured. The student can then more easily revisit that page and study the material again.

Evaluation 1: 5–10 min.

Finally, emphasize to students the importance of answering the two questions posed in *Reflection*. They are designed to help students assign real-life value to their classroom work.

Instructor's Notes for Unit 3 Team Project, Pronunciation, and Learner Log

_____

_____

_____

_____

_____

_____

_____

_____

_____

_____

_____

_____

_____

_____

_____

_____

_____

_____

_____

LESSON PLAN

Objective:
Identify resources in a community
Key vocabulary:
education, Employment Development Center, health, local government, recreation, transportation, Little League baseball, skate park, Superior Court

Pre-Assessment: Use the *Stand Out* ExamView® Pro *Test Bank* for Unit 4. (*optional*)

Warm-up and Review: 5–10 min.

Write *community* on the board. Ask students what the word means to them.

Introduction: 1 min.

Tell students that *Community* is the title of this unit. Ask them what they think they will be learning about.

State the Objective: *Today you will identify resources in an imaginary community and then think of similar resources in your own community.*

Presentation 1: 10–15 min.

A **The Sanchez family has just bought a home in Loronado. They are trying to learn about all the available resources in their community. Which category does each place belong to? Make a list on a separate sheet of paper. Then think of one thing you can do at each place.**

Write the word *resources* on the board and ask the students to help you define it.

Practice 1: 15–20 min.

Have students focus on the chart with the major headings and go over each heading. Explain how *City Clerk* fits under local government and *Skate Park* fits under recreation.

Evaluation 1: 10–15 min.

Ask volunteers to write their lists on the board.

Presentation 2: 5–10 min.

Ask students: *What can you do at the City Clerk's office?* Help them come up with a few different answers.

Practice 2: 10–15 min.

Tell students to look at the places they listed in the chart above in groups. Have them think of one thing they can do at each place.

Evaluation 2: 10–15 min.

Have each group report to the class.

Pronunciation: An optional pronunciation activity is found on the final page of this unit. This pronunciation activity may be introduced during any lesson in this unit, especially if students need practice with word linking. (See pages 80 and 80a for Unit 4 Pronunciation.)

STANDARDS CORRELATIONS

CASAS: 2.1.1
SCANS: **Interpersonal** Participates as a Member of a Team, Teaches Others New Skills, Works with Cultural Diversity **Information** Acquires and Evaluates Information, Organizes and Maintains Information, Interprets and Communicates Information, Uses Computers to Process Information (optional)
Technology Applies Technology to Task (optional)
Basic Skills Reading, Writing, Listening, Speaking

Thinking Skills Decision Making
Personal Qualities Sociability
EFF: **Communication** Read with Understanding, Speak So Others Can Understand, Listen Actively
Decision Making Solve Problems and Make Decisions
Interpersonal Guide Others, Cooperate with Others
Lifelong Learning Learn through Research, Use Information and Communications Technology (optional)

Community

GOALS

- Identify resources in a community
- Use embedded questions
- Read a community bulletin board
- Identify and access library services
- Interpret a road map
- Volunteer in your community
- Interpret location/event descriptions

LESSON 1

Your community

GOAL ▶ Identify resources in a community | *Life skill*

A The Sanchez family has just bought a home in Loronado. They are trying to learn about all the available resources in their community. Which category does each place belong to? Make a list on a separate sheet of paper. Then think of one thing you can do at each place.

Education	Employment	Health	Local government	Recreation	Transportation
High School	*Employment Development Department*	*Health Clinic*	City Clerk	Skate Park	*Bus Transit*

(Sample answers above.)

Community Resources

Balboa Park Museum	555-2939	71852 Orange Ave
Bus Transit	555-2678	35984 First Street
Chamber of Commerce	555-4671	72064 Orange Ave
City Clerk	555-8403	63246 Fifth Street #1
Department of Motor Vehicles	555-0013	54679 Fourth Street
Employment Development Department	555-5334	94678 Orange Ave
Health Clinic	555-8473	26489 First Street
High School	555-1238	34658 Loro Road
Hospital	555-7623	79346 Orange Ave
Little League Baseball	555-7300	66554 Third Street
Orange Adult School	555-9134	46589 Fourth Street
Public Library	555-0507	34661 Loro Road
Public Pool	555-4499	56321 Third Street
Senior Center	555-7342	97685 Sixth Street
Skate Park	555-6482	35211 Fourth Street
Superior Court	555-1796	96345 Orange Ave
Village Elementary School	555-8462	34660 Loro Road

Where is Consuela?
What information can she find here?

B **Consuela Sanchez needs some help, so she's at the Loronado Welcome Center. Read the conversation below.**

Consuela: Hi. We just moved to Loronado and I'm looking for a place to <u>get a job</u>. Can you help me?

Receptionist: Of course. Why don't you try the <u>Employment Development Department</u>? It's located on <u>Orange Avenue</u>.

Consuela: Great! Thanks.

C **With a partner, practice the conversation above, but change the <u>underlined</u> information. Use the expressions below and the information on the previous page. There may be more than one possible answer.**

1. take some English classes
2. get a bus schedule
3. use a computer
4. volunteer
5. check out some books

6. get medical help
7. register my little boy for school
8. go swimming
9. look at some art
10. sign up for baseball

D **Now practice the same conversation, but this time ask about *your* town or city. Try to find a location and street for each activity above. Write down the information you find out. If your partner doesn't know, ask other students until you get an answer.**

 E **Active Task:** Use the phone book or the Internet to find other locations to do the above activities. Report back to the class.

Presentation 3: 5–10 min.

B **Consuela Sanchez needs some help, so she's at the Loronado Welcome Center. Read the conversation below.**

Practice 3: 10–15 min.

C **With a partner, practice the conversation above, but change the <u>underlined</u> information. Use the expressions below and the information on the previous page. There may be more than one possible answer.**

Help students by demonstrating the first change.

D **Now practice the same conversation, but this time ask about *your* town or city. Try to find a location and street for each activity above. Write down the information you find out. If your partner doesn't know, ask other students until you get an answer.**

Evaluation 3: 10–15 min.

Ask volunteers to perform their dialogs for the class.

Application: 20–25 min.

Have students make a chart of community resources, like the one they completed in exercise A, identifying resources in their own communities.

 Refer to the *Stand Out Actvity Bank 4 CD-ROM*, Unit 4 Worksheet 1 (three pages), for a template and directed exercises to expand a Class Telephone Directory. *(optional)*

Optional Computer Activity: Have students create this chart on the computer. Show them how to make each column a different color. (See Teaching Hints for suggestions on how to use computers in the classroom.)

E **Active Task: Use the phone book or the Internet to find other locations to do the above activities. Report back to the class.**

Refer to the *Stand Out Activity Bank 4 CD-ROM*, Unit 4 for the Active Task Checklist. *(optional)*

Remind students to use this checklist as they complete Active Tasks for Lessons 1, 2, 3, 4, 5, 6, and 7.

Instructor's Notes for Lesson 1

LESSON PLAN

Objective:
Use embedded questions
Key vocabulary:
embedded, conversational phrase,
transfer, school counselor

Warm-up and Review: 5–10 min. 1.5+

Ask students who completed the Active Task
from the previous lesson to share what they
found out.

Introduction: 10–15 min. 1.5+

Ask students the following questions: *Do you
know if there's a library near here? Can you tell
me when the post office opens?* Ask some other
questions just so students can hear embedded
questions.

State the Objective: *Today you will learn how to
use embedded questions.*

Presentation 1: 5–10 min. 1.5+

**Ⓐ In each of the questions below,
there are two questions. Can you find
them? The first one has been done as
an example.**

Go over the example with the students.

Practice 1: 5–10 min. 1.5+

**Ask the students to come up with three examples
of their own.** Give them a few minutes and then
ask some of the students to write their questions
on the board. Now ask the class to find the two
questions in each question, just as they did in
exercise A.

Evaluation 1: 20–30 min. 1.5+

Go over the answers as a class.

Presentation 2: 5–10 min. 1.5+

**Ⓑ When two questions are combined,
they are called *embedded questions*.
One question is embedded in the
other. Study the chart.**

Review the chart with the class. Assist students in
practicing by beginning with introductory
questions and giving them a topic to make a
question about.

STANDARDS CORRELATIONS

CASAS: 0.1.2
SCANS: **Information** Acquires and Evaluates Information,
Basic Skills Reading, Writing, Listening, Speaking
Thinking Skills Creative Thinking, Decision Making,
Problem Solving, Reasoning

Personal Qualities Sociability
EFF: **Communication** Convey Ideas in Writing, Speak So
Others Can Understand, Listen Actively, Observe Critically
Interpersonal Cooperate with Others

Can you tell me when the library opens?

GOAL ▶ **Use embedded questions**   *Grammar*

> Do you know if there is a library near here?

A **In each of the questions below, there are two questions. Can you find them? The first one has been done as an example.**

EXAMPLE:
Do you know if there is a library near here?
First question: ***Do you know?*** Second question: ***Is there a library near here?***

1. Can you show me where Orange Avenue is?

   First question: *Can you show me?*

   Second question: *Where is Orange Avenue?*

2. Can you tell me when the post office opens?

   First question: *Can you tell me?*

   Second question: *When does the post office open?*

B **When two questions are combined, they are called *embedded questions.* One question is embedded in the other. Study the chart.**

Introductory question	Embedded question	Rule
Can you show me	where *Orange Avenue* is?	In an embedded question, the subject comes *before* the verb.
Do you know	if there <u>is</u> a library near here?	For *yes/no* questions, use *if* before the embedded question.
Can you tell me	when the library <u>opens</u>?	For questions with *do*, take out *do* and use the normal form of the verb.

Why do we use embedded questions? When you are talking to someone you don't know very well, it sounds more polite to put a question into a conversational phrase.

Expressions used to introduce embedded questions	
Could you tell me . . . ?	Would you show me . . . ?
Can you explain . . . ?	Do you know . . . ?

C **Change the following questions to embedded questions, using the expressions in the box.**

EXAMPLE:

What is the name of the local adult school?

Do you know what the name of the local adult school is?

1. What is the address of the public pool?

   Could you tell me what the address of the public pool is?

2. Where is Loronado?

   Do you know where Loronado is?

3. Do you have running shoes?

   Could you tell me if you have running shoes?

4. What time does the library close?

   Do you know what time the library closes?

5. Is Orange Adult School on this street?

   Could you tell me if Orange Adult School is on this street?

6. How can I register for classes?

   Can you explain how I can register for classes?

7. Where do you take your papers for recycling?

   Would you show me where you take your papers for recycling?

8. Is your restaurant open on Sunday?

   Could you tell me if your restaurant is open on Sunday?

   (Answers may vary. Possible answers above.)

D **On a separate sheet of paper, make a list of five questions you could ask a school counselor (using embedded questions). Examples: what classes to take, which colleges to transfer to, how to get a high school diploma.**

(Answers will vary.)

E **Active Task:** Make an appointment with a school counselor and ask him or her the questions you wrote. Then report back to the class.

Practice 2: 10–15 min.

C **Change the following questions to embedded questions, using the expressions in the box.**

Refer to the *Stand Out Activity Bank 4 CD-ROM,* Unit 4 Worksheet 2 (two pages), for additional exercises about embedded questions. *(optional)*

Evaluation 2: 10–15 min.

Call on individuals to write their questions on the board. Evaluate as a class.

Refer to *Stand Out Grammar Challenge 4,* Unit 4 pages 25–27 for more practice with embedded questions. *(optional)*

Presentation 3: 5–10 min. **3**

Question Formation Circle: Have students get into groups of four or five. Each student must contribute a word ultimately to form an embedded question. Ask each group to designate a leader. The leader will start. Example:

Leader: *Do*

Student 2: *you*

Student 3: *know*

Student 4: *what*

Leader: *time*

Student 2: *the*

Student 3: *bank*

Student 4: *closes?*

The person who finishes the question must write it on a piece of paper or on the board.

Practice 3: 10–15 min. **3**

Have students repeat this activity until you tell them to stop.

Evaluation 3: 10–15 min. **3**

Ask groups to demonstrate for the class.

Application: 20–25 min.

D **On a separate sheet of paper, make a list of five questions you could ask a school counselor (using embedded questions). Examples: what classes to take, which colleges to transfer to, how to get a high school diploma.**

E **Active Task: Make an appointment with a school counselor and ask him or her the questions you wrote. Then report back to the class.**

Remind students to use the Active Task Checklist for Lesson 2.

Note: This would be a good opportunity for you to invite a school counselor to your class for students to ask questions, or at least to introduce them to the counselor's role.

Instructor's Notes for Lesson 2

_____

_____

_____

_____

_____

_____

_____

_____

_____

_____

_____

_____

_____

LESSON PLAN

Objectives:
Interpret a community bulletin board,
Make suggestions
Key vocabulary:
bulletin board, bulletin, suggestion,
local hangout, notices, flyers,
marathon, Bingo

Warm-up and Review: 5–10 min.

Ask students to take out the questions they prepared for a school counselor. Have students find a partner and practice asking and answering those questions.

Introduction: 10–15 min.

Write *bulletin board* **on the board.** Ask students what this is and what sort of information they might find on a bulletin board.

State the Objective: *Today you will practice reading a bulletin board and making and responding to suggestions. Then you will make your own bulletin board for this classroom.*

Presentation 1: 10–15 min.

A Consuela and her husband Ricardo are talking to their next-door neighbors. Read their conversation.

Ask students what suggestion Ricardo makes. Go over the phrases used to make and respond to suggestions, giving students examples of each one.

Practice 1: 15–20 min.

B With a partner, make new conversations. Use the topics below and suggestions from the chart. Follow the model in exercise A. Talk about places in your community.

Do the first one as an example with a student.

Evaluation 1: 10–15 min.

Ask volunteers to demonstrate their conversations to the class.

STANDARDS CORRELATIONS

CASAS: 2.5.4., 2.5.5
SCANS: **Resources** Allocates Materials and Facility Resources, Allocates Human Resources
Interpersonal Participates as a Member of a Team, Exercises Leadership, Works with Cultural Diversity
Information Acquires and Evaluates Information, Organizes and Maintains Information, Interprets and Communicates Information, Uses Computers to Process Information (optional)
Systems Monitors and Corrects Performance
Technology Applies Technology to Task (optional)
Basic Skills Reading, Writing, Listening, Speaking

Thinking Skills Creative Thinking, Decision Making, Problem Solving, Reasoning
Personal Qualities Sociability
EFF: **Communication** Read with Understanding, Convey Ideas in Writing, Speak So Others Can Understand, Listen Actively, Observe Critically
Decision Making Solve Problems and Make Decisions, Plan
Interpersonal Guide others, Resolve Conflict and Negotiate, Advocate and Influence, Cooperate with Others
Lifelong Learning Learn through Research, Use Information and Communications Technology (optional)

LESSON 3

Making suggestions

GOAL ▶ **Read a community bulletin board**   *Life skill*

> Where are Consuela and her husband?
> Who are they talking to?

A **Consuela and her husband, Ricardo, are talking to their next-door neighbors. Read their conversation.**

Ricardo: Let's find a good Italian restaurant. Can you think of where we could go?
Jim: Why don't we try this great little place called Island Pasta? It's a local hangout and the food is great!
Marie: I think they're closed tonight. How about going to Laredo's for a Mexican meal instead?
Consuela: Great idea!

B **With a partner, make new conversations. Use the topics below and suggestions from the chart. Follow the model in exercise A. Talk about places in your community.**

1. an inexpensive shoe store

2. a good movie for kids

3. a nice restaurant for your best friend's birthday dinner

4. a bookstore with a large selection of books

5. a good place to find really fresh fruit and vegetables

6. a place to eat Mexican food

7. a place to listen to good music

8. a bookstore to buy the required book for class

Suggestions	Responses
Why don't we . . . ?	Great idea!
We could . . .	Yes, let's do that!
How about . . . ?	Sure!
Do you want to . . . ?	No, I don't like that idea.
Let's . . .	Let's . . . instead.

COMMUNITY BULLETIN BOARD

1 Have you ever wanted to run a marathon?

Now's your chance! Run with a group of people just like you. Get advice from a group leader on fitness, health, and nutrition, and HAVE FUN! Call (777) 555-9768 for more info.

7 Basketball–Open Gym

The new downtown Recreation Center is where the action is! Come on down Monday and Wednesday afternoon, from 5-7 p.m. and join a game. Recreation Center, 4350 Third Street, (777) 555-6211

5 Did you hear your number?

BINGO

Sunday nights starting 4 p.m. Call Charlene for more info (777) 555-9728

2 Guitar Lessons

All levels
Must have a guitar
Music will be provided
Call to set up lessons
$20 a half hour

(777) 555-8697
(777) 555-8697
(777) 555-8697
(777) 555-8697
(777) 555-8697
(777) 555-8697

3 Summer Day Camp

Ages 3-6, 7-10, 11-14
Morning session 9-12 p.m.
Afternoon session 1-4 p.m.
June 25–August 24,
$60 a week per child.
Discounts available for more than one child.
Discounts available for morning and afternoon session.
See Activities Director to sign up.
Or call (777) 555-6211

9 Lost Black Cat

Answers to the name of Blackie. Reward $50 If found, please call:

(777) 555-967
(777) 555-967
(777) 555-967

C Read the notices on the community bulletin boards. Which notice is the most interesting to you? Why? Which notice is the least interesting to you? Why?

D Listen to the statements and write the correct number next to each notice.

(Answers set in bulletin board above and on page 67.)

Presentation 2: 5–10 min.

 C **Read the notices on the community bulletin board. Which notice is the most interesting to you? Why? Which notice is the least interesting to you? Why?**

Give students a chance to read the bulletin board on their own. Then ask them basic comprehension questions about the notices and flyers.

Practice 2: 10–15 min.

 D **Listen to the statements and write the correct number next to each notice.**

Remind students to look at the bulletin boards on both pages 66 and 67 (of the student book).

Evaluation 2: 10–15 min.

Go over the answers with the class.

Presentation 3: 5–10 min. `3`

Demonstrate how to do exercise E by making a statement about something on the bulletin board and asking a student to give you a suggestion. Then have two students demonstrate.

Practice 3: 15–20 min. `3`

E **Work in pairs. Student A, make a statement about one of the notices on the board. Student B, respond with a suggestion.**

Evaluation 3:

Observe the activity.

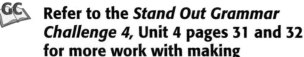 **Refer to the *Stand Out Grammar Challenge 4,* Unit 4 pages 31 and 32 for more work with making suggestions and modals.** *(optional)*

Application: 20–25 min. `L5+`

F **Make a Community Bulletin Board in your classroom. Think of things you could offer and make flyers.**

Encourage students to offer their own talents (musical, athletic, etc.) or items they want to sell.

Have students work in teams to create flyers. Make sure each team has a leader, a writer, and a designer.

Optional Computer Activity: Have students create flyers on the computer using different fonts, borders, shading, colors, and art. (See Teaching Hints for suggestions on how to use computers in the classroom.)

 G **Active Task: Go to a community center and look at the bulletin board. Make a list of activities posted and report back to your class.**

Remind students to use the Active Task Checklist for Lesson 3.

Refer to the *Stand Out Activity Bank 4 CD-ROM,* Unit 4 Worksheet 3, for more practice making suggestions. *(optional)*

Instructor's Notes for Lesson 3

COMMUNITY BULLETIN BOARD

1 **Intro to T'ai Chi'**
T'ai Chi Chih

Discover a wonderful form of exercise and meditation that is centuries old. Involve your mind, body, and spirit. All ages welcome.
Instructor: Mary Walker
Class Site: Room 209
Day: Thursday *Time:* 6 p.m.
Cost: $49/8 weeks
Begins September 4th

8 ## Arts and Crafts

Ever wanted to learn how to knit? Do needlepoint? Help your children with art projects? Make gifts for friends? Come join our craft group on Saturday mornings. There is a $5 material fee each day you attend. Come this Saturday! For more information, call Rick (777) 555-8693

6 ## Roommate wanted

Female, non-smoker, 1 bed, 1 bath, kitchen, garage $400 + sec deposit. Call Laura

Roommate (777) 555-9475
Roommate (777) 555-9475
Roommate (777) 555-9475

4 ## Summer Volleyball League

Got a group of people who want to play volleyball? Want to join a team that needs another player? Sign up for our summer volleyball league! All league games are on Thursday nights. For more information, call (777) 555-7809

Book Club

Do you like mysteries? Fiction? Romance? Non-fiction? Suspense? Come down to the Book Barn and join one of our Book clubs! Read a book every month and meet with others who share your passion to discuss it!
Book Barn, 4212 Loro Road, Tel. (777) 555-5630

E **Work in pairs. Student A, make a statement about one of the notices on the boards. Student B, respond with a suggestion.**

EXAMPLE:
Student A: I need a place to send my kids for the summer while I'm at work.
Student B: Why don't you phone the summer day camp?
Student A: That's a good idea.

F **Make a Community Bulletin Board in your classroom. Think of things you could offer and make flyers.**

G **Active Task:** Go to a community center and look at the bulletin board. Make a list of activities posted and report back to your class.

GOAL ▶ **Identify and access library services**   *Life skill*

 A **Discuss the following questions before you read.**

1. Have you been to your local library?

2. What services does it offer?   *(Answers will vary.)*

3. When is it open?

4. What kind of events are there?

 B **Read the following information from the Loronado library brochure.**

LORONADO PUBLIC LIBRARY

The mission of the Loronado Public Library is to offer an extensive collection of books, audio-visual, and other library and information resources to meet the informational, recreational, and cultural needs of Loronado community members and to actively promote reading and lifelong learning.

 Video Collection

We have an extensive video collection. You may check out two videos at a time for a two-week period.

 Literacy Program

Do you know someone who needs help learning to read? The Loronado Public Library offers a free literacy program with personal tutors to help anyone at any age learn to read. Inquire at the front office for more information.

 Computers

The library is online and you can have access to our entire catalogue of books as well as to the Internet. Use of computers is on a first-come, first-served basis and the time limit is 30 minutes when someone is waiting. Parents can be assured that we have computers in the children's reading room that are blocked from accessing inappropriate material.

 Reading Room

Come visit the Reading Room where

children of all ages can read and check out books. Every Tuesday and Friday, we have Story Time where a different children's book will be read. Preschool at 10:30 a.m. Toddlers at 11:00 a.m.

 Reference Section

Reference materials are books and journals that you can use while at the library. They may not be checked out.

 Be a Volunteer

We're always looking for volunteers to help out in the library. If you have a few free hours to spare, join us!

 Meeting Room

The Peterson Room is available for public meetings by reservation. Maximum seating 15.

LESSON PLAN

Objective:
Identify and access library services
Key vocabulary:
mission, collection, cultural needs, reference materials, on line, catalogue of books, first-come first-served, inappropriate material, accessing, literacy program, volunteers

Warm-up and Review: 5–10 min.

Ask the students to look at the bulletin board they made in the previous lesson. Have them ask other students which notices intrigued them most.

Introduction: 10–15 min.

A **Discuss the following questions before you read.**

Explore the questions as a class.

State the Objective: *Today you will read a library brochure and prepare to ask a librarian questions about available services.*

Presentation 1: 10–15 min.

Focus the students' attention on the brochure. Ask them to look at the main topics and guess what information they might find when they read the pamphlet.

Practice 1: 15–20 min.

B **Read the following information from the Loronado library brochure.**

Evaluation 1: 10–15 min.

Quiz the students by asking them comprehension questions about the information they just read. Go over any parts of the brochure they don't understand.

Optional Internet Activity: Have students go on the web site for their school library or local library. Ask them to find the same sort of information that they just read about in the brochure and make a comparison between the two. (See Teaching Hints for suggestions on how to use computers in the classroom.)

Refer to the *Stand Out Activity Bank 4 CD-ROM*, Unit 4 Worksheet 4, for additional exercises and comprehension questions about internet service at public libraries. *(optional)*

STANDARDS CORRELATIONS

CASAS: 2.5.4, 2.5.6
SCANS: **Interpersonal** Participates as a Member of a Team, Works with Cultural Diversity
Information Acquires and Evaluates Information, Interprets and Communicates Information
Technology Applies Technology to Task (optional)
Basic Skills Reading, Writing, Listening, Speaking
Personal Qualities Sociability

EFF: **Communication** Read with Understanding, Convey Ideas in Writing, Speak So Others Can Understand, Listen Actively
Decision Making Plan
Interpersonal Cooperate with Others
Lifelong Learning Learn through Research, Use Information and Communications Technology (optional)

Presentation 2: 5–10 min.

C Study the floor plan of the Loronado Public Library.

Practice 2: 10–15 min.

D Use the floor plan and the brochure to ask for and give information about the library.

Go over the example in exercise D and demonstrate with a few students.

Evaluation 2:

Observe the activity.

Presentation 3: 5–10 min.

Write the word _librarian_ on the board. Ask the students who this person is and what is involved in his or her job.

Practice 3: 10–15 min.

E With a partner, brainstorm five questions you might ask a librarian. Write them down and share them with the class.

Evaluation 3: 10–15 min.

Ask volunteers to share their questions with the class.

Application: 20–25 min.

F Of all the services listed on the pamphlet, which two are the most important to you? Why?

Have students brainstorm this question in small groups. Then have each student write a paragraph answering the questions. Have them share their paragraphs with their groups for peer correction.

G Active Task: Visit your local library and find out about their services. Ask the librarian some of the questions you wrote above and report back to the class. Remind students to use the Active Task Checklists for Lesson 4.

Optional Internet Activity: Have the students go to the web site of their local library. Have them see if there is an option for them to e-mail questions to the librarian. (See Teaching Hints for suggestions on how to use computers in the classroom.)

Instructor's Notes for Lesson 4

_____

_____

_____

_____

_____

_____

_____

_____

_____

_____

_____

_____

_____

_____

_____

_____

_____

_____

C **Study the floor plan of the Loronado Public Library.**

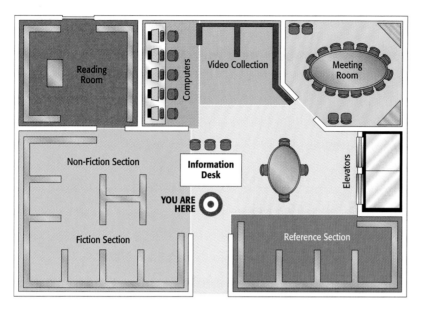

D **Use the floor plan and the brochure to ask for and give information about the library.**

EXAMPLE:
Student A: Where can I find a journal about computers?
Student B: Turn around and go straight ahead. That's our reference section.

E **With a partner, brainstorm five questions you might ask a librarian. Write them down and share them with the class.**

1. *Where can I find a book about gardening?*

2. *How can I get information about the American Red Cross?*

3. *Where is the children's section?*

4. *How do I look up books by this author?*

5. *Where can I find a phone book for San Diego?*

(Answers may vary. Possible answers above.)

F **Of all the services listed on the pamphlet, which two are the most important to you? Why?**

G **Active Task:** Visit your local library and find out about their services. Ask the librarian some of the questions you wrote above and report back to the class.

 **LESSON 5** How far is it?

GOAL ▶ Interpret a road map

Life skill

 A A legend helps you read the symbols on a road map. Write the correct words from the box next to the symbols below.

Legend of Map Symbols

✈ ___airport___   ⛨ 3   ___interstate highway___

H ___hospital___   ⑤   ___freeway___

▲ ___campground___   8   ___exit___

▮▮ ___state scenic highway___   ⊨   ___hotel/motel___

⑤ ___state highway___   R   ___rest area___

(Signs may vary in different regions of the U.S.)

hotel/motel
airport
hospital
rest area
campground
exit
state scenic highway
freeway
interstate highway
state highway

B **Look at the map on the next page and answer the following questions with a partner.**

1. Is there a hospital in Rose? *no*

2. What interstate has rest stops? *315*

3. Where is the nearest campground to Grandville? *Mountain State Park*

4. Which highways are scenic? *13, 15*

5. Is there an airport near Lake Ellie? *no*

C **Look at the highway map scale below and estimate the road distances on the map.**

1. How far is it from Grandville to Rose?
   ≈60 miles
2. How far is it from Poppington to Lake Ellie?
   ≈120 miles
3. How far is it from Loronado to Poppington?
   ≈30 miles
4. How far is it from Lake Ellie to Rose?
   ≈90 miles
5. How far is it from Grandville to Poppington?
   ≈90 miles
6. How far is it from Rose to Loronado?
   ≈90 miles

Highway Map Scale

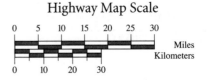

LESSON PLAN

Objective:
Interpret a road map
Key vocabulary:
freeway, interstate, airport, campground, rest area, scenic, map scale, speed limit

Warm-up and Review: 5–10 min.

Ask students if they have thought more about the library. Ask how many students plan to go to a library soon or how many use the library regularly now.

Optional Activity: Invite a librarian to come in, speak to your class, and help students fill out library card applications.

Introduction: 10–15 min.

Ask how many students drive. Ask how many students drive on the highway. Ask them how they know how to get where they need to go.

State the Objective: *Today you will read a road map and practice giving and receiving directions from one city to another.*

Presentation 1: 10–15 min.

A **A legend helps you read the symbols on a road map. Write the correct words from the box next to the symbols below.**

Do this activity as a class.

Practice 1: 5–10 min.

B **Look at the map on the next page and answer the following questions with a partner.**

Evaluation 1: 10–15 min.

Go over the answers as a class. Check comprehension by asking a few extra questions.

Presentation 2: 5–10 min.

Explain map scales and their purpose. Also, teach the word *approximate* and give an example of an approximate distance on student book page 71.

Practice 2: 10–15 min.

C **Look at the highway map scale below and estimate the road distances on the map.**

Allow *approximate* answers for the distances.

Optional Internet Activity: Have students go on the Internet and find a road map of their city. Ask them to find which symbols are on the map. (See Teaching Hints for suggestions on how to use computers in the classroom.)

Evaluation 2: 10–15 min.

Go over the answers together.

STANDARDS CORRELATIONS

CASAS: 1.9.1, 1.9.3, 1.9.4
SCANS: **Interpersonal** Participates as a Member of a Team, Teaches Others New Skills, Works with Cultural Diversity **Information** Acquires and Evaluates Information, Organizes and Maintains Information, Interprets and Communicates Information
Systems Understands Systems, Monitors and Corrects Performance
Technology Applies Technology to Task (optional)
Basic Skills Reading, Writing, Listening, Speaking

Thinking Skills Decision Making, Reasoning
Personal Qualities Sociability
EFF: **Communication** Read with Understanding, Convey Ideas in Writing, Speak So Others Can Understand, Listen Actively
Decision Making Solve Problems and Make Decisions, Plan
Interpersonal Guide Others, Cooperate with Others
Lifelong Learning Reflect and Evaluate, Learn through Research, Use Information and Communications Technology (optional)

Presentation 3: 15–20 min.

 D Listen to the following people giving directions. Where will the driver end up? Fill in the circle next to the correct answer.

Before the listening, review features on the map such as the symbols, the cities, the compass, and the road names. Play the tape a second time so students can check their answers.

Listen to the following people giving directions. Where will the driver end up? Fill in the circle next to the correct answer.

1. ○ Grandville   ○ Rose   ○ Lake Ellie   ● Loronado   ○ Poppington
2. ○ Grandville   ● Rose   ○ Lake Ellie   ○ Loronado   ○ Poppington
3. ● Grandville   ○ Rose   ○ Lake Ellie   ○ Loronado   ○ Poppington
4. ○ Grandville   ○ Rose   ○ Lake Ellie   ● Loronado   ○ Poppington

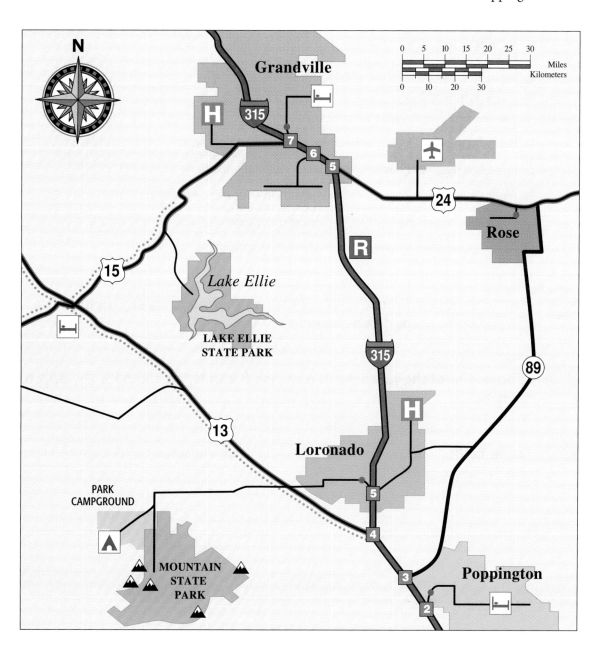

E Now practice giving directions to a partner and receiving directions by writing them down. Student A, look at the map on the previous page to give directions to the places below. Student B, write down what your partner says. If you get confused, ask your partner to slow down or repeat. Then change roles.

EXAMPLE:

From Rose to Grandville

Student A: I live in <u>Rose</u> and I need to get to <u>Grandville</u>. What's the best way to get there?

Student B: Take 24 West until it joins 315 North in Grandville. Follow 315 North and take Exit 7 off the Interstate.

Student A: About how far is it?

Student B: _____ miles.

Student A: Thank you so much.

(Answers may vary. Possible answers below.)

1. From Poppington to Lake Ellie

   Take 315 North to exit 4. Go north on route 13 for about 80 miles, then take 15 East. In about 25 miles you'll make a right turn onto the road to Lake Ellie.

2. From Loronado to Poppington

   Take 315 South and get off at exit 2.

3. From Lake Ellie to Rose

   Take 15 North to Grandville. Then take 315 South until exit 5 for 24 East. Follow 24 East for about 45 miles to Rose.

4. From Rose to Loronado

   Take 89 South until it ends at route 315. Take 315 North to exit 5 for Loronado.

5. From Grandville to Poppington

   Take 315 South to exit 2 for Poppington.

F Now look at the directions you wrote down and compare them to the map. Did you write them down correctly?

G Choose one of the journeys in exercise E and try to estimate the approximate driving time.

H **Active Task:** Call up your local supermarket or bookstore and ask for directions from your house. Write them down.

Practice 3: 20–25 min.

 E Now practice giving directions to a partner and receiving directions by writing them down. Student A, look at the map on the previous page to give directions to the places below. Student B, write down what your partner says. If you get confused, ask your partner to slow down or repeat. Then change roles.

Go over the example with students and show them how to do it by writing the directions on the board and having a pair of students perform the dialog.

Evaluation 3: 10–15 min.

F Now look at the directions you wrote down and compare them to the map. Did you write them down correctly?

Go over the answers as a class.

  Refer to the *Stand Out Activity Bank 4 CD-ROM,* Unit 4 Worksheet 5 (two pages), for additional direction-giving and map-reading skills including a supplemental listening activity about people calling for directions. *(optional)*

Application: 20–25 min.

G Choose one of the journeys in exercise E and try to estimate the approximate driving time.

Compare results to see if all students understand how to estimate. Next have students estimate all the driving times from exercise E with a partner. Compare rates as a class and discuss speed limits.

 H Active Task: Call up your local supermarket or bookstore and ask for directions from your house. Write them down.

Encourage students to do this by telling them you will ask them to turn in the directions when the class meets next. Remind students to use the Active Task Checklist for Lesson 5.

Instructor's Notes for Lesson 5

_____

LESSON PLAN

Objective:
Volunteer in your community
Key vocabulary:
volunteer, community organizations

Warm-up and Review: 5–10 min.

Ask students who completed the Active Task from the previous lesson to share their directions or experience with the class.

Introduction: 10–15 min.

A **Have you ever offered to help a friend or neighbor do something? Do you belong to any local community organizations where you help out in some way? If you answered *yes* to any of the questions above, you are a volunteer!**

Ask students these questions and go over the concept of volunteering.

State the Objective: *Today you will think about things you are good at, things you enjoy doing, and things you might want to learn to help you decide at what places you might become a volunteer.*

Presentation 1: 10–15 min.

B **Before you can volunteer, you need to think about what you can do or like to do. Look at the list below and check the things that you can do or like to do. Add your own ideas to the list.**

Do this exercise as a class. Go through each item on the list and make sure students understand what it entails. Have them put checks in the first two columns based on their preferences. Help them come up with some ideas of things they might write in on the last three lines.

Practice 1: 15–20 min.

C **Now interview your partner. Ask what he or she can do and likes to do and put checks in the appropriate columns. Use the following questions:**

Evaluation 1: 10–15 min.

Ask students to report what they learned about their partners. For example: *John, what does Sara like to do?*

STANDARDS CORRELATIONS

CASAS: 2.1.1, 7.5.1
SCANS: **Interpersonal** Participates as a Member of a Team, Exercises Leadership, Works with Cultural Diversity
Information Acquires and Evaluates Information, Organizes and Maintains Information, Interprets and Communicates Information, Uses Computers to Process Information (optional)
Technology Applies Technology to Task (optional)
Basic Skills Reading, Writing, Listening, Speaking
Thinking Skills Decision Making

Personal Qualities Responsibility, Self-Esteem, Sociability, Self-Management, Integrity/Honesty
EFF: **Communication** Read with Understanding, Convey Ideas in Writing, Speak So Others Can Understand, Listen Actively
Decision Making Solve Problems and Make Decisions, Plan
Interpersonal Cooperate with Others
Lifelong Learning Reflect and Evaluate, Learn through Research, Use Information and Communications Technology (optional)

GOAL ▶ Volunteer in your community | *Life skill*

A Have you ever offered to help a friend or neighbor do something? Do you belong to any local community organizations where you help out in some way? If you answered *yes* to any of the questions above, you are a volunteer!

B Before you can volunteer, you need to think about what you can do or like to do. Look at the list below and check the things that you can do or like to do. Add your own ideas to the list. *(Answers will vary.)*

Skills	I can	I like to	My partner can	My partner likes to
ask for money				
build structures				
clean				
cook				
give a speech				
keep track of money				
make phone calls				
organize				
plan a meeting				
plan a party				
put books in alphabetical order				
spend time with children				
talk to people				
teach someone English				
teach someone to read				
teach someone math				
use the computer				
_____				
_____				

C Now interview your partner. Ask what he or she can do and likes to do and put checks in the appropriate columns. Use the following questions:

Can you _____ ?

Do you like to _____ ?

D **Where are some places in your community you might be able to volunteer? With a group, make a list. Share your list with the class.**

(Answers may vary. Possible answers below.)

Places to Volunteer
library, school, hospital, animal shelter, senior center, homeless shelter, soup kitchen

E **Now look back at the checklist for you and your partner. Come up with one or two places each of you might like to volunteer based on your skills. Give your partner suggestions.**

Places I can volunteer	Places my partner can volunteer
1. *(Answers will vary.)*	1.
2.	2.

F **Now that you have two places you can volunteer, what's the next step? First of all, figure out how to contact them and find the person in charge of volunteering. Second, ask them if they need volunteers. If so, what type of help do they need? Third, find out what hours they need people.**

G **Come up with at least three questions you might ask when you visit or call the location.** *(Answers may vary. Possible answers below.)*

1. *Do you need volunteers?*

2. *What kind of skills do you need?*

3. *Is there a training program?*

 H **Active Task:** Find the phone number and/or address of two places you might volunteer in your phone directory or on the Internet. Visit the location or call and talk to someone. Ask them your three questions. Volunteer to help!

Presentation 2: 5–10 min.

Ask: *Who likes to spend time with children?* Have students raise their hands. Ask them: *Where are some places you might be able to work as a volunteer?* Make a list on the board.

Practice 2: 10–15 min.

D Where are some places in your community you might be able to volunteer? With a group, make a list. Share your list with the class.

Evaluation 2: 10–15 min.

Have each group share their list with the class.

 Refer to the *Stand Out Activity Bank 4 CD-ROM,* Unit 4 Worksheet 6 (two pages), for reading comprehension and vocabulary practice about volunteer opportunities. *(optional)*

Presentation 3: 5 min.

Have students look back at the checklists they made with a partner in exercise B. Ask them to think about places they might be able to volunteer.

Practice 3: 10–15 min.

E Now look back at the checklist for you and your partner. Come up with one or two places each of you might like to volunteer based on your skills. Give your partner suggestions.

Evaluation 3: 10–15 min.

Ask the pairs to report to the class.

Application: 20–25 min.

F Now that you have two places you can volunteer, what's the next step? First of all, figure out how to contact them and find the person in charge of volunteering. Second, ask them if they need volunteers. If so, what type of

help do they need? Third, find out what hours they need people.

Have students share ideas with and report back to their partners.

G Come up with at least three questions you might ask when you visit or call the location.

When students are finished, write some of the questions on the board to give students more ideas of what else they could ask.

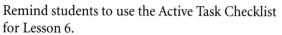 **H Active Task: Find the phone number and/or address of two places you might volunteer in your phone directory or on the Internet. Visit the location or call and talk to someone. Ask them your three questions. Volunteer to help!**

Remind students to use the Active Task Checklist for Lesson 6.

Optional Activity: Have students write a business letter to a place where they may want to volunteer to ask for more information. Introduce the idea of including a self-addressed stamped envelope to help ensure a reply.

Instructor's Notes for Lesson 6

_____

_____

_____

_____

_____

_____

_____

_____

_____

LESSON PLAN

Objective:
Interpret location/event descriptions
Key vocabulary:
visitor's guide

Warm-up and Review: 5–10 min. (1.5+)

Have a discussion about volunteering. Ask students if they went home and thought about it any more.

Introduction: 10–15 min. (1.5+)

Write *visitor's guide* **on the board.** Ask students what it means.

State the Objective: *Today you will read and interpret a visitor's guide and then research information about your own city that could be included in such a guide.*

Presentation 1: 10–15 min. (1.5+)

Ask students what information they might find in a visitor's guide. Ask them to imagine they are visiting a new city. What sort of information would help them in a visitor's guide?

Practice 1: 15–20 min. (1.5+)

A **Read the information from the Loronado Visitor's Guide.**

Go over the entries with the students and help them with any vocabulary problems they might encounter (bestsellers, Victorian historical landmark home, reunions, etc.).

B **Make a list of what type of information you can find in the descriptions.**

Suggest one or two besides *address:* products, hours, dates, and so on.

Evaluation 1: 10–15 min. (1.5+)

Have volunteers write their lists on the board. Ask them if there is additional information they think should be included in the descriptions.

STANDARDS CORRELATIONS

CASAS: 2.1.1, 2.6.1
SCANS: **Interpersonal** Participates as a Member of a Team, Teaches Others New Skills, Exercises Leadership, Works with Cultural Diversity
Information Acquires and Evaluates Information, Organizes and Maintains Information, Interprets and Communicates Information, Uses Computers to Process Information (optional)
Technology Applies Technology to Task (optional)

Basic Skills Reading, Writing, Listening, Speaking
Thinking Skills Creative Thinking, Decision Making
Personal Qualities Responsibility, Sociability
EFF: **Communication** Read with Understanding, Convey Ideas in Writing, Speak So Others Can Understand, Listen Actively
Interpersonal Cooperate with Others
Lifelong Learning Learn through Research, Use Information and Communications Technology (optional)

 **Where can we get good French food?**

GOAL ▶ Interpret location/event descriptions | *Life skill*

A Read the information from the Loronado Visitor's Guide.

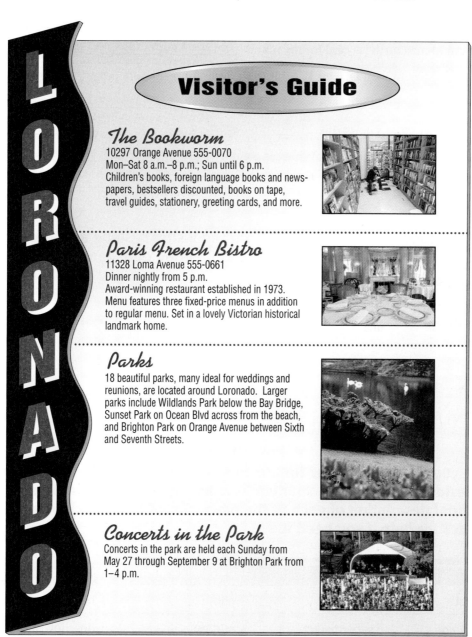

Visitor's Guide

The Bookworm
10297 Orange Avenue 555-0070
Mon–Sat 8 a.m.–8 p.m.; Sun until 6 p.m.
Children's books, foreign language books and newspapers, bestsellers discounted, books on tape,
travel guides, stationery, greeting cards, and more.

Paris French Bistro
11328 Loma Avenue 555-0661
Dinner nightly from 5 p.m.
Award-winning restaurant established in 1973.
Menu features three fixed-price menus in addition
to regular menu. Set in a lovely Victorian historical
landmark home.

Parks
18 beautiful parks, many ideal for weddings and
reunions, are located around Loronado. Larger
parks include Wildlands Park below the Bay Bridge,
Sunset Park on Ocean Blvd across from the beach,
and Brighton Park on Orange Avenue between Sixth
and Seventh Streets.

Concerts in the Park
Concerts in the park are held each Sunday from
May 27 through September 9 at Brighton Park from
1–4 p.m.

B Make a list of what type of information you can find in the descriptions.

address	merchandise	phone number
hours	services	picture

C **Have your partner look at the Visitor's Guide and ask him or her the following questions. Write down what he or she says.** *(Answers may vary. Possible answers below.)*

1. Where can I go for a delicious French meal? *the Paris French Bristo*

2. I'm planning a wedding with a friend. Do you know of a good location?
   Sunset Park, Wildlands Park, or Brighton Park

3. Where can I find a birthday card for my mom? *the Bookworm*

4. Do you know where I can take my kids for some entertainment on Sunday?
   a concert at Brighton Park

5. Where can I get today's newspaper? *the Bookworm*

6. My sister will be here on April 23. What can we do? *eat at the Paris French Bistro, shop at the Bookworm, visit a park*

D **Write three questions of your own about the Visitor's Guide and ask your partner for the information. Try to write embedded questions.**

Question: *Do you know where I can buy a book on tape?*

Answer: *The Bookworm*

Question: *Can you tell me what time the concert in the park begins?*

Answer: *1 P.M.*

Question: *Do you know the address of the Paris French Bistro?*

Answer: *11328 Loma Avenue*

(Answers may vary. Possible answers above.)

E **Imagine you are a staff writer for a community brochure that will be given to all the residents in your city. Your editor asks you to find the information and write a brief description of each of the places listed below. Ask other classmates for help if you need it.**

Locations		Information needed	
restaurant	bookstore	name	hours
public library	supermarket	address	description
park	your school	phone number	special events

 F **Active Task:** Go the Visitor's Bureau in your city or look on the Internet to find a Visitor's Guide for your city. What information does it have?

Presentation 2: 5 min.

Ask students some basic questions about the Loronado Visitor's Guide such as, *When are the concerts in the park? Where is The Bookworm located?*

Practice 2: 10–15 min.

C Have your partner look at the Visitor's Guide and ask him or her the following questions. Write down what he or she says.

D Write three questions of your own about the Visitor's Guide and ask your partner for the information. Try to write embedded questions.

Refer to *Stand Out Grammar Challenge 4,* Unit 4 pages 25–26 for more practice. *(optional)*

Evaluation 2: 10–15 min.

Go over the answers to exercise C and have students share the questions they wrote for exercise D.

Presentation 3: 5–10 min.

Refer to the *Stand Out Activity Bank 4 CD-ROM,* Unit 4 Worksheet 7, for a Visitor's Guide supplemental listening activity during which students listen to information about Loronado and fill in what they hear. Print out a copy of the worksheet for each student. Have them read through to guess what they will be listening for. (See Teaching Hints for more on focused listening.)

Practice 3: 10–15 min.

Play the recording for students one time to see how much they can fill in. Have them share their answers with another student to see if someone else got something they missed. Play the recording again if necessary.

Evaluation 3: 10–15 min.

Go over the answers as a class. Play the recording one more time.

Refer to the *Stand Out Activity Bank 4 CD-ROM,* Unit 4 Worksheet 8 (two pages), for additional reading and question writing activities. *(optional)*

Application: 20–25 min.

E Imagine you are a staff writer for a community brochure that will be given to all the residents in your city. Your editor asks you to find the information and write a brief description of each of the places listed below. Ask other classmates for help if you need it.

Have students work in teams on this project. They may want to consult the telephone directory or use the Internet to find the needed information.

Optional Activity: Once students have gathered the information, ask each group to make a flyer or poster for one of the locations. This can be done with classroom art supplies or on the computer. Have each group share their creation.

F Active Task: Go to the Visitor's Bureau in your city or look on the Internet to find a Visitor's Guide for your city. What information does it have?

Remind students to use the Activity Task Checklist for Lesson 7.

Instructor's Notes for Lesson 7

_____

_____

_____

_____

_____

_____

_____

_____

_____

LESSON PLAN

Objective:
Review all previous unit objectives
Key vocabulary:
Review all previous unit vocabulary

Warm-up and Review: 5–10 min.

Ask students to take out a piece of paper and write down everything they've learned in this unit. Give them a few minutes and then invite everyone to share. Make a list on the board.

Introduction: 5–10 min.

Write *evaluation* and *review* on the board. Ask students what these words mean and what their purpose is.

State the Objective: *Today we will review all that we have done in the past unit in preparation for the application project to follow.* Ask students as a class to recall all the goals of this unit without looking at their books. Then remind them of the goals they haven't mentioned.

Unit goals: *Identify resources in a community, Use embedded questions, Read a community bulletin board, Identify and access library services, Read a road map, Volunteer in your community, Interpret location/event descriptions.*

Presentation, Practice, and Evaluation 1:

Do the Learner Log on page 80. Notes are next to the page.

Presentation 2: 5–10 min.

Preview the instructions for exercises A, B, and C.

Practice 2: 25–40 min.

A Imagine you just moved into your neighborhood. Write four questions you might ask your new neighbor about different places to go. Then practice asking a partner those questions. Write down the suggestions your partner gives you.

B Now ask your partner to give you directions from the school to the four places he or she suggested. Write down the directions he or she gives you on a separate sheet of paper and double-check them with your partner.

C You are visiting the public library for the first time. Write three questions you might ask the librarian.

Evaluation 2: 10–15 min.

Observe the activities. Have volunteers write their questions on the board.

Review

A Imagine that you just moved into your neighborhood. Write four questions you might ask your new neighbor about different places to go. Then practice asking a partner those questions. Write down the suggestions your partner gives you. *(Answers will vary.)*

Questions	Suggestions
1. _____ _____ _____	1. _____ _____ _____
2. _____ _____ _____	2. _____ _____ _____
3. _____ _____ _____	3. _____ _____ _____
4. _____ _____ _____	4. _____ _____ _____

B Now ask your partner to give you directions from the school to the four places he or she suggested. Write down the directions he or she gives you on a separate sheet of paper and double-check them with your partner.

C You are visiting the public library for the first time. Write three questions you might ask the librarian. *(Answers will vary.)*

1. _____

2. _____

3. _____

D You have learned a lot in this unit about different places in the community that you can visit, volunteer, or do things at. Make a list of all the places in your community that you visit. *(Answers will vary.)*

Restaurants I eat at: _____

_____

Stores I shop at: _____

_____

Places that provide free services: _____

_____

Places I volunteer: _____

_____

Places my family and I go to school: _____

_____

Other: _____

_____

E Now make a list of places you haven't been but would like to go.

Restaurants _____ *(Answers will vary.)* _____

Stores _____

Places that provide free services _____

Places to volunteer _____

Places to go to school _____

Other _____

F Make a list of ways you can get information about the places you listed above. (All of this information will help you with your team project.)

1. *Find the number in the phone book and call.* _____

2. *Look up information on the Internet.* _____

3. *Visit in person and ask questions.* _____

4. *Ask a neighbor or friend for information.* _____

(Answers may vary. Possible answers above.)

Presentation 3: 5–10 min.   **3**

Go over the instructions for exercises D, E, and F.

Practice 3: 10–15 min.   **3**

 D **You have learned a lot in this unit about different places in the community that you can visit, volunteer, or do things at. Make a list of all the places in your community that you visit.**

E **Now make a list of the places you haven't been but would like to go.**

F **Make a list of ways you can get information about the places you listed above. (All of this information will help you with your team project.)**

Evaluation 3: 10–15 min.   **3**

Go over responses as a class.

Application: 1–2 days   **1.5⁺**

The Team Project Activity on the following page is the Application Activity to be done on the next day.

Post-Assessment: Use the *Stand Out* ExamView® Pro *Test Bank* for Unit 4. *(optional)*

Note: With the *Stand Out* ExamView® Pro *Test Bank* you can design a post-assessment that focuses on what students have learned. It is designed for three purposes:

- To help students practice taking a test similar to current standardized tests.
- To help the teacher evaluate how much the students have learned, retained, and acquired.
- To help students see their progress when they compare their scores to the pre-test they took earlier.

Instructor's Notes for Unit 4 Review

LESSON PLAN • Unit 4: Community   TEAM PROJECT

Unit 4 Application Activity

> **TEAM PROJECT**
> **CREATE A COMMUNITY PAMPHLET**
> Objective:
> Project designed to apply all the
> objectives of this unit.
> Product:
> A community pamphlet

Introduction: 1–2 min.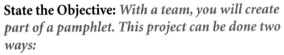

State the Objective: *With a team, you will create part of a pamphlet. This project can be done two ways:*

1) Each team creates its own pamphlet.

2) Each team creates a portion of a pamphlet and all parts will be combined at the end.

Note: Shorter classes can do this project over two periods.

Stage 1: 5–10 min.

Form a team with four or five students. Choose positions for each member of your team. Have students decide who will take which position as described on the student page. Provide well-defined directions on the board for how teams should proceed. Explain to the students that all the students do every task. The students don't go to the next stage until the previous one is complete.

Stage 2: 10–15 min.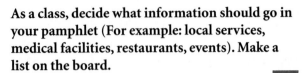

As a class, decide what information should go in your pamphlet (For example: local services, medical facilities, restaurants, events). Make a list on the board.

Stage 3: 5–10 min.

Decide if each team will create its own pamphlet or if each team will work on a portion of the pamphlet. (If the second option is chosen, decide what section each team will work on.)

Stage 4: 20–45 min.

Create the pamphlet or portion of the pamphlet. Make sure to include addresses, phone numbers, and basic information. (Use the phone book or Internet if you need to.)

Stage 5: 10–15 min.

Put your pamphlet together. Pamphlets can be created on the computer using templates or can be handwritten and photocopied. Recommend students use art, photos, maps, and charts in the pamphlets.

Stage 6: 10–15 min.

Present your pamphlet or portion of your pamphlet to the class. Make copies for the whole class. Share the pamphlets with other classes.

STANDARDS CORRELATIONS

CASAS: 4.8.1, 4.8.5, 4.8.6
SCANS: **Resources** Allocates Materials and Facility Resources, Allocates Human Resources
Interpersonal Participates as a Member of a Team, Teaches Others New Skills, Exercises Leadership, Works with Cultural Diversity
Information Acquires and Evaluates Information, Organizes and Maintains Information, Interprets and Communicates Information, Uses Computers to Process Information (optional)
Systems Understands Systems, Monitors and Corrects Performance, Improves and Designs Systems
Technology Applies Technology to Task (optional)
Basic Skills Reading, Writing, Listening, Speaking

Thinking Skills Creative Thinking, Decision Making, Problem Solving, Seeing Things in the Mind's Eye, Knowing How to Learn, Reasoning
Personal Qualities Responsibility, Self-Esteem, Sociability, Self-Management, Integrity/Honesty
EFF: **Communication** Read with Understanding, Convey Ideas in Writing, Speak So Others Can Understand, Listen Actively, Observe Critically
Decision Making Solve Problems and Make Decisions, Plan
Interpersonal Guide Others, Resolve Conflict and Negotiate, Advocate and Influence, Cooperate with Others
Lifelong Learning Take Responsibility for Learning, Reflect and Evaluate, Learn through Research, Use Information and Communications Technology (optional)

T E A M
P R O J E C T

Create a community pamphlet

With a team, you will create a community pamphlet or part of a pamphlet. This project can be done two ways:

1. Each team creates its own pamphlet.

2. Each team creates a portion of a pamphlet and all parts will be combined at the end.

1. Form a team with four or five students. Choose positions for each member of your team.

Position	Job Description	Student Name
Student 1 Leader	See that everyone speaks English. See that everyone participates.	
Student 2 Community Representative	Take notes and write information for pamphlet.	
Student 3 Artist	Design and add art to pamphlet.	
Students 4/5 Member(s)	Help community representative and designer with their work.	

2. As a class, decide what information should go in your pamphlet (For example: local services, medical facilities, restaurants, events). Make a list on the board.

3. Decide if each team will create its own pamphlet or if each team will work on a portion of the pamphlet. (If the second option is chosen, decide what section each team will work on.)

4. Create your pamphlet or portion of the pamphlet. Make sure to include addresses, phone numbers, and basic information. (Use the phone book or Internet if you need to.)

5. Put your pamphlet together.

6. Present your pamphlet or portion of your pamphlet to the class.

PRONUNCIATION

Word Linking. Listen to the sentences below and notice how the words *could, would,* and *did* are linked to the following word *you.* They sound like *kudju, wudju,* and *didju.* Listen again and repeat. Make new sentences to practice these sounds.

1. Could you tell me when the store opens?

2. Would you show me where the elevators are?

3. Did you find the phone number?

LEARNER LOG

In this unit, you learned many things about community. How comfortable do you feel doing each of the skills listed below? Rate your comfort level on a scale of 1 to 4.

1 = Not so comfortable **2** = Need more practice **3** = Comfortable **4** = Very comfortable

If you circle 1 or 2, write down the page number where you can review this skill.

Life Skill	Comfort Level				Page(s)
I can identify and ask for resources in a community.	1	2	3	4	61, 62, 77
I can ask about resources in a community.	1	2	3	4	62, 63
I can identify recreational programs.	1	2	3	4	61
I can read a community bulletin board.	1	2	3	4	66, 67
I can understand library resource information.	1	2	3	4	68
I can identify and access library services.	1	2	3	4	68, 69, 77
I can interpret a road map.	1	2	3	4	71
I can give and receive directions using a road map.	1	2	3	4	71, 72, 77
I can volunteer in my community.	1	2	3	4	73, 74
I can read and interpret location and event descriptions.	1	2	3	4	75, 76
I can create location descriptions.	1	2	3	4	76

Grammar					
I can use embedded questions to ask for information.	1	2	3	4	63, 64
I can make suggestions.	1	2	3	4	65

Reflection

Complete the following statements with your thoughts from this unit. *(Answers will vary.)*

I learned _____

I would like to find out more about _____

I am still confused about _____

Unit 4 Pronunciation and Learner Log

Pronunciation: 10–15 min.
(optional)

Word linking

Listen to the sentences below and notice how the words *could, would,* and *did* are linked to the following word *you*. They sound like *kudju, wudju,* and *didju*. Listen again and repeat. Make new sentences to practice these sounds.

Play the recording and pause after each question. Ask students to repeat. Have students find other examples of similar questions in the unit.

For additional pronunciation practice: Write the following sentences on the board. Remind students of similar sound changes in the following types of questions. Have them practice saying the words in each question clearly and distinctly. Then contrast this by saying them rapidly and smoothly, with all the words running together as in normal speech. Then have students make up their own examples.

1. *Did you know who the librarian was?*
2. *Would you show me how to drive there?*
3. *Could you tell us where the library is?*
4. *Did you know why it closed early?*
5. *Would you tell me what time it opens?*
6. *Could you explain why we have to go?*

Learner Log:

Presentation 1: 5–10 min.

If needed, review the purpose of the Learner Log. Make sure students understand how to rate the comfort level they feel in reaching the individual goals listed under *Life Skill, Grammar,* and *Academic Skill.* They should rate their comfort level on a scale of 1 to 4:

1. Not so comfortable
2. Need more practice
3. Comfortable
4. Very comfortable

Practice 1: 5–10 min.

If a student circles 1 or 2, he or she should enter the page number on which the skill is featured. The student can then more easily revisit that page and study the material again.

Evaluation 1: 5–10 min.

Finally, emphasize to students the importance of answering the two questions posed in *Reflection.* They are designed to help students assign real-life value to their classwork.

Instructor's Notes for Team Project, Pronunciation, and Learner Log

_____

_____

_____

_____

_____

_____

_____

_____

_____

_____

_____

_____

_____

_____

_____

_____

LESSON PLAN

Objectives:
Identify healthy vs. unhealthy habits,
Make a bar graph, Calculate
percentages
Key vocabulary:
health, healthy, unhealthy, percentage,
habits, poll, junk food

Pre-Assessment: Use the *Stand Out* ExamView® Pro *Test Bank* for Unit 5. *(optional)*

Warm-up and Review: 2–5 min.

Write *health* on the board. Ask students what the word means to them.

Introduction: 10–15 min.

Write *healthy* and *unhealthy* on the board. Ask students the difference between these words and have them give you some examples.

State the Objective: *This unit focuses on health and the things you need to know to live a healthy life. Today you will identify healthy and unhealthy habits, calculate percentages of people who have healthy habits, and make a bar graph of the healthy habits of students in this class.*

Presentation 1: 10–15 min.

A What are the following people doing? Which activities are healthy? Which activities are unhealthy? Make two lists below.

Do this exercise as a class.

Practice 1: 15–20 min.

B Can you think of other healthy or unhealthy activities? Add a good and a bad habit to your list.

Have students do this in small groups.

Evaluation 1: 10–15 min.

Have each group report to the class and record results on the board.

Refer to the *Stand Out Activity Bank 4 CD-ROM*, Unit 5 Worksheet 1, for supplemental listening exercises about healthy and unhealthy habits. *(optional)*

Pronunciation: An optional pronunciation activity is found on the final page of this unit. This pronunciation activity may be introduced during any lesson in this unit, especially if students need practice with word linking. (See pages 100 and 100a for Unit 5 Pronunciation.)

STANDARDS CORRELATIONS

CASAS: 3.5.8, 3.5.9, 6.4.3, 6.7.2
SCANS: **Interpersonal** Participates as a Member of a Team, Works with Cultural Diversity
Information Acquires and Evaluates Information, Organizes and Maintains Information, Interprets and Communicates Information, Uses Computers to Process Information (optional)
Systems Understands Systems
Technology Applies Technology to Task (optional)
Basic Skills Reading, Writing, Arithmetic, Listening, Speaking

Thinking Skills Creative Thinking, Decision Making, Problem Solving, Seeing Things in the Mind's Eye, Knowing How to Learn, Reasoning
Personal Qualities Sociability, Integrity/Honesty
EFF: **Communication** Read with Understanding, Speak So Others Can Understand, Listen Actively
Decision Making Use Math to Solve Problems and Communicate, Solve Problems and Make Decisions, Plan
Interpersonal Cooperate with Others
Lifelong Learning Learn through Research, Use Information and Communications Technology (optional)

Health

GOALS

- Make a bar graph
- Use the present perfect continuous
- Use indirect speech
- Fill out a health insurance form
- Read for detail
- Interpret medicine labels
- Write a summary

Health habits

 GOAL ▷ **Make a bar graph**

Academic skill

A **What are the following people doing? Which activities are healthy? Which activities are unhealthy? Make two lists below.**

Healthy habits	Unhealthy habits
exercising	*eating while working*
eating fruit	*eating junk food*
(Answers will vary.)	

B **Can you think of other healthy or unhealthy activities? Add a good and a bad habit to your list.**

C Ms. Tracy's 25 students took a poll in their class to find out what bad health habits they have. They presented their results in the form of a bar graph. Read the bar graph and answer the questions.

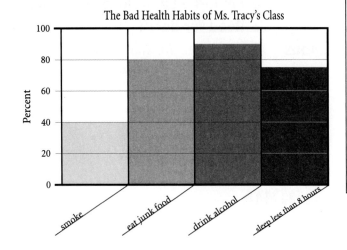

The Bad Health Habits of Ms. Tracy's Class

How to Calculate Percentage

1. First, find out the total number of students in your class.
2. Then divide the total number of students into the number of students who answered the question yes.

   EXAMPLE: In a class of 25 students, 15 students exercise.

   $$25 \overline{)\,15.00} \quad \begin{array}{r} .60 \\ \underline{15\,00} \\ 00 \end{array}$$

3. Move the decimal over two places to the right to get the percentage.

   .60 = 60%

1. What percentage of students eat junk food? _80%_

2. What percentage of students sleep less than eight hours? _75%_

3. What percentage of students *don't* smoke? _60%_

4. What percentage of students *don't* drink alcohol? _10%_

5. What is the worst health habit Ms. Tracy's class shares? _____*drink alcohol*_____

D With a group of students, make a list of four good health habits and take a poll in your class. Make sure you ask every student in the class. Based on your findings, make a bar graph.

Example question: Do you exercise?

(Answers will vary.)

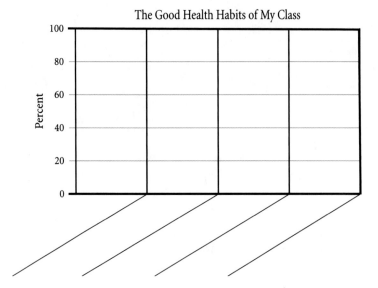

The Good Health Habits of My Class

Active Task: Take a poll among your family and friends of the health habits in exercise D. Make a bar graph.

Presentation 2: 5–10 min.

Ask students to raise their hands if they eat junk food. Count and write the number on the board. Ask one student to tell you the total number of students in the class. Now ask students what percentage of them eat junk food. See if anyone can figure it out. Then show students how to calculate percentage using the steps on page 82.

Ask students to scan the bar graph in exercise C and guess the meaning of the information it presents.

Practice 2: 10–15 min.

C Ms. Tracy's 25 students took a poll in their class to find out what bad health habits they have. They presented their results in the form of a bar graph. Read the bar graph and answer the questions.

Evaluation 2: 10–15 min.

Go over the answers as a class.

Presentation 3: 5–10 min.

Refer to the *Stand Out Activity Bank 4 CD-ROM,* Unit 5 Worksheet 2, for an activity called *My Health Habits,* in which students have to answer questions about their personal health habits and make a bar graph. *(optional)*

Make one copy for each student in the class and go over the instructions.

Practice 3: 10–15 min.

Have students answer the questions and complete the bar graph for *My Health Habits.*

Evaluation 3: 10–15 min.

Have students compare their graphs with those of others in the class.

Application: 20–25 min.

D With a group of students, make a list of four good health habits and take

a poll in your class. Make sure you ask every student in the class. Based on your findings, make a bar graph.

Optional Computer Activity: Have students create their bar graphs on the computer. (See Teaching Hints for suggestions on how to use computers in the classroom.)

E Active Task: Take a poll among your family and friends of the health habits in exercise D. Make a bar graph.

Refer to the *Stand Out Activity Bank 4 CD-ROM,* Unit 5 Active Task Checklist. *(optional)*

Remind students to use this checklist as they complete Active Tasks in Lessons 1, 3, 4, 5, 6, and 7.

Instructor's Notes for Lesson 1

_____

_____

_____

_____

_____

_____

_____

_____

_____

_____

_____

_____

_____

_____

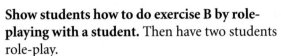

LESSON PLAN

Objectives:
Communicate symptoms to a doctor,
Use present perfect and present
perfect continuous
Key vocabulary:
symptoms, diagnosis, bronchitis,
muscle spasm, flu, common cold, faint,
dizzy, ache, hurt, throw up

Warm-up and Review: 5–10 min.

Ask students about their friends' and families'
healthy and unhealthy habits.

Introduction: 10–15 min.

Tell students about a family member or friend
who is or was sick recently. Make someone up if
you have to. Ask students: *Who should this person
see to get help?* (The doctor.) *What should this
person tell the doctor?* (His or her symptoms.)

State the Objective: *Today you will learn how to
use present perfect and present perfect
continuous to communicate your symptoms to
the doctor.*

Presentation 1: 10–15 min.

A Read the conversation between the doctor and patient.

Ask volunteers to role-play the conversation. Then
have students find partners and practice the
conversation. When they finish, have them switch
roles.

Note: See Teaching Hints for further ways of using
dialogs in class.

Practice 1: 15–20 min.

**Show students how to do exercise B by role-
playing with a student.** Then have two students
role-play.

B Practice the conversation with a partner. Then practice the conversation again, replacing the underlined parts with the information below.

Have each student alternate being the doctor and
patient. If pairs finish early, encourage them to
come up with additional symptoms and
diagnoses.

Evaluation 1: 10–15 min.

Ask volunteer pairs to role-play for the class.

STANDARDS CORRELATIONS

CASAS: 3.1.1
SCANS: **Interpersonal** Participates as a Member of a
Team, Works with Cultural Diversity
Information Acquires and Evaluates Information
Systems Monitors and Corrects Performance
Basic Skills Reading, Writing, Listening, Speaking

Thinking Skills Decision Making, Reasoning
Personal Qualities Sociability
EFF: **Communication** Read with Understanding, Speak So
Others Can Understand, Listen Actively
Interpersonal Cooperate with Others

LESSON 2 What's the problem?

GOAL ▶ **Use the present perfect continuous**   *Grammar*

Who are the people in
the picture?
What are they saying?

A **Read the conversation between the doctor and patient.**

Doctor: Hello, John. What seems to be the problem?
John: Well, I've been coughing a lot.
Doctor: Anything else?
John: Yes, my chest has been hurting, too.
Doctor: It sounds like you might have bronchitis. I'd like to do some tests to be sure, and then I'll
give you a prescription to relieve your symptoms.
John: Thanks, Doc.

B **Practice the conversation with a partner. Then practice the conversation
again, replacing the underlined parts with the information below.**

Symptom no. 1	Symptom no. 2	Diagnosis
1. I've been blowing my nose a lot.	My back has been aching.	common cold
2. My leg's been hurting.	I haven't been walking properly.	muscle spasm
3. I've been throwing up.	I've been feeling faint and dizzy.	flu

GOAL ▶ Use the present perfect continuous *Grammar*

C Study the chart with your teacher.

Present perfect continuous		
Example	**Form**	**When do you use it?**
I *have been studying* for three hours. The president *has been speaking* since 9 A.M.	*Affirmative sentence* has/have + been + present participle	To emphasize the duration of an activity or state that started in the past and continues in the present
You've *been going* to the movies a lot lately. He *hasn't been working* late recently.	*Negative sentence* has/have + not + been + present participle	To show that an activity has been in progress recently
How long *have they lived / been living* here? They *have lived / have been living* here since 2000.	*Question* has/have + subject + been + present participle	With some verbs (*work, live, teach*), there is no difference in meaning between the present perfect and the present perfect continuous.

Note: Some verbs are not usually used in the continuous form, e.g., *be, believe, hate, have, know, like, want.*

(Answers may vary. Possible answers below.)

D Complete the following sentences using the present perfect continuous and suitable time expressions.

for + period of time	*since* + point in time
two weeks five days a month a long time a while	Tuesday 5:30 P.M. 1964 last night I was a child

1. We _____*have been studying*_____ (study) English for ___*a month*___.
2. The kids _____*have been sleeping*_____ (sleep) since ___*last night*___.
3. The couple ___*has been traveling*___ (travel) in Mexico for ___*five days*___.
4. I ___*have been working*___ (work) at the same job for ___*a long time*___.
5. How long ___*have you been teaching*___ (you/teach) math?
6. Satomi ___*has not been feeling well*___ (feel well/not) since ___*Tuesday*___.
7. The boy ___*has been reading*___ (read) since ___*5:30 P.M.*___.
8. Enrico ___*has been playing piano*___ (play piano) for ___*two weeks*___.
9. Minh ___*has been thinking*___ (think) about changing jobs for ___*a while*___.
10. ___*Have they been living*___ (they/live) in New York for ___*a long time*___?

84 UNIT 5 • Lesson 2

Presentation 2: 10–15 min.

C Study the chart with your teacher.

Practice 2: 10–15 min.

D Complete the following sentences using the present perfect continuous and suitable time expressions.

Review *for* and *since* expressions with the students. Have them think of more time expressions to use with *for* or *since*.

Evaluation 2: 10–15 min.

Go over the answers as a class.

 Refer to *Stand Out Grammar Challenge 4,* Unit 5 pages 33–35 for more practice with forms of the present perfect continuous. *(optional)*

Presentation 3: 5–10 min. **L5+**

E **Now review the present perfect with your teacher.**

Practice 3: 10–15 min. **3**

F **Choose the present perfect or the present perfect continuous to complete these sentences.**

Evaluation 3: 10–15 min. **3**

Go over the completed sentences as a class.

GC **Refer to *Stand Out Grammar Challenge 4,* Unit 5 pages 36–37 for more review of the present perfect.** *(optional)*

Application: 20–25 min. **L5+**

G **Work in groups of three or four. Ask and answer questions using How long . . . ? Use the present perfect or present perfect continuous.**

Walk around and observe each group.

AB **Refer to the *Stand Out Activity Bank 4 CD-ROM,* Unit 5 Worksheet 3 (two pages), for additional practice with present perfect and present perfect continuous.** *(optional)*

Instructor's Notes for Lesson 2

E Now review the present perfect with your teacher.

Present perfect simple		
Example	**Form**	**When do you use it?**
He *has seen* the doctor. *Have* you *called* your mother? She *has* never *broken* her arm.	*Affirmative Sentence* *has/have* + past participle	When something happened (or didn't happen) at an unspecified time in the past
I *have moved* four times in my life. She *has been* to the hospital many times.	*Negative Sentence* *has/have* + *not* + past participle *or* *has/have* + *never* + past participle	When something happened more than once in the past (and could possibly happen again in the future)
They *have lived* here for ten years. I *have had* bronchitis since last week.	*Question* *has/have* + subject + past participle	When something started at a specific time in the past and continues in the present

F Choose the present perfect or the present perfect continuous to complete these sentences.

1. They _____*have been*_____ (be) to New York several times.

2. Marco _____*has had*_____ (have) three jobs since 1995.

3. She _____*has been giving*_____ (give) me a lot of help since I moved here.

4. I _____*haven't been studying*_____ (study) Spanish recently.

5. _____*Have you seen*_____ (you/see) the Tower of Pisa in Italy?

6. _____*Have you been waiting*_____ (you/wait) for a long time?

7. Santiago _____*hasn't missed*_____ (miss/not) any classes this week.

8. We _____*have been living*_____ (live) here for three years.

9. John _____*has been talking*_____ (talk) to the doctor for 20 minutes.

10. How long _____*have you known*_____ (you/know) Maria?

G Work in groups of three or four. Ask and answer questions using *How long . . . ?* Use the present perfect or present perfect continuous.

EXAMPLES:
How long have you been studying English?
How long have you been at this school?

What did she say?

GOAL ▶ **Use indirect speech**

> What are Rosa and her friend talking about? What do you think they are saying?

 A **Listen to the following conversation between Rosa and her doctor. Number the sentences in the correct order.**

___1___ "I can give you some more tests."

___5___ "The most important thing is to stay active."

___2___ "You have to come back in two weeks."

___3___ "If you do more exercise, your cholesterol should go down."

___4___ "If you don't stop eating junk food, you will have serious health problems."

 B **Now listen to Rosa reporting her conversation to her friend. Fill in the missing words.**

1. The doctor said that she ___could___ give ___me___ some more tests.

2. The doctor told me that the most important thing ___was___ to stay active.

3. The doctor said that ___I___ ___would___ ___have___ to come back in two weeks.

4. The doctor told me that if ___I___ ___did___ more exercise, ___my___ cholesterol should go down.

5. The doctor said that if ___I___ ___didn't___ stop eating junk food, ___I___ ___would___ have serious health problems.

 C **What differences do you notice between the sentences in exercise A and exercise B? Study the chart below with your teacher.**

Direct speech	Indirect speech	Rule
"You have to exercise more."	The doctor *told me* (that) I had to exercise more.	Change pronoun.
"The most important thing is to stay active."	The doctor *said* (that) the most important thing *was* to stay active.	Change present tense to past tense.

LESSON PLAN

Objective:
Use indirect speech
Key vocabulary:
treatment, cholesterol, obstetrician,
podiatrist, chiropractor, dentist,
pediatrician, junk food, prenatal

Warm-up and Review: 5–10 min.

Review present perfect and present perfect continuous with students by asking them some basic information questions. For example: *How long have you lived in the United States? How long have you been studying English?* Briefly review the rules with students if necessary.

Introduction: 10–15 min.

Ask students to recall the Active Task in Lesson 1, in which they were supposed to go home and talk to their family members and friends about health habits. Ask one student what responses he or she received. For example: *What did your sister say about her health habits?* If the student rephrases what the sister said using indirect speech, great. If not, rephrase it. For example, *So your sister <u>told you</u> she exercises three times a week.* You are subtly introducing the idea of indirect speech.

State the Objective: *Today you will learn how to use indirect speech to tell someone what the doctor said to you.*

Presentation 1: 10–15 min.

Have students look at the picture of Rosa and her friend on p. 86. Ask students the questions in the box: *What are these people talking about? What do you think they are saying?*

Practice 1: 15–20 min.

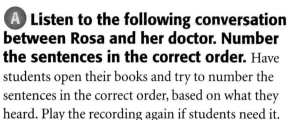

A Listen to the following conversation between Rosa and her doctor. Number the sentences in the correct order. Have students open their books and try to number the sentences in the correct order, based on what they heard. Play the recording again if students need it.

B Now listen to Rosa reporting her conversation to her friend. Fill in the missing words.

Evaluation 1: 10–15 min.

Go over the answers to both exercises by playing the recording again and having students check their work.

Presentation 2: 10–15 min.

C What differences do you notice between the sentences in exercise A and exercise B? Study the chart below with your teacher. Allow students time to look at the different patterns before studying the chart.

Practice 2: 10–15 min.

Have students rewrite the sentences in exercise A using indirect speech, as if they were the ones who went to the doctor. For example: *The doctor said he could give me more tests.*

Evaluation 2: 10–15 min.

Ask volunteers to write their sentences on the board. Have the class evaluate the sentences based on the rules they just learned.

Refer to *Stand Out Grammar Challenge 4*, Unit 5 pages 38–40 for more practice with indirect speech. *(optional)*

STANDARDS CORRELATIONS

CASAS: 3.1.1
SCANS: **Interpersonal** Participates as a Member of a Team, Works with Cultural Diversity
Information Acquires and Evaluates Information
Systems Monitors and Corrects Performance
Basic Skills Reading, Writing, Listening, Speaking

Thinking Skills Decision Making, Reasoning
Personal Qualities Sociability
EFF: **Communication** Read with Understanding, Speak So Others Can Understand, Listen Actively
Interpersonal Cooperate with Others

Presentation 3: 5–10 min.   `3`

D Match the type of doctor with the type of treatment he or she provides.

Go over the vocabulary words in the box.

Practice 3: 10–15 min.   `3`

E Read each statement below. Decide what kind of doctor said each statement and use indirect speech to tell your partner what each person said. Then write the sentences below.

Review the example together.

Evaluation 3: 10–15 min.   `3`

Ask volunteers to read their statements aloud.

Application: 20–25 min.   `1.5+`

F Active Task: Think of a conversation you had recently with a friend, family member, co-worker, or your teacher. Tell your partner what the person said to you.

Walk around the room and listen to each pair. Remind students to use the Active Task Checklist for Lesson 3.

Refer to the *Stand Out Activity Bank 4 CD-ROM,* Unit 5 Worksheet 4, for additional practice with indirect speech. (*optional*)

Instructor's Notes for Lesson 3

D **Match the type of doctor with the treatment he or she provides.**

| dentist | chiropractor | podiatrist | pediatrician | obstetrician |

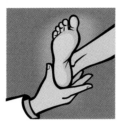
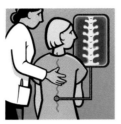

obstetrician   *podiatrist*   *chiropractor*   *dentist*   *pediatrician*

E **Read each statement below. Decide what type of doctor said each statement and use indirect speech to tell your partner what each person said. Then write the sentences below.**

EXAMPLE:
"You are in perfect health!"
The doctor told me I was in perfect health.

1. "You need to brush your gums and floss your teeth every day."

   The dentist told me I needed to brush my gums and floss my teeth every day.

2. "Your children are eating too many sweets and sugary foods. They need to eat more fruits and vegetables."

   The pediatrician told me my children were eating too many sweets and sugary foods. They need to eat more fruits and vegetables.

3. "It is good idea to go to prenatal classes for at least three weeks."

   The obstetrician told me it was a good idea to go to prenatal classes for at least three weeks.

4. "The shoes you are wearing aren't good for your feet."

   The podiatrist told me the shoes I was wearing weren't good for my feet.

5. "You'll hurt your back if you don't bend your knees to lift heavy objects."

   The chiropractor told me I'd hurt my back if I didn't bend my knees to lift heavy objects.

F **Active Task:** Think of a conversation you had recently with a friend, family member, co-worker, or your teacher. Tell your partner what the person said to you.

LESSON 4 Do you want dental coverage?

GOAL ▶ **Fill out a health insurance form**   *Life skill*

A **If you were looking for a good health insurance company, what things would you look for? Check ✓ which of the items below would be most important for you and then share your answers with the class.** *(Answers will vary.)*

❏ dental coverage   ❏ low deductible

❏ prescription plan   ❏ low co-pay

❏ vision plan   ❏ good choice of providers

❏ low premium   ❏ good reputation

B **Skim the health insurance application on this page and the next page. Put a check ✓ next to every part you can answer. Underline parts you are not sure about.** *(Answers will vary.)*

Employee Applicant Information:

First Name: _____ Middle Name: _____ Last Name: _____

Home Address: Street: _____ City: _____ State: ____ Zip Code: _____

Sex: ____ Male ____ Female

Social Security Number: _____

Date of birth: (mm/dd/yyyy) _____

Marital Status: ____ Married ____ Single

Work Phone: _____ Home Phone: _____

Job Title: _____

Hours Worked per Week: _____ Annual Salary: _____

Tobacco: Have you or your spouse used any tobacco products in the past 12 months?

Employee: ____ Yes ____ No

Spouse: ____ Yes ____ No

Dental: Do you want Dental Coverage? ____ Yes ____ No

Prescription Card: Do you want a Prescription Card? ____ Yes ____ No

Dependants: Dependants you want covered on this policy.

Spouse: _____

Date of birth: (mm/dd/yyyy) ____ Sex: ____ Male ____ Female

Child #1: _____

Date of birth: (mm/dd/yyyy) ____ Sex: ____ Male ____ Female

Child #2: _____

Date of birth: (mm/dd/yyyy) ____ Sex: ____ Male ____ Female

LESSON PLAN

Objective: Interpret and fill out a health insurance form

Key vocabulary: coverage, prescription plan, vision, premium, deductible, co-pay, providers, reputation, spouse, dependants, stroke, intestinal, colon, kidney, muscular, circulatory, cancer, diabetes, respiratory, mental, emotional, liver, hernia, thyroid, allergy, digestive system, joint, asthma, reproductive organs, ulcer, arthritis, high blood pressure, HIV, AIDS

Warm-up and Review: 5–10 min.

Review indirect speech by asking some students to tell you about conversations they had with people before class.

Introduction: 10–15 min.

Ask students to raise their hands if they have health insurance. Ask how many have it through their work or through a special program, and how many pay for it individually. Ask students who don't have health insurance why they don't.

State the Objective: *Today we will talk about what to look for in a health insurance company and practice filling out health insurance paperwork.*

Presentation 1: 10–15 min.

Ask students what qualities they would look for in a health insurance company. Make a list on the board.

Practice 1: 15–20 min.

A If you were looking for a good health insurance company, what things would you look for? Check ✓ which of the items below would be most important for you and then share your answers with the class.

Review each item with students explaining the difficult vocabulary or have the class come up with definitions together.

Evaluation 1: 10–15 min.

Have students share their answers with the class. Now ask students to rate each item 1–8 based on its importance, 1 being the most important.

Optional Internet Activity: Have students research different insurance companies and the benefits they offer. (See Teaching Hints for more suggestions on how to use computers in the classroom.)

Presentation 2: 5–10 min.

Go over the instructions for exercise B, giving students an example of something to check and something to underline. You may want to put the application on an overhead transparency to make it easier to explain.

Practice 2: 10–15 min.

B Skim the health insurance application on this page and the next page. Put a check ✓ next to every part you can answer. Underline parts you are not sure about.

STANDARDS CORRELATIONS

CASAS: 3.2.3
SCANS: **Interpersonal** Participates as a Member of a Team, Teaches Others New Skills, Works with Cultural Diversity **Information** Acquires and Evaluates Information, Interprets and Communicates Information, Uses Computers to Process Information (optional) **Technology** Applies Technology to Task (optional) **Basic Skills** Reading, Writing, Listening, Speaking

Thinking Skills Decision Making, Knowing How to Learn **Personal Qualities** Responsibility, Sociability *EFF:* **Communication** Read with Understanding, Speak So Others Can Understand, Listen Actively **Interpersonal** Guide others, Cooperate with Others **Lifelong Learning** Take Responsibility for Learning, Learn through Research, Use Information and Communications Technology (optional)

Evaluation 2: 10–15 min.

C **Work in pairs and use a dictionary to help you understand the parts of the form that you underlined.**

Presentation 3: 5–10 min.

Write the two questions from exercise D on the board. Tell students they will work in small groups of four or five to come up with the most reasonable answers they can. Each group will have to write its answers on the board for the class to evaluate.

Practice 3: 10–15 min.

D **Why do you think health insurance companies need this information? Why is it important to have health insurance?**

Have students work in groups of four or five to come up with answers to the questions. Walk around and help students.

Evaluation 3: 10–15 min.

Have each group report to the class. Volunteers can write responses on the board.

Application: 20–25 min.

Have students fill out the application in their book. Remind students that they don't need to write real information about themselves for this class if they don't feel comfortable. Health and financial information is considered very private in the U.S.

Note: Shorter classes will need to complete Practice 2 before they fill out the application.

 E **Active Task: Find a health insurance application form from a health insurance company or from the Internet. Fill out the application. (Don't send it in unless you're sure you want to get health insurance through them!)**

Remind students to use the Active Task Checklist for Lesson 4.

Refer to the *Stand Out Activity Bank 4 CD-ROM*, Unit 5 Worksheet 4 (two pages), for a discussion, reading, vocabulary work, and comprehension questions about an HMO. *(optional)*

Instructor's Notes for Lesson 4

_____

_____

_____

_____

_____

_____

_____

_____

_____

_____

_____

_____

_____

_____

_____

_____

_____

_____

_____

_____

_____

_____

A-1: Within the last four (4) years, have you or any dependent received or been recommended to have treatment for any disorders or conditions of the following? Please check all that apply.
❑ Back   ❑ Stroke   ❑ Intestinal   ❑ Colon
❑ Kidney   ❑ Muscular   ❑ Heart or Circulatory ❑ Cancer
❑ Diabetes   ❑ Respiratory   ❑ Mental or Emotional   ❑ Liver

A-2: Within the last four (4) years, have you or any dependent used drugs not prescribed by a physician, been advised to have treatment or been treated for drug abuse or alcoholism, or been a member of Alcoholics Anonymous?
❑ Yes ❑ No

A-3: Have you or any dependent ever had a positive blood test indicating HIV antibodies or been treated and/or advised by a medical practitioner as having Acquired Immune Deficiency Syndrome (AIDS), AIDS Related Complex (ARC), or any other immune system deficiency?
❑ Yes ❑ No

A-4: Have you or any dependent been hospitalized, had surgery, or had more than $5000 in medical expenses in the last twelve (12) months?
❑ Yes ❑ No

A-5: Are you or any dependent pregnant? ❑ Yes ❑ No
If "Yes," what is your estimated due date? _____

A-6: Within the last four (4) years, have you or any dependent received or been recommended to have treatment for any disorders or conditions of the following? Please check all that apply.
❑ Ear   ❑ Hernia   ❑ Thyroid   ❑ Breast
❑ Eye   ❑ Allergy   ❑ Digestive System ❑ Joint
❑ Asthma   ❑ Reproductive Organs ❑ Ulcer   ❑ Arthritis
❑ High Blood Pressure

A-7: Within the last four (4) years, have you or any dependent received treatment or been advised to seek treatment for any reason not already mentioned?
❑ Yes ❑ No

Employee Name: _____

Date: (mm/dd/yyyy) _____

C Work in pairs and use a dictionary to help you understand the parts of the form that you underlined.

D Why do you think health insurance companies need this information? Why is it important to have health insurance?

E **Active Task:** Find a health insurance application form from a health insurance company or from the Internet. Fill out the application. (Don't send it in unless you're sure you want to get health insurance through them!)

Reading nutrition labels

GOAL ▶ **Read for detail**

Academic skill

A Do you always read the nutrition label on food that you buy? What do you usually read first on the label? Why?

B Look at the nutrition label below. Answer the questions.

1. How many calories are in one serving of this product? How many of those calories are from fat?
2. How much protein is in this product?
3. What vitamins or minerals does this product contain?
4. How many carbohydrates are in one serving of this product?
5. How much fat is in one serving of this product? How much of the fat is saturated?
6. What is one serving of this product?

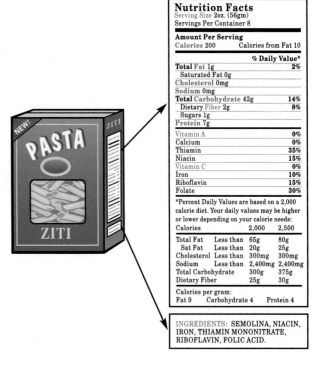

Nutrition Facts
Serving Size 2oz. (56gm)
Servings Per Container 8

Amount Per Serving

Calories 200   Calories from Fat 10

	% Daily Value*
Total Fat 1g	2%
Saturated Fat 0g	
Cholesterol 0mg	
Sodium 0mg	
Total Carbohydrate 42g	14%
Dietary Fiber 2g	8%
Sugars 1g	
Protein 7g	
Vitamin A	0%
Calcium	0%
Thiamin	35%
Niacin	15%
Vitamin C	0%
Iron	10%
Riboflavin	15%
Folate	30%

*Percent Daily Values are based on a 2,000 calorie diet. Your daily values may be higher or lower depending on your calorie needs:

Calories	2,000	2,500
Total Fat	Less than 65g	80g
Sat Fat	Less than 20g	25g
Cholesterol	Less than 300mg	300mg
Sodium	Less than 2,400mg	2,400mg
Total Carbohydrate	300g	375g
Dietary Fiber	25g	30g

Calories per gram:
Fat 9   Carbohydrate 4   Protein 4

INGREDIENTS: SEMOLINA, NIACIN, IRON, THIAMIN MONONITRATE, RIBOFLAVIN, FOLIC ACID.

C Match the highlighted words from the label with the definitions below.

1. This is the amount of food that a person actually eats at one time. _____*Serving size*_____

2. This type of nutrient indicates the salt content of food. _____*Sodium*_____

3. This ingredient of food is not digested, but it aids digestion. _____*Fiber*_____

4. These indicate the total amount of energy supplied by a kind of food. _____*Calories*_____

5. This helps to build and repair muscles. It is found mainly in meat, fish, eggs, beans, and cheese.
_____*Protein*_____

6. These are whatever is contained in a type of food. _____*Ingredients*_____

7. This is a type of fat. It can contribute to heart disease. _____*Saturated fat*_____

8. This is the best source of energy and can be found in breads, grains, fruits, and vegetables.
_____*Carbohydrate*_____

9. Eating too much of this can cause heart disease. _____*Cholesterol*_____

10. These nutrients help to keep your body healthy. _____*Vitamin A, Vitamin C*_____

LESSON PLAN

Objective:
Read and interpret nutritional information
Key vocabulary:
fat, sodium, calories, carbohydrates, serving size, protein, ingredients, cholesterol, fiber, FDA, vitamins, minerals

Warm-up and Review: 5–10 min.

Look over the health insurance form from the previous lesson. See if students have any questions. Ask students to explain the different parts of the form.

Introduction: 10–15 min.

Write *nutrition* **on the board.** Ask students what this means to them. Ask them how they can find the nutritional information of certain foods.

Optional Activity: Pass around some cans or food packages to show them examples of nutrition labels.

State the Objective: *Today you will learn about the nutritional information found on product labels and practice reading nutritional labels.*

Presentation 1: 10–15 min.

Write the following words on the board and see if students can help you define them: *fat*, *sodium*, *calories*, *protein*. Accept all answers at this point and don't correct students. Write answers on the board.

Practice 1: 10–15 min.

A Do you always read the nutrition label on food that you buy? What do you usually read first on the label? Why?

Discuss answers as a class.

B Look at the nutrition label below. Answer the questions.

Have students work with a partner to answer exercises B and C.

Evaluation 1: 10–15 min.

C Match the highlighted words from the label with the definitions below.

Go over the answers for exercises B and C as a class. Check definitions from Presentation 1 and revise as needed.

STANDARDS CORRELATIONS

CASAS: 3.5.1
SCANS: **Interpersonal** Teaches Others New Skills, Works with Cultural Diversity
Information Acquires and Evaluates Information, Interprets and Communicates Information, Uses Computers to Process Information (optional)
Systems Understands Systems, Monitors and Corrects Performance
Technology Selects Technology, Applies Technology to Task, Maintains and Troubleshoots Equipment (optional)

Basic Skills Writing, Reading, Listening, Speaking
Thinking Skills Seeing Things in the Mind's Eye, Knowing How to Learn, Reasoning
EFF: **Communication** Read with Understanding, Speak So Others Can Understand, Listen Actively
Decision Making Solve Problems and Make Decisions
Lifelong Learning Take Responsibility for Learning, Learn through Research, Use Information and Communications Technology (optional)

Presentation 2: 15–20 min.

D **Read the following information about food labels.**

Have students first read the selection to themselves. Then call on students to read each part aloud. After each student is finished, go over what was just read, checking for comprehension and answering any questions students might have.

Practice 2: 5–10 min.

E **How much do you know about nutrition? Fill in the circle under *True* or *False* for each statement below.**

Evaluation 2: 5 min.

Go over the answers as a class.

Presentation and Practice 3: 15–20 min.

 Refer to the *Stand Out Activity Bank 4 CD-ROM,* Unit 5 Worksheet 6 (three pages), for more practice reading nutrition labels. *(optional)*

Have the students work in pairs to interpret nutrition labels. Assign *one* label per pair. Then have pairs meet in groups with others who have their same label to compare answers.

Evaluation 3: 10–15 min.

The class should come together to discuss answers. At this point all students should receive all three nutrition labels and record answers. Discuss the problems with reading the nutrition labels and any new vocabulary.

Application: 15–20 min.

 F **Active Task: Read the food labels of your favorite products or look them up on the Internet. Share the information with your class.**

Remind students to use the Active Task Checklist.

 Refer to the *Stand Out Activity Bank 4 CD-ROM,* Unit 5 Worksheet 7, for a nutrition label quiz. *(optional)*

Instructor's Notes for Lesson 5

_____

_____

_____

_____

_____

_____

_____

_____

_____

_____

_____

_____

_____

_____

_____

_____

_____

_____

_____

_____

_____

_____

_____

_____

_____

D **Read the following information about food labels.**

Reading Nutritional Information on Food Labels

Knowing how to read the food label on packaged foods can help you build better eating habits. Here's a rundown of the basics you'll find on a food label and how you can use the information to improve your daily diet:

1. **Serving Size** The serving sizes on the label are supposed to be close to "real life" serving sizes - no more listing a teaspoon of dressing when most of us use a tablespoon. The information on the rest of the label is based on data for one serving. Remember, a package may contain more than one serving.

2. **Calories** The number of calories tells you how many calories are in one serving. The number of calories from fat tells you how many calories come from fat. Try to find foods with low amounts of calories from fat.

3. **Fat** This is where you look if you are trying to count fat grams. Total fat is important to watch, but saturated fat is particularly bad for you. Saturated fat raises your blood cholesterol level and that could lead to heart troubles.

4. **Cholesterol** Along with saturated fat, cholesterol amounts are important for anyone concerned about heart disease. High levels of cholesterol can lead to serious heart problems later in life.

5. **Sodium** Sodium (or salt) levels are important to monitor if you have high blood pressure.

6. **Carbohydrates** These fit into two categories: complex carbohydrates (dietary fiber) and simple carbohydrates (sugars). Diets high in complex carbohydrates have been shown to fight cancer and heart disease. Simple carbohydrates are good for energy, but eat too much of them and you can expect your waistline to grow.

7. **Fiber** Fiber consists of complex carbohydrates that cannot be absorbed by the body. It aids digestion and can help to lower blood cholesterol. High fiber foods include fruits, vegetables, brown rice, and whole grain products.

8. **Protein** The food label doesn't specify a daily percentage or guideline for protein consumption because so much depends on individual needs. An athlete needs more than an office worker, but in a typical 2,000-calorie diet, most people need no more than 50 grams of protein per day.

9. **Vitamins and Minerals** The FDA requires only Vitamin A, Vitamin C, Iron, and Calcium on this label, although food companies can voluntarily list others. The FDA feels these four vitamins and minerals are particularly important in order to maintain a healthy diet. Try and get 100 percent of each every day.

10. **Ingredients** These are listed on a food label by weight from the most to the least. This section can alert you to any ingredients you may want to avoid because of food allergies.

E **How much do you know about nutrition? Fill in the circle under *True* or *False* for each statement below.**

	True	False
1. Reading food labels can help to improve your eating habits.	●	○
2. Diets high in complex carbohydrates can help to fight cancer and heart disease.	●	○
3. Saturated fat lowers your blood cholesterol level.	○	●
4. You should watch your sodium intake if you have high blood pressure.	●	○
5. Most people need at least 100 grams of protein per day.	○	●
6. Simple carbohydrates are good for energy.	●	○
7. Foods with fiber can help to lower cholesterol.	●	○

  F **Active Task:** Read the food labels of your favorite products or look them up on the Internet. Share the information with your class.

Take two aspirin

GOAL ▶ Interpret medicine labels | *Life skill*

A Identify the medicines in the pictures below. Are they usually prescription or non-prescription? What illnesses or conditions are they used for?

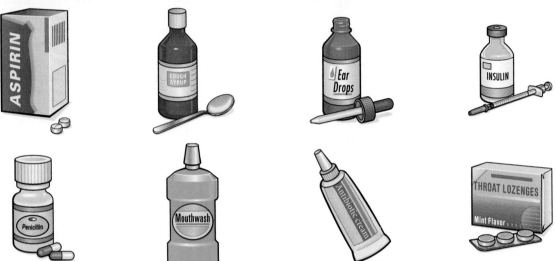

B Make two lists of brand names of different medications below.

Prescription drugs	Non-prescription drugs
(Answers will vary.)	

C Now look at each drug on your lists. What is each one used for? Why is each one prescription or non-prescription? Discuss it with your group and then share your answers with the class.

D **Active Task:** Find out at the library or on the Internet which of the following drugs are prescription and which are non-prescription. What are they used for?

| aspirin | penicillin | antihistamine | ibuprofen | codeine | valium |

LESSON PLAN

Objectives:
Identify prescription vs. non-prescription drugs, Interpret directions on medicine labels

Key vocabulary:
drugs, prescription, non-prescription, brand, indications, warning, exceed, overdose

Warm-up and Review: 5–10 min.

Ask students to share what they found when they did the Active Task from the previous lesson.

Introduction: 10–15 min.

Ask students the following questions and write their answers on the board. *What medicine do you take if you have a cold? What medicine do you take if you have a cough? What medicine do you take if you have a sore throat?*

State the Objective: *Today you will identify prescription and non-prescription drugs and read medicine labels.*

Presentation 1: 10–15 min.

A **Identify the medicines in the pictures below. Are they usually prescription or non-prescription? What illnesses or conditions are they used for?**

Do this activity as a class.

Practice 1: 15–20 min.

Have students form small groups. Give them an example of a brand name for a prescription drug.

B **Make two lists of brand names of different medications below.**

C **Now look at each drug on your lists. What is each one used for? Why is each one prescription or non-prescription? Discuss it with your group and then share your answers with the class.**

Evaluation 1: 10–15 min.

Have each group share their answers.

D **Active Task: Find out at the library or on the Internet which of the following drugs are prescription and which are non-prescription. What are they used for?**

Remind students to use the Active Task Checklist for Lesson 6.

STANDARDS CORRELATIONS

CASAS: 3.3.1, 3.3.2, 3.3.3
SCANS: **Interpersonal** Participates as a Member of a Team, Teaches Others New Skills, Works with Cultural Diversity **Information** Acquires and Evaluates Information, Organizes and Maintains Information, Interprets and Communicates Information, Uses Computers to Process Information (optional) **Technology** Applies Technology to Task (optional) **Basic Skills** Reading, Listening, Speaking

Thinking Skills Creative Thinking, Decision Making, Reasoning **Personal Qualities** Sociability
EFF: **Communication** Read with Understanding, Speak So Others Can Understand, Listen Actively **Decision Making** Solve Problems and Make Decisions **Interpersonal** Advocate and Influence, Cooperate with Others **Lifelong Learning** Learn through Research, Use Information and Communications Technology (optional)

Presentation 2: 5–10 min.

Write *indication*, *warning*, and *direction* on the board. Have students help you define each of these in the context of a medicine label.

Practice 2: 5–10 min.

E Below is a list of phrases you might find on a medicine label. Decide if each phrase is an indication, a direction, or a warning. Fill in the circle under the correct answer.

Evaluation 2: 10–15 min.

Go over the answers as a class. Discuss any questions about the vocabulary in exercise E.

Presentation 3: 5 min.

Have students look at the medicine labels in exercise F. Ask students, *What are the medicines for?*

Practice 3: 10–15 min.

F Read the medicine labels and answer the questions below.

Evaluation 3: 10–15 min.

Go over the answers as a class.

 Refer to the *Stand Out Activity Bank 4 CD-ROM,* Unit 5 Worksheet 8 (three pages), for an additional exercise reading medicine labels. *(optional)*

As in Lesson 5, students work in pairs on one of the three medicine labels provided. Then ask the pairs to meet in small groups with others who worked on the same label. Distribute all labels to the class and have each group report the answers. Discuss new vocabulary.

Application: 20–25 min.

Note: Shorter classes can do exercise F for their Application Activity.

G Active Task: At home or on the Internet, look at the labels of drugs that you or your family members take. Answer the questions above for each drug.

Remind students to use the Active Task Checklist for Lesson 6.

Instructor's Notes for Lesson 6

E **Below is a list of phrases you might find on a medicine label. Decide if each phrase is an indication, a direction, or a warning. Fill in the circle under the correct answer.**

	Indication	Direction	Warning
1. Do not exceed two doses in any 24-hour period. Use only as directed.	○	○	●
2. Temporarily relieves common cold/flu symptoms.	●	○	○
3. Take two tablespoons in dose cup provided.	○	●	○
4. For the temporary relief of minor aches and pains.	●	○	○
5. Adults: Take one tablet every 4 to 6 hours.	○	●	○
6. In case of accidental overdose, contact a poison control center immediately.	○	○	●

F **Read the medicine labels and answer the questions below.**

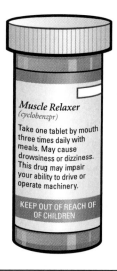

Muscle Relaxer
(cyclobenzpr)

Take one tablet by mouth three times daily with meals. May cause drowsiness or dizziness. This drug may impair your ability to drive or operate machinery.

KEEP OUT OF REACH OF OF CHILDREN

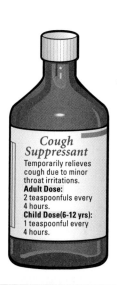

Cough Suppressant
Temporarily relieves cough due to minor throat irritations.
Adult Dose:
2 teaspoonfuls every 4 hours.
Child Dose(6-12 yrs):
1 teaspoonful every 4 hours.

	Muscle relaxer	Cough suppressant
1. How often can you take this medicine?	*3 times a day*	*every 4 hours*
2. Can you drive a car or operate machinery while taking this drug?	*no*	*yes*
3. Do you have to take this drug with food?	*yes*	*no*
4. Can children take this medicine?	*no*	*yes*
5. What symptoms will this drug relieve?	*muscle tension*	*coughing*

G **Active Task:** At home or on the Internet, look at the labels of drugs that you or your family members take. Answer the questions above for each drug.

The common cold

 What do you know about the common cold? Discuss each of the topics below.

Does Vitamin C Have a Role? How Can We Prevent Colds? What Are Cold Symptoms?
What Is the Treatment? The Problem How Do Colds Spread?

 Read the article and write the correct heading for each paragraph.

The Common Cold

The Problem

In the course of a year, individuals in the United States suffer 1 billion colds, according to some estimates. Children have about six to ten colds a year. In families with children in school, the number of colds per child can be as high as 12 a year. Adults average about two to four colds a year. Women, especially those aged 20 to 30 years, have more colds than men, possibly because of their closer contact with children. On average, individuals older than 60 have less than one cold a year.

What Are Cold Symptoms

Symptoms of the common cold usually begin two to three days after infection and often include sneezing, sore throat, cough, and headache. Fever is usually slight but can climb to 102 degrees Fahrenheit in infants and young children. Cold symptoms can last from two to fourteen days, but two-thirds of people recover in a week. If symptoms occur often or last much longer than two weeks, they may be the result of an allergy rather than a cold.

How Do Colds Spread?

Depending on the virus type, any or all of the following routes of transmission may be common:
- Touching infectious respiratory secretions on skin and on environmental surfaces and then touching the eyes or nose.
- Inhaling relatively large particles of respiratory secretions transported briefly in the air.
- Inhaling droplet nuclei: smaller infectious particles suspended in the air for long periods of time.

How Can We Prevent Colds?

Hand-washing is the simplest and most effective way to keep from getting rhinovirus colds. Not touching the nose or eyes is another. Individuals with colds should always sneeze or cough into a facial tissue and promptly throw it away. If possible, one should avoid close, prolonged exposure to persons who have colds. Cleaning environmental surfaces with a virus-killing disinfectant might help prevent spread of infection.

What Is the Treatment?

Only symptomatic treatment is available for uncomplicated cases of the common cold: bed rest, plenty of fluids, gargling with warm salt water, petroleum jelly for a raw nose, and aspirin or acetaminophen to relieve headache or fever.

Does Vitamin C Have a Role?

Many people are convinced that taking large quantities of vitamin C will prevent colds or relieve symptoms. To test this theory, several large-scale, controlled studies involving children and adults have been conducted. To date, no conclusive data has shown that large doses of vitamin C prevent colds.

Source: The National Institute of Allergy and Infectious Diseases of The National Institutes of Health. Fact Sheet: **The Common Cold**. June 1996. Last revised May 1998. (Online) http://www.niaid.nih.gov/factsheets/cold.htm

LESSON PLAN

Objectives:
Interpret a reading about the common cold, Write a summary
Key vocabulary:
common cold, role, prevent, treatment, spread, infection, recover, virus, respiratory, resistance, allergy, rhinovirus, title, source, author, citation, vitamin C, aspirin

Warm-up and Review: 5–10 min.

Ask students if they looked at any medicine labels at home and, if so, what they found.

Introduction: 10–15 min.

Write *the common cold* on the board. Ask students why we call the cold "common." Ask students to describe the symptoms of a cold.

State the Objective: *Today you will read an article on the common cold and practice writing a summary.*

Presentation 1: 10–15 min.

A What do you know about the common cold? Discuss each of the topics below.

Practice 1: 15–20 min.

B Read the article and write the correct heading for each paragraph.

Evaluation 1: 10–15 min.

Go over the answers as a class and answer any questions students may have about the article. Remind them that it is not necessary to understand every word, just the main ideas.

STANDARDS CORRELATIONS

CASAS: 7.2.1, 7.4.2
SCANS: **Information** Acquires and Evaluates Information, Organizes and Maintains Information, Interprets and Communicates Information, Uses Computers to Process Information (optional)
Systems Monitors and Corrects Performance
Technology Applies Technology to Task (optional)
Basic Skills Reading, Writing, Listening, Speaking

Thinking Skills Creative Thinking, Decision Making, Knowing How to Learn, Reasoning
EFF: **Communication** Read with Understanding, Convey Ideas in Writing, Observe Critically
Decision Making Solve Problems and Make Decisions, Plan
Lifelong Learning Take Responsibility for Learning, Learn through Research, Use Information and Communications Technology (optional)

Presentation 2: 5–10 min.

Do exercises C and D as class.

C What is the title and source of the article?

D Summarize the main topic of the article in one sentence.

Practice 2: 10–15 min.

E Write one sentence to summarize each paragraph by completing the sentences below.

Remind students that summarizing does not mean copying the exact words from the article.

Evaluation 2: 10–15 min.

Ask volunteers to write their sentences on the board. As a class, analyze the sentences and decide which ones are better and why.

Presentation 3: 5–10 min.

Explain to students that when writing a summary of something not authored by them, they should indicate that by using phrases such as *The author states that . . .* or *The article says . . . .*

Practice 3: 10–15 min.

F Rewrite two of the sentences from exercise E starting with *The author states that . . .* or *The article says that . . . .*

Give students an example.

G What is a summary? Why do we write summaries? Why are they useful? Discuss as a class.

Have students discuss these questions as a class.

Evaluation 3: 10–15 min.

Ask volunteers to write their summary sentences on the board. Evaluate them as a class.

C **What is the title and source of the article?**

The Common Cold; The National Institute of Health

D **Summarize the main topic of the article in one sentence.** *(Answers may vary. Possible answer below.)*

The article describes __*the causes, symptoms, treatment, and prevention of the common cold.*__

_____

E **Write one sentence to summarize each paragraph by completing the sentences below.** *(Answers will vary.)*

Paragraph 1: Colds are a problem because _____

_____

Paragraph 2: The symptoms include _____

_____

Paragraph 3: Colds are spread by _____

_____

Paragraph 4: Some ways of preventing colds are _____

_____

Paragraph 5: Some ways of treating a cold are _____

_____

Paragraph 6: Vitamin C _____

_____

F **Rewrite two of the sentences from exercise E starting with *The author states that . . .* or *The article says that . . . .*** *(Answers will vary.)*

1. _____

_____

2. _____

_____

G **What is a summary? Why do we write summaries? Why are they useful? Discuss as a class.**

(Definition: A brief statement of important ideas, facts, and actions.)

H   **When you write a summary, follow these rules.**

Rules for writing a summary

1. Read the article carefully.

2. Make a brief outline.

    I. Main idea

        A. Important supporting point

        B. Important supporting point

        C. Important supporting point

3. Identify the main idea and write it first.

4. Identify only the most important supporting points, and omit unnecessary details.

5. Don't repeat ideas.

6. Don't change the author's meaning.

7. Use your own words, but don't include your own ideas or comments.

8. Mention the source of the selection and the author at the beginning.

9. Present the ideas in the order in which they were discussed in the article.

10. Remind the reader that you are summarizing someone else's ideas by using citation expressions. (See box.)

How to cite sources in summaries

The author . . .

says that	emphasizes that
states that	argues that
explains that	maintains that
points out that	highlights the fact that
mentions that	concludes that

I   **Follow the rules above and use your answers from page 96 to write a summary of the article on a separate sheet of paper.**

    Active Task: Find an interesting article in the newspaper or on the Internet. Write a summary using the guidelines above.

Application: 20–25 min.

Note: Shorter classes may want to do exercises E and F first and then do the application for homework.

H When you write a summary, follow these rules.

Go over the rules with the class, answering any questions students may have.

I Follow the rules above and use your answers from page 95 to write a summary of the article on a separate sheet of paper.

Below is an example summary of article, "The Common Cold," Unit 5 lesson 7 page 94. Refer students to *Stand Out Student Book 4,* page 169 for the same summary.

"The article *The Common Cold,* published by The National Institute of Allergy and Infectious Diseases (NIAID) in 1996, describes the causes, symptoms, prevention, and treatment of the common cold. The author states that colds are one of the commonest illnesses in children and adults. The symptoms include difficulty in breathing, sneezing, sore throat, cough, and headache. Colds are spread by catching viruses that are present on things we touch and in the air we breathe. The article emphasizes that washing our hands and not touching our noses and mouths are two of the best ways to prevent catching a cold. The author points out that if we do get a cold, the only way to treat it is by relieving the symptoms: sleep, drinking lots of water, gargling with salt water, and taking aspirin for the headaches. Claims that vitamin C can help prevent colds have not been proven."

Have students compare their summaries to this. How do they differ?

J Active Task: Find an interesting article in the newspaper or on the Internet. Write a summary using the guidelines above.

Remind students to use the Active Task Checklist for Lesson 7.

Refer to the *Stand Out Activity Bank 4 CD-ROM,* Unit 5 Worksheet 9, for a summary writing checklist. *(optional)*

Remind students to use this checklist after they write their first draft.

Instructor's Notes for Lesson 7

_____
_____
_____
_____
_____
_____
_____
_____
_____
_____
_____
_____
_____
_____
_____
_____
_____
_____
_____
_____
_____
_____
_____

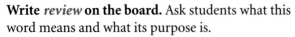

LESSON PLAN

Objective:
Review all previous unit objectives
Key vocabulary:
Review all previous unit vocabulary

Warm-up and Review: 5–10 min.

Ask volunteers to share their summaries from the previous lesson.

Introduction: 5–10 min.

Write *review* on the board. Ask students what this word means and what its purpose is.

State the Objective: *Today we will review all that we have done in the past unit in preparation for the application project to follow.* Ask students as a class to recall all the goals of this unit without looking at their books. Then remind them of the goals they haven't mentioned.

Unit goals: *Make a bar graph, Use the present perfect continuous, Use indirect speech, Fill out a health insurance form, Read for detail, Interpret medicine labels, Write a summary.*

Presentation, Practice, and Evaluation 1:

Do the Learner Log on page 100. Notes are next to the page.

Presentation 2: 5–10 min.

Go over the instructions to exercises A and B. Have students turn back in their books if they need help.

Practice 2: 10–15 min.

A What are three good health habits discussed in this unit?

B What are three bad health habits discussed in this unit?

Evaluation 2: 10–15 min.

Ask volunteers to share their answers with the class.

Presentation 3: 5–10 min.

Review the present perfect, present perfect continuous, and indirect speech if necessary.

Practice 3: 10–15 min.

C Complete these sentences using the present perfect or present perfect continuous.

D Change the following sentences from direct speech to indirect speech.

Evaluation 3: 10–15 min.

Go over the answers as a class.

Refer to *Stand Out Grammar Challenge 4*, Unit 5, pages 33–40 for review practice. *(optional)*

STANDARDS CORRELATIONS

CASAS: 7.1.4, 7.2.1, 7.4.1, 7.4.2
SCANS: **Interpersonal** Participates as a Member of a Team, Teaches Others New Skills, Works with Cultural Diversity **Information** Acquires and Evaluates Information, Organizes and Maintains Information **Systems** Understands Systems, Monitors and Corrects Performance **Basic Skills** Reading, Writing, Listening, Speaking **Thinking Skills** Creative Thinking, Decision Making, Seeing

Things in the Mind's Eye, Knowing How to Learn, Reasoning **Personal Qualities** Responsibility, Self-Esteem, Sociability, Self-Management, Integrity/Honesty **EFF: Communication** Convey Ideas in Writing, Speak So Others Can Understand, Listen Actively **Decision Making** Solve Problems and Make Decisions **Interpersonal** Guide Others, Cooperate with Others **Lifelong Learning** Take Responsibility for Learning, Reflect and Evaluate, Learn Through Research

A What are three good health habits discussed in this unit? *(Answers will vary.)*

1. _____

2. _____

3. _____

B What are three bad health habits discussed in this unit? *(Answers will vary.)*

1. _____

2. _____

3. _____

C Complete these sentences using the present perfect or present perfect continuous.

1. I (not / eat) _____*haven't eaten*_____ meat for three years.

2. Sara (go) _____*has been going*_____ to yoga classes since September.

3. Andres (drink) _____*has drank*_____ two liters of water today.

4. I (not / sleep) _____*haven't been sleeping*_____ well recently.

5. I (never / smoke) _____*have never smoked*_____ a cigarette.

6. Why (you / choose) _____*have you chosen*_____ such a stressful job?

D Change the following sentences from direct speech to indirect speech.

1. "My daughter is sick."

   Maria said _*her daughter was sick.*_____

2. "We won't be able to come to the meeting."

   Luis and Ricardo told me _*they weren't able to come to the meeting.*_____

3. "You have to take two pills every day."

   The doctor told me _*I had to take two pills every day.*_____

4. "Your son is eating too much sugar."

   The pediatrician said _*my son was eating too much sugar.*_____

5. "My back has been hurting for two months."

   I told the chiropractor _*my back had been hurting for two months.*_____

Review

E **Make a list of ten new vocabulary words you used this unit.** *(Answers will vary.)*

1. _____   6. _____
2. _____   7. _____
3. _____   8. _____
4. _____   9. _____
5. _____   10. _____

F **Make word families for four of the words from your list.** *(Answers will vary.)*

Noun	Verb	Adjective	Adverb
1.			
2.			
3.			
4.			

G **Find words in this unit to complete the following sentences. The answers are all names of different kinds of food nutrients.**

1. _____*Sodium*_____ indicates the amount of salt content in your food.

2. _____*Calories*_____ are the amount of energy supplied by a kind of food.

3. _____*Protein*_____ helps to build and repair muscles.

4. _____*Saturated*_____ fat is a type of fat that causes heart disease.

H **Complete the sentences below. Share your answers with a group of students and choose the best answer in the group. Report your answers to the class.**

1. We need health insurance forms when we _*need to apply for coverage in case we become ill.*_
   _____

2. We need to read nutrition labels if we want to _*eat a healthy diet.*_
   _____

3. It is important to understand medicine labels because _*we must be sure to take the correct*_
   *dosage.*

4. It is useful to write summaries because _*it helps us to remember information.*_

(Answers may vary. Possible answers above.)

Presentation 4: 10–20 min.

E Make a list of ten new vocabulary words you used in this unit.

F Make word families for four of the words from your list.

G Find words in this unit to complete the following sentences. The answers are all names of different kinds of food nutrients.

Review exercises E, F, and G briefly with the class.

Practice 4: 10–15 min.

H Complete the sentences below. Share your answers with a group of students and choose the best answer in the group. Report your answers to the class.

Evaluation 4: 5–10 min.

Have students with the strongest sentences write the sentences on the board. Read and review with the class.

Application: 1–2 days

The Team Project Activity on the following page is the Application Activity to be done on the next day.

Post-Assessment: Use the *Stand Out* ExamView® Pro *Test Bank* for Unit 5. (*optional*)

Note: With the *Stand Out* ExamView® Pro *Test Bank* you can design a post-assessment that focuses on what students have learned. It is designed for three purposes:

- To help students practice taking a test similar to current standardized tests.
- To help the teacher evaluate how much the students have learned, retained, and acquired.
- To help students see their progress when they compare their scores to the pre-test they took earlier.

Instructor's Notes for Unit 5 Review

_____

_____

_____

_____

_____

_____

_____

_____

_____

_____

_____

_____

_____

_____

_____

_____

_____

_____

_____

_____

_____

_____

_____

_____

_____

Unit 5 Application Activity

> ### TEAM PROJECT: CREATE A COMMUNITY HEALTH PAMPHLET
>
> Objective:
> Project designed to apply all the objectives of this unit.
> Product:
> A health pamphlet

Introduction: 1 min.

Student teams will create a pamphlet on good health practices to distribute to the community.

Note: Shorter classes can do this project over two periods.

State the Objective: *With a team, you will create a pamphlet to distribute to the community about good health practices.*

Stage 1: 5 min.

Form a team with four or five students. Choose positions for each member of your team.

Have students decide who will take which position as described on the student page. Provide well-defined directions on the board for how teams should proceed. Explain to the students that all the students do every task. The students don't go to the next stage until the previous one is complete.

Stage 2: 10–15 min.

With your team, decide what information should go in your pamphlet. (Ideas: good health habits, nutrition, reading medicine labels, etc.)

Have each team report to the class.

Stage 3: 60–75 min.

Write the text and decide on the art to use in your pamphlet.

Allow students to choose between handwriting and finding or creating their own art work *or* typing the pamphlet on the computer and using clipart or pictures they scan in.

Stage 4: 10–15 min.

Put your pamphlet together.

Stage 5: 10–15 min.

Present your pamphlet to the class.

If possible make copies for everyone or prepare transparencies of student work. Share presentations with another class (optional).

STANDARDS CORRELATIONS

CASAS: 4.8.1, 4.8.5, 4.8.6
SCANS: **Resources** Allocates Materials and Facility Resources, Allocates Human Resources
Interpersonal Participates as a Member of a Team, Teaches Others New Skills, Exercises Leadership, Works with Cultural Diversity
Information Acquires and Evaluates Information, Organizes and Maintains Information, Interprets and Communicates Information, Uses Computers to Process Information (optional)
Systems Understands Systems, Monitors and Corrects Performance, Improves and Designs Systems
Technology Applies Technology to Task (optional)
Basic Skills Reading, Writing, Listening, Speaking

Thinking Skills Creative Thinking, Decision Making, Problem Solving, Seeing Things in the Mind's Eye, Knowing How to Learn, Reasoning
Personal Qualities Responsibility, Self-Esteem, Sociability, Self-Management, Integrity/Honesty
EFF: **Communication** Read with Understanding, Convey Ideas in Writing, Speak So Others Can Understand, Listen Actively, Observe Critically
Decision Making Solve Problems and Make Decisions, Plan
Interpersonal Guide Others, Resolve Conflict and Negotiate, Advocate and Influence, Cooperate with Others
Lifelong Learning Take Responsibility for Learning, Reflect and Evaluate, Learn through Research, Use Information and Communications Technology (optional)

Create a community health pamphlet

With a team, you will create a pamphlet to distribute to the community about good health practices.

1. Form a team with four or five students. Choose positions for each member of your team.

Position	Job Description	Student Name
Student 1 Leader	See that everyone speaks English. See that everyone participates.	
Student 2 Secretary	Take notes and write information for pamphlet.	
Student 3 Designer	Design and add art to pamphlet.	
Students 4/5 Member (s)	Help secretary and designer with their work.	

2. With your team, decide what information should go in your pamphlet. (Ideas: good health habits, nutrition, reading medicine labels, etc.)

3. Write the text and decide on the art to use in your pamphlet.

4. Put your pamphlet together.

5. Present your pamphlet to the class.

PRONUNCIATION

Word Linking. In spoken English, the pronoun *he* often loses its initial /h/ sound when it is linked to the previous word. Listen and repeat.

1. Is he taking any medication? (*izzy*)
2. Has he been ill for a long time? (*hazzy*)
3. Does he often go to the doctor? (*duzzy*)
4. Did he give you some advice? (*diddy*)

5. Isn't he going to take sick leave? (*izzeny*)
6. Hasn't he phoned yet? (*hazzeny*)
7. Doesn't he have insurance? (*duzzeny*)
8. Didn't he tell you about the pills? (*diddeny*)

LEARNER LOG

In this unit, you learned many things about health. How comfortable do you feel doing each of the skills listed below? Rate your comfort level on a scale of 1 to 4.

1 = Not so comfortable **2** = Need more practice **3** = Comfortable **4** = Very comfortable

If you circle 1 or 2, write down the page number where you can review this skill.

Life Skill	Comfort Level	Page(s)
I can identify good and bad health habits.	1 2 3 4	81
I can report illness and symptoms.	1 2 3 4	83
I can interpret and fill out health insurance forms.	1 2 3 4	88, 89
I can identify vitamins and nutritional content of foods.	1 2 3 4	90
I can interpret nutritional information.	1 2 3 4	91
I can identify prescription and non-prescription drugs.	1 2 3 4	92
I can interpret instructions on medicine labels.	1 2 3 4	93

Grammar	Comfort Level	Page(s)
I can use the present perfect and the present perfect continuous.	1 2 3 4	84, 85
I can use indirect speech to report a conversation with the doctor.	1 2 3 4	86, 87

Academic Skill	Comfort Level	Page(s)
I can interpret information about the common cold.	1 2 3 4	94, 95
I can write a summary.	1 2 3 4	95, 96

Reflection

Complete the following statements with your thoughts about this unit. *(Answers will vary.)*

I learned _____

I would like to find out more about _____

I am still confused about _____

Unit 5 Pronunciation and Learner Log

Pronunciation: 10–15 min.
(optional)

Word linking

In spoken English, the pronoun *he* often loses its initial /h/ sound when it is linked to the previous word. Listen and repeat.

Play the recording and pause after each question. Ask students to repeat. Have students practice saying the words in each question clearly and distinctly. Contrast this by saying the words rapidly and smoothly, with all the words running together as in normal speech. Then practice again, having students substitute the word "she" instead of "he" in each of the sentences.

For additional pronunciation practice: Write the following sentences on the board or on a transparency and have students practice saying the words in each question clearly and distinctly. Contrast this by saying the words rapidly and smoothly, with all the words running together as in normal speech. Practice again, having students substitute the word "she" instead of "he" in each of the sentences. Then have students make up their own examples.

1. *When is he (izzy) leaving?*
2. *How long has he (hazzy) been here?*
3. *Where does he (duzzy) work?*
4. *When did he (diddy) start school?*

Learner Log

Presentation 1: 10–15 min.

If needed, review the purpose of the Learner Log. Make sure students understand how to rate the comfort level they feel in reaching the individual goals listed under *Life Skill, Grammar,* and *Academic Skill.* They should rate their comfort level on a scale of 1 to 4:

1. Not so comfortable
2. Need more practice
3. Comfortable
4. Very comfortable

Practice 1: 10–15 min.

If a student circles 1 or 2, he or she should enter the page number on which the skill is featured. The student can then more easily revisit that page and study the material again.

Evaluation 1: 5–10 min.

Finally, emphasize to students the importance of answering the two questions posed in *Reflection.* They are designed to help students assign real-life value to their classroom work.

Instructor's Notes for Unit 5 Team Project, Pronunciation, and Learner Log

_____

_____

_____

_____

_____

_____

_____

_____

_____

_____

_____

_____

_____

_____

LESSON PLAN

Objectives:
Identify skills, Complete a skills inventory
Key vocabulary:
skills, qualities, traits, (list of skills in exercise A), breaks, suitable, stressful, file, interests

Pre-Assessment: Use the *Stand Out* ExamView® Pro *Test Bank* for Unit 6. *(optional)*

Warm-up and Review: 5–10 min.

Have students get into small groups and discuss their current jobs or those they have held in the past. Groups should make a list of all jobs mentioned.

Introduction: 10–15 min.

Write *skills* on the board. Explain what skills are in relation to various jobs. Discuss related words such as *qualities*, *traits*, and *habits*. Ask students what skills or qualities they think a teacher needs. Help them make a list on the board. Now ask students in groups to discuss a few of the jobs they wrote down and what skills might be needed to do each of those jobs.

State the Objective: *Today you will think of what skills you have and what jobs you might be good at that require those skills.*

Presentation 1: 10–15 min.

A Read the list of characteristics that employers look for in good employees. Which ones describe you? Discuss each of them with your class and check the ones that apply to you.

Practice 1: 15–20 min.

B Are there other personal skills or qualities that aren't listed above?

You may need to help students brainstorm other skills or qualities.

Evaluation 1: 10–15 min.

C Why is each of the above skills important? Discuss what jobs might be good for a person with each skill.

Do this as a class. Write responses in categories on the board.

Refer to the *Stand Out Activity Bank 4 CD-ROM*, Unit 6 Worksheet 1, for vocabulary practice about skills and interests. *(optional)*

Pronunciation: An optional pronunciation activity is found on the final page of this unit. This pronunciation activity may be introduced during any lesson in this unit, especially if students need practice understanding and pronouncing contractions. (See pages 120 and 120a for Unit 6 Pronunciation.)

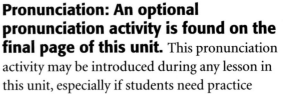

STANDARDS CORRELATIONS

CASAS: 4.1.9, 4.4.2
SCANS: **Information** Acquires and Evaluates Information, Interprets and Communicates Information
Basic Skills Reading, Writing, Listening, Speaking
Thinking Skills Decision Making, Reasoning

Personal Qualities Responsibility, Self-Esteem, Sociability
EFF: **Communication** Read with Understanding, Speak So Others Can Understand, Listen Actively
Decision Making Solve Problems and Make Decisions
Lifelong Learning Reflect and Evaluate

UNIT 6

Getting Hired

GOALS

- Complete a skills inventory
- Use adjective clauses
- Conduct a job search
- Use the past perfect
- Write a resume
- Write a cover letter
- Prepare for a job interview

LESSON 1 — What skills do you have?

GOAL ▶ Complete a skills inventory   *Vocabulary*

A   **Read the list of characteristics that employers look for in good employees. Which ones describe you? Discuss each of them with your class and check the ones that apply to you.** *(Answers will vary.)*

- ❑ dependable
- ❑ detail-oriented
- ❑ efficient
- ❑ flexible
- ❑ good with numbers
- ❑ great with people

- ❑ hard-working
- ❑ open-minded
- ❑ patient
- ❑ a problem solver
- ❑ a quick learner
- ❑ reliable

- ❑ responsible
- ❑ self-motivated
- ❑ a team player
- ❑ well-organized
- ❑ willing to accept responsibility
- ❑ works well under pressure

B   **Are there other personal skills or qualities that aren't listed above?**

_____ *(Answers will vary.)* _____

_____

_____

_____

_____

_____

_____

C   **Why is each of the above skills important? Discuss what jobs might be good for a person with each skill.**

D **Match the sentences below with words from exercise A.**

1. Suzanne works long hours and never takes any breaks. _____ *hard-working* _____

2. You can always count on Linh. _____ *dependable/reliable* _____

3. Tran isn't afraid of making decisions. _____ *willing to accept responsibility* _____

4. Li is always calm, even when it's very stressful. _____ *works well under pressure* _____

5. You never have to explain anything to Vlasta twice. _____ *a quick learner* _____

6. Chan can always find any file immediately. _____ *efficient/well-organized* _____

7. Arnold takes time to explain everything carefully to every customer. _*great with people/patient*_

8. Let's ask Phuong. She's good at thinking of different solutions. _____ *a problem solver* _____

E **Listen to four people describe their skills and interests. Take notes in the first column. Then suggest a job for each of them in the second column.**

Lam	Skills and interests	Most suitable job
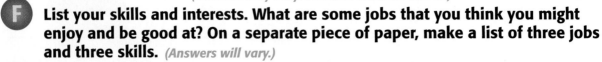	*loves being outdoors* *hard worker* *likes to use hands* *doesn't mind taking orders*	*gardener; grounds keeper*
Lilia	*loves working with people* *likes to help people* *not good with numbers* *works hard* *learns quickly*	*customer service representative*
Morteza	*engineering skills* *good at technical things* *knows about computers* *prefers to works alone*	*computer repair technician*
Hilda	*well-organized* *detail-oriented* *good with numbers* *creative*	*bookkeeper*

(Answers may vary. Possible answers above.)

F **List your skills and interests. What are some jobs that you think you might enjoy and be good at? On a separate piece of paper, make a list of three jobs and three skills.** *(Answers will vary.)*

G **Active Task:** Ask your family and friends what they think your best skills are.

Presentation 2: 5–10 min.

Read the first sentence from exercise D to students. Ask them which skill or quality applies to Suzanne.

Practice 2: 10–15 min.

D Match the sentences below with words from exercise A.

Tell students that more than one skill or quality may apply.

Evaluation 2: 10–15 min.

Go over the answers as a class.

Presentation 3: 5–10 min.

Have students look at the chart in exercise E. Ask them what they think they will hear.

Practice 3: 10–15 min.

E Listen to four people describe their skills and interests. Take notes in the first column. Then suggest a job for each of them in the second column.

Evaluation 3: 10–15 min.

Go over the answers as a class.

Application: 20–25 min.

F List your skills and interests. What are some jobs that you think you might enjoy and be good at? On a separate piece of paper, make a list of three jobs and three skills.

G Active Task: Ask your family and friends what they think your best skills are.

Refer to the *Stand Out Activity Bank 4 CD-ROM,* Unit 6 Active Task Checklist. *(optional)*

Remind students to use this checklist as they complete Active Tasks for Lessons 1, 2, 3 (two tasks), and 5.

Instructor's Notes for Lesson 1

LESSON PLAN

Objectives:
Identify job responsibilities, Use adjective clauses
Key vocabulary:
job titles and responsibilities, (job titles listed in exercise B), adjective clauses

Warm-up and Review: 5–10 min.

Ask a few students to report on their skills and interests. Then ask the class what jobs would best suit those students. Write the jobs on the board.

Introduction: 10–15 min.

Have students look at each job title on the board and ask them to give you a brief description of what a person with that job does.

State the Objective: *Today you will learn how to use adjective clauses to describe what people do for a living.*

Presentation 1: 10–15 min.

A Look at the pictures. What jobs are the people doing? Discuss with a partner.

Ask students what each job entails. Do this with two or three other occupations to get them thinking about job responsibilities.

Practice 1: 15–20 min.

B Below is a list of job titles and responsibilities. Work in groups of three and ask each other questions to complete the missing information. Then add two of your own job titles to the list.

Evaluation 1: 10–15 min.

Go over the answers as a class.

C From the list above, choose three jobs that you would like to have. What skills do you have that would be necessary for each of these jobs?

Ask volunteers to supply answers for each job on the board.

STANDARDS CORRELATIONS

CASAS: 4.1.8
SCANS: **Interpersonal** Participates as a Member of a Team, Teaches Others New Skills, Works with Cultural Diversity **Information** Acquires and Evaluates Information, Organizes and Maintains Information, Interprets and Communicates Information
Systems Monitors and Corrects Performance
Basic Skills Reading, Writing, Listening, Speaking
Thinking Skills Creative Thinking, Decision Making, Reasoning

Personal Qualities Responsibility, Self-Esteem, Sociability, Integrity/Honesty
EFF: **Communication** Read with Understanding, Convey Ideas in Writing, Speak So Others Can Understand, Listen Actively, Observe Critically
Decision Making Solve Problems and Make Decisions
Interpersonal Cooperate with Others
Lifelong Learning Reflect and Evaluate

LESSON 2 — What does an accountant do?

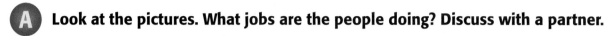

GOAL ▶ **Use adjective clauses** *Grammar*

A Look at the pictures. What jobs are the people doing? Discuss with a partner.

B Below is a list of job titles and responsibilities. Work in groups of three and ask each other questions to complete the missing information. Then add two of your own job titles to the list. *(Answers may vary. Possible answers below.)*

Job title	Job responsibilities
accountant	*manages finances*
administrative assistant	*writes correspondence, schedules appointments*
assembler	*puts things together*
cashier	*handles customer payment for goods*
computer technician	**repairs computers**
delivery person	*drives truck, makes deliveries*
dental assistant	*assists dentist, cleans teeth*
garment worker	*sews clothing*
gas station attendant	*pumps gas, takes payment*
hairdresser	**cuts hair**
homemaker	*cooks meals, takes care of children and house*
lawyer	*represents people in court*
police officer	*arrests criminals, directs traffic*
postal worker	*sorts and delivers mail*
receptionist	*answers telephone, takes messages*
salesperson	*sells merchandise to customers*
security guard	*protects store or bank from theft*

C From the list above, choose three jobs that you would like to have. What skills do you have that would be necessary for each of these jobs?

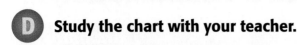
D **Study the chart with your teacher.**

Adjective clauses		
Restrictive adjective clauses	A homemaker is a person *who maintains a home and a family.* I applied for the job *which was in the paper on Sunday.*	*Restrictive adjective clauses* give essential information about the noun they refer to. They cannot be omitted without losing the meaning of the sentence. They do not need commas.
Non-restrictive adjective clauses	My brother-in-law, *who owns his own business,* works very hard. I quit my job, *which I never really liked anyway.*	*Non-restrictive adjective clauses* give extra non-essential information about the noun they refer to. They can be omitted. They need commas.

E **With a partner, make sentences using adjective clauses with the information from the previous page.**

EXAMPLE:
Student A: A person who takes care of the home and the family is a _____.
Student B: Homemaker.

F **Look at exercise F on page 102 where you wrote three job titles and your skills for each of those jobs. Make sentences about your partner using non-restrictive adjective clauses.**

Job title	Skills	Sentence
Ex. *car salesperson*	*likes talking to people, knows a lot about cars*	*Aaron, who likes talking to people and knows a lot about cars, would make a great car salesman.*

G **Write down two sentences about your job (or a job you would like to have). Give the sentences to your partner to combine into one sentence using an adjective clause.** *(Answers may vary. Possible answers below.)*

Sentence 1: ___*I am a chef.*_____

Sentence 2: ___*I am creative with food.*_____

Combined sentence: ___*I am a chef who is creative with food.*_____

H **Active Task:** Talk to three different people about their jobs. Ask them what their job title is and what their responsibilities are.

Presentation 2: 5–10 min.

 D **Study the chart with your teacher.**

Practice 2: 10–15 min.

E **With a partner, make sentences using adjective clauses with the information from the previous page.**

Go over the example with students and then let them work with their partners.

Evaluation 2: 10–15 min.

Ask volunteers to make sentences including adjective clauses about the job titles and responsibilities from exercise B.

 Refer to *Stand Out Grammar Challenge 4,* Unit 6 pages 41–43 for more practice with adjective clauses. *(optional)*

Presentation 3: 5–10 min.

Go over the example in exercise F with students. Then call on a student to share what he or she wrote down as a possible job title and related skills in exercise F on page 102. Help the class make the information into a sentence with an adjective clause about the student.

Practice 3: 10–15 min.

F **Look at exercise F on page 102 where you wrote three job titles and your skills for each of those jobs. Make sentences about your partner using non-restrictive adjective clauses.**

Evaluation 3: 10–15 min.

Ask volunteers to write their sentences from exercise F on the board.

Application: 20–25 min.

G **Write down two sentences about your job (or a job you would like to have). Give the sentences to your partner to combine into one sentence using an adjective clause.**

Have students repeat this exercise about other students in the class as many times as you want.

 H **Active Task: Talk to three different people about their jobs. Ask them what their job title is and what their responsibilities are.**

Ask students to write sentences with adjective clauses about the people they spoke with and then have students share sentences with the class. Remind students to use the Active Task Checklist.

 Refer to the *Stand Out Activity Bank 4 CD-ROM,* Unit 6 Worksheet 2 (two pages), for additional exercises with adjective clauses. *(optional)*

Instructor's Notes for Lesson 2

_____

_____

_____

_____

_____

_____

_____

_____

_____

_____

_____

_____

_____

_____

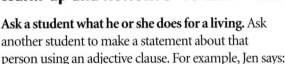

LESSON PLAN

Objective: Conduct a job search
Key vocabulary: duties, qualifications, salary, contact

Warm-up and Review: 5–10 min.

Ask a student what he or she does for a living. Ask another student to make a statement about that person using an adjective clause. For example, Jen says: *I'm a seamstress. I sew clothes.* The other student says: *Jen is a seamstress who sews clothes.*

Introduction: 10–15 min.

Call on individual students who have jobs and ask them how they found their jobs.

State the Objective: *Today you will learn how to conduct a job search and how to learn about different companies.*

Presentation 1: 10–15 min.

A **What is the best way to look for a job?**

Do this exercise as a class. Once you have made a list, ask for a show of hands of how many students found their jobs each way. Review percentages by having students calculate the percentage of the class that found their job each way. Reminder: Divide total number of students into the number of responses.

Practice 1: 15–20 min.

B **What are some things you need to think about before you begin your job search? Make a list.**

Have students work in small groups.

Evaluation 1: 10–15 min.

Ask a representative from each group to share their information with the class. Have them make a list on the board.

Presentation 2: 5–10 min.

C **When you find a job opportunity, what information should you find out? Discuss the meaning of each of the following.**

Do this as a class.

Practice 2: 10–15 min.

D **Think about the job you have now. (Some of you may be students or homemakers. This is your job. If you are retired, think about your last job.) Fill in the chart below with information about your job.**

Evaluation 2: 10–15 min.

Ask students to report to the class.

E **Active Task: Look in the paper or on the Internet for a job that interests you and find out as much of the above information as you can. Share your findings with the class.**

This can be done in class or for homework. Remind students to use the Active Task Checklist for Lesson 3. There are two Active Tasks in Lesson 3.

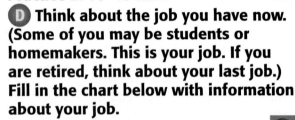

STANDARDS CORRELATIONS

CASAS: 4.1.3
SCANS: **Interpersonal** Participates as a Member of a Team, Works with Cultural Diversity
Information Acquires and Evaluates Information, Organizes and Maintains Information, Interprets and Communicates Information, Uses Computers to Process Information (optional)
Technology Applies Technology to Task (optional)
Basic Skills Reading, Writing, Arithmetic, Listening, Speaking
Thinking Skills Decision Making, Problem Solving, Reasoning

Personal Qualities Sociability
EFF: **Communication** Read with Understanding, Convey Ideas in Writing, Speak So Others Can Understand, Listen Actively
Decision Making Use Math to Solve Problems and Communicate, Solve Problems and Make Decisions
Interpersonal Cooperate with Others
Lifelong Learning Take Responsibility for Learning, Learn through Research, Use Information and Communications Technology (optional)

LESSON 3 Looking for a job

GOAL ▶ **Conduct a job search**　　　　　　　*Life skill*

A **What is the best way to look for a job?**

_____ *(Answers will vary.)* _____

_____

_____

B **What are some things you need to think about before you begin your job search? Make a list.**

EXAMPLE: ***What hours can I work?***

1. _How far can I commute?_

2. _What are my skills?_

3. _What salary do I want?_

4. _Do I want a temporary or permanent position?_

5. _(Answers may vary. Possible answers above.)_

C **When you find a job opportunity, what information should you find out? Discuss the meaning of each of the following.**

- job title
- hours
- duties
- contact
- qualifications
- phone
- job location
- salary

D **Think about the job you have now. (Some of you may be students or homemakers. This is your job. If you are retired, think about your last job.) Fill in the chart below with information about your job.**

Information about your job	
Job title	*(Answers will vary.)*
Job location	
Job duties	
Qualifications	
Hours	
Salary	

E **Active Task:** Look in the paper or on the Internet for a job that interests you and find out as much of the above information as you can. Share your findings with the class.

F **Imagine you want to work for a company. It is important to find out some information about the company or business that you might work for. Fill in the chart below with your own ideas.**

(Answers will vary. Possible answers below.)

What kind of information is useful?	Where can you find this information?
Ex. *How many employees work for the company?*	*in the company brochure or on the Internet*
1. *What kind of business is it?*	1. *company web site or brochure*
2. *How long has the company been in business?*	2. *company web site or brochure*
3. *Are there branch offices in other locations?*	3. *company web site or brochure*
4. *What is the company's mission?*	4. *company web site or brochure*
5. *How does the company compare to its competition?*	5. *an Internet search for the type of business*

G **Think about the company or business you work for now. Tell your partner about it. Make sure your partner is prepared to share this new information with the class.**

  H **Active Task:** Think of a company or business you have heard of and do some research on it. Find information in the library or on the Internet. Share your findings with the class.

Presentation 3: 5–10 min.

 Imagine you want to work for a company. It is important to find out some information about the company or business that you might work for. Fill in the chart below with your own ideas.

Go over the first example with students.

Practice 3: 10–15 min.

Have students work in small groups to complete the chart.

Evaluation 3: 10–15 min.

Have someone from each group write their ideas on the board.

 Refer to the *Stand Out Activity Bank 4 CD-ROM,* Unit 6 Worksheet 3 (two pages), for additional exercises on job searches. *(optional)*

Application: 20–25 min. (1.5+)

G Think about the company or business you work for now. Tell your partner about it. Make sure your partner is prepared to share this new information with the class.

 H Active Task: Think of a company or business you have heard of and do some research on it. Find information in the library or on the Internet. Share your findings with the class.

Remind students to use the second Active Task Checklist for Lesson 3.

Instructor's Notes for Lesson 3

LESSON PLAN

Objective:
Use past perfect to talk about educational and occupational history
Key vocabulary:
certificate, computer repair, troubleshooting, financial company, school district, past perfect, assemble

Warm-up and Review: 5–10 min.

Ask which students completed the Active Task from the previous lesson by doing some research on a company. Have them share what they found with the class.

Introduction: 10–15 min.

Have students look in their books at the picture of Ranjit. Ask them to speculate about him: where he is from, what he does, etc.

State the Objective: *Today you will use the past perfect to talk about your job and education history.*

Presentation 1: 10–15 min.

A **Read about Ranjit.**

Have students read the passage first by themselves, and then read it as a class.

Practice 1: 15–20 min.

B **Answer the following questions about Ranjit.**

C **Think about your own job history. Make a list of jobs below starting with the most recent first.**

Evaluation 1: 10–15 min.

Go over the answers to exercise B as a class. Then ask two volunteers to come to the board and list their job history.

STANDARDS CORRELATIONS

CASAS: 4.6.5
SCANS: **Information** Acquires and Evaluates Information, Organizes and Maintains Information, Interprets and Communicates Information
Systems Monitors and Corrects Performance
Basic Skills Reading, Writing, Listening, Speaking

Thinking Skills Decision Making, Reasoning
EFF: **Communication** Read with Understanding, Convey Ideas in Writing, Speak So Others Can Understand, Listen Actively, Observe Critically
Decision Making Solve Problems and Make Decisions

My job, then and now

GOAL ▶ **Use the past perfect**

A **Read about Ranjit.**

Ranjit Ghosh is from south India. He moved to the United States seven years ago. In India, he attended the National Computer School and received a certificate in computer repair. His first job was troubleshooting computer repairs for a financial company. After he moved to the United States, he started assembling computers and was able to use the skills he had learned during his course. Although he loves his job now, he needed another job to pay the bills. In addition to assembling, he also repairs computers in the evenings for another company. Ranjit is busy, but he is doing what he loves.

B **Answer the following questions about Ranjit.**

1. Ranjit has had three jobs. List them below with the most recent first.

   a. *He repairs computers.*

   b. *He assembles computers.*

   c. *He was troubleshooting computer repairs in India.*

2. Where did he go to school and what did he receive? *He received a certificate in computer repair from the National Computer School in India.*

3. Why does Ranjit have two jobs in the United States? *He has two jobs to be able to earn enough money to pay the bills.*

C **Think about your own job history. Make a list of jobs below starting with the most recent first.** *(Answers will vary.)*

Job History	
1. _____	4. _____
2. _____	5. _____
3. _____	6. _____

D Read the two sentences below. In each sentence, there are two things that happened. Which happened first? Write *first* or *second* under each idea.

Ranjit had attended school in India before he came to the United States.

_____*first*_____   _____*second*_____

Before Ranjit was hired to assemble computers, he had worked in computer repair.

_____*second*_____   _____*first*_____

Past perfect and simple past		
Example	**Form**	**Rule**
Before Ranjit moved to the United States, he *had lived* in India. = First he lived in India (past perfect) and then he moved to the United States. (simple past)	*had* + past participle	When describing two events that happened in the past, use the *past perfect* for the event that happened first.

E Combine the sentences below into one sentence using the past perfect for the event that happened first.

EXAMPLE:
(first) Santiago studied to be a teacher.
(second) Santiago was hired by the school district.

Santiago had studied to become a teacher before he was hired by the school district. *or*
After Santiago had studied to become a teacher, he was hired by the school district.

(first) Carolina worked as a cashier.
(second) Carolina became a food server.

Carolina had worked as a cashier before she became a food server. or
After Carolina had worked as a cashier, she became a food server.

(first) Benjamin got his high school diploma.
(second) Benjamin enrolled in college classes.

Benjamin had gotten his high school diploma before he enrolled in college classes. or
After Benjamin had gotten his high school diploma, he enrolled in college classes.

(first) Sandeep made money working for someone else.
(second) Sandeep opened his own dry cleaning business.

Sandeep had made money working for someone else before he opened his own dry cleaning business. or
After Sandeep had made money working for someone else, he opened his own dry cleaning business.

F Look back to exercise C where you wrote your personal job history. On a separate piece of paper, write two sentences using the past perfect. Read your sentences aloud to the class. *(Answers will vary.)*

Presentation 2: 5–10 min.

D **Read the two sentences below. In each sentence, there are two things that happened. Which happened first? Write *first* or *second* under each idea.**

Go through these examples with students and then explain past perfect using the chart in the book.

Practice 2: 10–15 min.

Ask students in pairs to write two sentences about Ranjit using the past perfect. When they are finished, have them share their two sentences with another pair of students. Have each group of four choose one sentence that they will share with the class.

Evaluation 2: 10–15 min.

Ask a representative from each group of four to write the chosen sentence on the board. Have the class evaluate.

 Refer to *Stand Out Grammar Challenge 4*, Unit 6 pages 44–46 for more practice with past perfect. *(optional)*

Presentation 3: 5–10 min.

Preview the instructions and the example in exercise E with students.

Practice 3: 10–15 min.

E **Combine the sentences below into one sentence using the past perfect for the event that happened first.**

Evaluation 3: 10–15 min.

Call on individual students to write their answers on the board.

 Refer to the *Stand Out Activity Bank 4 CD-ROM*, Unit 6 Worksheet 4 for an additional exercise with past perfect. *(optional)*

Application: 20–25 min.

F **Look back to exercise C where you wrote your personal job history. On a separate piece of paper, write two sentences using past perfect. Read your sentences aloud to the class.**

Instructor's Notes for Lesson 4

> ## LESSON PLAN
>
> Objective:
> Write a resume
> Key vocabulary:
> resume, keyboarding, fluent, Hindi,
> hobbies, degree, computer-literate,
> award

Warm-up and Review: 5–10 min.

Review the past perfect. Ask students to write an original sentence using past perfect about their job history. Have volunteers write their sentences on the board.

Introduction: 10–15 min.

Ask students what a *resume* is. Ask them what the difference is between a job application and a resume. Pass around sample resumes if you have them.

Optional Internet Activity: Have students do a search for resumes on the Internet and print out some that they find.

State the Objective: *Today you will write a resume.*

Presentation 1: 10–15 min.

Ⓐ Read Ranjit's resume.

Check students' comprehension by asking them information questions about the resume.

STANDARDS CORRELATIONS

CASAS: 4.1.2
SCANS: **Interpersonal** Participates as a Member of a Team, Works with Cultural Diversity
Information Acquires and Evaluates Information, Organizes and Maintains Information, Interprets and Communicates Information, Uses Computers to Process Information (optional)
Technology Applies Technology to Task (optional)
Basic Skills Reading, Writing, Listening, Speaking
Thinking Skills Creative Thinking, Decision Making, Problem

Solving, Seeing Things in the Mind's Eye, Reasoning
Personal Qualities Responsibility, Self-Esteem, Sociability, Self-Management, Integrity/Honesty
EFF: **Communication** Read with Understanding, Convey Ideas in Writing, Speak So Others Can Understand, Listen Actively
Decision Making Solve Problems and Make Decisions, Plan
Interpersonal Cooperate with Others
Lifelong Learning Use Information and Communications Technology (optional)

LESSON 5 Resumes

GOAL ▶ Write a resume

 Life skill

A **Read Ranjit's resume.**

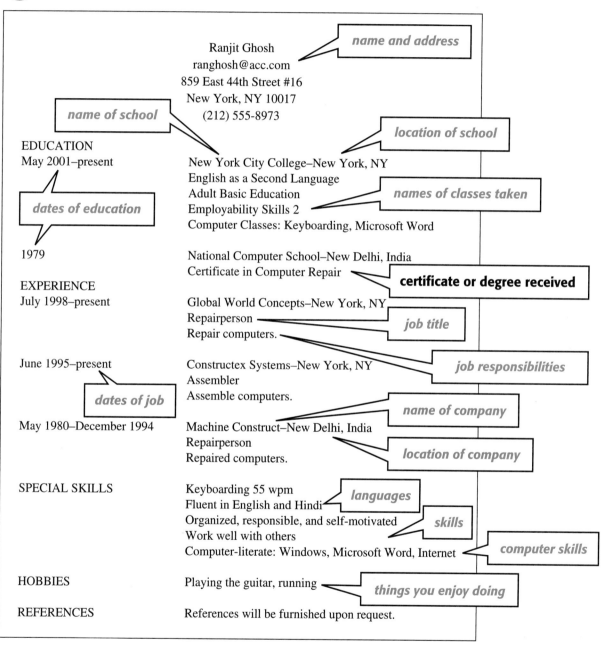

Ranjit Ghosh
ranghosh@acc.com
859 East 44th Street #16
New York, NY 10017
(212) 555-8973

name and address

EDUCATION
May 2001–present   New York City College–New York, NY
                          English as a Second Language
                          Adult Basic Education
                          Employability Skills 2
                          Computer Classes: Keyboarding, Microsoft Word

name of school

location of school

names of classes taken

dates of education

1979   National Computer School–New Delhi, India
                          Certificate in Computer Repair

certificate or degree received

EXPERIENCE
July 1998–present   Global World Concepts–New York, NY
                          Repairperson
                          Repair computers.

job title

job responsibilities

June 1995–present   Constructex Systems–New York, NY
                          Assembler
                          Assemble computers.

name of company

dates of job

May 1980–December 1994   Machine Construct–New Delhi, India
                          Repairperson
                          Repaired computers.

location of company

SPECIAL SKILLS   Keyboarding 55 wpm
                          Fluent in English and Hindi
                          Organized, responsible, and self-motivated
                          Work well with others
                          Computer-literate: Windows, Microsoft Word, Internet

languages

skills

computer skills

HOBBIES   Playing the guitar, running

things you enjoy doing

REFERENCES   References will be furnished upon request.

B Can you identify the following parts of a resume? Use the words below to label the resume on the previous page.

- certificate or degree received
- dates of job
- computer skills
- dates of education
- job responsibilities

- name of company
- location of company
- names of classes taken
- skills
- name of school

- job title
- location of school
- languages
- things you enjoy doing
- name and address

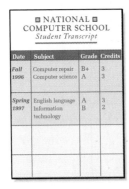

transcript

letter of recommendation

resume

degree certificate

award

C Why is it important to put each piece of information on your resume? Discuss the reasons with a group and make notes next to each item on the list in exercise B.

D On a separate piece of paper, make a list of the following things: *(Answers will vary.)*

1. schools you have attended

2. classes you have taken

3. certificates or degrees you have received

4. awards you have received

5. names and locations of companies you have you worked for

6. job titles and responsibilities you have had

7. special skills you have (see page 101)

8. things you enjoy doing

Practice 1: 15–20 min.

B Can you identify the following parts of a resume? Use the words below to label the resume on the previous page.

Evaluation 1: 10–15 min.

Go over the answers as a class. It would be a good idea to put up a transparency of the resume so students can come up and label the various parts.

Presentation 2: 10–15 min.

C Why is it important to put each piece of information on your resume? Discuss the reasons with a group and make notes next to each item on the list in exercise B.

Go through each part in exercise B and explain why each item is important.

Practice 2: 10–15 min.

D On a separate piece of paper, make a list of the following things:

See student page 110. Have each student make his or her own personalized list.

Evaluation 2: 10–15 min.

Check with students to see if they understand all categories. Call on a few volunteers to report what they wrote for different items in exercise D.

Presentation 3: 5–10 min.

Ask students why it is important to list the languages that they speak on their resumes. Review the major categories of a resume (Education, Experience, Special Skills, Hobbies, References) and ask them where language skills belong on the resume. Talk about where internships, awards, objectives, athletic abilities, and talents should go.

Practice 3: 10–15 min.

Go over the five documents pictured and make sure students know the significance and resume location of each document.

Evaluation 3: 10–15 min.

Call on different students to report what they wrote for certain items in exercise D and have them name other things about themselves they might include in the five major resume categories. List these on the board.

Application: 20–25 min.

E **Using the information you wrote for task D, write your resume on the lines below.**

Optional Computer Activity: Have students enter their resumes on the computer. Show them how to use the resume templates that come with many word processing programs. Focus on formatting to show students how to make their resumes easy to read.

F **Active Task: Go to the library or use the Internet to find tips on how to write your resume. Type your resume.**

Remind students to use the Active Task Checklist for Lesson 5.

Refer to the *Stand Out Activity Bank 4 CD-ROM,* Unit 6 Worksheet 5, for more practice with resumes. *(optional)*

Instructor's Notes for Lesson 5

E **Using the information you wrote for task D, write your resume on the lines below.**

_____ (name)

_____

_____

_____

_____

EDUCATION

_____   *(Answers will vary.)* _____

_____   _____

_____   _____

EXPERIENCE

_____   _____

_____   _____

_____   _____

SPECIAL SKILLS   _____

_____

_____

HOBBIES   _____

REFERENCES   _____

_____

  F **Active Task:** Go to the library or use the Internet to find tips on how to write your resume. Type your resume.

GOAL ▶ **Write a cover letter**

Life skill

 A **Read the cover letter that Ranjit wrote to send with his resume. What is the purpose of a cover letter?**

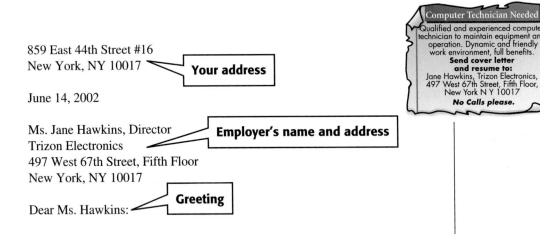

859 East 44th Street #16
New York, NY 10017 — **Your address**

June 14, 2002

Ms. Jane Hawkins, Director — **Employer's name and address**
Trizon Electronics
497 West 67th Street, Fifth Floor
New York, NY 10017

Dear Ms. Hawkins: — **Greeting**

I am writing in response to the ad for computer technician advertised in the *New York Gazette* this past Sunday. I have the education and qualifications you are looking for and would be an asset to your team.

As you can see from my enclosed resume, I have a certificate in computer repair and experience working with computers. I'm a hard worker and willing to learn new things. Trizon Electronics is a well-known, well-respected company which I feel could teach me a lot. My schedule is flexible and I'd be willing to work whenever you need me.

Thank you for taking the time to consider my application. I will follow up next week with a phone call. I look forward to meeting you and discussing any opportunities there may be for me at your company.

Sincerely,

Closing

Ranjit Ghosh
Ranjit Ghosh

Suggest next steps

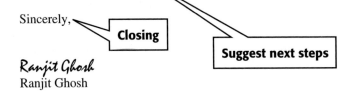

Computer Technician Needed
Qualified and experienced computer technician to maintain equipment and operation. Dynamic and friendly work environment, full benefits.
Send cover letter and resume to:
Jane Hawkins, Trizon Electronics, 497 West 67th Street, Fifth Floor, New York N Y 10017
No Calls please.

LESSON PLAN

Objective:
Write a cover letter
Key vocabulary:
cover letter, Director, Ms, asset,
warehouse, RN, paperwork, vital signs,
complaints, supervise, outgoing, handle

Warm-up and Review: 5–10 min.

Ask students to share their resumes with the
person sitting next to them.

Introduction: 10–15 min.

Write *cover letter* on the board. Ask if students
know what this is and what its purpose is. Ask if
students have written cover letters before.

State the Objective: *Today you will write a cover
letter to go along with your resume.*

Presentation 1: 10–15 min.

**Have students look at the cover letter in their
books.** Ask them some basic comprehension
questions, such as, *Who wrote the letter? Who did
he write the letter to? When did he write the
letter? Where is the company located?*

Practice 1: 15–20 min.

**(A) Read the cover letter that Ranjit
wrote to send with his resume. What is
the purpose of a cover letter?**

Have students read the letter to themselves and
then discuss it as a class.

Evaluation 1: 10–15 min.

Answer any questions students might have. Ask
students what things Ranjit said in his letter that
are important.

STANDARDS CORRELATIONS

CASAS: 4.1.2
SCANS: **Interpersonal** Participates as a Member of a
Team, Works with Cultural Diversity
Information Acquires and Evaluates Information,
Interprets and Communicates Information, Uses
Computers to Process Information (optional)
Systems Monitors and Corrects Performance
Technology Applies Technology to Task (optional)
Basic Skills Reading, Writing, Listening, Speaking
Thinking Skills Creative Thinking, Decision Making, Reasoning

Personal Qualities Responsibility, Self-Esteem, Sociability,
Integrity/Honesty
EFF: **Communication** Read with Understanding, Convey
Ideas in Writing, Speak So Others Can Understand, Listen
Actively, Observe Critically
Decision Making Solve Problems and Make Decisions, Plan
Interpersonal Cooperate with Others
Lifelong Learning Reflect and Evaluate, Use Information
and Communications Technology (optional)

Presentation 2: 10–15 min. 2+

Ask volunteers to read each of the job ads to the class.

Practice 2: 10–15 min. 2+

B Read the following job descriptions. Choose one of the jobs that you would like to apply for.

Have student work in small groups to talk about each ad. After analyzing all of the ads, each student should choose a job that he or she would like to apply for.

Evaluation 2: 10–15 min. 2+

Have students report their choices to the class. Ask them why they chose the job they did. Ask them if they think they have the necessary skills for that job.

Note: There is no Practice 3 for this lesson. Have students begin working on the Application activity. Longer classes will have more time to peer edit, type, and perfect their letters in class. Shorter classes may have to do some work at home.

Application: 20–25 min. 15+

C On a separate sheet of paper, write a cover letter to apply for one of the jobs above. Follow the model on page 112.

Optional Computer Activity: Have students type their cover letters using one of the business letter templates that comes with many word processing programs.

Refer to the *Stand Out Activity Bank 4 CD-ROM,* Unit 6 Worksheet 6, for a cover letter template and exercise. *(optional)*

Instructor's Notes for Lesson 6

B Read the following job descriptions. Choose one of the jobs that you would like to apply for.

 Work Solutions Inc.

Company Name: Healthy Living (61835 Valley Road, Grand Rapids, MI 49504)
Company Description: A company that produces and sells vitamins
Job Title: Warehouse Supervisor
Job Description: In charge of packaging orders in the warehouse. Must be able to supervise 20 employees. No experience with vitamins necessary, but warehouse experience would be helpful.

Company Name: Medical Valley Hospital (875 Washington Ave., Portland, OR 79468)
Job Title: Nurse's Aide
Job Description: Help the RNs take care of the patients. Fill out basic paperwork regarding patients, be able to take vital signs. No experience necessary—will train. Looking for someone who is friendly, patient, and likes working with sick people.

Company Name: Auto Land (75436 Harbor Blvd., Costa Mesa, CA 92627)
Company Description: Used car company
Job Title: Salesperson
Job Description: Selling cars. Must be good with people and outgoing. No sales experience necessary.

Company Name: Choicemart (876 San Miguel Street, Houston, TX 77042)
Job Title: Customer Service Representative
Job Description: Handle customer complaints, help customers fill out proper paperwork to file complaint, enter the complaint information into the computer, and set up meetings to discuss the complaints with the proper department. Must have good oral and written communication skills. Must be good with people and have the ability to handle angry customers. Basic computer skills helpful.

Company Name: Villa Italia (756 Fifth Ave., New York, NY 10019)
Job Title: Food Server
Job Description: Serve food to customers. Must have restaurant experience, but serving experience not necessary. Will train.

C On a separate sheet of paper, write a cover letter to apply for one of the jobs above. Follow the model on page 112. *(Answers will vary.)*

GOAL ▶ **Prepare for a job interview**   *Life skill*

A **Now that you have written your resume and your cover letter, it's time to get ready for the big interview! The best way to prepare for an interview is to practice.**

First, look at some sample interview questions. How would you answer each of them? Discuss each question with your group and then write out your answers on a separate piece of paper.

1. Tell me about yourself.

2. Why are you applying for this job?

3. Why do you think you would be good at this job?

4. What is your greatest strength?

5. What is your greatest weakness?

6. Do you prefer to work alone or with other people?

7. Why did you leave your last job?

8. What did you do at your last job?

9. Describe a situation where you had a conflict with another employee. How did you solve it?

10. What special skills do you have that would benefit our company?

11. What is your present salary?

12. What did you like most about your last job?

13. Do you have any questions?
    (Answers will vary.)

B **With a partner, practice asking and answering the interview questions. It is OK to look at the answers you wrote for now.**

LESSON PLAN

Objectives:
Practice responding to interview questions, Interview for a job, Interview another student, Fill out an evaluation form

Key vocabulary:
strength, weakness, conflict, benefit (v.), eye contact, voice level, facial expressions, posture, willingness, self-evaluate, impression, mock, criteria, applicant, handshake

Warm-up and Review: 5–10 min.

Ask some students to read their cover letters aloud.

Introduction: 10–15 min.

Tell students they have found the job they want, filled out the application, written their resume and cover letter, and sent everything in. Ask: *What's the next step?*

State the Objective: *Today you will practice interviewing for a job.*

Presentation 1: 10–15 min.

A Now that you have written your resume and your cover letter, it's time to get ready for the big interview! The best way to prepare for an interview is to practice.

Before reading the questions, have a brief discussion with students about interviewing for jobs. Ask how many of them practice before they interview. Discuss the importance of practicing.

Practice 1: 20–25 min.

(Exercise A. continued)

First, look at some sample interview questions. How would you answer each of them? Discuss each question with your group and then write out your answers on a separate sheet of paper. Have each student write out his or her own answers.

Evaluation 1: 10–15 min.

Go over some of the questions and ask students how they would answer them. Discuss what makes a good answer and what makes a poor one.

Presentation 2: 5–10 min.

Have a student ask you some of the interview questions. Give responses that you would give in a real interview.

Practice 2: 15–20 min.

B With a partner, practice asking and answering the interview questions. It is OK to look at the answers you wrote for now.

Evaluation 2:

Observe the pairs.

STANDARDS CORRELATIONS

CASAS: 4.1.5, 4.1.7
SCANS: **Interpersonal** Participates as a Member of a Team, Teaches Others New Skills, Exercises Leadership, Works with Cultural Diversity
Information Acquires and Evaluates Information, Organizes and Maintains Information, Interprets and Communicates Information
Systems Monitors and Corrects Performance
Basic Skills Reading, Writing, Listening, Speaking
Thinking Skills Creative Thinking, Decision Making, Problem Solving, Reasoning

Personal Qualities Responsibility, Self-Esteem, Sociability, Self-Management, Integrity/Honesty
EFF: **Communication** Read with Understanding, Convey Ideas in Writing, Speak So Others Can Understand, Listen Actively, Observe Critically
Decision Making Solve Problems and Make Decisions, Plan
Interpersonal Guide Others, Advocate and Influence, Cooperate with Others
Lifelong Learning Take Responsibility for Learning, Reflect and Evaluate

Presentation 3: 5–10 min.

C In addition to your answers, job interviewers are also looking for other qualities. Read the list below. How would you rate on each of the qualities?

Go through the list with students, explaining each item and how they should rate themselves. For example, demonstrate an excellent handshake, a medium handshake, and a fair handshake. Have students discuss or practice each item with you so they understand what it means to be excellent.

Practice 3: 10–15 min.

D Looking at the list above, which two are you best at?

E Which two do you need to work on the most?

Ask students to complete exercise D and E individually.

Evaluation 3: 10–15 min.

Ask some volunteers to say which items they are best at and which ones they need to work on the most. You may want to speak about your own qualities if students hesitate.

Application: 20–25 min.

F Now it's time to practice. You will be interviewing for the job that you wrote your cover letter for. Work with a partner. Then switch roles.

Explain each role to students and what they are supposed to do. If students need more of an explanation, ask for a volunteer to help demonstrate.

(Application continues on page 116a.)

C In addition to your answers, job interviewers are also looking for other qualities. Read the list below. How would you rate on each of the qualities?

Handshake	○ Fair	○ Good	○ Excellent
Clothing	○ Fair	○ Good	○ Excellent
Eye contact with interviewer	○ Fair	○ Good	○ Excellent
Voice level (volume)	○ Fair	○ Good	○ Excellent
Facial expressions	○ Fair	○ Good	○ Excellent
Posture / body position	○ Fair	○ Good	○ Excellent
Self-confidence / comfort level	○ Fair	○ Good	○ Excellent
Willingness to volunteer information	○ Fair	○ Good	○ Excellent
Appropriateness of responses to questions	○ Fair	○ Good	○ Excellent
Ability to self-evaluate	○ Fair	○ Good	○ Excellent

(Answers will vary.)

D Looking at the list above, which two are you best at?

1. _____ *(Answers will vary.)* _____

2. _____

E Which two do you need to work on the most?

1. _____ *(Answers will vary.)* _____

2. _____

F Now it's time to practice. You will be interviewing for the job that you wrote your cover letter for. Work with a partner. Then switch roles.

Student A: Interviewer

Ask your partner at least ten of the questions on page 114. When the interview is over, fill out the Mock Interview Evaluation Form sheet on the next page in your partner's book.

Student B: Interviewee

Do your best to answer the questions without looking at your notes and try to rate highly on each of the qualities listed above.

Fill out the mock evaluation form about your partner. Then switch roles.

(Answers will vary.)

Mock Interview Evaluation Form

Name of applicant: _____

Name of interviewer: _____

Date of interview: _____

Job applied for: _____

Rate the applicant on each of the following questions by writing <u>Excellent</u>, <u>Good</u>, or <u>Fair</u>.

What kind of impression did this person make? _____

Did the person give answers that would make an employer want to hire him or her?

_____

Did the person have a friendly, enthusiastic, and positive attitude?

_____

What suggestions can you give this person for how to make a better impression?

_____

Rate the applicant on the criteria below on a scale of 1 to 5.
(1=poor and 5=excellent)

CRITERIA	RATING				
	1	2	3	4	5
1. Handshake	—	—	—	—	—
2. Appearance	—	—	—	—	—
3. Eye contact with interviewer	—	—	—	—	—
4. Voice level (volume)	—	—	—	—	—
5. Facial expressions	—	—	—	—	—
6. Posture / body position	—	—	—	—	—
7. Self-confidence / comfort level	—	—	—	—	—
8. Willingness to volunteer information	—	—	—	—	—
9. Appropriateness of responses to questions	—	—	—	—	—
10. Effectiveness in describing strengths, skills, and abilities	—	—	—	—	—
11. Overall evaluation	—	—	—	—	—

Comments: _____

_____

_____

(Application continued from page 115a)

G Fill out the mock evaluation form about your partner. Then switch roles.

Make sure students exchange books so partners write out the answers. This provides students with realistic feedback.

The interview and evaluation process will be discussed in the Review.

 Refer to the *Stand Out Activity Bank 4 CD-ROM*, Unit 6 Worksheet 7, for a supplemental listening exercise and discussion about interviews and evaluations. *(optional)*

 Refer to the *Stand Out Activity Bank 4 CD-ROM*, Unit 6 Worksheet 8, for activities related to writing thank you letters after interviews. *(optional)*

Instructor's Notes for Lesson 7

LESSON PLAN

Objective:
Review all previous unit objectives
Key vocabulary:
Review all previous unit vocabulary

Warm-up and Review: 5–10 min.

Have students discuss the interview process from the last lesson. Ask them how they would improve next time.

Introduction: 2–5 min.

Write *evaluation* and *review* on the board. Ask students what these words mean and what their purpose is.

State the Objective: *Today we will review all that we have done in the past unit in preparation for the application project to follow.* Ask students as a class to recall all the goals of this unit without looking at their books. Then remind them of the goals they haven't mentioned.

Unit goals: *Complete a skills inventory, Use adjective clauses, Conduct a job search, Use the past perfect, Write a resume, Write a cover letter, Prepare for a job interview.*

Presentation, Practice, and Evaluation 1:

Do the Learner Log on page 120. Notes are next to the page.

Presentation 2: 5–10 min.

Preview exercises A, B, C, D with students.

Practice 2: 20–30 min.

A If you want to get a job, what are all the things you need to do from beginning to end? Make a list.

B List three skills that you have. List three skills that you need to work on.

C Complete the following sentences by yourself.

D What should you put on your resume? Make a list.

Evaluation 2: 15–20 min.

Ask volunteers to share their lists.

STANDARDS CORRELATIONS

CASAS: 7.1.4, 7.2.1, 7.4.1, 7.4.2
SCANS: **Interpersonal** Participates as a Member of a Team, Teaches Others New Skills, Works with Cultural Diversity
Information Acquires and Evaluates Information, Organizes and Maintains Information
Systems Understands Systems, Monitors and Corrects Performance
Basic Skills Reading, Writing, Listening, Speaking
Thinking Skills Creative Thinking, Decision Making, Seeing

Things in the Mind's Eye, Knowing How to Learn, Reasoning
Personal Qualities Responsibility, Self-Esteem, Sociability, Self-Management, Integrity/Honesty
EFF: **Communication** Convey Ideas in Writing, Speak So Others Can Understand, Listen Actively
Decision Making Solve Problems and Make Decisions
Interpersonal Guide Others, Cooperate with Others
Lifelong Learning Take Responsibility for Learning, Reflect and Evaluate, Learn through Research

A **If you want to get a job, what are all the things you need to do from beginning to end? Make a list.** *Possible answers:*

1. *write a resume*
2. *look for available position*
3. *research the company*
4. *write a cover letter*
5. *apply for the job*
6. *make a follow-up call*
7. *prepare for interview*
8. *interview*

B **List three skills that you have. List three skills that you need to work on.**

1. *(Answers will vary.)*
2. _____
3. _____

1. _____
2. _____
3. _____

C **Complete the following sentences by yourself.**

My three best skills are that I'm _____ *(Answers will vary.)* _____

_____

I need to work on being more _____

_____

D **What should you put on your resume? Make a list.** *(Answers will vary. Possible answers below.)*

name

address/phone/e-mail

education (dates, name of school, degree or

certificate)

work experience (dates, names of employers,

job titles, job duties)

personal interests

skills

 In this unit, you learned many things about getting a job. With a group discuss each of the following. Come up with one sentence about why each is important. Share your answers with the class.

Knowing my skills is important because _it helps me describe why I would make a good employee._

Knowing my interests is important because _it helps me to decide what kind of job I would like._

Finding information about the job I want is important because _it will tell me if I am qualified for that job._

Finding information about the company I am applying to is important because _I can show that I am prepared for the interview._

Writing a resume is important because _it summarizes your education and skills for the employer._

Writing a cover letter is important because _it introduces you to the employer._

Practicing interviewing is important because _it will help you to give a better impression._

(Answers may vary. Possible answers above.)

 Combine the two sentences using an adjective clause.

1. I need to find a new job. I know it will be hard to find a new job.

   I need to find a new job, which I know will be hard.

2. Many companies are looking for employees with strong communication skills. Many companies hire customer service personnel.

   Many companies hire customer service personnel who have strong communications skills.

 Combine the two ideas using past perfect.

(first) Dinora finished her ESL classes.

(second) Dinora started taking classes for her AA Degree.

   Dinora had finished her ESL classes before she started taking classes for her AA degree.

(first) Eric applied for a small business loan.

(second) Eric opened his business.

   Eric had applied for a small business loan before he opened his business.

(Answers may vary. Possible answers above.)

Presentation 3: 5–10 min. `3`

Preview exercises E, F, and G with students.

Practice 3: 10–15 min. `3`

E **In this unit, you learned many things about getting a job. With a group, discuss each of the following. Come up with one sentence about why each is important. Share your answers with the class.**

F **Combine the two sentences using an adjective clause.**

 Refer to *Stand Out Grammar Challenge 4*, Unit 6 pages 41–43 for more practice with adjective clauses. *(optional)*

G **Combine the two ideas using past perfect.**

 Refer to *Stand Out Grammar Challenge 4*, Unit 6 pages 44–46 for more practice with past perfect. *(optional)*

Evaluation 3: 10–15 min. `3`

Students share answers with the class. Invite students to write answers on the board.

Application: 1–2 days `L5+`

The Team Project Activity on the following page is the Application Activity to be done on the next day.

 Post-Assessment: Use the *Stand Out* ExamView® Pro *Test Bank* for Unit 6. *(optional)*

Note: With the *Stand Out* ExamView® Pro *Test Bank* you can design a post-assessment that focuses on what students have learned. It is designed for three purposes:

• To help students practice taking a test similar to current standardized tests.

• To help the teacher evaluate how much the students have learned, retained, and acquired.

• To help students see their progress when they compare their scores to the pre-test they took earlier.

Instructor's Notes for Unit 6 Review

_____

_____

_____

_____

_____

_____

_____

_____

_____

_____

_____

_____

_____

_____

_____

_____

_____

_____

_____

_____

Unit 6 Application Activity

> TEAM PROJECT:
> CREATE AN APPLICATION PORTFOLIO
> Objective: Project designed to apply all the objectives of this unit.
> Products: A job application portfolio, a mock job, ad, and interview

Introduction: 5 min.

Individual students will create their own job application portfolio. Then, in teams, students will come up with a job title, write an ad for it, and interview students to fill the position.

Note: Shorter classes can do this project over two periods.

State the Objectives: *By yourself, you will create a job application portfolio, which will contain all the information you need to apply for a job and go on a practice interview. With a team, you will create a job, write a brief job advertisement, and interview students.*

Stage 1: 5–10 min.

Make a list of all the information you want to include in your portfolio. Have some students report to class what they have on their lists.

Stage 2: 45–60 min.

Create the different parts of your portfolio. All portfolios must include the following: a resume, a cover letter or application letter, sample interview questions and answers. (Other possible items: certificates, awards, transcripts, performance reviews, letters of recommendation.)

Stage 3: 5 min.

Form a team with four or five students. Choose positions for each member of your team.

Stage 4: 15–30 min.

Decide what company you are and for what position you are hiring. Write a job advertisement for the position. Put all teams' job advertisements on one page to be distributed to the class. Compile all the ads onto one page to be given to each student.

Stage 5: 15–20 min.

Prepare a list of interview questions that you will ask the applicants.

Stage 6: 10–15 min.

Decide what you are looking for in an employee, and create an evaluation form.

Stage 7: 20–30 min.

Interview and evaluate the applicants. Each student must interview for one of the jobs. Appointments must be set up by each team to interview applicants, each of whom will present his or her portfolio. You may have to help students coordinate this so as not to waste too much time.

Stage 8: 15–20 min.

Choose the best person for the job. Have each team come to a decision and then report its choice to the class. If time, have students say which company they'd most like to work for.

STANDARDS CORRELATIONS

CASAS: 4.8.1, 4.8.5, 4.8.6
SCANS: **Resources** Allocates Materials and Facility Resources, Allocates Human Resources
Interpersonal Participates as a Member of a Team, Teaches Others New Skills, Exercises Leadership, Works with Cultural Diversity
Information Acquires and Evaluates Information, Organizes and Maintains Information, Interprets and Communicates Information, Uses Computers to Process Information (optional)
Systems Understands Systems, Monitors and Corrects Performance, Improves and Designs Systems
Technology Applies Technology to Task (optional)
Basic Skills Reading, Writing, Listening, Speaking

Thinking Skills Creative Thinking, Decision Making, Problem Solving, Seeing Things in the Mind's Eye, Knowing How to Learn, Reasoning
Personal Qualities Responsibility, Self-Esteem, Sociability, Self-Management, Integrity/Honesty
EFF: **Communication** Read with Understanding, Convey Ideas in Writing, Speak So Others Can Understand, Listen Actively, Observe Critically
Decision Making Solve Problems and Make Decisions, Plan
Interpersonal Guide Others, Resolve Conflict and Negotiate, Advise and Influence, Cooperate with Others
Lifelong Learning Take Responsibility for Learning, Reflect and Evaluate, Learn through Research, Use Information and Communications Technology (optional)

TEAM PROJECT

Create an application portfolio

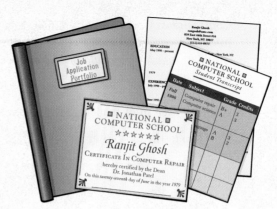

By yourself, you will create a job application portfolio, which will contain all the information you need to apply for a job and go on a practice interview.

With a team, you will create a job, write a brief job advertisement, and interview students.

1. Make a list of all the information you want to include in your portfolio.

2. Create the different parts of your portfolio. All portfolios must include the following: a resume, a cover letter or application letter, sample interview questions and answers. (Other possible items: certificates, awards, transcripts, performance reviews, letters of recommendation.)

3. Form a team with four or five students. Choose positions for each member of your team.

Position	Job Description	Student Name
Student 1 Leader	See that everyone speaks English. See that everyone participates.	
Student 2 Secretary	Take notes and write job advertisement.	
Student 3 Spokesperson	Ask interview questions.	
Students 4/5 Member (s)	Help secretary and spokesperson with their work.	

4. Decide what company you are and for what position you are hiring. Write a job advertisement for the position. Put all teams' job advertisements on one page to be distributed to the class.

5. Prepare a list of interview questions that you will ask the applicants.

6. Decide what you are looking for in an employee, and create an evaluation form.

7. Interview and evaluate the applicants.

8. Choose the best person for the job.

PRONUNCIATION

Contractions. Would and *had* can both have the contraction *'d* in spoken English and in informal written style. Read the examples below and decide if the contraction *'d* stands for *would* or *had*. Write *would* or *had* in the spaces below. Then listen and repeat each sentence.

1. I'd worked in Australia for three months before I started to feel homesick. _____ *had* _____

2. I'd go to the job center and ask for an application if I were you. _____ *would* _____

3. She'd like to get a job in engineering when she graduates. _____ *would* _____

4. They'd offered him a job before he finished his degree. _____ *had* _____

LEARNER LOG

In this unit, you learned many things about getting hired. How comfortable do you feel doing each of the skills listed below? Rate your comfort level on a scale of 1 to 4.

1 = Not so comfortable **2** = Need more practice **3** = Comfortable **4** = Very comfortable
If you circle 1 or 2, write down the page number where you can review this skill.

Vocabulary	**Comfort Level**				**Page(s)**
I can identify job skills and job titles.	1	2	3	4	*102, 103*

Life Skill					
I can complete a skills inventory.	1	2	3	4	*101*
I can identify job titles and responsibilities.	1	2	3	4	*103*
I can conduct a job search.	1	2	3	4	*105, 106*
I can conduct a company search.	1	2	3	4	*106*
I can write down my job history.	1	2	3	4	*107*
I can identify the parts of a resume.	1	2	3	4	*109*
I can write a resume.	1	2	3	4	*110, 111*
I can write a cover letter.	1	2	3	4	*112, 113*
I can prepare for a job interview.	1	2	3	4	*114, 115*
I can practice interviewing.	1	2	3	4	*116*

Grammar					
I can use adjective clauses.	1	2	3	4	*104*
I can use the past perfect.	1	2	3	4	*108*

Reflection
Complete the following statements with your thoughts about this unit. *(Answers will vary.)*

I learned _____

I would like to find out more about _____

I am still confused about _____

Unit 6 Pronunciation and Learner Log

Pronunciation: 10–15 min.
(optional)

Contractions

Would and *had* can both have the contraction *'d* in spoken English and in informal written style. Read the examples below and decide if the contraction *'d* stands for *would* or *had*. Write *would* or *had* in the spaces below. Then listen and repeat each sentence.

Play the recording and pause after each sentence. Ask students to write the answers in their books. Write the answers on the board or on a transparency. Have students find other examples of these contractions in the unit.

For additional pronunciation practice: Divide the class into two teams. Have each team think of five sentences containing the contracted form of *would* and five sentences containing the contracted form of *had.* Walk around and listen while students are creating the sentences to check if they have understood. Then have each team read out their sentences. The other team will have to identify which word has been used.

Learner Log

Presentation 1: 5–10 min.

If needed, review the purpose of the Learner Log. Make sure students understand how to rate the comfort level they feel in reaching the individual goals listed under *Life Skill, Grammar,* and *Academic Skill.* They should rate their comfort level on a scale of 1 to 4:

1. Not so comfortable

2. Need more practice

3. Comfortable

4. Very comfortable

Practice 1: 5–10 min.

If a student circles 1 or 2, he or she should enter the page number on which the skill is featured. The student can then more easily revisit that page and study the material again.

Evaluation 1: 5–10 min.

Finally, emphasize to students the importance of answering the two questions posed in *Reflection*. They are designed to help students assign real-life value to their classroom work.

Instructor's Notes for Unit 6 Team Project, Pronunciation, and Learner Log

_____

_____

_____

_____

_____

_____

_____

_____

_____

_____

_____

_____

_____

_____

_____

_____

_____

LESSON PLAN

Objective:
Identify appropriate workplace behavior
Key vocabulary:
appropriate, inappropriate, shower, groom, make-up, shave, press/iron, mechanic, fingernails

Pre-Assessment: Use the *Stand Out* ExamView® Pro *Test Bank* for Unit 7. (optional)

Warm-up and Review: 5–10 min. **1.5+**

Have students look at the picture in their books on page 121. Ask them what is wrong with this picture, if anything.

Introduction: 10–15 min. **1.5+**

Write *appropriate* and *inappropriate* on the board. See if students know what these words mean. Ask them if the picture shows *appropriate* or *inappropriate* workplace behavior.

State the Objective: *In this unit, you will learn about workplace behavior and things you need to do to be a good employee and keep your job (or maybe get a better one!). Today we will identify appropriate and inappropriate workplace behavior, including how you should dress on the job.*

Presentation 1: 10–15 min. **1.5+**

A Imagine that you are at work. Think carefully about each situation below and decide if it is appropriate (A) or inappropriate (I). Write *A* or *I* next to each statement.

Go through each situation with students, clarifying when they don't understand. Have them write *A* or *I* in the space provided without sharing their decision with the class.

Practice 1: 15–20 min. **1.5+**

B Discuss your answers with a group and think of three more examples of appropriate and inappropriate workplace behavior. Share your ideas with the class.

Evaluation 1: 10–15 min. **1.5+**

Have students share their responses with the class. Ask if any group had disagreements about whether a situation was appropriate or inappropriate.

Pronunciation: An optional pronunciation activity is found on the final page of this unit. This pronunciation activity may be introduced during any lesson in this unit, especially if students need practice with using intonation in tag questions. (See pages 140 and 140a for Unit 7 Pronunciation.)

STANDARDS CORRELATIONS

CASAS: 4.4.1
SCANS: **Interpersonal** Participates as a Member of a Team, Works with Cultural Diversity
Information Acquires and Evaluates Information, Organizes and Maintains Information, Interprets and Communicates Information
Basic Skills Reading, Writing, Listening, Speaking
Thinking Skills Creative Thinking, Decision Making,

Problem Solving, Reasoning
Personal Qualities Sociability, Self-Management
EFF: **Communication** Read with Understanding, Convey Ideas in Writing, Speak So Others Can Understand, Listen Actively, Observe Critically
Decision Making Solve Problems and Make Decisions
Interpersonal Advocate and Influence, Cooperate with Others

On the Job

G O A L S

- Discuss appropriate workplace behavior
- Use the passive voice
- Communicate problems to a supervisor
- Use tag questions
- Discuss workplace ethics
- Work out meanings from context
- Write a letter asking for a raise

LESSON 1

Can I wear this to work?

GOAL ▶ Discuss appropriate workplace behavior   *Life skill*

 A Imagine that you are at work. Think carefully about each situation below and decide if it is appropriate (A) or inappropriate (I). Write *A* or *I* next to each statement.

___A___ Ask a co-worker for help.

___A___ Ask for a raise.

___A___ Call in sick (when you are really sick).

___I___ Send personal e-mails.

___I___ Sit on your desk.

___I___ Smoke while you're working.

___I___ Talk to a friend on the phone.

___I___ Do Internet research for your child's school project.

___I___ Take products home for your friends and family.

___A___ Talk to your supervisor about a problem with a co-worker.

___I___ Arrive at work a few minutes late.

___A___ Tell your supervisor you don't understand something he or she said.

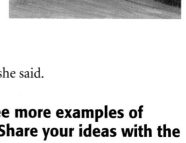

B Discuss your answers with a group and think of three more examples of appropriate and inappropriate workplace behavior. Share your ideas with the class.

C Read each of the situations below and decide if it is appropriate or inappropriate. Why do you think personal grooming is important in the workplace? Discuss the situations with your partner.

> **groom – v.** to take care of your own appearance by keeping your body, clothes, and hair clean and neat   **n. – grooming**

Alison is an administrative assistant in an office building. She runs every morning before she goes to work. Usually she gets home in time to shower, but this morning she is late. She has to decide between changing her clothes and having breakfast. She decides to skip breakfast today and shower and change into her work clothes.

Alison

Ross

Ross is a mechanic who worked a 14-hour shift yesterday. He was so tired that he went to bed in his work clothes. When he got up in the morning, he didn't have time to shower, but he washed his face, shaved, and put on a clean shirt. He didn't have time to clean his fingernails, but he knew they'd be getting dirty again anyway.

D On a separate sheet of paper, draw a diagram like the one below. Complete the diagram with facts about workplace grooming. Remember that some things are true for both men and women. *(Answers will vary.)*

Men
close shave and trim beard

Both
pressed/ironed clothing

Women
not too much perfume

Presentation 2: 5–10 min.

Write *groom* and *grooming* on the board. Help students understand the meanings of these words by giving them an example of good grooming (taking a shower), and bad grooming (not putting on a clean shirt). See if students can help you come up with a few more examples.

Practice 2: 10–15 min.

C Read each of the situations below and decide if it is appropriate or inappropriate. Why do you think personal grooming is important in the workplace? Discuss the situations with your partner.

Have students do this exercise by themselves. When they are finished, have them share their answers with the person next to them.

Evaluation 2: 10–15 min.

Go over the answers with students and ask them why they chose *appropriate* or *inappropriate*.

As a class, discuss why personal grooming is important in the workplace.

Presentation 3: 5–10 min.

Draw a Venn diagram on the board like the one in the book. Go over the examples given in the book and show students how to fill in the Venn diagram.

Practice 3: 10–15 min.

D On a separate sheet of paper, draw a diagram like the one below. Complete the diagram with facts about workplace grooming. Remember that some things are true for both men and women.

Have students do this exercise in small groups.

Evaluation 3: 10–15 min.

Ask a volunteer from each group to come to the board and fill in something on the diagram that was discussed in his or her group. Tell students not to write something that has already been written. Continue with students until all of their ideas are on the board.

Application: 20–25 min.

In groups, have students make a list of Employee Rules and Regulations that deal with workplace behavior. Write number 1, below, on the board for them and tell them to come up with at least ten rules and regulations.

1. Arrive at work on time.

Optional Computer Activity: Have students create their list of rules on the computer using a word processing program. Show students how to format their list using numbers or bullets. (See Teaching Hints for more suggestions on using computers in the classroom.)

Refer to the *Stand Out Activity Bank 4 CD-ROM,* Unit 7 Worksheet 1 (two pages), for activities about appropriate behavior and classroom/work rules. *(optional)*

Instructor's Notes for Lesson 1

_____

_____

_____

_____

_____

_____

_____

_____

_____

_____

_____

_____

_____

```
LESSON PLAN
Objective:
Use the passive voice in the simple past
Key vocabulary:
passive voice, active voice,
misunderstanding, signature, past
participle, memo
```

Warm-up and Review: 5–10 min.

Ask a representative from each group to read their list of Employee Rules and Regulations compiled in the previous lesson. Have a class discussion on which three rules are the most important.

Introduction: 10–15 min.

Have students look at the picture in their books on page 123. As a class discuss the boxed questions: *Where are these people? What are they talking about? What can you see on the desk?*

Write the following sentence on the board: *The note <u>was put</u> on the desk by his supervisor.* Underline *was put* and ask students if they know what verb tense this is.

State the Objective: *Today, you will use the passive voice to discuss things that happen at work.*

Presentation 1: 10–15 min.

 A Listen and read the conversation.

Play the recording for students and ask them to follow along in their books.

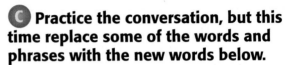 **B Answer the questions about the conversation with a partner.**

Have students work in pairs, and then go over the answers as a class.

Go over the instructions for exercise C and show students how to substitute the words in the dialog. (See Teaching Hints for suggestions on presenting dialogs.)

Practice 1: 15–20 min.

C Practice the conversation, but this time replace some of the words and phrases with the new words below.

Have students practice the conversation twice with one partner (switching roles) and then have them find two or three other partners to repeat the process.

Evaluation 1: 10–15 min.

Ask two or three pairs of students to demonstrate for the class. Get students used to being in front of the class by asking them to come to the front of the room when they present.

STANDARDS CORRELATIONS

CASAS: 0.1.2, 0.1.6
SCANS: **Interpersonal** Participates as a Member of a Team
Information Acquires and Evaluates Information, Interprets and Communicates Information
Systems Monitors and Corrects Performance
Basic Skills Reading, Writing, Listening, Speaking

Thinking Skills Decision Making
Personal Qualities Sociability
EFF: **Communication** Read with Understanding, Convey Ideas in Writing, Speak So Others Can Understand, Listen Actively
Interpersonal Cooperate with Others

LESSON 2

The note was written by Jim.

GOAL ▶ **Use the passive voice**   *Grammar*

 A **Listen and read the conversation.**

Raquel: Did you see the note I put on your desk?

Bruno: Was that note from you? I thought it was put there by Jim.

Raquel: Actually, the note was written by Jim but I taped it to your desk. I wanted to make sure you got it before you left for lunch.

Bruno: I did get it. The orders were sent to me yesterday and I'll have them ready for your signature before I leave today.

Raquel: Great! I'll sign them in the morning, and then you can send them to the Finance Department. Make sure they are sent by Package Express.

Bruno: I'll take care of it right away.

> Where are these people?
> What are they talking about?
> What can you see on the desk?

B **Answer the questions about the conversation with a partner.**

1. Who are the two people in the conversation? Who is the supervisor? *a supervisor and an employee; Raquel*

2. What is the misunderstanding? *The misunderstanding is about who left the note.*

3. What was sent to Bruno? *The orders were sent to Bruno.*

C **Practice the conversation, but this time replace some of the words and phrases with the new words below.**

desk	→	computer
note	→	memo
lunch	→	the day
Finance Department	→	Human Resources
right away	→	as soon as possible

D **Look at the sentences below. Compare the sentences in the passive voice with those in the active voice. What is the difference?**

Passive voice	Active voice
The note was put there by Raquel.	Raquel put the note there.
The note was written by Jim.	Jim wrote the note.
The orders were sent yesterday. (We don't know who sent them.)	They sent the orders yesterday.

Passive subject	*be*	Past participle	(*by* + person or thing)	Example sentence
I, he, she , it	was	written	by Jim	The note was written by Jim.
you, we, they	were	sent		The orders were sent yesterday. (We don't know who sent them.)

Use the passive voice to emphasize the object of the action or when the doer of the action is unknown or unimportant. To make an active sentence into a passive sentence, switch the subject and the object, and change the verb to the correct tense of *be* + the past participle. The word *by* is used before the doer of the action.

 E **Change the following sentences from active voice to passive voice. Think of your own ideas for the final sentence.**

EXAMPLE:
Our delivery person brought twelve bottles of water this morning.
Twelve bottles of water were brought by our delivery person this morning.

1. The receptionist bought all the supplies.

   All the supplies were bought by the receptionist.

2. The repairperson fixed the copy machine.

   The copy machine was fixed by the repairperson.

3. Our supervisor wrote some new regulations.

   Some new regulations were written by our supervisor.

4. Someone stole his money and driver's license.

   His money and driver's license were stolen.

5. A nurse took my blood pressure.

   My blood pressure was taken by a nurse.

6. *(Answers will vary.)*

Presentation 2: 5–10 min.

** D Look at the sentences below. Compare the sentences in the passive voice with those in the active voice. What is the difference?**

Go over the chart with students, making sure they understand how to form passive voice.

Practice 2: 10–15 min.

E Change the following sentences from active voice to passive voice. Think of your own ideas for the final sentence.

Go over the example with students and perhaps the first sentence if you think they need more guidance.

 Refer to the *Stand Out Activity Bank 4 CD-ROM,* Unit 7 Worksheet 2, for additional practice with passive voice. *(optional)*

Evaluation 2: 10–15 min.

Call on individual students to come to the board and write their sentences. Have the class evaluate.

 Refer to *Stand Out Grammar Challenge 4,* Unit 7 pages 49–51 for more about passive voice. *(optional)*

Presentation 3: 5–10 min.

On the *Stand Out Activity Bank 4 CD-ROM,* Unit 7 Worksheet 3 is an exercise in which students have to decide if a sentence is written in active voice or passive. Print out a copy for each student and review directions.

Practice 3: 10–15 min.

Decide whether each sentence is active or passive. Then change the sentence to active or passive voice (whatever it is not). Have students complete this worksheet by themselves.

Evaluation 3: 10–15 min.

Go over the answers as a class. Have students suggest sentences where the class responds "active" or "passive."

Application: 20–25 min.

Below is a list of questions written in both active and passive voice. Have students answer them in the passive voice. There are two ways to do this activity:

1) Ask a volunteer to stand. Read him or her the question and have him or her answer the question in passive voice.

2) Dictate the questions to students (see Teaching Hints for suggestions on dictation) and have them answer the questions in passive voice on their paper.

1. When were you born?

2. Who raised you?

3. Who taught the last class you took?

4. When was your house or apartment built?

5. When did you register for school?

6. When were you hired for your current job?

7. Where did you buy your book for this class?

8. Who wrote your textbook?

9. When was your textbook written?

10. When did you learn how to read?*

(*This one is tricky because students will have to change the verb from *learn* to *was taught.*)

```
Instructor's Notes for Lesson 2
_____

_____

_____

_____

_____

_____

_____

_____

_____

_____
```

LESSON PLAN

Objective:
Communicate problems to a
supervisor
Key vocabulary:
get someone's attention, politely,
excuse me, pardon me, flow chart,
solution, construction, shipment,
lumber, doorframes, co-worker, receipt,
urgent, addressee, overtime, install

Warm-up and Review: 5–10 min.

Review the difference between active and passive
voice by using the questions from the
application activity in the previous lesson. If you
didn't do the dictation, this would be good time to
do it for review.

Refer to *Stand Out Grammar Challenge 4,* Unit 7 pages 49–51 for review practice with the passsive voice. *(optional)*

Introduction: 10–15 min.

Ask students to tell you about some problems
they might face at work, possibly with a co-
worker or supervisor. Ask the class for
suggestions on how to solve these problems.

State the Objective: *Today you will learn how to
communicate problems to a supervisor. You will*

*read a flow chart and practice with some
example problems.*

Presentation 1: 10–15 min.

A Listen to the conversation.

Have students close their books. Play the
recording for them. Ask them some basic
comprehension questions about what they heard.
Now have them open their books and follow along
as you play the recording a second time.

Practice 1: 15–20 min.

B With a partner, answer the following questions about the conversation.

Have students discuss the questions with the
person sitting next to them.

Evaluation 1: 10–15 min.

Go over the questions as a class. Review the chart
as a class and practice these expressions.

Optional Activity: Have students work in pairs as
supervisor and worker. Have the worker tell the
supervisor a problem, but begin with an
attention-getting expression. Have the supervisor
repeat the problem with an expression from the
right and then make a suggestion. Reverse roles.

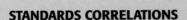

STANDARDS CORRELATIONS

CASAS: 4.4.1, 4.8.1, 4.8.5, 7.3.2, 7.4.8
SCANS: **Resources** Allocates Human Resources
Interpersonal Participates as a Member of a Team,
Teaches Others New Skills, Exercises Leadership, Works
with Cultural Diversity
Information Acquires and Evaluates Information,
Organizes and Maintains Information, Interprets and
Communicates Information, Uses Computers to Process
Information (optional)
Systems Understands Systems, Monitors and Corrects
Performance
Technology Applies Technology to Task (optional)
Basic Skills Reading, Listening, Speaking

Thinking Skills Creative Thinking, Decision Making,
Problem Solving, Seeing Things in the Mind's Eye, Knowing
How to Learn, Reasoning
Personal Qualities Responsibility, Self-Esteem, Sociability,
Self-Management, Integrity/Honesty
EFF: **Communication** Read with Understanding, Speak So
Others Can Understand, Listen Actively, Observe Critically
Decision Making Solve Problems and Make Decisions, Plan
Interpersonal Resolve Conflict and Negotiate, Advocate
and Influence, Cooperate with Others
Lifelong Learning Take Responsibility for Learning, Reflect
and Evaluate, Use Information and Communications
Technology (optional)

Taking action

GOAL ▶ **Communicate problems to a supervisor** | **Life skill**

A **Listen to the conversation.**

Construction worker: Excuse me, do you have a second?

Supervisor: Sure. What is it?

Construction worker: Well, there's a small problem. The shipment of lumber didn't arrive, so we have to stop construction until it gets here. What would you like us to do?

Supervisor: There's nothing else you can do while you are waiting for it?

Construction worker: No. We need that lumber to start working on the door frames.

Supervisor: OK. Well, why don't you guys take lunch early, and I'll call and see where the lumber is?

Construction worker: OK, so you want all of us to go on lunch break right now, while you call and find out where the lumber is?

Supervisor: That's right.

Construction worker: When should we come back?

Supervisor: In about an hour.

Construction worker: Thank you. See you in an hour.

B **With a partner, answer the following questions about the conversation.**

1. What is the problem? *A shipment of lumber didn't arrive, so work must stop.*

2. What does the employee say to get the supervisor's attention? *Excuse me.*

3. Does the supervisor understand the problem? *Yes.*

4. What does she suggest they do to solve the problem? *The workers will take a break while she calls to find out where the shipment is.*

How to get someone's attention politely	How to check that you have understood
Excuse me, sir/ma'am/ (name). Do you have a minute? Pardon me, sir/ma'am/ (name). Can I talk to you for a second?	Let me make sure I understand you. What you are saying is . . . So what we/I should do is . . .

C Read the flow chart below. Do you agree with each step?

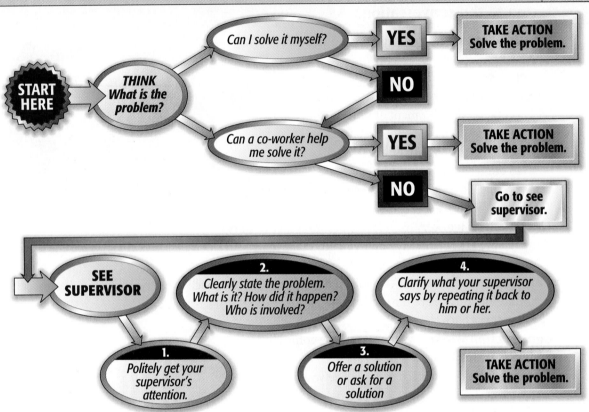

How to Communicate a Problem to Your Supervisor

START HERE

THINK What is the problem?

Can I solve it myself?

YES → TAKE ACTION Solve the problem.

NO

Can a co-worker help me solve it?

YES → TAKE ACTION Solve the problem.

NO → Go to see supervisor.

SEE SUPERVISOR

1. Politely get your supervisor's attention.

2. Clearly state the problem. What is it? How did it happen? Who is involved?

3. Offer a solution or ask for a solution

4. Clarify what your supervisor says by repeating it back to him or her.

TAKE ACTION Solve the problem.

D Discuss these questions with a partner.

1. If you can solve the problem by yourself, what should you do? *Take action and solve the problem.*

2. If a co-worker can help you solve the problem, what should you do? *With your co-worker's help, solve the problem.*

3. When you go to see your supervisor, what is the first thing you should do? What is the last thing you should do? *Politely get his or her attention. Clarify what he or she says by repeating it back.*

How to suggest a solution
Why don't we/I . . .
What if we/ I . . .
Would it work if we/ I . . .

E Look at the conversation on the previous page. Did the construction worker follow the steps in the flow chart? *Yes.*

Presentation 2: 5–10 min.

Read the flow charts below. Do you agree with each step?

Go through the flow chart with students, making sure they understand how to follow it. It will be easier to explain if you put up a transparency of the chart.

Practice 2: 10–15 min.

D Discuss these questions with a partner.

E Look at the conversation on the previous page. Did the construction worker follow the steps in the flow chart?

Evaluation 2: 10–15 min.

Go over the questions as a class.

Optional Computer Activity: Show students how to create a flow chart on the computer using arrows and text boxes. Have them recreate the one on page 126.

Presentation 3: 5–10 min.

Look at situation 1 in exercise F with the class. Take students through the flow chart on page 126 and have them come up with a decision about what Renee should do.

Practice 3: 10–15 min.

F With a group, read each situation below. Following the steps in the flow chart on page 126, discuss what you would do if you were in that situation. Do the first one with your class as an example.

Evaluation 3: 10–15 min.

Call on different groups to report what should be done in each situation.

Application: 20–25 min.

G Separate your class into two groups. Read your group's directions.

Group A: Supervisors

As a group, discuss how you would solve each of the problems in exercise H below. Be prepared to communicate this to the employee when he or she asks you.

Group B: Employees

As a group, discuss what you would say to your supervisor about each of the problems in exercise H below. Remember the four steps from the flow chart.

H When you are ready, each employee from Group B should find a supervisor from Group A to talk to about the first problem. You must talk to a different supervisor about each problem.

I Now, switch! The supervisors will become employees, and the employees will become supervisors.

Refer to the *Stand Out Activity Bank 4 CD-ROM,* Unit 7 Worksheet 4, for a supplemental listening and group activity on finding solutions to problems. *(optional)*

Instructor's Notes for Lesson 3

F With a group, read each situation below. Following the steps in the flow chart on page 126, discuss what you would do if you were in that situation. Do the first one with your class as an example.

1. Renee is a cashier in a fast-food restaurant. A customer just came up to the counter and told her that she gave him the wrong change. He doesn't have his receipt and she doesn't remember helping him. What should she do?

2. Mikhail came back from lunch and found a message marked *urgent* that wasn't addressed to him on his desk. He doesn't recognize the name of the addressee so he doesn't know what to do with it. What should he do?

3. James and Sara assemble telephones. For this particular group of phones, they have an uneven number of parts and aren't able to finish 20 of the phones. What should they do?

G Separate your class into two groups. Read your group's directions.

Group A: Supervisors
As a group, discuss how you would solve each of the problems in exercise H below. Be prepared to communicate this to your employee when he or she asks you.

Group B: Employees
As a group, discuss what you would say to your supervisor about each of the problems in exercise H below. Remember the four steps from the flow chart.

H When you are ready, each employee from Group B should find a supervisor from Group A to talk to about the first problem. You must talk to a different supervisor about each problem.

1. You just received your paycheck and you notice that you didn't get paid for the overtime hours you worked.

2. There is an emergency phone call for you, but if you leave your place, you will throw off the assembly line.

3. You are out installing cable TV at a customer's home and the customer is unhappy with your service.

I Now, switch! The supervisors will become employees, and the employees will become supervisors.

LESSON 4 You speak English, don't you?

GOAL ▶ Use tag questions | *Grammar*

A Compare these two questions. Which question is a tag question?

"Is Eric looking for new employees for his company?"

I have no idea, but I want to know.

"Eric is looking for new employees for his company, isn't he?"

I'm not 100% sure, but I think this is true.

B Read the questions and answers about rules for tag questions.

Tag question: *Eric is looking for new employees for his company, isn't he?*

Q: Why is this called a tag question?
A: Because it's a question tagged onto the end of a sentence.

Q: When do we use tag questions?
A: When we are almost sure something is true, but we want to check and make sure.

Q: When I'm asking a tag question, how do I know if the tag should be positive or negative?
A: If the sentence is positive, the tag is negative. If the sentence is negative, the tag is positive.

Q: What verb tense do I use in the tag?
A: Use the same verb tense in the tag that is used in the beginning of the statement.

C Study the chart with your teacher.

Positive statement	Tag	Negative statement	Tag
She works,	doesn't she?	She doesn't work,	does she?
She is working,	isn't she?	She isn't working,	is she?
She worked,	didn't she?	She didn't work,	did she?
She will work,	won't she?	She won't work,	will she?
She is going to work,	isn't she?	She isn't going to work,	is she?
She has worked,	hasn't she?	She hasn't worked,	has she?
She had worked,	hadn't she?	She hadn't worked,	had she?

LESSON PLAN
Objective:
Use tag questions
Key vocabulary:
tag, positive, negative

Warm-up and Review: 5–10 min.

Talk about the Application Activity from the previous lesson with students. Ask them if it was easy or difficult and if they now think they feel better prepared to talk to a supervisor at work about a problem.

Introduction: 10–15 min.

A Compare these two questions. Which question is a tag question?

Have students read the two questions and the thought bubbles coming from the woman. Ask students how the two questions differ.

State the Objective: *Today, you will use tag questions.*

Presentation 1: 10–15 min.

B Read the questions and answers about rules for tag questions.

First, have students read the questions and answers silently to themselves. Then go through the rules as a class, calling on two students to read each question and answer.

C Study the chart with your teacher.

Using the examples in the chart, go back through the rules in exercise B. To check for students' comprehension, have them close their books. Read the portion of the tag question without the tag to

students and see if they can come up with the tag. Have students practice this same activity with a partner.

Prepare students for exercise D on the next page by telling them they will hear some tag questions and have to circle the tag they hear. (See Teaching Hints for suggestions on focused listening.)

Refer to *Stand Out Grammar Challenge 4,* Unit 7 pages 53–55 for instruction and practice with tag questions. *(optional)*

STANDARDS CORRELATIONS

CASAS: 0.1.2, 0.1.6
SCANS: **Interpersonal** Participates as a Member of a Team
Information Acquires and Evaluates Information, Interprets and Communicates Information
Systems Monitors and Corrects Performance
Basic Skills Reading, Writing, Listening, Speaking

Thinking Skills Decision Making
Personal Qualities Sociability
EFF: **Communication** Read with Understanding, Convey Ideas in Writing, Speak So Others Can Understand, Listen Actively
Interpersonal Cooperate with Others

Practice 1: 15–20 min. `1.5+`

D Listen to the tag questions and fill in the circle next to the tag that you hear.

E Complete each of the following questions with the correct tag.

Do the first one with students.

Evaluation 1: 10–15 min. `1.5+`

Go over the answers to each exercise.

Presentation 2: 5–10 min. `1.5+`

For this next exercise, a student will read the statements in exercise E aloud to his or her partner, and the partner will have to complete the statement with the correct tag. Demonstrate with a student.

Example:

Student A: He isn't being promoted . . .

Teacher: . . . is he?

Practice 2: 10–15 min. `2+`

Have students read the statements for their partners to complete. The student who is completing the sentence should have his or her book closed. Have students switch roles and repeat.

Evaluation 2: 10–15 min. `2+`

Have all students close their books. Review by doing the same exercise with students, only this time, you read the statement and call on a student to complete it.

Presentation 3: 5–10 min. `3`

For this next exercise, you will dictate the listening exercises from exercise D. Prepare students for the dictation. (See Teaching Hints for suggestions on dictation.)

Practice 3: 10–15 min. `3`

Dictate the following tag questions to students, but don't give them the tag.

1. He sent the package yesterday, _____?

2. We'll get our paychecks tomorrow, _____?

3. They didn't unload those boxes yet, _____?

4. Martina hasn't ever assembled computers, _____?

5. You're just learning about tag questions, _____?

Have students complete the statements.

Extra practice: Have students take the tag questions in exercise D and/or exercise E and make the positive ones negative and the negative ones positive.

Refer to the *Stand Out Activity Bank 4 CD-ROM,* Unit 7 Worksheet 5, for additional practice with tag questions. *(optional)*

Evaluation 3: 10–15 min. `3`

Go over the answers as a class.

Application: 20–25 min. `1.5+`

F Write four tag questions you might be able to use at your work. If you don't have a job, write tag questions you could use at home or at school.

Ask volunteers to write their tag questions on the board.

Instructor's Notes for Lesson 4

_____

_____

_____

_____

_____

_____

_____

_____

_____

_____

GOAL ▶ Use tag questions

Grammar

D **Listen to the tag questions and fill in the circle next to the tag that you hear.**

1. ○ did he ● didn't he ○ don't he ○ doesn't he
2. ○ won't she ○ will she ● won't we ○ don't we
3. ● did they ○ did he ○ didn't they ○ didn't he
4. ○ hasn't she ○ did she ○ didn't she ● has she
5. ○ are you ● aren't you ○ don't you ○ were you

E **Complete each of the following questions with the correct tag.**

1. He isn't being promoted, _____*is he?*_____

2. Lisa and Jack have never missed a day of work, _____*have they?*_____

3. Maria lives near her job, _____*doesn't she?*_____

4. Our computers will be repaired next week, _____*won't they?*_____

5. My assistant is going to get a new office, _____*isn't she?*_____

6. She didn't finish her work, _____*did she?*_____

7. The supervisor said to wait until tomorrow to finish, _____*didn't she?*_____

8. The machine broke down, _____*didn't it?*_____

9. Roberto had worked in a restaurant before, _____*hadn't he?*_____

10. We'll have a business meeting next week, _____*won't we?*_____

F **Write four tag questions you might be able to use at your work. If you don't have a job, write tag questions you could use at home or at school.**

EXAMPLE:
She left the package at the office, didn't she?

1. _**(Answers will vary.)**_____

2. _____

3. _____

4. _____

LESSON 5 **What should you do?**

GOAL ▶ Discuss workplace ethics | *Life skill*

> **ethics – n.** moral rules or principles of behavior for deciding what is right and wrong **adj. – ethical**

A Each situation below describes an ethical question that you might face at work or at school. What would you do? Check ✓ your answers and discuss them with a partner. *(Answers may vary.)*

1. You pay the cashier at the supermarket and she gives you change from $20 instead of the $10 you gave her. What would you do?

   _____ Tell her.   _____ Just forget about it.

2. It's the night before the final exam at your school and you haven't had much time to study. A classmate has stolen the answers to the exam and offers to share them with you. What would you do?

   _____ Say no.   _____ Borrow the answers from him.

3. You go shopping and buy some books. When you get home, you realize that the clerk put an extra book in your bag that you didn't pay for. What would you do?

   _____ Go back to the store and give the book back.   _____ Keep it.

B In the examples above, you know what you should do, but do you always do it? Sometimes, the decision is not that easy, but there are steps you can take to help you make a good decision.

> **Steps for Making an Ethical Decision**
>
> 1. Identify the ethical issue or problem.
> 2. List the facts that are most relevant to your decision.
> 3. Identify the people who might be affected by your decision and how.
> 4. Explain what each person would want you to do about the issue.
> 5. List three different decisions you could make and what the outcome of each decision would be.
> 6. Decide what you will do.

C Using the steps above, discuss one of the situations in exercise A with a group and decide what would be the best thing to do.

LESSON PLAN

Objective:
Discuss workplace ethics
Key vocabulary:
ethics, ethical, dilemmas, relevant, outcome, clerk, policy, refurbish, depleted

Warm-up and Review: 5–10 min. `1.5+`

Review tag questions. Ask volunteers to share the questions they wrote for the Application Activity in the prior lesson.

Introduction: 10–15 min. `1.5+`

Write *ethics* and *ethical* on the board. Tell the following story: *Imagine that last week you received $500 extra in your paycheck. Your boss hasn't said anything about bonuses or raises. None of your co-workers are talking about bonuses. You really need the money. Will you tell your supervisor about the extra money or keep it until somebody asks you?*

Discuss good and poor decisions with students and define *ethics*.

State the Objective: *Today you will look at ethical dilemmas and learn steps you can follow to make good decisions.*

Presentation 1: 5 min. `1.5+`

Tell students that they are presented with a choice in each situation in exercise A. Have them think hard about each circumstance and make an honest decision.

Practice 1: 15–20 min. `1.5+`

A **Each situation below describes an ethical question that you might face at work or at school. What would you do? Check ✓ your answers and discuss them with a partner.**

Have each student complete this exercise alone and then find a partner to share answers. Remind students that there is no right or wrong answer and that they should try to answer truthfully.

Evaluation 1: 10–15 min. `1.5+`

Take a poll and see if the class agrees on the decisions.

Presentation 2: 5–10 min. `1.5+`

B **In the examples above, you know what you should do, but do you always do it? Sometimes, the decision is not that easy, but there are steps you can take to help you make a good decision.**

Go through each step with students. Then choose one situation in exercise A. Go through each of the steps for making an ethical decision and see if the class can agree on a decision.

Practice 2: 10–15 min. `2+`

C **Using the steps above, discuss one of the situations in exercise A with a group and decide what would be the best thing to do.**

Have students choose one of the problems that you didn't do as an example. This may be difficult for them, so walk around and help.

Evaluation 2: 10–15 min. `2+`

Observe the groups working out their dilemmas. Discuss after the groups have come to a conclusion. Do all groups agree?

STANDARDS CORRELATIONS

CASAS: 4.8.1, 4.8.5, 4.8.6, 7.2.2, 7.2.5, 7.2.7, 7.3.2, 7.3.4
SCANS: **Interpersonal** Participates as a Member of a Team, Exercises Leadership, Works with Cultural Diversity **Information** Acquires and Evaluates Information **Basic Skills** Reading, Writing, Listening, Speaking **Thinking Skills** Creative Thinking, Decision Making, Problem Solving, Seeing Things in the Mind's Eye, Reasoning **Personal Qualities** Responsibility, Self-Esteem, Sociability,

Self-Management, Integrity/Honesty
EFF: **Communication** Read with Understanding, Convey Ideas in Writing, Speak So Others Can Understand, Listen Actively, Observe Critically **Decision Making** Solve Problems and Make Decisions, Plan **Interpersonal** Guide Others, Resolve Conflict and Negotiate, Advocate and Influence, Cooperate with Others **Lifelong Learning** Reflect and Evaluate

Presentation 3: 5–10 min.

Put students who don't normally work together into groups of four or five. Tell groups they will choose an ethical dilemma and go through the steps listed on page 130 to reach a decision. Tell them all group members must agree on a single decision, so it may take some negotiating.

Practice 3: 10–15 min.

D With a group, choose one of the ethical situations below.

Have each group read through the situations and choose one to work on. Have each group report their decision to the class.

E For the situation you have chosen, follow the steps for making an ethical decision on page 130. On a separate piece of paper, answer each of the questions below before you make your final decision.

Each group should have a reporter to write down the answers to the questions and the group's final decision.

Evaluation 3: 10–15 min.

Have each group choose a representative to report their decision to the class.

Application: 20–25 min. 1.5+

F Write a description of a situation where you had to make an ethical choice. What did you do? How did you feel afterward?

You may need to help students brainstorm if they are having trouble thinking of something to write about.

 Refer to the *Stand Out Activity Bank 4 CD-ROM,* Unit 7 Worksheet 6 (two pages), for a reading and discussion questions about an ethical dilemma. *(optional)*

Instructor's Notes for Lesson 5

With a group, choose one of the ethical situations below.

1.
Ricardo, the night security guard, has access to all of the buildings at night. It is a slow night and he wants to check his personal e-mail using one of the available computers. The company has a strict policy about e-mail being used for business purposes only, but Ricardo is the only person in the building.

3.
Kimberly, who works as a receptionist in the front office, has access to the copy machine to make copies for other employees. Her daughter, Alyse, needs some copies for a school project. She brought her own paper and needs 200 copies for her class. Alyse needs to have the copies or she will fail the project and possibly not pass the class. The company copier does not require a security code and they don't keep track of who made how many copies.

2.
Emilia is a janitor who is in charge of cleaning the restrooms and refilling all of the depleted supplies. She is the only one with a key to the supply closet. Her husband is very sick, and she is having trouble making enough money to support her family. Often times they can't afford food and they can't afford to buy toilet paper and soap.

4.
Brandon works in Quality Control, helping refurbish used computers. Once a year, his supervisor gives away computers to a local elementary school. He doesn't keep any records of this and Brandon really needs a computer for his son who is just starting high school. His supervisor asks him to deliver twelve computers to the local school.

E **For the situation you have chosen, follow the steps for making an ethical decision on page 130. On a separate piece of paper, answer each of the questions below before you make your final decision.**

1. What is the ethical problem?

2. What are the relevant facts?

3. Which people are involved and how would each person be affected? *(Answers will vary.)*

4. What would each person want you to do?

5. What are three different possible decisions?

6. What is your final decision?

F **Write a description of a situation where you had to make an ethical choice. What did you do? How did you feel afterward?**
(Answers will vary.)

LESSON 6 Women at work

GOAL ▶ **Work out meanings from context** | *Academic skill*

A **What is most important to you in your job? Number the items 1–9 (1 = most important). Then explain your choices to a partner.**

_____ relationships with co-workers   _____ career opportunities   _____ working hours

_____ interesting work   _____ distance from home   _____ salary

_____ vacations   _____ benefits   _____ working environment

(Answers will vary.)

B **Read the following article about getting a raise. Underline the advice that could be useful for you.**

How to Ask for a Raise

Men are still earning more than women—lots more. According to the most recent Census Bureau data, the pay gap between men and women is 27%—a woman earns 73 cents for every dollar a man earns. What does that mean? A woman works four weeks to earn as much as her male counterpart earns in three weeks.

How can women close the gap? Knock on the boss's door and ask for a raise, because getting the raise is not as difficult as it might seem. Here are 10 tips to assist women in negotiating the annual raise.

1. **Be a star performer.** Make yourself indispensable to the company. Document your successes by saving e-mails and letters, and compiling them into a portfolio. Make sure to take this with you when you go to your boss.
2. **Research.** Know what other men and women in your field are paid.
3. **Focus on your contributions to the company.** While the raise is certainly important to you, do not focus on how it will help your credit card debt.
4. **Be informed.** Know the company's policy on raises by asking your human resources director.
5. **Timing is everything.** Don't ask when the office is hectic. Wait until the pace has slowed down and the moment is right.
6. **Do your homework.** Rehearse and prepare responses to counter any objections your boss might have. Know ahead of time what the difficult questions might be and have your answers ready!
7. **Rehearse.** If you can, act out the scenario with a friend or colleague. This will help you to become more comfortable when you are actually doing the asking.
8. **Be a professional.** Ask for a formal meeting with your boss.
9. **Cover your bases.** Make four points about your contribution prior to asking for the raise. Illustrate your ability:
   • to find solutions,
   • to go above and beyond your job responsibilities,
   • to help others, and most importantly,
   • to increase the company's profitability.
10. **Don't take no for an answer.** Negotiate more vacation time, stock options, 401K contributions, or flex time. Set goals and ask for another review in three months.

LESSON PLAN

Objectives:
Identify ways to ask for a raise, Read for understanding, Work on meanings from context
Key vocabulary:
benefits, working environment, close the gap, cover your bases, contributions to the company, star performer, document, vacations, counterpart, Census Bureau data, rehearse, indispensable, portfolio, debt, colleague, negotiate, flex time, raise

Warm-up and Review: 5–10 min.

Ask volunteers to describe the ethical situations they wrote about in the previous lesson.

Introduction: 10–15 min.

A What is most important to you in your job? Write the numbers 1–9 below. (1 = most important) Then explain your choices to a partner.

Tell students to rate their choices with 1 as most important and 9 as least important. Take a brief class poll on the most important aspects of a job.

State the Objectives: *Today you will read about asking for a raise and learn how to work out meanings of words you don't understand from context.*

Presentation 1: 10–15 min.

Have students look at the article title, "How to Ask for a Raise." Have them speculate on what they think the article might contain.

Practice 1: 15–20 min.

B Read the following article about getting a raise. Underline the advice that could be useful for you.

Encourage students to read for overall understanding and not to worry about every single word and phrase. At this time, don't help students with unfamiliar words or phrases.

Evaluation 1: 10–15 min.

Review the article as a class by reading the numbered headings and asking volunteers to rephrase what each tip means. Again, vocabulary will be reviewed in Practice 2 if students don't yet understand.

STANDARDS CORRELATIONS

CASAS: 4.1.6, 4.4.2, 7.2.1, 7.2.4
SCANS: **Interpersonal** Participates as a Member of a Team, Works with Cultural Diversity
Information Acquires and Evaluates Information, Organizes and Maintains Information, Interprets and Communicates Information
Basic Skills Reading, Listening, Speaking
Thinking Skills Decision Making,
Personal Qualities Responsibility, Self-Esteem, Sociability,

Self-Management
EFF: **Communication** Read with Understanding, Speak So Others Can Understand, Listen Actively
Decision Making Solve Problems and Make Decisions, Plan
Interpersonal Resolve Conflict and Negotiate, Cooperate with Others
Lifelong Learning Reflect and Evaluate, Learn through Research

Presentation 2: 5–10 min.

C Practice working out meaning from context. Use the following steps.

Call on one student to tell you the first unknown word(s) he or she found in the article. Go through each step with students using this example.

Practice 2: 10–15 min.

Have students individually try to work out the meaning of the words and phrases that they underlined. Check to see that all students understand the process.

Evaluation 2: 10–15 min.

Have students tell you which phrases or words they worked on and have them take you and the class through the process of working out the meaning through context.

Presentation 3: 5–10 min.

Go over the instructions for exercises D and E with students and help them understand the examples.

Practice 3: 10–15 min.

D Look at these words from the article. Each word has two meanings. Find the word and choose the correct meaning in this context.

Have students return to the article and underline the sentence where the word appears on page 132.

E What are the opposites of the words below?

Have students locate other words with similar prefixes in the reading. Can they guess the opposite of those words as well?

F Discuss the following questions with a group.

Evaluation 3: 10–15 min.

Go over the answers to D and E as a class. Make a list of prefixes.

C   **Practice working out meaning from context. Use the following steps.**

1. Skim through the article again and circle any words or phrases that you don't understand.

2. Now look at the context and see if you can figure out the meaning on your own. Ask students next to you for help if you need it.

3. Is it necessary to understand these phrases or can you still get the general idea?

4. Ask your teacher or use a dictionary for help with any phrases that you can't figure out.

D   **Look at these words from the article. Each word has two meanings. Find the word and choose the correct meaning in this context.**

EXAMPLE:
document
○ paper   ● prove

1. **illustrate**

   ● give evidence   ○ draw pictures

2. **counter**

   ● respond to   ○ work surface

3. **contributions**

   ○ money   ● work or effort

4. **field**

   ● specialization   ○ grassy area

E   **What are the opposites of the words below?**

EXAMPLE:
necessary ➡ ***unnecessary***

1. dispensable ➡ ___*indispensable*___

2. important ➡ ___*unimportant*___

3. comfortable ➡ ___*uncomfortable*___

4. formal ➡ ___*informal*___

F   **Discuss the following questions with a group.**

1. This article focuses on how women should ask for a raise. Do you think these same ideas apply to men? Why or why not?

2. Which aspect of asking for a raise do you think is the most difficult? Take a poll in your group.

G Nabil met with his boss yesterday to ask for a raise. Read about his experience.

Nabil has been working for EJ Electronics as an assembler for two years. In the past year, he has come up with new ways to make the assembly line more efficient and helped increase productivity in his department. Nabil thinks he deserves a raise. He has friends that work at other electronics companies and he has been finding out what different employees are paid. He believes that with his experience and his contributions to the company, his boss should give him a raise.

First, Nabil went to see Heidi in Human Resources and asked her what procedures he needed to follow to ask for a raise. She suggested that he make an appointment with his boss. So last week, he asked his boss if the two of them could sit down and have a meeting. When his boss agreed, he began to gather his paperwork: job evaluations, memos from his supervisor about the new assembly line configurations, his "Employee of the Month" award, and records of his attendance at work. He sat down and thought about all the questions his boss might ask him and he wrote out detailed answers. Then he asked his cousin to practice asking him those questions.

H Look back at the article on page 132. How did Nabil follow each point from the article? Some things are not mentioned in the story about Nabil. How do you think he handled those aspects of asking for a raise?

I Imagine you are Nabil. Practice the conversation he might rehearse with his cousin. Then act out the conversation with his boss.

J **Active Task:** Find a friend or family member and rehearse asking for a raise.

Application: 20–30 min.

G Nabil met with his boss yesterday to ask for a raise. Read about his experience.

Have students read this to themselves.

H Look back at the article on page 132. How did Nabil follow each point from the article? Some things are not mentioned in the story about Raj. How do you think he handled those aspects of asking for a raise?

Refer to the *Stand Out Activity Bank 4 CD-ROM,* Unit 7 Worksheet 7, for a chart that you can print out for students to fill in. Have students complete this exercise by themselves before they share their answers with other students.

I Imagine you are Nabil. Practice the conversation he might rehearse with his cousin. Then act out the conversation with his boss.

Pair students up to practice asking for a raise. Tell them to switch roles after they have practiced once. Ask the students to imagine the boss says *No!*

J Active Task: Find a friend or family member and rehearse asking for a raise.

Refer to the *Stand Out Activity Bank 4 CD-ROM,* Unit 7 Active Task Checklist.

Remind students to use this checklist as they complete this Active Task. (optional)

Refer to the *Stand Out Activity Bank 4 CD-ROM,* Unit 7 Worksheet 8, for a self-evaluation table about asking for a raise. *(optional)*

Instructor's Notes for Lesson 6

LESSON PLAN

Objective:
Write a letter asking for a raise
Key vocabulary:
raise, reviews from supervisors, deserve

Warm-up and Review: 5–10 min. (1.5⁺)

Ask a volunteer to come to the front of the class and practice asking you for a raise. Do this with a few students if you have time.

Introduction: 10–15 min. (1.5⁺)

Ask students: *What's another way to ask for a raise?* (Write a letter.) *What do you think you should put in a letter like this?* Make a list of responses on the board.

State the Objective: *Today you will write a letter asking for a raise.*

Presentation 1: 10–15 min. (1.5⁺)

(A) Discuss these questions with your group.

Practice 1: 15–20 min. (1.5⁺)

(B) Many people hesitate to ask for a raise. Can you think of some reasons why? Make a list below.

(C) Let's get ready to ask for a raise! First of all, answer the following questions on a separate piece of paper. (If you are a homemaker or a student, imagine that you get paid for what you do and are asking for more money.)

Go through each question with students, giving an example of a possible answer where necessary. Then have them work individually to answer the questions.

(D) You can ask for a raise in person or by writing a letter. What do you think the advantages and disadvantages of each are?

In small groups, have students complete the chart at the bottom of the page or on a separate piece of paper.

Evaluation 1: 5–10 min. (3)

Write the chart on the board and have students come up and fill it in with notes from their group discussions.

STANDARDS CORRELATIONS

CASAS: 4.4.1, 4.4.2
SCANS: **Interpersonal** Participates as a Member of a Team, Works with Cultural Diversity
Information Organizes and Maintains Information, Interprets and Communicates Information, Uses Computers to Process Information (optional)
Systems Monitors and Corrects Performance
Technology Applies Technology to Task (optional)
Basic Skills Reading, Writing, Listening, Speaking
Thinking Skills Creative Thinking, Decision Making,

Reasoning
Personal Qualities Responsibility, Self-Esteem, Sociability, Self-Management, Integrity/Honesty
EFF: **Communication** Read with Understanding, Convey Ideas in Writing, Speak So Others Can Understand, Listen Actively
Decision Making Solve Problems and Make Decisions, Plan
Interpersonal Cooperate with Others
Lifelong Learning Use Information and Communications Technology (optional)

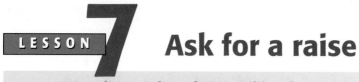

Ask for a raise

GOAL ▶ Write a letter asking for a raise

Life skill

A **Discuss these questions with your group.**

1. Have you ever received a raise at your job? If yes, what was it for?

2. Have you ever asked for a raise? If yes, did you get it? If no, did your manager or supervisor explain to you why you didn't get it?

   (Answers will vary.)

B **Many people hesitate to ask for a raise. Can you think of some reasons why? Make list below.** *(Answers may vary. Possible answers below.)*

They don't feel they deserve it; they are afraid the answer will be no; they are nervous about

talking with their supervisor.

C **Let's get ready to ask for a raise! First of all, answer the following questions on a separate piece of paper. (If you are a homemaker or a student, imagine that you get paid for what you do and are asking for more money.)**

1. Do you deserve a raise? Why or why not?

2. How long have you been working at your job?

3. When was the last time you got a raise?   *(Answers will vary.)*

4. Have you been working harder or working more hours?

5. Have you been given more responsibilities?

6. Have you gotten good reviews from your supervisors?

D **You can ask for a raise in person or by writing a letter. What do you think the advantages and disadvantages of each are?**

(Answers will vary. Sample answers below.)

Ask for a raise in person		Ask for a raise by writing	
Advantages	Disadvantages	Advantages	Disadvantages
easy to ask and answer questions; friendly;	*may be inconvenient time for boss;*	*record of request including date; convenient for boss;*	*too formal;*

E **Read the letter that Rogelio wrote to his supervisor asking for a raise.**

August 14, 2002

Dear Mr. Michalski,

　　I'm writing this letter to ask you to consider giving me a raise. I have been working at Mitchell George Manufacturing for five years and I really like my job here. I started out as a warehouse packer, and now I work in the shipping department.

　　I feel like I deserve a raise because in the past year I have been given more responsibilities on my shift. I have trained ten new employees and become a team leader. I have increased efficiency in my department by implementing a new flow system that helps us pack and ship the boxes in less time. Therefore, I hope that you will consider giving me a raise.

　　I would like to sit down and discuss this with you as soon as it is convenient for you. Thank you for your time.

Sincerely,
Rogelio Rodriguez

F **Read the letter again and check which of the following Rogelio included in his letter.**

✔ date	✔ what his job is
✔ a thank you to his supervisor for reading the letter	✔ how his job has changed since he has been there
✔ greeting	✔ things he has done to help the company
✔ reason for writing the letter	✔ closing
✔ how long he has been working for the company	

G **Write a letter asking for a raise. Include each part mentioned above.**

Presentation 2: 5–10 min.

Write this question on the board: *Do you deserve a raise?* Make sure students understand *deserve*. Ask students if any of them feel they deserve a raise at their job. If they say *yes*, ask them, *Why?*

If no one says yes, ask students to give you good reasons for getting a raise.

Practice 2: 10–15 min.

E **Read the letter that Rogelio wrote to his supervisor asking for a raise.**

Have students read the letter to themselves. When they are finished, ask them such basic comprehension questions about the letter as: *How long has Rogelio been working at the company? How many new employees has he trained?*

Evaluation 2: 10–15 min.

Ask some students to share their answers with the class.

Presentation 3: 5–10 min.

To review ask students, *What are some ways to ask for a raise?* (Answer: In person or by writing a letter.) Ask students which way they think is better.

Have students make a list of things *not* to say or do when asking for a raise.

Practice 3: 5–10 min.

F **Read the letter again and check which of the following Rogelio included in his letter.**

Students can do this exercise individually.

Evaluation 3:

Observe exercise F and the letter writing in the Application below. Have students use the worksheet below.

Application: 20–25 min.

G **Write a letter asking for a raise. Include each part mentioned above.**

Have students follow Rogelio's letter as an example.

Refer to the *Stand Out Activity Bank 4 CD-ROM,* Unit 7 Worksheet 9, for a self-editing checklist for the letter. *(optional)*

Optional Computer Activity: Have students enter their business letters on the computer, making sure they use all of the correct formatting. Show them how to use a business letter template, available in most word-processing programs.

Optional Internet Activity: Have students write their letter as an e-mail and send it to you.

Instructor's Notes for Lesson 7

LESSON PLAN

Objective:
Review all previous unit objectives
Key vocabulary:
Review all previous vocabulary

Introduction: 5–10 min.

Write *evaluation* and *review* on the board.
Review with students what these words mean and
what their purpose is.

State the Objective: *Today we will review all that
we have done in the past unit in preparation for
the application project to follow.*

 **Refer to *Stand Out Grammar
Challenge 4*, Unit 7 pages 49–51, to
review the passive voice and Unit 7
pages 53–55 to review tag questions.**
(optional)

Ask students as a class to recall all the goals of this
unit without looking at their books. Then remind
them of the goals they haven't mentioned.

Unit goals: *Discuss appropriate workplace
behavior, Use the passive voice, Communicate
problems to a supervisor, Write a letter asking for
a raise, Use tag questions, Discuss workplace
ethics, Work out meanings from context.*

Presentation, Practice, and Evaluation 1:

Do the Learner Log on page 140. Notes are
adjacent to the page.

Presentation 2: 5–10 min.

Review tag questions and passive voice by going
back to pages 124 and 128.

Practice 2: 10–15 min.

A **Add tags to the following
statements to make tag questions.**

B **Take each group of words and
write a sentence in the passive voice.
You may have to add some words.**

Go over the example before students begin.

C **Match the questions and the
answers below.**

Evaluation 2: 10–15 min.

Go over the answers as a class.

STANDARDS CORRELATIONS

CASAS: 7.1.4, 7.2.1, 7.4.1, 7.4.2
SCANS: **Interpersonal** Participates as a Member of a Team,
Teaches Others New Skills, Works with Cultural Diversity
Information Acquires and Evaluates Information,
Organizes and Maintains Information
Systems Understands Systems, Monitors and Corrects
Performance
Basic Skills Reading, Writing, Listening, Speaking
Thinking Skills Creative Thinking, Decision Making, Seeing

Things in the Mind's Eye, Knowing How to Learn, Reasoning
Personal Qualities Responsibility, Self-Esteem, Sociability,
Self-Management, Integrity/Honesty
EFF: **Communication** Convey Ideas in Writing, Speak So
Others Can Understand, Listen Actively
Decision Making Solve Problems and Make Decisions
Interpersonal Guide Others, Cooperate with Others
Lifelong Learning Take Responsibility for Learning, Reflect
and Evaluate, Learn through Research

Review

A. Add tags to the following statements to make tag questions.

1. In this unit, we were taught how to read a flow chart, _____*weren't we?*_____

2. They understand how to make ethical decisions, _____*don't they?*_____

3. You have learned how to ask for a raise, _____*haven't you?*_____

4. They didn't study computer science in school, _____*did they?*_____

5. In the next unit, our teacher will teach us about civics, _____*won't he/she?*_____

6. Tag questions are easy, _____*aren't they?*_____

B. Take each group of words and write a sentence in the passive voice. You may have to add some words.

EXAMPLE:
new office building / build / Lynn Street
A new office building was built on Lynn Street.

1. childcare workers / give / a raise

   The childcare workers were given a raise.

2. machines / repair / mechanics

   The machines were repaired by the mechanics.

3. roses / cut / gardeners

   The roses were cut by the gardeners.

4. this computer / buy / the finance department

   This computer was bought by the finance department.

5. reports / write / two weeks ago

   These reports were written two weeks ago.

6. package / sent / express mail

   The package was sent by express mail.

C. Match the questions and the answers below.

_d_ 1. Why don't we phone human resources?

_c_ 2. Could I speak to you for a second?

_b_ 3. So what we should do is find another office?

_a_ 4. What should we do if we run out of supplies?

a. Let me know right away.

b. That's right.

c. Yes, what do you need?

d. That's a good idea.

D Recall what you learned about each of the following topics. Without looking back in the book, what is the most important thing you learned about each?

Topic	The most important thing I learned
Workplace behavior and grooming	*(Answers will vary.)*
Communicating problems to supervisors	
Workplace ethics	
Asking for a raise	

E Explain what you wrote in the chart to a partner. If your partner wrote something different, add his or her idea to your chart.

F Make a list of four new words or phrases from this unit that you'd like to use. Write a definition and sentence for each. *(Answers will vary.)*

1. Word: _____

   Definition: _____

   Sentence: _____

2. Word: _____

   Definition: _____

   Sentence: _____

3. Word: _____

   Definition: _____

   Sentence: _____

4. Word: _____

   Definition: _____

   Sentence: _____

Presentation 3: 5–10 min. **3**

Go over the instructions for exercises D and E. If students are having trouble, give them an example of something they could write in the chart.

Practice 3: 10–15 min. **3**

 Recall what you learned about each of the following topics. Without looking back in the book, what is the most important thing you learned about each?

 Explain what you wrote in the chart to a partner. If your partner wrote something different, add his or her idea to your chart.

F **Make a list of four new words or phrases from this unit that you'd like to use. Write a definition and sentence for each.**

Evaluation 3: 10–15 min. **3**

Ask a few students to write their sentences on the board. Evaluate as a class.

Application: 1–2 days **1.5+**

The Team Project Activity on the following page is the Application Activity to be done on the next day.

TB

Post-Assessment: Use the *Stand Out* ExamView® Pro *Test Bank* for Unit 7. (optional)

Note: With the *Stand Out* ExamView® Pro *Test Bank* you can design a post-assessment that focuses on what students have learned. It is designed for three purposes:

- To help students practice taking a test similar to current standardized tests.
- To help the teacher evaluate how much the students have learned, retained, and acquired.
- To help students see their progress when they compare their scores to the pre-test they took earlier.

Instructor's Notes for Unit 7 Review

_____

_____

_____

_____

_____

_____

_____

_____

_____

_____

_____

_____

_____

_____

_____

_____

_____

_____

_____

_____

_____

_____

_____

_____

_____

Unit 7 Application Activity

> **TEAM PROJECT:**
> **SOLVE A COMPANY PROBLEM**
> Objective:
> Project designed to apply all the objectives of this unit.
> Product:
> A handout for the class

Introduction: 2–5 min.

Student teams will form action committees to solve a company problem.

They will create a handout explaining the process they went through to come up with their solutions.

State the Objective: *With a team, you will solve a company problem in an action committee and create a handout for the class.*

Note: Shorter classes can do this project over two periods.

Stage 1: 5 min.

Form a human resources action committee with four or five students. Choose positions for each member of your team.

Have students decide who will take which position as described on the student page. Provide well-defined directions on the board for how teams should proceed. Explain to the students that all the students do every task. The students don't go to the next stage until the previous one is complete.

Stage 2: 5 min.

With your group, carefully read the problem below.

Stage 3: 15–20 min.

Use the steps for making an ethical decision on page 130 to go through each possible solution.

Stage 4: 10–15 min.

Make a final decision.

Stage 5: 20–30 min.

Create a handout explaining the process you went through to come up with your decision.

Stage 6: 10–15 min.

Report your final decision to the class.

Consider videotaping the student reports. Students will prepare better for formal presentations if they are videotaped. Another approach would be for students to videotape themselves and polish their presentations.

STANDARDS CORRELATIONS

CASAS: 4.8.1, 4.8.5, 4.8.6
SCANS: **Resources** Allocates Materials and Facility Resources, Allocates Human Resources
Interpersonal Participates as a Member of a Team, Teaches Others New Skills, Exercises Leadership, Works with Cultural Diversity
Information Acquires and Evaluates Information, Organizes and Maintains Information, Interprets and Communicates Information, Uses Computers to Process Information (optional)
Systems Understands Systems, Monitors and Corrects Performance, Improves and Designs Systems
Technology Applies Technology to Task (optional)
Basic Skills Reading, Writing, Listening, Speaking

Thinking Skills Creative Thinking, Decision Making, Problem Solving, Seeing Things in the Mind's Eye, Knowing How to Learn, Reasoning
Personal Qualities Responsibility, Self-Esteem, Sociability, Self-Management, Integrity/Honesty
EFF: **Communication** Read with Understanding, Convey Ideas in Writing, Speak So Others Can Understand, Listen Actively, Observe Critically
Decision Making Solve Problems and Make Decisions, Plan
Interpersonal Guide Others, Resolve Conflict and Negotiate, Advocate and Influence, Cooperate with Others
Lifelong Learning Take Responsibility for Learning, Reflect and Evaluate, Learn through Research, Use Information and Communications Technology (optional)

T E A M
P R O J E C T

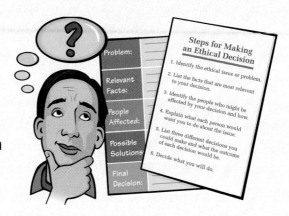

Solve a company problem

With a team, you will solve a company problem in an action committee and create a handout for the class.

1. Form a human resources action committee with four or five students. Choose positions for each member of your team.

Position	Job Description	Student Name
Student 1 Leader	See that everyone speaks English. See that everyone participates.	
Student 2 Secretary	Take notes and write information for handout.	
Student 3 Spokesperson	Report your decision to the class.	
Students 4/5 Member (s)	Help secretary and spokesperson with their work.	

2. With your group, carefully read the problem below.

3. Use the steps for making an ethical decision on page 130 to go through each possible solution.

4. Make a final decision.

5. Create a handout explaining the process you went through to come up with your decision.

6. Report your final decision to the class.

Company: RB Aerospace—Refurbishes and designs airplane interiors

Problem: A group of employees discovers that the quality of some of the parts they are using is not up to standard. They are worried that this may cause safety problems when the aircraft is in use. They have mentioned it to the quality control supervisor, but the factory is on a tight schedule and if they don't deliver this contract on time, they may lose future contracts.

PRONUNCIATION

Intonation. In tag questions, a rising intonation often indicates that you are unsure of the answer, and a falling intonation indicates that you are almost sure of the answer. Listen to these examples and decide if they are rising or falling. Draw arrows on the sentences as in the examples.

1. You work in the library, don't you?
2. She is an engineer, isn't she?
3. He hasn't applied yet, has he?
4. We called them, didn't we?
5. You weren't in the office, were you?
6. He wasn't fired, was he?

LEARNER LOG

In this unit, you learned many things about being on the job. How comfortable do you feel doing each of the skills listed below? Rate your comfort level on a scale of 1 to 4.
1 = Not so comfortable **2** = Need more practice **3** = Comfortable **4** = Very comfortable
If you circle 1 or 2, write down the page number where you can review this skill.

	Comfort Level	Page(s)
Vocabulary		
I can use vocabulary to ask for a raise.	1 2 3 4	132, 133
Life Skill		
I can discuss workplace behavior and grooming.	1 2 3 4	121, 122
I can communicate problems to a supervisor.	1 2 3 4	125, 126, 127
I can discuss workplace ethics.	1 2 3 4	130
I can make ethical decisions.	1 2 3 4	131
I can write a letter asking for a raise.	1 2 3 4	135, 136
Grammar		
I can use the passive voice in the simple past.	1 2 3 4	124
I can use tag questions.	1 2 3 4	128, 129
Academic		
I can interpret a flow chart.	1 2 3 4	126, 127
I can work out meanings from context.	1 2 3 4	132, 133
I can analyze what I've read.	1 2 3 4	133

Reflection
Complete the following statements with your thoughts from this unit. *(Answers will vary.)*

I learned _____

I would like to find out more about _____

I am still confused about _____

Unit 7 Pronunciation and Learner Log

Pronunciation: 10–15 min. (optional)

Intonation

In tag questions, a rising intonation often indicates that you are unsure of the answer, and a falling intonation indicates that you are almost sure of the answer. Listen to these examples and decide if they are rising or falling. Draw arrows on the sentences as in the example.

Play the recording for students, pausing after each sentence. Have them mark the sentences with either rising or falling intonation. Then have them practice saying what they heard.

For additional pronunciation practice: Have students make two lists of statements about their partner. The first list should have five statements that they are sure of (e.g., *She is a student.*) and the second list should contain five statements that they are not sure of (e.g., *She is going to the library after class today.*). In pairs, students practice asking (and answering) checking and confirming questions using the correct intonation.

Learner Log

Presentation 1: 5–10 min.

If needed, review the purpose of the Learner Log. Make sure students understand how to rate the comfort level they feel in reaching the individual goals listed under *Life Skill, Grammar,* and *Academic Skill.* They should rate their comfort level on a scale of 1 to 4:

1. Not so comfortable
2. Need more practice
3. Comfortable
4. Very comfortable

Practice 1: 5–10 min.

If a student circles 1 or 2, he or she should enter the page number on which the skill is featured. The student can then more easily revisit that page and study the material again.

Evaluation 1: 5–10 min.

Finally, emphasize to students the importance of answering the two questions posed in *Reflection*. They are designed to help students assign real-life value to their classroom work.

Instructor's Notes for Unit 7 Team Project, Pronunciation, and Learner Log

_____

_____

_____

_____

_____

_____

_____

_____

_____

_____

_____

_____

_____

_____

_____

_____

_____

_____

_____

_____

LESSON PLAN

Objectives:
Understand civic responsibility and interpret official forms
Key vocabulary:
civic responsibility, registration, ticket, jaywalking, public transportation, jury summons, notify

Pre-Assessment: Use the *Stand Out* ExamView® Pro *Test Bank* for Unit 8. *(optional)*

Warm-up and Review: 5–10 min.

Ask students to recall what they studied in the **workplace units.** Have them make a list of the most important things they learned. Review their points that are related to workplace responsibility.

Introduction: 10–15 min.

Ask students the following questions and ask for a show of hands:

How many of you drive a car?
How many of you have a driver's license?
How many of you vote?
How many of you pay taxes?

State the Objectives: *Today you will define civic responsibility and identify the responsibilities you have here in the United States. In the rest of the unit, you will learn how to handle those responsibilities.*

Presentation 1: 10–15 min.

Ⓐ Why are these things important? Complete the sentences below.

Have students use the words from the vocabulary box to name the documents pictured. Complete this vocabulary exercise as a class. Some students may want to discuss personal experiences dealing with these civic forms. Allow only one example for each form as students will have a chance to share experiences later in the lesson.

Pronunciation: An optional pronunciation activity is found on the final page of this unit. This pronunciation activity may be introduced during any lesson in this unit, especially if students need practice with rising and falling intonation to indicate degree of importance in information. (See pages 160 and 160a for Unit 8 Pronunciation.)

STANDARDS CORRELATIONS

CASAS: 5.6.3
SCANS: **Interpersonal** Participates as a Member of a Team, Works with Cultural Diversity
Information Acquires and Evaluates Information, Organizes and Maintains Information, Interprets and Communicates Information
Basic Skills Reading, Writing, Listening, Speaking
Thinking Skills Creative Thinking, Reasoning

Personal Qualities Responsibility, Sociability, Self-Management
EFF: **Communication** Read with Understanding, Convey Ideas in Writing, Speak So Others Can Understand, Listen Actively
Decision Making Plan
Interpersonal Cooperate with Others

UNIT 8

Civic Responsibility

GOALS

- Understand civic responsibility
- Apply for a driver's license
- Respond to a jury summons
- Fill out a tax form
- Interpret a flow chart
- Write a letter about a community problem
- Use passive modals

Responsibilities

GOAL ▶ Understand civic responsibility

Life skill

A Why are these things important? Complete the sentences below.

car registration	jury summons	taxes	driver's license	traffic ticket

1. A _____*driver's license*_____ permits you to drive a car.

2. _____*Taxes*_____ help pay for government programs.

3. A _____*car registration*_____ shows that you have paid to register your car with the state.

4. A _____*traffic ticket*_____ indicates that you have violated a traffic law.

5. A _____*jury summons*_____ notifies you that the court needs you to appear for jury selection.

B **A group of students from all over the country are attending a workshop about civic responsibility in the United States. Read their conversation and see if you can define *civic responsibility* with your teacher.**

Bita: I never realized how difficult it would be to get adjusted to life in the United States. There are so many things to do.

Consuela: I know. Getting a driver's license and registering my car was very complicated.

Ranjit: In New York we have good public transportation, so I don't have to worry about a car. But I did get a jury summons the other day and I didn't know what I was supposed to do with it.

Ricardo: I got one of those last year and I couldn't understand it, so I threw it away.

Bita: You threw it away? You can't do that. You have to respond.

Consuela : What about tickets? The other day, I got a ticket for jaywalking. I want to fight it, but I don't know where to go.

Ranjit: I think you have to go to court, don't you?

Bita: The most confusing thing I've had to do is pay taxes. Can't they make those forms easier to understand?

Consuela: I agree. Last year, we paid someone to do our taxes.

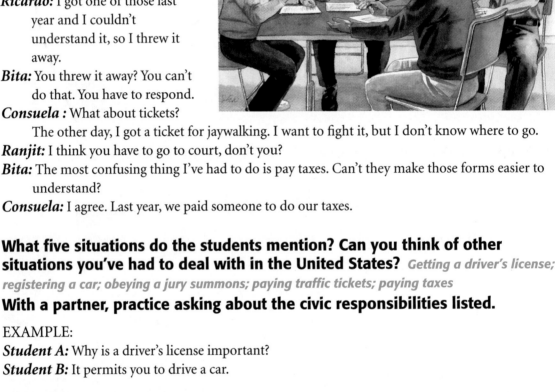

C **What five situations do the students mention? Can you think of other situations you've had to deal with in the United States?** *Getting a driver's license; registering a car; obeying a jury summons; paying traffic tickets; paying taxes*

D **With a partner, practice asking about the civic responsibilities listed.**

EXAMPLE:
Student A: Why is a driver's license important?
Student B: It permits you to drive a car.

E **Have you had to deal with the civic responsibilities listed above? What other responsibilities have you had to deal with? Make a list.** *(Answers may vary. Sample answers below.)*

registering to vote	*having car insurance*
applying for a social security number	*filling out census forms*
sending children to school	*reporting a car accident to police*

F **Active Task:** Talk to a friend or family member about civic responsibility.

Practice 1: 15–20 min.

B **A group of students from all over the country are attending a workshop about civic responsibility in the United States. Read their conversation and see if you can define *civic responsibility* with your teacher.**

Have four volunteers read the conversation aloud. As a class, brainstorm the definition of civic responsiblity.

C **What five situations do the students mention? Can you think of other situations you've had to deal with in the United States?**

Have students get in small groups to find the five situations listed in the conversation. Then have each group list more situations its members have had to deal with.

Evaluation 1: 5–10 min.

After students meet, ask groups to name the situations from the dialog while you list them on the board. Then ask representatives of each group to come up and write the other situations their group came up with.

Presentation 2: 5–10 min.

With the class decide which situations on the board reflect civic responsibility.

Practice 2: 10–15 min.

On a separate sheet of paper, have students write five sentences about the importance of their individual civic responsibilities. Example: *My driver's license permits me to drive a car.*

Evaluation 2: 10–15 min.

Ask volunteers to read their sentences aloud.

 Refer to *Stand Out Grammar Challenge 4*, Unit 8 page 57–59 for practice with related verbs, word order with infinitives, and causative verbs. *(optional)*

Presentation 3: 5–10 min.

D **With a partner, practice asking about the civic responsibilities listed.**

Go over the example with students.

Practice 3: 10–15 min.

E **Have you had to deal with the civic responsibilities listed above? What other responsibilities have you had to deal with? Make a list.**

Evaluation 3: 10–15 min.

Ask for students to help you increase the list of civic responsibilities. Write the list on the board.

 Refer to the *Stand Out Activity Bank 4 CD-ROM*, Unit 8 Worksheet 1, for more exercises on civic responsibility. *(optional)*

Application: 20–25 min.

Have students create a list of interview questions about civic responsibility to ask three classmates. The list should have at least five questions. Write this example question on the board: *Do you have a driver's license?* Give students some time to write their interview questions and then have them walk around and interview at least three students.

F **Active Task: Talk to a friend or family member about civic responsibility.**

Tell students to do this for homework because you will be asking them about it at the next class period.

 Refer to the *Stand Out Activity Bank 4 CD-ROM*, Unit 8 Active Task Checklist. *(optional)*

Remind students to use this checklist as they complete Active Tasks for Lessons 1, 2, and 7.

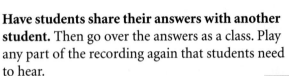

LESSON PLAN

Objective:
Apply for a driver's license
Key vocabulary:
apply, pass, suspended, expire, operate, organ donor

Warm-up and Review: 5–10 min.

Call on students to report their conversations with a friend or family member about civic responsibility.

Introduction: 10–15 min.

A Do you have a driver's license? How did you get it? Share your experience with a group of students.

Have students discuss these questions in small groups.

State the Objective: *Today you will learn what you need to know to apply for a driver's license.*

Presentation 1: 10–15 min.

Have students look at the picture on page 143. Ask: *What is happening in the picture?*

Prepare students for focused listening by reading through the questions in exercise B so they know what to listen for. (See Teaching Hints for more suggestions on focused listening.)

Practice 1: 15–20 min.

 ### B Bita telephones Consuela to ask about how to get a driver's license.

Listen to the conversation and write answers (in your own words) to each of Bita's questions.

You may need to play the recording more than once.

Optional Activity: Have students close their books and just listen to the recording without writing anything. Then have them open their books and fill in whatever they can remember.

Evaluation 1: 10–15 min.

Have students share their answers with another student. Then go over the answers as a class. Play any part of the recording again that students need to hear.

Presentation 2: 5–10 min.

Go over the instructions to exercise C and demonstrate the activity with a student.

Practice 2: 10–15 min.

C With a partner, practice asking and answering the questions above.

Evaluation 2:

Observe and listen to the pairs.

Optional Internet Activity: Have students go on the Internet and research how to get a driver's license in their city. (See Teaching Hints for more suggestions on using computers in the classroom.)

STANDARDS CORRELATIONS

CASAS: 1.9.2
SCANS: **Interpersonal** Participates as a Member of a Team, Works with Cultural Diversity
Information Acquires and Evaluates Information, Organizes and Maintains Information, Interprets and Communicates Information, Uses Computers to Process Information (optional)
Systems Monitors and Corrects Performance
Technology Applies Technology to Task (optional)
Basic Skills Reading, Writing, Listening, Speaking

Personal Qualities Responsibility, Self-Esteem, Sociability, Self-Management, Integrity/Honesty
EFF: **Communication** Read with Understanding, Convey Ideas in Writing, Speak So Others Can Understand, Listen Actively
Interpersonal Guide Others, Cooperate with Others
Lifelong Learning Take Responsibility for Learning, Learn through Research, Use Information and Communications Technology (optional)

LESSON 2

A driver's license

GOAL ▶ Apply for a driver's license

Life skill

A Do you have a driver's license? How did you get it? Share your experience with a group of students.

B Bita telephones Consuela to ask about how to get a driver's license. Listen to the conversation and write answers (in your own words) to each of Bita's questions.

1. If I already have my driver's license from another country, do I still have to take the test?
   Yes, you have to take both written and driving tests.

2. How do I prepare for the written test? _Go to the DMV and get a Driver's Handbook to study the rules of the road._

3. How many questions are on the test? _In California, there are 36._

4. How many questions do I have to get correct? _You can miss five questions._

5. What if I don't pass it the first time? _You may take the test two more times._

6. What do I need to know about the driving test? _You need to make an appointment, and a licensed driver must accompany you._

7. How do I apply for the license? _Fill out an application at the DMV and turn it in._

8. Do I need to make an appointment to turn in my application? _No, you don't._

9. What do I have to do when I turn in my application? _You take the written test, take a vision exam, give proof of your social security number and birthdate, and have your picture taken._

10. How much does it cost? _It costs $12._

   (Answers may vary. Possible answers above.)

C With a partner, practice asking and answering the questions above.

Bita went to the Department of Motor Vehicles (DMV) and got a driver's license application. Fill out the application with help from your teacher.

DRIVER'S LICENSE APPLICATION

Name: *(Answers will vary.)*

Street/PO Box

City	State	Zip

Date of Birth	Sex: ❑ Male ❑ Female	Height	Weight

License Number	Social Security No.	Restricted Code

	Eye Color ❑ Blue ❑ Brown ❑ Black ❑ Green ❑ Gray ❑ Violet ❑ Hazel

Do you have any condition which might affect your ability to operate a motor vehicle, such as:

❑ Seizures or Unconsciousness	❑ Hearing or Vision Problem	❑ Have Your Driving Privileges
❑ Mental Disability	❑ Alcohol or Drug Problem	Ever Been Suspended?

***If any of the above are checked, a letter of explanation must accompany this application. Failure to do so may delay your license.

I certify that the above statements are true. Do you wish to be an organ donor? ❑ Yes ❑ No

Signed X	Date

Please check one of the following:
❑ Regular Driver's License (Class E)
❑ Out-of-State Transfer
   (Must surrender license from other state.)
❑ Applicant Under Age of 18
   *Must Provide School Enrollment Form
   *License Will Expire on 21st Birthday

DUPLICATE LICENSE FEE: $5.00
❑ Duplicate License
❑ Duplicate Class D License
❑ Address change: If you move, you must change your address on your driver's license within twenty days.
❑ Name Change: _____
                          FORMER NAME
*You must attach a copy of your marriage certificate, divorce decree, court order or birth certificate when changing your name.

DEPARTMENT USE ONLY
Your birth certificate must be shown to the examining officer as proof of your age.
The Applicant Named in This Application Passed the Examination Conducted.
At _____ Detachment This _____ Day of _____ 20 ___

Examiner   Unit Number

Restrictions _____

E **With a group, write a paragraph or make a chart that explains step-by-step how to get a driver's license. Compare your paragraph or chart with another group's.**

F **Active Task:** Go to the DMV and pick up a driver's handbook and a driver's license application.

Presentation 3: 5–10 min.   `3`

 D Bita went to the Department of Motor Vehicles (DMV) and got a driver's license application. Fill out the application with help from your teacher.

Make a transparency of this page to use on the overhead projector as you work through the vocabulary.

Practice 3: 10–15 min.   `3`

 E With a group, write a paragraph or make a chart that explains step-by-step how to get a driver's license. Compare your paragraph or chart with another group's.

Allow groups to decide if they want to write a paragraph or make a chart. Discuss the differences between the two and which might be a better way to present certain types of information.

Optional Computer Activity: Have students create their paragraph or chart on the computer. Suggest students add art if it helps explain the steps. (See Teaching Hints for suggestions on using computers in the classroom.)

Evaluation 3: 10–15 min.   `3`

Have students read paragraphs or present their charts.

 ## Application: 20–25 min.   `1.5⁺`

 F Active Task: Go to the DMV and pick up a driver's handbook and a driver's license application.

Optional Internet Activity: Have students go on-line and find a driver's license application to print out and fill in.

Remind students to use the Active Task Checklist for Lesson 2.

 Refer to the *Stand Out Activity Bank 4 CD-ROM,* Unit 8 Worksheet 2 (two pages), for exercises and information on driving safety. *(optional)*

Instructor's Notes for Lesson 2

_____
_____
_____
_____
_____
_____
_____
_____
_____
_____
_____
_____
_____
_____
_____
_____
_____
_____
_____
_____
_____
_____
_____
_____
_____
_____
_____
_____

LESSON PLAN

Objective:
Respond to a jury summons
Key vocabulary:
fair trial, jury, judge, jury selection,
accused of a crime, case, qualifications,
disqualify, attorney, juror, witness

Warm-up and Review: 5–10 min.

Quiz students on the procedures they learned in the previous lesson by asking them to take out a sheet of paper and write down answers to the following questions:

1. *If you already have your driver's license from another country, do you still have to take the test?*

2. *How do you prepare for the written test?*

3. *How many questions are on the test?*

4. *How many questions do you have to get correct?*

5. *What if you don't pass it the first time?*

6. *How do you apply for the license?*

7. *Do you need to make an appointment to turn in your application?*

8. *What do you have to do when you turn in your application?*

9. *How much does it cost?*

Introduction: 10–15 min.

Write *jury duty* **on the board.** See if students can define this for you. Then ask if any students have had experience with jury duty or have received a jury summons in the mail.

State the Objective: *Today you will learn what to do when you receive a jury summons in the mail.*

Presentation 1: 10–15 min.

A Bita and Ranjit are chatting about jury duty in the United States. Read their conversation.

Ask two volunteers to read the conversation aloud.

Practice 1: 15–20 min.

B Discuss the following terms with your teacher. See if you can work out their meanings from the conversation above and by looking at the picture.

See if students can work out the meanings on their own before you begin a class discussion.

Have students read the conversation and underline any unfamiliar words or phrases. Have them again work out the meanings alone, then as a class.

Optional Internet Activity: Have students do some research on the Internet about jury duty in the United States.

Evaluation 1: 10–15 min.

Go over the meanings of unfamiliar words and phrases.

STANDARDS CORRELATIONS

CASAS: 5.3.3, 5.6.3
SCANS: **Interpersonal** Participates as a Member of a Team, Teaches Others New Skills, Works with Cultural Diversity **Information** Acquires and Evaluates Information, Organizes and Maintains Information, Interprets and Communicates Information, Uses Computers to Process Information (optional) **Technology** Applies Technology to Task (optional) **Basic Skills** Reading, Listening, Speaking

Thinking Skills Decision Making, Reasoning
Personal Qualities Responsibility, Sociability, Self-Management, Integrity/Honesty
EFF: **Communication** Read with Understanding, Speak So Others Can Understand, Listen Actively
Interpersonal Cooperate with Others
Lifelong Learning Take Responsibility for Learning, Learn through Research, Use Information and Communications Technology (optional)

GOAL ▶ Respond to a jury summons

Life skill

A **Bita and Ranjit are chatting about jury duty in the United States. Read their conversation.**

Ranjit: Bita, you said we shouldn't throw away a jury summons like Ricardo did. Can you tell me what I'm supposed to do with it?

Bita: Sure. I've had at least three of them.

Ranjit: What are they about, anyway?

Bita: Well, in the United States, anyone accused of a crime has the right to a fair trial, which means a judge and twelve people on a jury listen to the case and make a decision.

Ranjit: Oh, I get it. So can anyone be on a jury?

Bita: No, you have to meet certain qualifications.

Ranjit: Like what?

Bita: First of all, you have to be a U.S. citizen and a resident of the county where the trial is taking place. Also, you have to be able to understand and speak enough English to participate in the jury selection and the trial.

Ranjit: Well, I think I can speak and understand enough English, but I'm not a citizen yet. Does that disqualify me?

Bita: I'm afraid so.

Ranjit: Too bad. It sounds interesting to participate in a trial. So what do I do with this form?

Bita: There should be a series of yes or no questions on it. Answer each of the questions truthfully. Then explain at the bottom why you are not qualified to participate. Some people who are citizens can be excused for other reasons, like financial hardship, medical conditions, or being older than 65. So just fill out the form and then send it back in within 10 days.

Ranjit: That's it?

Bita: That's it. Easy, huh?

B **Discuss the following terms with your teacher. See if you can work out their meanings from the conversation above and by looking at the picture.**

trial	judge
accused of a crime	jury
jury selection	qualifications
attorney	witness
juror	

Go over the jury summons with your teacher.

JURY SUMMONS

Please bring this upper portion with you when you report for jury duty.

| JUROR | You are hereby notified that you have been selected for jury service in the State Trial Courts of _____ County. You are ordered to appear at the court for the following days: *May 3, 4, 5*

Your Group Number: 75
Your Juror Number: 567 |

JUROR QUALIFICATION FORM

DETACH THIS HALF AND RETURN BY MAIL WITHIN 10 DAYS

Name _____

Address _____

City/State/Zip _____

Home Phone _____ Date of Birth _____

Employer _____

Occupation _____

Work Phone _____

Answer each of the following questions under penalty of perjury.

1. Are you a citizen of the United States? ☐ yes ☐ no
2. Are you currently a resident of _____ County? ☐ yes ☐ no
3. Are you 18 years of age or older? ☐ yes ☐ no
4. Do you read, write, speak, and understand the English language?
   (If another person filled out this form, please provide their name, address, and the reasons in the space provided below.) ☐ yes ☐ no
5. Have you ever been convicted or plead guilty to theft or any felony offense? ☐ yes ☐ no
6. Do you have a physical or mental disability that would interfere with or prevent you from serving as a juror? ☐ yes ☐ no
7. Are you 65 years of age or older? ☐ yes ☐ no

If you answered NO to questions 1, 2, 3, or 4, you are automatically excused from jury duty. Please write your reason below and send in the form.

Reason I cannot serve on jury duty: _____

_____

_____

D **Fill out this jury summons with your personal information. What should you do with this form when you have filled it out?** *(Answers will vary.)*

146 **UNIT 8 • Lesson 3**

Presentation 2: 5–10 min.

C Go over the jury summons with your teacher.

Take the students step by step through the jury summons, explaining each part.

Practice 2: 10–15 min.

Have students practice asking and answering the seven *yes/no* questions on the Juror Qualification Form with at least three other students. Demonstrate by asking the first two questions to a student.

Evaluation 2:

Walk around the class and listen.

Presentation 3: 5–10 min.

Have students look back at the conversation on page 145 and write down five questions that Ranjit asks. Have students write the questions as if they were going to ask them. Help them by writing a few of them on the board, such as: *What should I do with my jury summons?* or *Can anyone be on a jury?* Point out that they may have to add information to a question in order for it to make sense. For example, instead of *Like what?* they should write, *What are the qualifications?*

Practice 3: 10–15 min.

Have students interview three students about the jury process and write down their answers. Don't let students being interviewed look in their books for help.

Evaluation 3: 10–15 min.

Ask students if all of the people they interviewed gave the same answers. Have some students share answers with the class.

Application: 20–25 min.

D Fill out this jury summons with your personal information. What should you do with this form when you have filled it out?

Refer to the *Stand Out Activity Bank 4 CD-ROM,* Unit 8 Worksheet 3 (three pages), for reading and comprehension questions about jury duty. *(optional)*

Instructor's Notes for Lesson 3

Go through each portion of the tax form with students, making sure they understand each part.

** Consuela and Ricardo both work and are filing the same tax return. Put a check in the correct box for them. Which box would you check if this were your tax return? Discuss the choices with your teacher.**

** Consuela is filing the tax return for herself, Ricardo, and their three children, Erica, Frankie, and Justin. Fill out the *Exemptions* portion above with information from the Sanchez family. How many exemptions will they get?**

Evaluation 1: 10–15 min.

Go over the answers as a class.

LESSON PLAN

Objective:
Fill out tax forms
Key vocabulary:
income, W2 form, owe, refund, overpaid, tax return, joint, separate, exemption, spouse, dependent, withhold, Internal Revenue Service

Warm-up and Review: 5–10 min. (1.5⁺)

Review the jury summons process with students by calling on them to explain what to do if they receive a jury summons in the mail. If they don't give you enough information, ask for more. Pretend you don't understand the process.

Introduction: 10–15 min. (1.5⁺)

Invite students to share their experiences filling out tax forms.

State the Objective: *Today you will practice filling out tax forms.*

Presentation 1: 10–15 min. (1.5⁺)

A This year Ricardo and Consuela have decided to fill out their own tax forms. Look at the words below and discuss them with your teacher. Look at page 163 to check their meanings.

Practice 1: 15–20 min. (1.5⁺)

B Read each portion of the form on the following two pages and do the exercises that follow.

STANDARDS CORRELATIONS

CASAS: 5.4.1, 5.4.3
SCANS: **Information** Acquires and Evaluates Information, Uses Computers to Process Information (optional)
Systems Understands Systems
Technology Applies Technology to Task (optional)
Basic Skills Reading, Writing, Arithmetic, Listening, Speaking
Thinking Skills Decision Making, Problem Solving, Seeing Things in the Mind's Eye, Reasoning

Personal Qualities Responsibility, Self-Esteem, Self-Management, Integrity/Honesty
EFF: **Communication** Read with Understanding, Speak So Others Can Understand, Listen Actively
Decision Making Use Mathematics in Problem Solving and Communication, Solve Problems and Make Decisions
Lifelong Learning Take Responsibility for Learning, Learn through Research, Use Information and Communications Technology (optional)

GOAL ▶ **Fill out a tax form**

A This year Ricardo and Consuela have decided to fill out their own tax forms. Look at the words below and discuss them with your teacher. Look at page 163 to check their meanings.

income	W2 form	owe	refund	overpaid	tax return
exemption	spouse	dependent	withhold	joint or separate	

B Read each portion of the form on the following two pages and do the exercises that follow.

Form **1040** U.S. Individual Income Tax Return **2003**

Label L A B E L H E R E

Your first name and initial: Consuela E. Last name: Sanchez Your social security number: xxx xx xxxx

If a joint return, spouse's first name and initial: Ricardo H. Last name: Sanchez Spouse's social security number: xxx xx xxxx

Home address (number and street): 2000 Second Avenue Apt. no. # 1

City, town or post office, state, and ZIP code: Loronado, CA 92117

▲ **Important!** ▲ You must enter your SSN(s) above.

Filing Status

Check only one box.

1		Single
2	✓	Married filing joint return (even if only one had income)
3		Married filing separate return. Enter spouse's ss# above and full name here. ▶ _____
4		Head of household
5		Qualifying widow(er) with dependent child (year spouse died _____)

C Consuela and Ricardo both work and are filing the same tax return. Put a check in the correct box for them. Which box would you check if this were your tax return? Discuss the choices with your teacher.

Exemptions

6a ☑ **Yourself.** If your parent (or someone else) can claim you as a dependent on his or her tax return, **do not** check box 6a

b ☑ **Spouse**

c ☑ **Dependents**

(1) First name	Last name	(2) SS#	(3) Relationship to you
Erica	Sanchez		daughter
Frankie	Sanchez		son
Justin	Sanchez		son

d   Total number of exemptions claimed   5

D Consuela is filing the tax return for herself, Ricardo, and their three children, Erica, Frankie, and Justin. Fill out the *Exemptions* portion above with information from the Sanchez family. How many exemptions will they get?

They will get 5 exemptions.

E **Look at the information below and answer the following questions.**

Income	7	Wages, salaries, tips, etc. Attach Form(s) W–2	7	40,968	79
	8	Taxable interest	8	36	79
	9	Add the amounts for lines 7 and 8. This is your total income.	9	41,005	58

1. How much did the Sanchez family earn at their jobs last year? _____ *$40,968.79* _____

2. How much interest did they get from their savings? _____ *$36.79* _____

3. What is their total income? _____ *$41,005.58* _____ Write this number in the form.

F **Help Consuela fill out the *Tax and Credits* portion below by following the instructions on each line. You will need to consult the tax schedule below to fill in line 15.**

Tax and Credits	10	Amount from line 9	10	41,005	58
	11	Enter your standard deduction from the left.	11	7,350	00
Standard Deduction Single: $4,400 Head of Household: $6,450 Married Filing Jointly or Qualifying Widow(er): $7,350 Married Filing Separately: $3,675	12	Subtract line 11 from line 10	12	33,655	58
	13	If line 10 is less than $96,700, multiply $2,800 by the total number of exemptions claimed on line 6d	13	14,000	00
	14	Subtract line 13 from line 12. This is your taxable income. If line 13 is more than line 12, enter 0.	14	19,655	58
	15	Tax (see tax schedule)	15	2,951	00
Payments	16	Federal income tax withheld from forms W–2	16	3320	38
Refund	17	If line 16 is more than line 15, subtract line 15 from line 16. This is the amount you overpaid. You will receive a refund.	17	369	38
Amount You Owe	18	If line 15 is more than line 16, subtract line 16 from line 15. This is the amount you owe.	18		

G **Will the Sanchez family owe taxes or get a refund?**

_____ *get a refund* _____

2003 Tax Table

At least	But less than	Single	Married filing jointly	Married filing separately	Head of a houshold
			Your tax is—		
19,000					
19,400	19,450	2,914	2,914	2,914	2,914
19,450	19,500	2,921	2,921	2,921	2,921
19,500	19,550	2,929	2,929	2,929	2,929
19,550	19,600	2,936	2,936	2,936	2,936
19,600	19,650	2,944	2,944	2,944	2,944
19,650	19,700	2,951	2,951	2,951	2,951
19,700	19,750	2,959	2,959	2,959	2,959
19,750	19,800	2,966	2,966	2,966	2,966

Presentation 2: 5–10 min.

Now, have the students complete the math portion of the presentation. First ask students where they should get the numbers to fill in on the tax forms. (Answer: W2s, tax schedules, tax forms)

Practice 2: 10–15 min.

Go through each portion of the tax form with students, making sure they understand each part.

E **Look at the information below and answer the following questions.**

F **Help Consuela fill out the *Tax and Credits* portion below by following the instructions on each line. You will need to consult the tax schedule below to fill in line 15.**

Evaluation 2: 10–15 min.

Go over the answers as a class. Put up the transparency of the tax forms from *Stand Out* student book page 148 to make the discussion clearer.

G **Will the Sanchez family owe taxes or get a refund?**

Presentation 3: 5–10 min.

Refer to the *Stand Out Activity Bank 4 CD-ROM,* Unit 8 Worksheet 4 (two pages) for an exercise where students can practice tax form calculations. Print out a copy for each student and go over the instructions. (optional)

Practice 3: 10–15 min.

In teams, have students complete the worksheet.

Evaluation 3: 10–15 min.

Ask a volunteer from each team to come up to the board and do one of the calculations. Review all vocabulary as a class.

Application: 20–25 min.

(1.5+)

(H) Imagine that you are single and have no dependents. Fill out the tax form below. Sample numbers have been filled in for you.

Optional Internet Activity: Have student go on-line to find the tax forms they need to fill out. (See Teaching Hints for more suggestions on using computers in the classroom.)

Instructor's Notes for Lesson 4

Imagine that you are single and have no dependents. Fill out the tax form below. Sample numbers have been filled in for you. *(Answers will vary.)*

Form **1040** U.S. Individual Income Tax Return 2003

Label

LABEL HERE

Your first name and initial	Last name	Your social security number
If a joint return, spouse's first name and initial	Last name	Spouse's social security number
Home address (number and street).		Apt. no.
City, town or post office, state, and ZIP code		▲ **Important!** ▲ You must enter your SSN(s) above.

Filing Status

Check only one box.

1 ☐ Single
2 ☐ Married filing joint return (even if only one had income)
3 ☐ Married filing separate return. Enter spouse's ss# above and full name here. ▶
4 ☐ Head of household
5 ☐ Qualifying widow(er) with dependent child (year spouse died   )

Exemptions

6a ☐ **Yourself.** If your parent (or someone else) can claim you as a dependent on his or her tax return, **do not** check box 6a
b ☐ **Spouse**
c ☐ **Dependents**

(1) First name Last name	(2) SS#	(3) Relationship to you

d Total number of exemptions claimed

Income

7	Wages, salaries, tips, etc. Attach Form(s) W–2	7	29,654	32
8	Taxable interest	8	12	70
9	Add the amounts for lines 7 and 8. This is your total income.	9		

Tax and Credits

Standard Deduction
Single: $4,400
Head of Household: $6,450
Married Filing Jointly or Qualifying Widow(er): $7,350
Married Filing Separately: $3,675

10	Amount from line 9	10		
11	Enter your standard deduction from the left.	11		
12	Subtract line 11 from line 10	12		
13	If line 10 is less than $96,700, multiply $2,800 by the total number of exemptions claimed on line 6d	13		
14	Subtract line 13 from line 12. This is your taxable income. If line 13 is more than line 12, enter 0.	14		
15	Tax (see tax schedule)	15		

Payments

| 16 | Federal income tax withheld from forms W–2 | 16 | 3,320 | 38 |

Refund

| 17 | If line 16 is more than line 15, subtract line 15 from line 16. This is the amount you overpaid. You will receive a refund. | 17 | | |

Amount You Owe

| 18 | If line 15 is more than line 16, subtract line 16 from line 15. This is the amount you owe. | 18 | | |

2003 Tax Table

At least	But less than	Single	Married filing jointly	Married filing separately	Head of a houshold
		Your tax is—			
24,000					
24,400	24,450	3,664	3,664	3,892	3,664
24,450	24,500	3,671	3,671	3,906	3,671
24,500	24,550	3,679	3,679	3,919	3,679
24,550	24,600	3,686	3,686	3,933	3,686
24,600	24,650	3,694	3,694	3,947	3,694
24,650	24,700	3,701	3,701	3,961	3,701
24,700	24,750	3,709	3,709	3,974	3,709
24,750	24,800	3,716	3,716	3,988	3,716

Elections

GOAL ▶ **Interpret a flow chart**

A **The students are chatting about local elections. Read their conversation. Do you agree with the speakers? Why is it important to understand the electoral process?**

Ranjit: Elections for a new mayor are coming up here in New York. Have any of you participated in an election before?

Bita: I have. I just became a U.S. citizen last year, so I finally got to vote.

Ricardo: So if we're not citizens, we don't need to pay attention to the elections, do we?

Bita: Oh, I disagree. Even when I wasn't a citizen, I participated in local town meetings and city council meetings.

Consuela: Why?

Bita: Because I live in this community just like everyone else, and I want my voice to be heard.

Ranjit: I agree with you, Bita. I think it's important that we voice our opinions on local issues in our community. I've been listening to the candidates' speeches to see who I would vote for. But I don't really understand how the election process works.

Bita: Let's look at the chart our teacher gave us.

B **Read the flow chart and discuss it with your class.**

LESSON PLAN

Objective:
Interpret a flow chart on the electoral process
Key vocabulary:
elected, position, step down, term, ballots, announce, nomination, candidate, campaign

Warm-up and Review: 5–10 min.

Talk about filling out tax forms. Do students think they can do it by themselves next time?

Introduction: 10–15 min.

Ask students who the *president* **is.** Ask students who the *vice president* is. Ask students how these people were chosen to lead our country.

State the Objective: *Today you will learn the steps of the electoral process.*

Presentation 1: 10–15 min.

Have a brief discussion about local elections and what happens in a community when elections are coming up (ad campaigns, voter registration drives, etc.).

Practice 1: 15–20 min.

 The students are chatting about local elections. Read their conversation. Do you agree with the speakers? Why is it important to understand the electoral process?

Have students read the conversation to themselves. Then call on two students to read the conversation aloud. Answer any questions students have about what they read.

Evaluation 1: 10–15 min.

Discuss the questions as a class, checking for comprehension.

Presentation 2: 5–10 min.

 Read the flow chart and discuss it with your class.

STANDARDS CORRELATIONS

CASAS: 5.1.4
SCANS: **Interpersonal** Participates as a Member of a Team, Works with Cultural Diversity
Information Acquires and Evaluates Information, Organizes and Maintains Information, Interprets and Communicates Information, Uses Computers to Process Information (optional)
Systems Monitors and Corrects Performance
Technology Applies Technology to Task (optional)
Basic Skills Reading, Writing, Listening, Speaking

Thinking Skills Decision Making, Seeing Things in the Mind's Eye
Personal Qualities Sociability
EFF: **Communication** Read with Understanding, Convey Ideas in Writing, Speak So Others Can Understand, Listen Actively
Decision Making Plan
Interpersonal Cooperate with Others
Lifelong Learning Learn through Research, Use Information and Communications Technology (optional)

Practice 2: 10–15 min.   **2⁺**

C **Explain the words in the box to your partner. Then have your partner explain the electoral process to you using these words.**

Evaluation 2: 10–15 min.   **2⁺**

Observe the pairs. Ask a few volunteers to explain the electoral process to the class.

Presentation 3: 5–10 min.   **3**

Have students look back at the flow chart on page 150. Instead of discussing the content this time, discuss the presentation of the chart.

Practice 3: 10–15 min.   **3**

In groups of four or five, have students recreate the flow chart on page 150. Ask them to be creative and think of a different way to present the same information.

Optional: Let students use computers to create their presentations. (See Teaching Hints for suggestions on using computers in the classroom.)

Evaluation 3: 10–15 min.   **3**

Have each group share their flow chart. Have the class vote on the best re-creation.

Refer to the *Stand Out Activity Bank 4 CD-ROM,* Unit 8 Worksheet 5, for more about the electoral process, specifically about registering to vote. *(optional)*

Application: 20–25 min.   **1.5⁺**

D **Write a paragraph about the electoral process. Use some of these sequencing transitions in your paragraph.**

If there's time, have students peer-correct one another's work.

Refer to the *Stand Out Activity Bank 4 CD-ROM,* Unit 8 Worksheet 6 (two pages), for a self-editing and a peer-editing checklist. *(optional)*

Instructor's Notes for Lesson 5

C Explain the words in the box to your partner. Then have your partner explain the electoral process to you using these words.

elected	position	to step down	term	ballots	to announce

D Write a paragraph about the electoral process. Use some of these sequencing transitions in your paragraph.

Next,	Finally,	First of all,
After that,	In conclusion,	Secondly,
At the next stage,	In summary,	Thirdly,

(Answers will vary.)

_____

_____

_____

_____

_____

_____

_____

_____

_____

_____

_____

_____

_____

_____

_____

_____

_____

_____

Problems in your community

| GOAL ▶ | Write a letter about a community problem | *Life skill* |

A Look at the photos below and identify what these local community problems might be. Discuss some possible solutions for each problem with your group.

1.

3.

2.

4.

B List each problem below. Write one solution for each problem.

(Answers may vary. Possible answers below.)

Problems	Solutions
1. *graffiti*	*repaint*
2. *traffic jams*	*improve public transportation*
3. *litter*	*community clean-up program*
4. *overcrowded schools*	*build new schools*

C Share your solutions with the class and, as a class, come up with the best solution for each problem.

LESSON PLAN

Objective:
Write a letter about a community problem
Key vocabulary:
graffiti, garbage, overcrowded, freeway, gang, street corner, local official, facts, anecdotes

Warm-up and Review: 5–10 min.

Without looking at their books, ask students to write down the six steps of the electoral process. Go over the answers as a class. How many students got them right?

Introduction: 10–15 min.

Ask students: *What are some problems in your community that you would like solved?* Write the problems that they mention on the board.

State the Objective: *Today you will come up with solutions for different community problems and write a business letter to a local official.*

Presentation 1: 10–15 min.

Ⓐ Look at the photos below and identify what these local community problems might be. Discuss some possible solutions for each problem with your group.

As a class, discuss each photo. List the four problems on the board.

Practice 1: 15–20 min.

In small groups, have students discuss each problem and come up with a list of solutions. Each group should assign a member to take notes and a spokesperson to report to the class.

Evaluation 1: 10–15 min.

Have a spokesperson from each group report their solutions for each problem to the class. Make a list of all the solutions on the board.

Presentation 2: 5 min.

Tell students they will complete the next exercise individually, writing down each problem and choosing just one solution that they think is best.

Practice 1 differs from Practice 2 in that students choose from all of the possble solutions in Practice 2.

Practice 2: 10–15 min.

Ⓑ List each problem below. Write one solution for each problem.

Evaluation 2: 15–20 min.

Ⓒ Share your solutions with the class and, as a class, come up with the best solution for each problem.

Ask each student to choose the problem that interests them the most. Have a few students volunteer their answers.

STANDARDS CORRELATIONS

CASAS: 5.6.1
SCANS: **Interpersonal** Participates as a Member of a Team, Works with Cultural Diversity
Information Acquires and Evaluates Information, Organizes and Maintains Information, Interprets and Communicates Information, Uses Computers to Process Information (optional)
Technology Applies Technology to Task (optional)
Basic Skills Writing, Listening, Speaking
Thinking Skills Creative Thinking, Decision Making, Problem

Solving, Seeing Things in the Mind's Eye, Reasoning
Personal Qualities Responsibility, Sociability
EFF: **Communication** Convey Ideas in Writing, Speak So Others Can Understand, Listen Actively, Observe Critically
Decision Making Solve Problems and Make Decisions, Plan
Interpersonal Resolve Conflict and Negotiate, Advocate and Influence, Cooperate with Others
Lifelong Learning Reflect and Evaluate, Learn through Research, Use Information and Communications Technology (optional)

Presentation 3: 5–10 min.   **3**

Go through each item required in exercise D and ask students why this information is important to include in a business letter to a local official.

Practice 3: 15–20 min.   **3**

D **Prepare to write a business letter about a problem in your community. Choose one of the problems you discussed with your group or a problem in your own community. Before writing the letter, fill in the information below.**

Evaluation 3:   **3**

Walk around helping students and developing ideas, and think of the best person to contact about the problem.

Application: 20–25 min.   **1.5⁺**

Note for shorter classes: It will be easier for students to write the letter if they have completed exercise D in class or as homework first.

E **Choose one of the problems and solutions that you discussed on the previous page and write a letter to a local official. Format it like a business letter.**

Optional Activity: Have students use the Internet or the phone book to find the name and address of the official to whom they will send their letter to. Then have students actually mail their letters.

 Refer to the *Stand Out Activity Bank 4 CD-ROM,* Unit 8 Worksheet 7, for an editing checklist to use with your letter. *(optional)*

Instructor's Notes for Lesson 6

Prepare to write a business letter about a problem in your community. Choose one of the problems you discussed with your group or a problem in your own community. Before writing the letter, fill in the information below.

Date: _____*(Answers will vary.)*_____

Your name and address: _____

_____

Official's name and address (Research this information.): _____

_____

State the problem: _____

_____

_____

_____

Facts or anecdotes about the problem: _____

_____

_____

_____

Suggested solutions: _____

_____

_____

Closing: _____

E **Choose one of the problems and solutions that you discussed on the previous page and write a letter to a local official. Format it like a business letter.** *(Answers will vary.)*

LESSON 7 What's your platform?

GOAL ▶ Use passive modals   *Grammar*

A Listen to the speeches from three people running for mayor of your city. For the first speech, put a check next to everything the candidate promises to do for you. For the second two speeches, write down what they promise to do for you. You will hear each speech two times.

Antonio Juliana promises to:

❏ clean up the streets

❏ lower tuition fees

❏ improve public transportation

☑ decrease gang violence

☑ get kids off the streets

☑ help the homeless people

❏ increase environmental awareness

Antonio Juliana

Gary Hurt promises to:

1. clean up the beaches

2. *improve public*
   transportation

3. *create parks*

Gary Hurt

Kwan Tan

Kwan Tan promises to:

1. *build more schools*

2. *lower community college tuition*

3. *implement education standards*

4. *start a parent-teacher program*

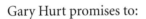

B Who would you vote for if you were interested in:

the environment? *Gary Hurt*

education? *Kwan Tan*

safe streets? *Antonio Juliana*

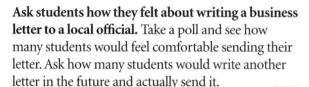

LESSON PLAN

Objectives:
Use passive modals, Write and give a speech
Key vocabulary:
running for office, tuition, gang violence, homeless, environmental awareness, implement, standards, invest

Warm-up and Review: 5–10 min. `1.5+`

Ask students how they felt about writing a business letter to a local official. Take a poll and see how many students would feel comfortable sending their letter. Ask how many students would write another letter in the future and actually send it.

Introduction: 10–15 min. `1.5+`

Ask students if they know who the mayor of their city is. Ask them if they have ever seen him or her on TV or in the newspaper. See what they know about their mayor.

State Objective: *Today you will hear speeches from three different mayoral candidates, analyze the speeches, and write your own speech to give to the class.*

Presentation 1: 10–15 min. `1.5+`

Prepare students for the listening exercise by telling them they will hear speeches from three different mayoral candidates. Go over the list of promises under *Antonio Juliana,* explaining each promise. (See Teaching Hints for suggestions on focused listening.)

Practice 1: 15–20 min. `1.5+`

A Listen to the speeches from three people running for mayor of your city. For the first speech, put a check next to everything the candidate promises to do for you. For the second two speeches, write down what they promise to do for you. You will hear each speech two times.

B Who would you vote for if you were interested in the environment? education? safe streets?

Have students do this exercise alone and then have them share their answers with a partner.

Evaluation 1: 10–15 min. `1.5+`

Go over the answers as a class.

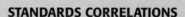

STANDARDS CORRELATIONS

CASAS: 5.1.4, 5.1.6
SCANS: **Interpersonal** Participates as a Member of a Team, Exercises Leadership, Works with Cultural Diversity
Information Acquires and Evaluates Information, Organizes and Maintains Information, Interprets and Communicates Information
Systems Monitors and Corrects Performance
Technology Applies Technology to Task (optional)
Basic Skills Reading, Writing, Listening, Speaking
Thinking Skills Creative Thinking, Decision Making

Personal Qualities Responsibility, Self-Esteem, Sociability, Self-Management, Integrity/Honesty
EFF: **Communication** Read with Understanding, Convey Ideas in Writing, Speak So Others Can Understand, Listen Actively, Observe Critically
Decision Making Solve Problems and Make Decisions, Plan
Interpersonal Advocate and Influence, Cooperate with Others
Lifelong Learning Reflect and Evaluate, Learn through Research, Use Information and Communications Technology (optional)

Presentation 2: 5–10 min.

Read Kwan Tan's speech.

Read Kwan's speech to your students. Ask them some basic comprehension questions about it.

Practice 2: 10–15 min.

Go over the first example in exercise D with students. This may be too difficult for them to do without presenting the chart in exercise E on the next page, so do that first if you need to.

Ⓓ Write sentences to describe the issues Kwan Tan wants to change. Use noun clauses following the example below.

Evaluation 2: 10–15 min.

Have students write their answers on the board. If there are a lot of mistakes, go immediately to exercise E, present it, and then have students go back to this exercise and try to fix their mistakes.

C Read Kwan Tan's speech.

Good evening, and thank you for coming tonight! This community has given me so many opportunities and, in running for mayor, I hope to give something back to the city that welcomed me as an immigrant, educated me through my teen years, and supported me as I opened my first business.

First on my agenda is education. I will make sure your tax dollars are used to build more schools, so our children won't have to sit in overcrowded classrooms. I'll lower the tuition at our community colleges, so all of us will have a chance to continue our education. I'll implement standards to ensure that schools are teaching our kids what they need to know. I'll start a parent-involvement program that encourages parents to participate actively in their kids' schools. Our children are the future of our community, and we should invest time and money in their success.

Vote for me on Election Day and you'll have schools and a community to be proud of!

D Write sentences to describe the issues Kwan Tan wants to change. Use noun clauses following the example below.

EXAMPLE:
Kwan Tan wants to build more schools.
She thinks that **more schools should be built.** *(Possible answers below.)*

1. Kwan Tan wants to lower tuition fees at community colleges.

She says that _tuition fees at community colleges should be lowered._

2. Kwan Tan wants to implement standards in schools.

She thinks that _standards should be implemented in schools._

3. Kwan Tan wants to encourage parents to participate in their kids' schools.

She believes that _parents should participate in their kids' schools._

4. Kwan Tan wants to invest time and money in children.

She emphasizes that _we should invest time and money in children._

E Study the chart below with your teacher.

Passive modals				
Passive subject	**Modal**	***be***	**Past participle**	**Example sentence**
Schools	should	be	built	More schools should be built.
Taxes	need to	be	increased	Taxes need to be increased.
Children	must	be	protected	Children must be protected.
Parents	have to	be	involved	Parents have to be involved.

F Think of three problems you would like to solve in your community. Write three sentences using passive modals.

1. _____ *(Answers will vary.)* _____

2. _____

3. _____

G Kwan's election speech has three parts. Look for each part in her speech on page 155.

Introduction She introduces herself and explains why she is running for office.

Body She tells her audience what she plans to do if she is elected.

Conclusion She reminds her audience to vote and tells them once again what changes she will make to the community.

H Imagine you are running for mayor of your community. How would you introduce yourself? What problems would you like to solve? On a separate sheet of paper, write a speech that you would give if you were running for mayor. Practice it and give your speech to the class.

 I **Active Task:** Look in the newspaper or on the Internet to find who is mayor or who is running for mayor in your town or city. What issues are they concerned about? What problems do they want to solve?

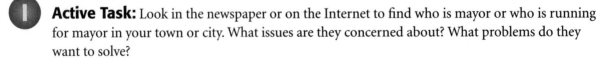

Presentation 3: 5–10 min.

E **Study the chart below with your teacher.**

Practice 3: 10–15 min.

F **Think of three problems you would like to solve in your community. Write three sentences using passive modals.**

 Refer to *Stand Out Grammar Challenge 4,* Unit 8 pages 61–63 for more practice with passive modals. *(optional)*

Evaluation 3: 10–15 min.

Ask volunteers to share their sentences with the class.

 Refer to the *Stand Out Activity Bank 4 CD-ROM,* Unit 8 Worksheet 8, for additional exercises with passive modals. *(optional)*

Application: 20–35 min.

G **Kwan's election speech has three parts. Look for each part in her speech on page 155.**

H **Imagine you are running for mayor of your community. How would you introduce yourself? What problems would you like to solve? On a separate sheet of paper, write a speech that you would give if you were running for mayor. Practice it and give your speech to the class.**

Give students an idea of how long their speech must be. Two to four minutes is probably reasonable if you have a large class. Depending on the amount of time you have, you may have to schedule the speeches over the next couple of class periods to give everyone a chance.

 I **Active Task: Look in the newspaper or on the Internet to find who is mayor or who is running for mayor in your town or city. What issues are they concerned about? What problems do they want to solve?**

Remind students to use the Active Task Checklist for Lesson 7.

Instructor's Notes for Lesson 7

_____

_____

_____

_____

_____

_____

_____

_____

_____

_____

_____

_____

_____

_____

_____

_____

_____

_____

_____

_____

LESSON PLAN

Objective:
Review all previous unit objectives
Key vocabulary:
Review all previous vocabulary

Warm-up and Review: 5–10 min.

Ask students if they found any information about their mayor in the newspaper or on the Internet. What issues are important to this person? Be prepared to help students answer this question in case they didn't do any research for homework.

Introduction: 1 min.

Write *evaluation* **and** *review* **on the board.** Recall with students what these words mean and what their purpose is.

State Objective: *Today we will review all that we have done in the past unit in preparation for the application project to follow.*

Ask students as a class to recall all the goals of this unit without looking at their books. Then remind them of the goals they haven't mentioned.

Unit goals: *Understand civic responsibility, Apply for a driver's license, Respond to a jury summons, Fill out tax forms, Interpret a flow chart on the electoral process, Write a letter about a community problem, Use passive modals.*

Presentation, Practice, and Evaluation 1:

Do the Learner Log on page 160. Notes are adjacent to the page.

Presentation 2: 5–10 min.

Ask students what topics they learned about in this unit. Make a list on the board.

Go over the instructions for exercise A and B.

Practice 2: 10–15 min.

A Recall what you learned about each of the following topics. Without looking back in the book, what is the most important thing you learned about each?

B Are the following statements true or false?

C What are three problems in your community you'd like to solve? How would you solve them?

When students finish, ask a few volunteers to state one problem and other volunteers to guess at a solution for each.

Evaluation 2: 10–15 min.

Discuss the answers as a class.

Refer to *Stand Out Grammar Challenge 4*, Unit 8, pages 61–64 for review practice with passive modals. *(optional)*

STANDARDS CORRELATIONS

CASAS: 7.1.4, 7.2.1, 7.4.1, 7.4.2
SCANS: **Interpersonal** Participates as a Member of a Team, Teaches Others New Skills, Works with Cultural Diversity
Information Acquires and Evaluates Information, Organizes and Maintains Information
Systems Understands Systems, Monitors and Corrects Performance
Basic Skills Reading, Writing, Listening, Speaking
Thinking Skills Creative Thinking, Decision Making, Seeing

Things in the Mind's Eye, Knowing How to Learn, Reasoning
Personal Qualities Responsibility, Self-Esteem, Sociability, Self-Management, Integrity/Honesty
EFF: **Communication** Convey Ideas in Writing, Speak So Others Can Understand, Listen Actively
Decision Making Solve Problems and Make Decisions
Interpersonal Guide Others, Cooperate with Others
Lifelong Learning Take Responsibility for Learning, Reflect and Evaluate, Learn through Research

A Recall what you learned about each of the following topics. Without looking back in the book, what is the most important thing you learned about each?

Topic	The most important thing I learned
A jury summons	*(Answers will vary.)*
A driver's license	
Income tax	
Community problems	
The electoral process	

B Are the following statements true or false?

○ True	● False	You have to be 18 to apply for a driver's license.
● True	○ False	You must reply to a jury summons.
● True	○ False	You have to be a U.S. citizen to serve on a jury.
○ True	● False	Everyone must file his or her income tax return separately.
● True	○ False	If you pay too much tax, the government will give you a refund.
○ True	● False	Only U.S. citizens can get involved in the community.

C What are three problems in your community you'd like to solve? How would you solve them? *(Answers will vary.)*

Problem	Solution
1.	
2.	
3.	

D **Rewrite each of these sentences using a passive modal.**

1. We must protect the environment.

   The environment must be protected.

2. They should reduce our taxes.

   Our taxes should be reduced.

3. They need to invest money in our educational system.

   Money needs to be invested in our educational system.

4. We have to reduce the driving speed limit.

   The driving speed limit has to be reduced.

E **Make a list of three new words or phrases from this unit that you'd like to use. Write a definition and sentence for each.** *(Answers will vary.)*

1. Word: _____

   Definition: _____

   Sentence: _____

2. Word: _____

   Definition: _____

   Sentence: _____

3. Word: _____

   Definition: _____

   Sentence: _____

F **How have your learning strategies improved during this course? Make a list of ways you have improved your strategies for learning.**

Vocabulary: _____ *(Answers will vary.)* _____

_____

Grammar: _____

_____

Life Skills: _____

_____

Academic Skills: _____

_____

Presentation 3: 5–10 min.

D **Rewrite each of these sentences using a passive modal.**

Practice 3: 10–15 min.

E **Make a list of three new words or phrases from this unit that you'd like to use. Write a definition and sentence for each.**

F **How have your learning strategies improved during this course? Make a list of ways you have improved your strategies for learning.**

Provide students with an example like this: *Vocabulary—I can find the meaning of words in context without using a dictionary.*

Evaluation 3: 10–15 min.

Ask volunteers to write their answers on the board.

Application: 1–2 days

The Team Project Activity on the following page is the Application Activity to be done on the next day.

Post-Assessment: Use the *Stand Out* ExamView® Pro *Test Bank* for Unit 8. (optional)

Note: With the Stand Out ExamView® Pro Test Bank you can design a post-assessment that focuses on what students have learned. It is designed for three purposes:

• To help students practice taking a test similar to current standardized tests.

• To help the teacher evaluate how much the students have learned, retained, and acquired.

• To help students see their progress when they compare their scores to the pre-test they took earlier.

Instructor's Notes for Unit 8 Review

Unit 8 Application Activity

> **TEAM PROJECT:**
> **CONDUCT AN ELECTION**
>
> Objective: Project designed to apply all the objectives of this unit.
> Products: A ballot, a ballet box, a campaign speech, an election

Introduction: 2–5 min.

Student teams will choose a candidate for class president, prepare a ballot, and conduct an election.

Note: Shorter classes can do this project over two class periods.

State the Objective: *With a team you will prepare a candidate for an election. As a class, you will conduct an election.*

Stage 1: 5 min.

Form a campaign committee with four or five students. Choose positions for each member of your team.

Have students decide who will take which position as described on the student page. Provide well-defined directions on the board for how teams should proceed. Explain to the students that all the students do every task. The students don't go to the next stage until the previous one is complete.

Stage 2: 10–15 min.

With your team, decide who will be running for class president. Announce the nomination to the class.

Have each team select the member they think will make the best class president.

Stage 3: 15–20 min.

Members: Create a ballot with all the nominees' names on it. Make a ballot box for students to put their ballots in after they vote.

Assign one team to construct a ballot box.

Refer to the *Stand Out Activity Bank 4 CD-ROM*, Unit 8 Worksheet 9, for a sample ballot which can be altered into a template for your class. *(optional)*

Stage 4: 20–30 min.

Decide what issues are most important and write a campaign speech.

Set a time limit for presidential speeches.

Stage 5: 20–30 min.

Candidates give speeches to the class.

Optional Activity: Videotape the speeches.

Stage 6: 5–10 min.

Vote.

Pass out ballots to students, including the candidates, and have everyone secretly vote and put their completed ballots into the ballot box.

Optional Activity: Have students set up voting booths for privacy.

Stage 7: 10–15 min.

Count the ballots and announce the winner.

Have one member from each team, but none of the candidates, meet to tally the votes. Votes should be counted twice to make sure. Choose one member to announce the winner.

Optional Activity: Throw a victory party!

STANDARDS CORRELATIONS

CASAS: 4.8.1, 4.8.5, 4.8.6
SCANS: **Resources** Allocates Materials and Facility Resources, Allocates Human Resources
Interpersonal Participates as a Member of a Team, Teaches Others New Skills, Exercises Leadership, Works with Cultural Diversity
Information Acquires and Evaluates Information, Organizes and Maintains Information, Interprets and Communicates Information, Uses Computers to Process Information (optional)
Systems Understands Systems, Monitors and Corrects Performance, Improves and Designs Systems
Technology Applies Technology to Task (optional)
Basic Skills Reading, Writing, Listening, Speaking

Thinking Skills Creative Thinking, Decision Making, Problem Solving, Seeing Things in the Mind's Eye, Knowing How to Learn, Reasoning
Personal Qualities Responsibility, Self-Esteem, Sociability, Self-Management, Integrity/Honesty
EFF: **Communication** Read with Understanding, Convey Ideas in Writing, Speak So Others Can Understand, Listen Actively, Observe Critically
Decision Making Solve Problems and Make Decisions, Plan
Interpersonal Guide Others, Resolve Conflict and Negotiate, Advocate and Influence, Cooperate with Others
Lifelong Learning Take Responsibility for Learning, Reflect and Evaluate, Learn through Research, Use Information and Communications Technology (optional)

TEAM PROJECT

Conduct an election

With a team, you will prepare a candidate for an election. As a class, you will conduct an election.

1. Form a campaign committee with four or five students. Choose positions for each member of your team.

Position	Job Description	Student Name
Student 1 Leader	See that everyone speaks English. See that everyone participates.	
Student 2 Secretary	Take notes and write candidate's speech.	
Student 3 Presidential candidate	Give speech to class.	
Students 4/5 Member (s)	Help secretary and candidate with their work.	

2. With your team, decide who will be running for class president. Announce the nomination to the class.

3. Members: Create a ballot with all the nominees' names on it. Make a ballot box for students to put their ballots in after they vote.

4. Decide what issues are most important and write a campaign speech.

5. Candidates give speeches to the class.

6. Vote.

7. Count the ballots and announce the winner.

PRONUNCIATION

Intonation. We use a rising-falling intonation ⤴ when information is less important, and a falling intonation ⤵ when it is more important. Listen to each sentence below and mark the intonation of each clause with an arrow. Add your own example for number 4.

1. I don't believe in the death penalty, but I think violent criminals should be punished.

2. If more training were available, there wouldn't be so many unemployed people.

3. If people don't vote, they shouldn't complain about who gets elected.

4. _____ *(Answers will vary.)* _____

LEARNER LOG

In this unit, you learned many things about civic responsibility. How comfortable do you feel doing each of the skills listed below? Rate your comfort level on a scale of 1 to 4.

1 = Not so comfortable **2** = Need more practice **3** = Comfortable **4** = Very comfortable

If you circle 1 or 2, write down the page number where you can review this skill.

Life Skill	Comfort Level				Page(s)
I can apply for a driver's license.	1	2	3	4	144
I can respond to a jury summons.	1	2	3	4	146
I can fill out a tax form.	1	2	3	4	147, 148, 149
I can identify community problems and possible solutions.	1	2	3	4	152
I can write a letter to a local official about a community problem.	1	2	3	4	153
I can communicate opinions about community issues.	1	2	3	4	152, 153, 156

Grammar					
I can use noun clauses.	1	2	3	4	155
I can use passives with modals.	1	2	3	4	155, 156

Academic					
I can interpret a flow chart about the electoral process.	1	2	3	4	150
I can explain the electoral process.	1	2	3	4	151
I can understand key points of a speech.	1	2	3	4	154, 155
I can write a speech.	1	2	3	4	156

Reflection

Wow! You've finished Stand Out! You should be very proud of yourself. Remember, your learning doesn't stop just because you've finished this book. Learning is something that will continue for the rest of your life. And the skills that you've learned in this course will help you Stand Out in everything you do.

Good luck!

Unit 8 Pronunciation and Learner Log

Pronunciation: 10–15 min.
(optional)

Intonation

We use a rising-falling intonation when information is less important, and a falling intonation when it is more important. Listen to each sentence below and mark the intonation of each clause with an arrow. Add your own example for number 4.

Explain that we can use intonation to show the relative importance of different pieces of information. Play the recording and pause after each question. Ask students to repeat. Then have them make up their own sentences using themes from the unit.

For additional pronunciation practice: Have students listen to the mayoral candidates' speeches from Lesson 7 again. Have them identify where the pauses are and whether the intonation is falling or rising-falling. This activity will help students to identify thought groups and focused words and will be a useful skill if they have to prepare their own presentations or speeches.

Learner Log

Presentation 1: 10–15 min.

If needed, review the purpose of the Learner Log. Make sure students understand how to rate the comfort level they feel in reaching the individual goals listed under *Life Skill, Grammar,* and *Academic Skill.* They should rate their comfort level on a scale of 1 to 4:

1. Not so comfortable
2. Need more practice
3. Comfortable
4. Very comfortable

Practice 1: 10–15 min

If a student circles 1 or 2, he or she should enter the page number on which the skill is featured. The student can then more easily revisit that page and study the material again.

Evaluation 1: 5–10 min.

Finally, emphasize to students the importance of answering the two questions posed in *Reflection*. They are designed to help students assign real-life value to their classroom work.

Instructor's Notes for Unit 8 Team Project, Pronunciation, and Learner Log

_____

_____

_____

_____

_____

_____

_____

_____

_____

_____

_____

_____

_____

_____

_____

_____

_____

_____

_____

Stand Out 4 Vocabulary List

Pre-Unit
Learning strategies
conclusion sentence P5
draft P4
edit P4
errors P3
paragraph P5
strategies P3
support sentence P5
topic sentence P5
version P5
word family P6

Unit 1
Goals
achieve 6
advice 9
architect 4
brainstorm 6
counseling 9
determination 13
firm 4
immigrant 4
influence 13
intern 5
obstacle 6
overcome 6
partner 5
patience 13
qualifications 4
raise (a family) 4
retired 4
solution 6
suburban 4
surgeon 4
Time management
accomplish 15
allocate 15
burned out 16
combine 16
deadlines 16
effectively 16
organized 15
prioritize 16
realistic 15
sacrifice 15
schedule 15
set (a deadline) 16
simultaneously 16
urgency 16

Unit 2
Budgets
calculate 21
expenses 21
finances 21
spend 21
utilities 21
Making a purchase
bargain 23
clearance 23
consumer 23
guarantee 23
merchandise 23
merchant 23
pricing policy 23
purchase 23
refund 23
return 23
shipping costs 23
warranty 23
Credit cards
annual fee 28
application 27
apply 28
APR (annual percentage rate) 28
assets 28
bill 28
billing date 28
borrow 28
capacity 28
cash advance 28
character 28
charge 28
collateral 28
credit limit 28
creditworthiness 28
creditworthy 28
debit card 28
fixed rate 28
grace period 28
interest 28
introductory rate 28
issuer 28
late fee 28
payment 28
penalty 28
rebate 28
terminate 28
variable rate 28
Loans
afford 30
approve 30

credit check 30
deposit 30
down payment 30
financial commitment 30
financial planner 30
mortgage 30
purchase price 30

Unit 3
Housing
amenities 41
asking price 41
brand new 41
cozy 41
downtown 41
fireplace 41
ideal 45
location 41
market 41
master suite 41
negotiate 41
neighborhood 41
offer 41
price range 50
property 50
real estate agent 48
secluded 41
spacious 44
spectacular 41
suburban 41
view 41
Buying a home
assessor 55
closing 55
contract 56
cost comparison 55
debt 55
defect 56
first-time buyer 55
homebuyer 55
income 55
inspect 56
motivation 55
lender 55
upgrade 56

Unit 4
Community
bulletin board 66
community organization 73
literacy program 68
local government 61
recreation 61

transportation 61
visitor's guide 75
volunteer 68
Road maps
campground 70
freeway 70
highway 70
interstate 70
rest area 70
scenic 70

Unit 5
Health
bronchitis 83
chiropractor 87
cholesterol 86
floss 87
gums 87
junk food 86
muscle spasm 83
obstetrician 87
pediatrician 87
podiatrist 87
prenatal classes 87
Health insurance
co-pay 88
deductible 88
dental coverage 88
dependent 89
physician 89
pregnant 89
premium 88
prescription plan 88
provider 88
treatment 89
Nutrition
calories 90
carbohydrate 90
fiber 90
ingredients 90
protein 90
serving 90
sodium 90
vitamins 90
Medicines and illness
allergy 94
antibiotics 92
direction 93
discharge 94
dizziness 93
drowsiness 93
gargle 94
impair 93
indication 93
infection 94
non-prescription drugs 92
overdose 93

prescription drugs 92
prevent 94
relieve 93
respiratory 94
sneeze 94
symptom 93
virus 94
warning 93

Unit 6
Job skills
count on 102
detail-oriented 101
efficient 101
flexible 101
hard-working 101
open-minded 101
patient 101
responsible 101
self-motivated 101
well-organized 101
Jobs
accountant 103
administrative assistant 103
assembler 103
award 110
busboy 103
cashier 108
certificate 110
computer technician 103
conflict 114
cover letter 112
homemaker 103
interview 114
letter of recommendation 110
postal worker 103
references 109
resume 109
security guard 103
transcript 110

Unit 7
Workplace behavior
affect (be affected by a decision) 130
clarify 126
ethical 130
ethics 130
face (a problem) 130
get someone's attention 126
grooming 122
moral 130
offer 126
outcome 130
relevant 130
solve 126
suggest 126
take action 126

Asking for a raise
consider 136
contribution 132
counter (an objection) 132
counterpart 132
deserve 136
efficiency 136
field 132
flextime 132
formal 132
hectic 132
hesitate 135
illustrate 132
implement 136
increase 136
indispensable 132
procedures 134
productivity 134
set (a goal) 132
shift 136
train 136

Unit 8
Civic responsibility
accuse (be accused of a crime) 145
car registration 141
citizen 145
crime 145
driver's license 141
jaywalking 142
judge 145
juror 145
jury 145
jury summons 141
parking ticket 141
resident 145
trial 145
Income tax
deduction 148
exemption 147
file (a tax return) 147
filing status 147
income 147
joint return 147
owe 147
refund 147
spouse 147
tax return 147
tax schedule 149
withhold 147
Elections
agenda 155
announce 151
ballot 151
campaign 150
candidate 150
city council 150

elect (be elected mayor) 151
encourage 155
get involved in 157
increase 156
invest 155
involve 156
local election 150

lower 155
mayor 150
nominate (be nominated for a position) 150
overcrowded 155
position 150
protect 156

proud 155
reduce 158
run for (a position) 150
step down 150
term 150
voice (an opinion) 150
vote 150

Explanation of vocabulary used on income tax forms on page 147

dependent	person you support financially
exemption	amount of your income that won't be taxed. Each exemption represents an amount of money deducted from your taxable income for various reasons, such as number of dependents or disabilities.
file (verb)	send in a completed tax return
income	money earned from working or investments
joint return	when husband and wife declare their income together on the same form
overpaid	when too much tax was withheld by your employer during the year
owe (verb)	you need to pay more tax than the amount that was withheld
refund (noun)	amount of money that will be paid back to you by the government
spouse	husband or wife
tax return	form you fill out to declare your income each year and the federal or state tax you owe
W2 form	a form that your employer gives you to fill out for withholding payroll tax
withhold (verb)	deduct money from your paycheck

Stand Out 4 Irregular Verb List
The following verbs are used in *Stand Out 4* and have irregular past tense forms.

Base form	Simple past	Past participle	Base form	Simple past	Past participle	Base form	Simple past	Past participle
be	was, were	been	give	gave	given	sell	sold	sold
become	became	become	go	went	gone	send	sent	sent
begin	began	begun	grow	grew	grown	set	set	set
break	broke	broken	have	had	had	show	showed	showed/shown
bring	brought	brought	hold	held	held	sit	sat	sat
build	built	built	hurt	hurt	hurt	sleep	slept	slept
buy	bought	bought	keep	kept	kept	speak	spoke	spoken
catch	caught	caught	know	knew	known	spend	spent	spent
come	came	come	learn	learned	learned/learnt	spread	spread	spread
cost	cost	cost	lend	lent	lent	stand	stood	stood
do	did	done	lose	lost	lost	steal	stole	stolen
drink	drank	drunk	make	made	made	take	took	taken
drive	drove	driven	mean	meant	meant	teach	taught	taught
eat	ate	eaten	meet	met	met	tell	told	told
fall	fell	fallen	pay	paid	paid	think	thought	thought
feel	felt	felt	put	put	put	throw	threw	thrown
fight	fought	fought	read	read	read	wake	woke	woken
find	found	found	ride	rode	ridden	wear	wore	worn
fly	flew	flown	run	ran	ran	win	won	won
get	got	gotten	say	said	said	write	wrote	written

Grammar Reference

Used to					
	Subject			***used to* + base verb**	**Object**
	I			used to be	an architect.
	She	didn't		use to play	the piano.
Where	did they			use to live?	
Did	they			use to work	in a restaurant?

Used to + base verb expresses a past habit or state that is now different.

Adjective Clauses			
	Main clause	**Relative pronoun**	**Adjective clause**
Subject clause	This is the *place*	where	I grew up.
	She is the *person*	who	influenced me most.
	A journal is *something*	that (which)	can help you focus on important things.
Object clause	This is the *woman*	who (whom)	I met yesterday.
	Here is the *book*	that (which)	you bought this morning.

Adjective clauses describe the preceding noun. They can describe a subject noun or an object noun. If the noun being described is an object, the relative pronoun can be left out.

Restrictive and Non-Restrictive Adjective Clauses		
Restrictive adjective clauses	A homemaker is a person *who maintains a home and a family.* I applied for the job *that (which) was in the paper on Sunday.*	*Restrictive adjective clauses* give essential information about the noun they refer to. They cannot be omitted without losing the meaning of the sentence. They do not need commas.
Non-restrictive adjective clauses	My brother-in-law, *who owns his own business,* works very hard. I quit my job, *which I never really liked anyway.*	*Non-restrictive adjective clauses* give extra non-essential information about the noun they refer to. They can be omitted. They need commas.

Contrary-to-fact Conditionals	
Condition (*if* + past tense verb)	**Result (*would* + base verb)**
If she *got* a raise,	she *would buy* a new house.
If they *didn't spend* so much money on rent,	they *would have* more money for entertainment.
If I *were* a millionaire,	I'd *give* all my money to charity.
If John *weren't* so busy at work,	he *would spend* more time with his children.
Question forms	
If you *won* the lottery,	what *would* you *do*?
If you *won* the lottery,	*would* you *give up* your job?

Contrary-to-fact (or *unreal*) *conditional statements* are sentences that are not true. The *if*-clause can come in the first or second part of the sentence. In written English, use *were* (instead of *was*) for *if*-clauses with first- and third-person singular forms of *be*.

Questions with Comparative and Superlative Forms				
Question word	**Subject**	**Verb**	**Comparative or superlative form**	**Answer**
Which	one place house Ø	is has	*bigger?* *the closest* to work? *more* rooms? *the biggest* floor plan?	The condominium. The condominium *is bigger.* The condominium *is bigger than* the house.

Embedded Questions		
Introductory question	**Embedded question**	**Rule**
Can you show me	where *Orange Avenue* <u>is</u>?	In an embedded question, the subject comes before the verb.
Do you know	*if* there <u>is</u> a library near here?	For *yes/no* questions, use *if* before the embedded question.
Could you tell me	when the library <u>opens</u>?	For questions with *do*, take out *do* or *does* and use the normal form of the verb.

Grammar Reference

Present Perfect

Subject	*have*	Past participle	Point or period of time	Sentence
I	have	studied	for three months / since April	I have studied English for three months / since April.
She	hasn't	visited	for a long time / since last year	She hasn't visited the dentist for a long time / since last year.
Question word	***have***	**Subject**	**Past participle**	**Question**
How long	have	they	worked	How long have they worked here?

Use *present perfect* to describe an action that happened in the past and continues in the present, when something happened more than once in the past (and could possibly happen again in the future), or for something that happened at an unspecified time in the past.

Present Perfect Continuous

Subject	*have*	*been*	Present participle	Sentence
I	have	been	studying	I have been studying for three months / since April.
She	hasn't	been	working	She hasn't been working long.
Question word	***have***	**Subject**	***been***	**Present participle**
How long	have	they	been	waiting?

Use *present perfect continuous* to emphasize the duration of an activity or state that started in the past and continues in the present or to show that an activity has been in progress recently. **Note:** Some verbs are not usually used in the continuous form, such as *be, believe, hate, have, know, like,* and *want.*

Past Perfect

Subject	*had*	Past participle	Example sentence
I, you, he, she, it, you, we, they	had	lived	He had lived in India before he came to the United States.

When describing two events that happened in the past, use *past perfect* for the event that happened first.

Passive Voice

Passive subject	*be*	Past participle	(*by* + person or thing)	Sentence
It	was	written	by Jim	The note was written by Jim.
They	were	sent	(by unknown person)	The orders were sent yesterday.

Use *passive voice* to emphasize the object of the action or when the doer of the action is unknown or unimportant. To make an active sentence into a passive sentence, switch the subject and the object and then change the verb to the correct tense of *be* + past participle. The word *by* is used before the doer of the action.

Passive Modals

Passive subject	Modal	*be*	Past participle	Sentence
Schools	should	be	built	More schools should be built.
Taxes	need to	be	increased	Taxes need to be increased.
Children	must	be	protected	Children must be protected.
Parents	have to	be	involved	Parents have to be involved.

Question Tags

Positive statement	Tag	Negative statement	Tag
She works,	doesn't she?	She doesn't work,	does she?
They can type,	can't they?	You won't apply,	will you?

A *question tag* makes a sentence into a question. Negative tags follow positive statements. Positive tags follow negative statements. For main verbs, use the verb *do* in the tag. For *be* and modal verbs, repeat the verb in the tag. Use question tags to check if something is true or to ask for agreement.

Student Book 4 Listening Scripts with Supplemental Listenings from the *Activity Bank 4*

Track 1, Stand Out 4, Standards-Based English, by Staci Lyn Sabbagh and Rob Jenkins, copyright 2002, published by Heinle, a division of Thomson Learning, Inc. All rights reserved.

Unit 1 "Balancing Your Life"

Unit 1 Lesson 1 "Where did you use to study?"
(Track 1) Page 1, Lesson 1, Exercise A
Bita and Satoru are new students at Bellingham Adult School. Listen to their conversation on the first day of class.
Bita: Excuse me. Is this Miss Johnson's ESL class? I'm new here.
Satoru: I'm new here too. But I'm pretty sure this is her class. I used to attend this school five years ago, and this is where her class was.
Bita: Oh good. I used to go to school in the daytime before I got a new job. Now that I'm working during the day, I have to go to school at night. My other school doesn't offer night classes, so I had to leave there and come here.
Satoru: I used to go to school in the daytime too, but sometimes I take care of my grandchildren, so night classes are better for me. What kind of work do you do?
Bita: I used to be an architect in Iran. But I don't have the right qualifications to be an architect in the United States. So I'm doing administrative work for an engineering company until my English is good enough to go to college and get the right degree.
Satoru: Wow, I'm impressed.
Bita: Do you work?
Satoru: Not anymore. I used to work for a computer company, assembling computers, but now I just go to school and help my children with their children.
Bita: That's nice. I bet your children appreciate that. Why are you studying English?
Satoru: First of all, I want to help my grandchildren with their homework. But also, I figure since I live in this country, I should be able to speak the language. Don't you agree?
Bita: Completely!

Track 2, Page 1, Lesson 1, Exercise C
(Note: This recording is a repeat of the script in Exercise A above.)

Track 3, Unit 1 Lesson 2 "What are your goals?"
Page 5, Lesson 2, Exercise F
Listen to the conversation that Bita is having with her friend, Yoshiko, and fill in Bita's goal chart with the missing steps and dates.
Yoshiko: How long do you think it will take you to become an architect?
Bita: My goal is to become a partner in a firm by the year 2010.
Yoshiko: What'll you do first?
Bita: Well, the first thing I have to do is improve my English, which I plan to study for two more years. Then by fall of 2004, I'll be ready to register for college.
Yoshiko: How long will it take you to finish?
Bita: Well, usually a degree in architecture takes five or six years to complete, but some of the classes I took in my country will transfer so I should be able to do it faster. I plan get my degree in the spring of 2008.
Yoshiko: Then you can become an architect?
Bita: Not quite. Then I'll have to become an intern to get some practical experience and prepare for my licensing exams.
Yoshiko: Exams?
Bita: Yes, I'll have to take a series of tests before I can get my license to be an architect. Once I have my license, which I hope to get in the winter of 2009, I can apply to work as a partner in an architecture firm.

Yoshiko: Whew! That sounds like a lot of work!
Bita: It will be. But it'll be worth it in the end.

Track 4, Unit 1 Lesson 4 "What should I do?"
Page 9, Lesson 4, Exercise C
Listen to the following people talking to their friends about their problems. After you listen to each conversation, write the problem and two pieces of advice that each person receives.

Conversation 1:
Anna: How's Harry doing these days?
Miyuki: I don't know what to do about him. He can't seem to settle down. He's angry all the time and is always fighting with the other students. My husband has to go and talk to the principal almost every week.
Anna: How about talking to the guidance counselor?
Miyuki: I've tried that but he doesn't have any suggestions.
Anna: Why don't you go and observe some classes and get to know the teachers better. Maybe that would help.
Miyuki: Yes, that's a great idea.

Conversation 2:
Ron: What am I going to do? My new landlord doesn't like dogs and he wants me to get rid of Herbie!
Mike: You can't do that! Has he met Herbie? Does he know what a polite, friendly dog he is? Did you try introducing them?
Ron: No, that won't work. I don't think he likes any dogs. . . .
Mike: Ok, then why don't you start looking for another apartment?

Conversation 3:
Sue: How's your back these days Patti?
Patty: It's getting worse. I'm going to need an operation. But I don't have any insurance.
Sue: I guess you'll have to save up some money then.
Patty: Yes, it could get expensive.
Sue: Or how about finding a job that gives you health insurance?
Patty: Yes, that's what I'll have to do.

Track 5, Unit 1 Lesson 5 "What is most important to me?"
Page 10, Lesson 5, Exercise A
Look at the pictures and listen to Eliana talking about what is important to her. Then read the paragraphs below.
Eliana: This is a picture of the house where I grew up in Argentina. It's very important to me because it holds a lot of memories. This is the garden where I played with my brothers and sisters, and the veranda where I often sat with my parents in the evenings, listening to their stories and watching the stars and dreaming about my future.

This is the person who influenced me the most when I was young. She was my teacher in first grade and we stayed friends until I left home. She was always so calm and gave me good advice. She was the kind of person who is able to give you another perspective on a problem and makes you feel hopeful, no matter how troubled you are.

This is my daily journal. I use it to write about my feelings and hopes and it helps me to understand them better. Sometimes I just write about things that happened to me during the day. My journal is something which helps me to focus on the important things in my life.

Track 6, Page 20, Unit 1 Pronunciation
Sentence stress. We can use stress to emphasize words that we want to contrast and to make the meaning clearer. Listen and repeat the first sentence. Then listen to sentences 2, 3, and 4. Underline the stressed words.

1. **Last** year she studied **computers,** but **this** year she wants to study **accounting.**
2. They **used** to like **skiing,** but **now** they prefer **yoga.**
3. **Cooking** is my **job,** but **jewelry-making** is my **hobby.**
4. **We** weren't able to attend **college,** so we want our **children** to **graduate.**

(This is the end of Unit 1.)

AB Track 2, Stand Out 4 Standards-Based English by Staci Lyn Sabbagh and Rob Jenkins, Supplemental Listening Activities, copyright 2002, published by Heinle, a division of Thomson Learning, Inc. All rights reserved.

Supplemental Listening Activities for Unit 1

(AB Track 2), Page 9a, Unit 1, Lesson 4,
Supplemental Listening, Activity Bank Worksheet 6
You will hear the first part of a conversation where someone is asking for advice. Listen to each conversation and write down the goal and the obstacle or problem. Then brainstorm with a group about possible solutions.
1. Jenny and her Mom are talking about a problem at work.
Jenny: Mom, I need your help.
Mom: Sure, hon. What do you need?
Jenny: Well, I'm having this problem at work. I really want to get this promotion and I've been working really hard to show my boss that I can do the work.
Mom: So what's the problem?
Jenny: Well, one of my co-workers is up for the same promotion. The problem is that we are good friends and I think she will be really upset if I get the promotion and she doesn't. She's already been acting distant towards me since she found out we were up for the same position.
Mom: Hmm. That's a tough one.
Jenny: I know. What should I do?

2. Brad is talking to his counselor about a problem with his schedule.
Brad: Ms. Jacobs, can I talk to you for a second?
School counselor: Sure Brad. Come on in. What's up?
Brad: I've been looking over the schedule of classes for next semester. My plan was to graduate in May and I really can't afford to stay in school any longer. But one of the classes I need is only offered at night and that's when I work. I already asked my boss if I could have that night off for a couple of months while I finish school. But he said if I couldn't work that night, he'd have to find someone else to do my job. It's a very small company and there aren't enough employees to cover when people can't come to work. So I don't know what to do.
School counselor: Yeah, it's hard when you have a lot going on in your life and you can't rearrange your schedule. But I'm sure if we think hard enough, we can come up with a solution.
Brad: Really? I knew it was a good idea to come and see you.

AB Track 3, Now listen to the entire conversation and write down the advice that was given.
1. Jenny and her Mom are talking about a problem at work.
Jenny: Mom, I need your help.
Mom: Sure, hon. What do you need?
Jenny: Well, I'm having this problem at work. I really want to get this promotion and I've been working really hard to show my boss that I can do the work.
Mom: So what's the problem?
Jenny: Well, one of my co-workers is up for the same promotion. The problem is that we are good friends and I think she will be really upset if I get the promotion and she doesn't. She's already been acting distant towards me since she found out we were up for the same position.
Mom: Hmm. That's a tough one.
Jenny: I know. What should I do?

Mom: I think you should sit down and talk about it with her before your boss makes his decision. Explain to her how you're feeling and that you don't want this to affect your friendship. Tell her that you would be happy for her if she got the promotion and you hope that she would be happy for you if you got the promotion. That's what friends are for.
Jenny: You're right Mom. I should talk to her. I was a little bit hesitant because I'm not sure how she'd react but I do think it's the best thing to do. Thanks Mom. You always know just what to do.
Mom: Well, when you're as old as me, you have years of experience!

2. Brad is talking to his counselor about a problem with his schedule.
Brad: Ms. Jacobs, can I talk to you for a second?
School counselor: Sure Brad. Come on in. What's up?
Brad: I've been looking over the schedule of classes for next semester. My plan was to graduate in May and I really can't afford to stay in school any longer. But one of the classes I need is only offered at night and that's when I work. I already asked my boss if I could have that night off for a couple of months while I finish school. But he said if I couldn't work that night, he'd have to find someone else to do my job. It's a very small company and there aren't enough employees to cover when people can't come to work. So I don't know what to do.
School counselor: Yeah, it's hard when you have a lot going on in your life and you can't rearrange your schedule. But I'm sure if we think hard enough, we can come up with a solution.
Brad: Really? I knew it was a good idea to come and see you.
School counselor: Have you thought of looking for a different job?
Brad: Not really. I've been working for this company for over two years.
School counselor: Well is that the place you want to continue working after you graduate?
Brad: No, with my degree and computer skills I've learned from all the classes I've taken, I should be able to get a much better job.
School counselor: So how about looking for a different job for the next six months while you finish school?
Brad: OK, but where am I going to find a job for only six months?
School counselor: Well, they're always hiring students here on campus and they're very flexible because they know you're a student. In fact, I just found out that the library is hiring right now for a person to monitor the computer lab. I think that would be perfect for you.
Brad: Wow! That sounds like a great idea. And I'd be right here on campus so it would be easy to get to class on time. Thanks Ms. Jacobs. I'm going to go over to the library right now to apply.
School counselor: Good luck!

(End of Unit 1 Supplemental Listenings)

Track 7, Unit 2 "Personal Finance"

Unit 2 Lesson 1 "Money in, money out"
(Track 7) Page 21, Lesson 1, Exercise B
Listen to Sara and Todd Mason talk about their finances. Fill in the amounts.
Todd: I think it's time we sat down and made a family budget. As the kids grow older, we're going to need to budget our money more wisely.
Sara: Good idea. How should we start?
Todd: Well, let's make a list of everything we spend money on and then let's guess at how much we spend in each category. Then we'll save our receipts for the next month and see how much we actually spent.
Sara: OK, why don't we start with the cars? Since both of them are paid off, we don't have any loan payments, but we do have to pay for gas, insurance, and maintenance. I'd say we spend $200 a month on gas, $150 a month on insurance, and I don't know about maintenance, but it might come to $450 a month for everything.

Todd: That sounds right. Now let's talk about utilities. Rent is $1500 a month. I know that for sure!

Sara: Yeah, and I'd say we spend about $40 on gas, $100 on electricity, and $20 on water. That adds up to $160.

Todd: Don't forget cable, phone, and Internet. Cable is $50, phone $80, and Internet $30. That's $160 right there.

Sara: Wow, we spend money on a lot of things!

Todd: And we're not even finished! How much do you think we spend on food each month?

Sara: I spend about $400 a month on groceries and I'd say we spend about $200 going out to dinner.

Todd: What about school supplies and clothing?

Sara: School supplies could be about $60 a month and clothing about $200.

Todd: Are we forgetting anything?… oh, medical expenses. It's a good thing we have insurance but it doesn't pay for everything. I'd say we spend about $50 a month.

Sara: That sounds about right. And don't forget entertainment. Movies and taking the kids on trips soon adds up! I'd be willing to bet we spend at least $150 a month on those kinds of things. I'm afraid to add all this up!

Track 8, Page 22, Lesson 1, Exercise E

Listen to Sara and Todd talk about what they actually spent in the month of May. Write down their actual expenses in the third column.

Sara: I can't believe it's been a month since we sat down last time and wrote down our budget. Time flies!

Todd: Yep, it sure does. OK, since we've already totaled up the receipts, let's write down the total amount of money we spent last month in each category.

Sara: OK, I've got the auto expenses. We spent $212.43 on gas, $150 on insurance, and nothing on maintenance, so that's $362.43 total. That's less than we thought.

Todd: OK, rent and utilities. Obviously, rent is what we thought, $1500. Gas was $35.76, electricity was $150.02, and water was $22.34. That comes to $208.12. We were close on gas and water, but we were way off on the electricity.

Sara: I guess we're not used to that rate increase yet.

Todd: I don't think I'll ever get used to it. OK, cable was $50, phone was $155.72, and Internet was $30. That adds up to $235.72.

Sara: Not bad. I guess the bigger phone bill was because of all those calls you made to your mother last month. Maybe we can make her pay for it!

Todd: Oh, she'd love that! OK, what else?

Sara: I spent $359.81 last month on groceries and we spent about $300 going out to dinner. I guess we underestimated that one.

Todd: What about school supplies and clothing?

Sara: School supplies were about $30; clothing was $102.14. But I still think we should leave the clothing budget at $200 because the boys will be growing and need new clothes quite often.

Todd: Good idea. We spent $45.28 on medical expenses and $132.96 on entertainment.

Sara: All right. Let's add it up!

Track 9, Unit 2 Lesson 5 "Apply for a loan"
Page 30, Lesson 5, Exercise A

Todd and Sara are thinking of buying a house. Todd is worried about money, so he made an appointment with a financial planner to talk about a mortgage. Look at the expressions below and discuss them with your teacher. Then listen to Todd talking with the financial planner.

Part 1:

Todd: I really appreciate you taking time to talk to me.

Financial Planner: No problem, Todd.

Todd: Well, as I told you over the phone, the boys are starting to grow up and Sara and I would like to move into a permanent place of our own. We're just a little worried about how we're going to pay for it.

Financial Planner: I think it's great that you and Sara are ready to take the next step. But only you can decide if you're ready to buy a house. Here's what I tell all of my clients. First, you have to ask yourself three questions. Do you have money set aside for a down payment? Do you have enough money each month to make a loan payment? And are you ready to make a long-term financial commitment? If you can answer yes to all three of those questions, you are ready to buy a home.

Part 2:

Todd: How much will we need for a down payment?

Financial Planner: Well, that all depends on how much the house is that you want to buy. Also, you have to decide how much you want to put down. It's best if you can put 20% down but some people can only put 5% down. The more you put down, the lower your monthly payments will be.

Todd: OK, so if we can answer yes to all of those questions, what's the next step?

Financial Planner: First you need to determine how much you can afford to spend on a house. Next, you get approved for a loan of that amount. Third, start looking for a home in your price range. And fourth, make an offer on the house you want.

Todd: Looking for a home and making an offer are easy. But how do we figure out how much we can afford?

Financial Planner: The best thing to do is gather all the necessary paperwork and then we can determine how much you can spend.

Part 3:

Todd: What's the necessary paperwork?

Financial Planner: I'll need six things. I'll need your social security number to run a credit check, tax statements from the past two years, two of your most recent pay stubs, the most recent statements from all your bank accounts, your most recent credit card statements, and statements from any other loans that you have. Once I have those things, I should be able to determine what you purchase price can be. If not, I'll ask you for more information.

Todd: Is there anything else I need to know?

Financial Planner: That's it for now. Why don't you and Sara sit down and discuss the three questions we talked about. If the answer is yes to all three, start gathering that paperwork and give me a call.

Todd: Great! Thanks for all your help, Jim.

Track 10, Page 30, Lesson 5, Exercise B

Listen to the first part of the conversation again. What are the three questions Todd must ask himself? Write them below. (Note: the following three scripts are the same as the script in exercise A above.)

Part 1:

Todd: I really appreciate you taking time to talk to me.

Financial Planner: No problem, Todd.

Todd: Well, as I told you over the phone, the boys are starting to grow up and Sara and I would like to move into a permanent place of our own. We're just a little worried about how we're going to pay for it.

Financial Planner: I think it's great that you and Sara are ready to take the next step. But only you can decide if you're ready to buy a house. I'll tell you what I tell all of my clients, but you'll have to talk it over with Sara and make the final decision on your own. First, you have to ask yourself three questions. Do you have money set aside for a down payment? Do you have enough money each month to make a loan payment? And are you ready to make a long-term financial commitment? If you can answer yes to all three of those questions, you are ready to buy a home.

Track 11, Page 30, Lesson 5, Exercise C
What are the next steps Todd must take? Listen to what the financial planner says and write the four steps below.

Part 2:
Todd: How much will we need for a down payment?
Financial Planner: Well, that all depends on how much the house is that you want to buy. Also, you have to decide how much you want to put down. It's best if you can put 20% down but some people can only put 5% down. The more you put down, the lower your monthly payments will be.
Todd: OK, so if we can answer all of those questions with a yes, what's the next step?
Financial Planner: First you need to determine how much you can afford to spend on a house. Next, you get approved for a loan of that amount. Third, start looking for a home in your price range. And fourth, make an offer on the house you want.
Todd: Looking for a home and making an offer are easy. But how do we figure out how much we can afford?
Financial Planner: The best thing to do is gather all the necessary paperwork and then we can determine how much you can spend.

Track 12, Page 30, Lesson 5, Exercise D
Todd will need to give the financial planner six things. Do you remember what they are? Write them below. If you can't remember, listen again.

Part 3:
Todd: What's the necessary paperwork?
Financial Planner: I'll need six things. I'll need your social security number to run a credit check, tax statements from the past two years, two of your most recent pay stubs, the most recent statements from all your bank accounts, your most recent credit card statements, and statements from any other loans that you have. Once I have those things, I should be able to determine what your purchase price can be. If not, I'll ask you for more information.
Todd: Is there anything else I need to know?
Financial Planner: That's it for now. Why don't you and Sara sit down and discuss the three questions we talked about. If the answer is yes to all three, start gathering that paperwork and give me a call.
Todd: Great! Thanks for all your help, Jim.

Track 13, Page 40, Unit 2 Pronunciation
Word Linking. Listen to sentences 1-3 and notice how the word ending in /w/ is linked to the following word in each sentence. Then listen to sentences 4-6. Listen to how the /w/ sound is introduced to link words? Listen again and repeat. Make new sentences using this type of word linking.
1. How often do you make large purchases?
2. What do you know about personal finance?
3. Now is the time to check out our special offers.
4. I want to apply for a credit card.
5. It is so easy to borrow money.
6. Go online to check our prices.

(This is the end of Unit 2.)

AB Track 4, Supplemental Listening Activities for Unit 2

(AB Track 4) Page 34a, Unit 2, Lesson 7 Supplemental Listening, Activity Bank Worksheet 9
Listen to each conversation and fill in the table with the information you hear.

Conversation 1:
Customer: I purchased these shoes last week and my feet have had blisters ever since. They are very uncomfortable.
Clerk: I'm sorry ma'am. Maybe they are too small?
Customer: No, they fit perfectly but the back of the shoe rubs my heel when I walk.
Clerk: I'm very sorry. What would you like to do?

Customer: I'd like to get my money back.
Clerk: I'm sorry ma'am, but since the shoes have been worn, I can't do that. I can give you store credit though.
Customer: I guess that's OK.
Clerk: All right, let me take care of that for you.

Conversation 2:
Customer: Hello. I had you print these business cards for me but you put the wrong address. This is inexcusable and I need you to fix the cards as soon as possible!
Clerk: Really? Let me get out your original order form. Here it is. 42015 Lake Street.
Customer: No, that's not the correct address.
Clerk: But that's what you wrote on the order form. Look. We printed it exactly how you asked.
Customer: Oh, I guess I made a mistake. It should be 42105 Lake Street.
Clerk: OK. Well, we can fix that for you and I'll give you a 20% discount on the new order.
Customer: Thank you. That's very kind.

Conversation 3:
Customer: Excuse me, waiter? This steak isn't cooked enough.
Waiter: I'm sorry. Is it too pink?
Customer: Yes. I asked for medium well and I think this is medium rare.
Waiter: I apologize. I'll take it back right away and have the chef put it back on the grill. Can I get you anything else while you are waiting?
Customer: No, I'll be fine. Thanks.

(End of Unit 2 Supplemental Listenings)

Track 14, Unit 3 "Buying a home"

Unit 3 Lesson 2 "Bigger? Better?"
(Track 14) Page 43, Lesson 2, Exercise A
Listen to Joey and Courtney discuss two properties that Courtney looked at. As you listen, take notes about the *advantages* and *disadvantages* of each place.
Courtney: I went and looked at houses yesterday.
Joey: You did? How did it go?
Courtney: Well, I found two that I really liked. One was a three-bedroom house and the other was a two-bedroom condominium.
Joey: Which one did you like better?
Courtney: Well, they both have their plusses and minuses. The house is closer to my job than the condo. But the condo is in a much nicer neighborhood.
Joey: What about price?
Courtney: The condo is cheaper than the house but the condo has association fees.
Joey: Did you talk to any of the people who live in the area?
Courtney: Yep. I met one of the women who lives in the condominium complex and she looked in both neighborhoods as well when she was buying her place. She said the condominium complex is safer than the housing neighborhood because of the gate at the front. She also said that there are more children in the complex and that the neighbors seem to be friendlier because everyone lives so close together.

Track 15, Unit 3 Lesson 3 "Which one is safer?"
Page 45, Lesson 3, Exercise A
Sara and Courtney have been comparing notes on houses they've looked at. Listen to their conversation.
Courtney: Have you looked at any new houses this week?
Sara: Yes, I saw three places the other day. Look at this brochure!
Courtney: The Country Cottage, the Suburban Dream, and the Downtown Condo. I like the sound of the Country Cottage best. It sounds more comfortable than the others.
Sara: Yeah, and it's the closest to where we live now.

Courtney: Oh really? Which place is the safest?
Sara: Actually, I think the Suburban Dream is the safest.
Courtney: Which one has the biggest floor plan?
Sara: The Suburban Dream. That would be ideal for our family.
Courtney: Is it the most expensive?
Sara: Of course! I have expensive taste.

Track 16, Page 47, Lesson 3, Exercise G
Listen to the four advertisements for *Homes for Sale* and fill in the information you hear.

Home 1
Wanna live like a king? Then you can't pass up the Prince's Palace. Offered at a mere 1.2 million, this sprawling 15, 000 square foot palace is located at the top of a hill far away from other residences. Not only does it have every appliance you can think of, but all the rooms have beautiful hardwood floors. Wanna find out more about this princely estate? Call today!

Home 2
Always wanted to take a house and make it your own? Here's your chance! Settle in to this four-bedroom, 2, 000 square foot Fixer-Upper for only $150, 000. Located in a busy neighborhood with lots of other families, this place is perfect for a young family.

Home 3
Move out of the slow life and into the fast lane! A beautifully spacious 1,000 square foot studio apartment at the top of one of the city's newest high rises is just what you're looking for. The building has 24-hour security. Utility room with washers and dryers is in the basement. The owner wants to lease it for $2000 a month but is willing to sell. Hurry! This one will go fast!

Home 4
You've finally decided it's time to move out of the city and into the country. Well we've got the place for you. This three-bedroom rural residence is just what you need. It's a spacious 3, 500 square foot ranch-style home with a huge backyard and a pool. It's located at the end of a cul-de-sac where there are only five other homes. It is now being offered at $125, 000.

Track 17, Unit 3 Lesson 4 "Housing preferences"
Page 48, Lesson 4, Exercise A
Think about the following questions as you listen to the story about the Bwarie family.
1. Why is the Bwarie family looking for a new home?
2. What are they looking for in a new home?

The Bwarie family has outgrown their apartment. They have three children and a baby on the way and they are now renting a two-bedroom house. They've been putting away money every month from their paychecks and finally have enough money for a 10% down payment on a house. Every Sunday, the whole family piles into the car and they go look at properties for sale in the $100,000 to $120,000 price range. Until now, they have been doing this on their own. But now it's time to find a real estate agent.

However, before they meet with a real estate agent, they need to decide exactly what they want. Courtney and Joey Bwarie have thought long and hard about what they want to purchase. First of all, they want a house in a safe neighborhood that is within walking distance to their children's school. Second of all, they want four bedrooms, one for Courtney and Joey, one for the two boys and another for their daughter and the baby girl who will be born next month. The fourth room will be used as an office for Courtney, who works from home. As far as bathrooms, four would be ideal, but they could

survive with three if they had to. Some other things they would like are a big backyard for the children to play in and an attached two-car garage. Other amenities, such as air conditioning or a pool, are not important to them.

Now they know what they are looking for in a new home. That was the easy part. Finding a real estate agent, that's a different story!

Track 18, Page 60, Unit 3 Pronunciation
Intonation. Yes/no questions usually have a rising intonation. Information questions usually have a falling intonation. Listen to these examples. Underline the stressed words and draw arrows to show the intonation pattern that you hear.
1. Do you want a garage? [rising intonation]
2. Do they need air conditioning? [rising intonation]
3. Does it have a back yard? [rising intonation]
4. What type of property do you want? [falling intonation]
5. How many rooms does it have? [falling intonation]
6. Where is it located? [falling intonation]

(This is the end of Unit 3.)

Track 19, Unit 4 "Community"

(Track 19) Unit 4 Lesson 3 "Making suggestions"
Page 66, Lesson 3, Exercise D
Listen to the statements and write the correct number next to each notice.
1. I want to do individual exercises that will help me relax.
2. I've always wanted to learn how to play an instrument.
3. I need a place to send my kids for the summer while I'm at work.
4. Wouldn't it be fun to play on a team with other people?
5. There's gotta be something my grandma can do Sunday nights to keep herself busy.
6. I need to find a place to live.
7. Is there a gym around here where I can play basketball?
8. I've always wanted to learn some crafts.
9. Have you seen my cat?

Track 20, Unit 4 Lesson 5 "How far is it?"
Page 71, Lesson 5, Exercise D
Listen to the following people giving directions. Where will the driver end up? Fill in the circle next to the correct answer.
1. Since you'll be coming from Rose, get on 24 going west. Then take 315 South. You'll drive for a while and then get off at the first exit.
2. From Grandville, get on 315 South. Then take 24 East. You'll pass the airport. Get off right before 24 and 89 intersect.
3. If you're coming from Poppington, take 315 North. Then get on 13 West, the scenic route, and go on to 15 North. You'll pass by Lake Ellie, which might be a nice place to stop and have lunch. Then continue on 15 North till you get to 315 North. Take the first exit.
4. From Rose, take 89 South until you get to the first exit. Keep going till you get to the hospital.

Track 21, Page 80 Unit 4 Pronunciation
Word Linking. Listen to the sentences below and notice how the words *could, would,* and *did* are linked to the following word *you.* They sound like *kudju, wudju,* and *didju.* Listen again and repeat. Make new sentences to practice these sounds.
1. Could you tell me when the store opens?
2. Would you show me where the elevators are?
3. Did you find the phone number?

(This is the end of Unit 4.)

AB Track 5, Supplemental Listening Activities for Unit 4

(AB Track 5) Page 72a, Unit 4, Lesson 5, Supplemental Listening, Activity Bank Worksheet 5
Listen to each person call and ask for directions. Write down where they are coming from, where they are going to, and the directions. Use shorthand to write the directions.

Conversation 1:
Clerk: Pete's Hardware.
Woman: Um, yes, I was wondering if you could give me directions to your store.
Clerk: Sure. Where are you coming from?
Woman: I live over on Main and Wardlow, right near the 605.
Clerk: Well, it would probably be best if you get on 605 south. Then exit Carson and turn right. Go down about a mile and then turn left on Second Street. We're about a block down on the right hand side.
Woman: OK, so 605 south to Carson. Carson right to Second. Left on Second and then you're on the right side.
Clerk: Yep, you got it.
Woman: Thank you.

Conversation 2:
Librarian: Good morning. Loronado Public Library.
Boy: Hi, I need directions to the library.
Librarian: Well, you sound a little bit young to drive.
Boy: I am. I'm only twelve. But my mom said I can ride my bike to the library.
Librarian: Well that sounds like a great idea! Where do you live?
Boy: Our house is on Sandy Lane.
Librarian: OK, go down Sandy Lane until you hit Beach Way. Then turn right on Beach Way. Ride about four blocks until you get to Loro Road. Turn left. The library will be on your left-hand side. The address is 34660 Loro Road.
Boy: OK.
Librarian: Do you want to repeat that back to me?
Boy: Sure. Go down to Beach Way and turn right. Then go to Loro Road and turn left. The address is 34660 and you're on the left.
Librarian: You got it.
Boy: OK bye.
Librarian: Bye bye.

Conversation 3:
Receptionist: Recycling Center. How can I help you?
Man: Yes, do you take all types of recyclables?
Receptionist: We take glass, plastic, and aluminum.
Man: Great. Where are you located?
Receptionist: We are in the Briar Road Shopping Center on Briar Road.
Man: Can you tell me how to get there? I'll be coming from First Avenue and Harbor Blvd.
Receptionist: Sure. Get on Harbor Blvd. coming south. You'll drive about 3 miles before you get to Fairview. Turn left on Fairview and take it to Baker Avenue. On Baker, turn right. Then take Baker to Landing and turn left. We are on the corner of Baker and Landing in a big white building.
Man: OK, so I'll take Harbor south to Fairview and then turn left. Then I go to Baker and turn left.
Receptionist: No, turn right on Baker.
Man: Oh, OK. I wrote it down wrong. Right on Baker. Then left on Landing and it's on the corner of Baker and Landing.
Receptionist: Yes.

Man: Thank you. When do you close today?
Receptionist: We're open until 8 p.m. tonight.
Man: Great! I'll come by this afternoon.
Receptionist: OK, we'll see you then.

AB Track 6, Page 76a, Unit 4, Lesson 7, Supplemental Listening, Activity Bank Worksheet 7
Listen to the Visitors Guide on Loronado. Fill in the missing information.

Welcome to historic Loronado! Loronado has been around since 1910 when the first settlers came to live near the water. It started out with just one main street and now it has grown into a large metropolis with over 200, 000 people! We're so glad you chose Loronado as your vacation destination and we'd like to tell you about some of the fun things you can do.

First of all, to get an overview of the whole city, hop on the Little Blue Bus. This is a small trolley car that will take you all around the city and show you the sights. For only $5, you can stay on the Little Blue Bus all day. It stops at 10 different locations where you can get off and then get back on when you're ready to go to the next spot. This gives you a great overview of Loronado and will give you an idea of where you'd like to spend more time.

For all you art lovers out there, Loronado has a world famous art museum where many famous maritime paintings are housed. It's located on Grant Avenue in an old lighthouse. The museum is open daily from 10 to 4 and I promise you won't be disappointed!

I'm sure we have some shoppers out there. You should head over to Main Street where you'll find tons of clothing boutiques, book shops, music stores, antiques, and gift shops. Most of the stores are open Monday Through Friday from 10 A.M. to 9 P.M. and Saturday and Sunday from 12-5 P.M.

Come one, come all! The Loronado Players are in town doing a performance of Oklahoma! The Players perform in an old movie theater that has been renovated and it's a show that you won't want to miss. They perform every night except Monday at 8 P.M. Rush on over to get your tickets. Adults $45, seniors and children $25.

For those of you who just like to relax, take a stroll down by the water. Loronado is famous for its beautiful beaches and ocean breezes.

Kids, don't think we have forgotten about you. Head down to Sunset Park where there are rides and games every Saturday and Sunday. Spend the whole day there for just $10 and meet some new friends.

These are just a few things you can do while you're in town. For more information please visit our Visitor's Bureau. And don't forget to have a great time!

(End of Unit 4 Supplemental Listenings)

Track 22, Unit 5 "Health"

Unit 5 Lesson 2 "What's the problem?"
(Track 22) Page 83, Lesson 2, Exercise A
Read the conversation between the doctor and patient.
Doctor: Hello, John. What seems to be the problem?
John: Well, I've been coughing a lot.
Doctor: Anything else?
John: Yes, my chest has been hurting, too.
Doctor: It sounds like you might have bronchitis. I'd like to do some tests to be sure, and then I'll give you a prescription to relieve your symptoms.
John: Thanks, Doc.

Track 23, Unit 5 Lesson 3 "What did she say?"
Page 86, Lesson 3, Exercise A
Listen to the following conversation between Rosa and her doctor. Number the sentences in the correct order.
Doctor: Rosa, I can give you some more tests, but you'll have to come back in two weeks to get the results. Here's an information leaflet that tells you about exercises that will be good for your back and for your knees. If you do more exercise, your cholesterol should go down. The fact is, if you don't stop eating junk food, you'll have serious health problems. The most important thing is to stay active.

Track 24, Page 86, Lesson 3, Exercise B
Now listen to Rosa reporting her conversation to her friend. Fill in the missing words.
Friend: What did the doctor tell you, Rosa?
Rosa: She said she could give me some more tests.
Friend: Why? Are you very sick?
Rosa: Not now, but I might get sick. The doctor told me the most important thing was to stay active. She told me if I did more exercise, my cholesterol should go down. She said if I didn't stop eating junk food, I would have serious health problems. She said I would have to come back in two weeks.

Track 25, Page 100 Unit 5 Pronunciation
Word Linking. In spoken English, the pronoun *he* often loses its initial /h/ sound when it is linked to the previous word. Listen and repeat.
1. Is he (*izzy*) taking any medication?
2. Has he (*hazzy*) been ill for a long time?
3. Does he (*duzzy*) often go to the doctor?
4. Did he (*diddy*) give you some advice?
5. Isn't he (*izzeny*) going to take sick leave?
6. Hasn't he (*hazzeny*) phoned yet?
7. Doesn't he (*duzzeny*) have insurance?
8. Didn't he (*diddeny*) tell you about the pills?

(This is the end of Unit 5.)

AB Track 7, Supplemental Listening Activities for Unit 5

(AB Track 7) Page 81a, Unit 5, Lesson 1, Supplemental Listening, Activity Bank Worksheet 1
A. Listen to each person talk about his or her health habits. Check healthy or unhealthy.
Example: I'm addicted to cola. I probably drink at least four cans a day.
 1. I've been working so hard lately that I've only been getting four hours of sleep every night. I'm tired when I first wake, but once I have my coffee I'm OK.
 2. I'm training for a marathon right now so I run every morning before I go to school.
 3. I love fresh fruit and vegetables and I try to eat at least six servings of them a day.
 4. My husband I like to walk for an hour after dinner every night. It's a good chance for us to talk and unwind from the day.
 5. My new favorite food is French fries. I have some for lunch every day with my hamburger and then I usually drive thru and get some on my way home from work every night.
 6. My friends and I like to go out drinking and dancing every night. It's so much fun to hang out with my friends.
 7. I eat breakfast every morning before I leave the house. It gives me energy for the day.
 8. I've been a smoker ever since I was 16. I can't seem to kick the habit.
 9. There's this new yoga class at my gym that I've been taking three times a week.

10. I feel so much better when I drink water all day. I try to drink at least ten cups a day.

AB Track 8, Page 81a, Unit 5, Lesson 1, Supplemental Listening, Activity Bank Worksheet 1
B. Listen to the people again. What are their habits? Write them below. (Note: This rest of the script is the same as the script above.)

(End of Unit 5 Supplemental Listenings)

Track 26, Unit 6 "Getting Hired"

Unit 6 Lesson 1 "What skills do you have?"
(Track 26) Page 102, Lesson 1, Exercise E
Listen to four people describe their skills and interests. Take notes in the first column. Then suggest a job for each of them in the second column.
1. Lam: My name is Lam and I love to be outdoors. I'm a hard worker and like to work with my hands. I don't like to tell other people what to do, but I don't mind taking orders from my boss.
2. Lilia: Hello, I'm Lilia and I love working with people. I'm very customer service oriented and like to help people. I wouldn't make a good cashier because I'm not very good with numbers. But I'm willing to work hard and I learn quickly.
3. Morteza: My name is Morteza and I was an engineer in my country. Unfortunately, I don't have the right qualifications to do that here, but I'm very good at technical things. I know a lot about computers and really like working with them. I prefer to work alone because I'm not very good with people.
4. Hilda: Hi, I'm Hilda. I've never had a job before but I'm very organized and good with details. I've always taken care of the finances at our house, so I'm good with numbers. Also, I'm creative and like to come up with new ideas.

Track 27, Page 120 Unit 6 Pronunciation
Contractions. Would and *had* can both have the contraction *'d* in spoken English and in informal written style. Read the examples below and decide if the contraction *'d* stands for *would* or *had.* Write would or had in the spaces below. Then listen and repeat each sentence.
1. I'd worked in Australia for three months before I started to feel homesick. _____
2. I'd go to the job center and ask for an application, if I were you. _____
3. She'd like to get a job in engineering when she graduates. _____
4. They'd offered him a job before he finished his degree. _____

(This is the end of Unit 6.)

AB Track 9, Supplemental Listening Activities for Unit 6

(AB Track 9) Page 116a, Unit 6, Lesson 7, Supplemental Listening, Activity Bank Worksheet 7
Listen to the following job interviews. You will only hear a portion of each interview. Rate each interview according to what you hear. Circle your response.

Interview 1:
Interviewer: Jason, why don't you tell me a little about yourself.
Jason: Um, well . . . um, what do you want to know?
Interviewer: Well, how about telling me what got you interested in computers?
Jason: Computers are just cool. It's fun to play games on them.

Interviewer: OK. Why do you think you would be good at this job?
Jason: Well, I don't know if I'm going to be good until I try.

Interview 2:
Interviewer: Roseanne, why did you leave your last job?
Roseanne: Actually, the hours conflicted with my school classes and it's really important for me to finish my degree, so I eventually got a full-time job. This job appeals to me because the hours are flexible and I'm hoping if I get the job, you can work around my school schedule.
Interviewer: That's definitely possible. We have a lot of students who work here and we try to accommodate everyone's schedules as best we can. What special skills do you have that would benefit our company?
Roseanne: First of all, I'm great with people, which is why I like customer service jobs so much. I enjoy helping customers find what they are looking for. Also, I'm a good problem solver. I seem to be very successful handling customer complaints and making the customer feel like she got what she wanted in the end.
Interviewer: Those are two great qualities!

Interview 3:
Interviewer: What did you like most about your last job, Jose?
Jose: My last job was very challenging. I was always learning new things and every day was different. I hope that every job I have will teach me new things and open my eyes to new possibilities. I'm the kind of person who gets bored doing the same thing every day, so I like a challenge.
Interviewer: Well this job will definitely challenge you. Can I ask what your salary is at your current job?
Jose: Right now I'm making $35, 000 plus benefits.
Interviewer: And what would you expect to make here?
Jose: Well, since this job will require more responsibility on my part, and since I'd be managing other people, I would hope for at least $40, 000 plus benefits. Is that possible?
Interviewer: Well, I don't make the salary decisions, but this job will pay somewhere between 37 and 43, depending on experience. So what you want isn't that far off.

Interview 4:
Interviewer: Steve, can you describe a situation where you had a conflict with another employee?
Steve: Yes, actually this conflict is one of the reasons I'm looking for another job. Another employee at work and I were up for the same promotion. About two weeks before the boss was about to make his decision, I started getting reports saying that I was filling out my paperwork incorrectly. When I went in to the office to see what the problem was, I saw that someone had been changing what I had written.
Interviewer: How did you know who was doing it?
Steve: Well, it could only be this guy. He wanted the promotion really bad.
Interviewer: Did you confront him about it?
Steve: Yeah, actually I asked him about it at lunch one day. He said it wasn't him. But I knew he was lying.
Interviewer: So what did you do?
Steve: I took him outside and told him off.
Interviewer: Wasn't there another way to handle the situation?
Steve: No, not with this guy. That was the best way to get through to him. The only problem is I was on probation for getting into an argument with another guy. So since this was my second time, they fired me. So that's why I'm applying for this job.

(End of Unit 6 Supplemental Listenings)

Track 28, Unit 7 "On the Job"

Unit 7 Lesson 2 "The note was written by Jim."
(Track 28) Page 123, Lesson 2, Exercise A
Listen and read the conversation.
Raquel: Did you see the note I put on your desk?
Bruno: Was that note from you? I thought it was put there by Jim.
Raquel: Actually, the note was written by Jim but I taped it to your desk. I wanted to make sure you got it before you left for lunch.
Bruno: I did get it. The orders were sent to me yesterday and I'll have them ready for your signature before I leave today.
Raquel: Great! I'll sign them in the morning, and then you can send them to the Finance Department. Make sure they are sent by Package Express.
Bruno: I'll take care of it right away.

Track 29, Unit 7 Lesson 3 "Taking action"
Page 125, Lesson 3, Exercise A
Listen to the conversation.
Construction Worker: Excuse me. Do you have a second?
Supervisor: Sure. What is it?
Construction Worker: Well, there's a small problem. The shipment of lumber didn't arrive, so we have to stop construction until it gets here. What would you like us to do?
Supervisor: There's nothing else you can do, while you are waiting for it?
Construction Worker: No. We need that lumber to start working on the doorframes.
Supervisor: OK. Well why don't you guys take lunch early, and I'll call and see where the lumber is?
Construction Worker: OK, so you want all of us to go on lunch break right now, while you call and find out where the lumber is?
Supervisor: That's right.
Construction Worker: When should we come back?
Supervisor: In about an hour.
Construction Worker: Thank you. See you in an hour.

Track 30, Unit 7 Lesson 4 "You speak English, don't you?"
Page 129, Lesson 4, Exercise D
Listen to the tag questions and fill in the circle next to the tag that you hear.
1. He sent the package yesterday, didn't he?
2. We'll get our paychecks tomorrow, won't we?
3. They didn't unload those boxes yet, did they?
4. Martina hasn't ever assembled computers, has she?
5. You're just learning about tag questions, aren't you?

Track 31, Page 140 Unit 7 Pronunciation
Intonation. In tag questions, a rising intonation often indicates that you are unsure of the answer, and a falling intonation indicates that you are almost sure of the answer. Listen to these examples and decide if they are rising or falling. Draw arrows on the sentences as in the examples.
1. You work in the library, don't you? (rising)
2. She is an engineer, isn't she? (falling)
3. He hasn't applied yet, has he? (falling)
4. We called them, didn't we? (rising)
5. You weren't in the office, were you? (rising)
6. He wasn't fired, was he? (falling)

(This is the end of Unit 7.)

AB Track 10, Supplemental Listening Activities for Unit 7

(AB Track 10) Page 127a, Unit 7, Lesson 3, Supplemental Listening, Activity Bank Worksheet 4
Listen to the conversation between an employee and his supervisor.
Randy: Ron, do you have a minute?
Supervisor: Sure. What's up?
Randy: Well we have a little problem over in shipping. We just received a delivery that we've been expecting for three days. Because it was delayed, our guys haven't been able to assemble as many computers as they should have, so we're really behind.
Supervisor: But now the delivery's here, so what's the problem?
Randy: Well, we were so anxious to get the delivery that we quickly signed for it without really checking if all the parts were there. Now that we've gone through it, we see that there are over 200 missing parts.
Supervisor: Have you already spoken to Jim about this?
Randy: Yes. The first thing I did was ask Jim what we should do. Jim said that because we signed for it saying it was all there, there was nothing we could do. But I wanted to come and talk to you about it to see if you have a different solution.

AB Track 11, Page 127a, Unit 7, Lesson 3, Supplemental Listening, Activity Bank Worksheet 4
Now listen to the entire conversation. What was the solution? (Note: The following script is an extended version of the script above.)
Randy: Ron, do you have a minute?
Supervisor: Sure. What's up?
Randy: Well we have a little problem over in shipping. We just received a delivery that we've been expecting for three days. Because it was delayed, our guys haven't been able to assemble as many computers as they should have right now, so we're really behind.
Supervisor: But now the delivery's here, so what's the problem?
Randy: Well we were so anxious to get the delivery that we quickly signed for it without really checking if all the parts were there. Now that we've gone through it, we see that there are over 200 missing parts.
Supervisor: Have you already spoken to Jim about this?
Randy: Yes. The first thing I did was ask Jim what we should do. Jim said that because we signed for it saying it was all there, there was nothing we could do. But I wanted to come and talk to you about it to see if you have a different solution.
Supervisor: Actually, I do. We've been working with this company for a long time and I think if I call over there and tell them what happened, they'll believe that we're telling the truth. I'll see how fast they can send us those missing parts. I need you to get me an accurate list of what we need, so I can make that phone call.
Randy: OK, so let me make sure I'm clear on this. I'm going to make you a list of the parts we need and then you're going to call the delivery company and tell them about the mistake. Then hopefully they'll deliver the missing parts ASAP.
Supervisor: That's the plan!
Randy: I hope it works.
Supervisor: Me, too!
Randy: Thanks.

(End of Unit 7 Supplemental Listenings)

Track 32, Unit 8 "Civic Responsibility"

Unit 8 Lesson 2 "A driver's license"
(Track 32) Page 143, Lesson 2, Exercise B
Bita telephones Consuela to ask about how to get a driver's license. Listen to the conversation and write answers (in your own words) to each of Bita's questions.
Bita: Is this Consuela?
Consuela: Yes. Who's this?
Bita: This is Bita from Bellingham, Washington.
Consuela: Hi! How are you doing?
Bita: I'm OK. A little busy with work and school but I'm surviving. Hey, I was wondering if you could help me with something.
Consuela: Of course, what do you need?
Bita: Well, I think it's time for me to get a driver's license. Public transportation is taking up too much of my time and I need to be able to get around faster. I've been saving up to buy a car but I still have to get my license. And I remember the other day that you said you had gotten your license and registered your car, so I thought maybe you could give me some advice.
Consuela: Sure I can.
Bita: Well, I already have my driver's license from Iran. Do I still have to take the test?
Consuela: Yes, you'll have to take the written test and the driving test. Only people from other states in the United States can get the driving test waived.
Bita: OK, so I how do I prepare for the written test?
Consuela: First, you need to go to the DMV and get a Driver's Handbook to study the rules of the road for the written test.
Bita: How many questions are on the test?
Consuela: In California, the written test has 36 questions. In Washington, it may be different.
Bita: How many questions do I have to get correct? And what if I don' t pass it the first time?
Consuela: You can miss five. But you have three chances to pass the test, so if you don't pass the first time you can take it two more times.
Bita: OK. What about the driving test?
Consuela: First, you need to make an appointment. They won't let you test without one. Second, a licensed driver must accompany you to the DMV in the car that you'll use to take the test.
Bita: And then they test me on my driving skills?
Consuela: Yep.
Bita: That should be easy. I've been practicing with my brother for over a year. So how do I apply for the license?
Consuela: First, you have to get an application and fill it out. Then you have to take the application to the DMV.
Bita: OK, so what do I have to do next?
Consuela: Well, you have to take the written test, take a vision exam, show them proof of your social security number and your date of birth, give them your thumbprint, and have your picture taken.
Bita: How much does that cost?
Consuela: $12.
Bita: OK, I think I can do this,
Consuela: I know you can. Good luck! Call me and let me know how it goes.
Bita: I sure will. Thanks a lot, Consuela!
Consuela: Any time.

Track 33, Unit 8 Lesson 7 "What's your platform?"
Page 154, Lesson 7, Exercise A
Listen to the speeches from three people running for mayor of your city. For the first speech, put a check next to everything the candidate promises to do for you. For the second two speeches, write down what they promise to do for you. You will hear each speech two times.

Antonio Juliana: First of all, I want to thank you all for coming today. It is my pleasure to speak to you and I hope that you will vote for me come Election Day. I'll be brief and to the point. My biggest concern is our streets. There is too much gang violence and I want to wipe it out. I think we can start by getting our children off the streets and taking care of the homeless people. It's time for us to regain our streets and feel safe again. Once this happens, we can focus on other problems, like overcrowded schools and our public transportation system. I know you have a tough decision to make but I hope that when you go to the polls next Tuesday, you'll put a check next to my name, Antonio Juliana.
(This speech repeats.)

Gary Hurt: I have been waiting for this day. A day when I could appear before you and tell you what I'm going to do if elected. These are not empty promises but things that WILL HAPPEN if you elect Gary Hurt as your mayor. The environment will be my number one priority. Our beaches will be clean again. Our public transportation system will be so good that you won't want to drive your cars any more. I will use your tax dollars to create more parks and safe places for our children to play. Our city will be great once again if you vote for Gary Hurt!
(This speech repeats.)

Kwan Tan: Good evening and thank you for coming tonight! This community has given me so many opportunities and, in running for mayor, I hope to give something back to the city that welcomed me as an immigrant, educated me through my teen years, and supported me as I opened my first business.

First on my agenda is education. I will make sure your tax dollars are used to build more schools, so our children won't have to sit in overcrowded classrooms. I'll lower the tuition at our community colleges, so all of us will have a chance to continue our education. I'll implement standards to ensure that schools are teaching our kids what they need to know. I'll start a parent-teacher program that encourages parents to participate actively in their kids' schools. Our children are the future of our community and we should invest time and money in their success.

Vote for me on Election Day and you'll have schools and a community to be proud of!
(This speech repeats.)

Track 34, Page 160 Unit 8 Pronunciation
Intonation. We use a falling-rising intonation when information is less important, and a falling intonation when it is more important. Listen to each sentence below and mark the intonation of each clause with an arrow. Add your own example for number 4.
1. I don't believe in the death penalty, but I think violent criminals should be punished.
2. If more training were available, there wouldn't be so many unemployed people.
3. If people don't vote, they shouldn't complain about who gets elected.

(This is the end of Unit 8.)

Example summary of article *The Common Cold*, Unit 5, Lesson 7, page 95

The article *The Common Cold*, published by The National Institute of Allergy and Infectious Diseases (NIAID) in 1996, describes the causes, symptoms, prevention, and treatment of the common cold. The author states that colds are one of the most common illnesses in children and adults. The symptoms include difficulty in breathing, sneezing, sore throat, cough, and headache. Colds are spread by viruses that are present on things we touch and in the air we breathe. The article emphasizes that washing our hands and not touching our noses and mouths are two of the best ways to prevent catching a cold. The author points out that if we do get a cold, the only way to treat it is by relieving the symptoms: sleep, drinking lots of water, gargling with salt water, and taking aspirin for the headaches. Claims that vitamin C can help prevent colds have not been proven.

Stand Out 4 Skills Index

COMPUTERS

Computers can be used in many real-life, task-based ways. We can use this tool to enhance instruction in the context of the lesson. The instructor will find it more workable if he or she presents one computer application along with a related task so students have an opportunity to practice a little at a time. There are various applications that can be used in the classroom:

1. **Word processing** allows students to write paragraphs. They will have a finished product that can include pictures. The spell check feature can be on or off. If it is on, students become more aware of their errors and how they can fix them. Word processing also allows students to make brochures and other interesting products.

2. **Graphs** can be designed in a variety of ways, using spreadsheet programs and chart wizards. Students must understand the information in more detail to be able to develop such graphs—therefore, they receive additional practice in the concepts.

3. **Spreadsheets** allow students to sort and classify information. Spreadsheet templates can be designed by the teacher or the student to display information and calculate formulas.

4. The **Internet** allows students to obtain more information, opening discussion and applying many activities from the lessons to real-life situations.

5. **E-mail** can be used to open up pen pal opportunities, communicate with classmates, get to know other classrooms, and discuss progress and assignments with the teacher.

Suggestions for Using Computers:

- Let students have control of the keyboard. If you need to model the steps by using the student's keyboard, put the computer back where it was before modeling so the student can try the technique or assignment him- or herself.

- Have students work in pairs or small groups. Even when typing a composition, work is enhanced when students work with a partner.

- Allow students the freedom to make mistakes. This is how we learn best.

- Allow students to work at different paces.

- Help students learn to solve their own problems and to assist each other.

COOPERATIVE LEARNING

The purpose of cooperative learning is to create community in the classroom, allow students freedom to speak in smaller settings, provide forums for discussions, accomplish tasks that individuals cannot do alone, provide SCANS and EFF practice, and enhance instruction in a variety of ways.

Cooperative Learning Activities:

- **Corners activities** allow students to learn more about each other by self-classifying into various groups. A corners activity asks students to go to designated places in a room (often corners). Each location represents a certain characteristic or opinion. A discussion among the group members and/or between different groups usually follows.

- **Information gap activities** allow students to practice speaking and listening to each other, clarifying what they don't understand. An information gap activity requires a student to get missing information from another student to complete a task.

- **Jigsaw activities** allow students to become experts in one part of a given topic or task and share their expertise with other members of their group.

Cooperative Learning Suggestions:

1. Groups should be a manageable number, from three to five students.

2. Each member of the group should have a responsibility. Traditional responsibilities include Leader, Secretary, Time Keeper, and Spokesperson. In **Stand Out** team project activities, students choose responsibilities specific to the tasks.

3. Groups should have a task or a product that is recorded and reported.

4. Students should be encouraged to speak English. Some ways to do that are:

- Have a leader whose task it is to make sure everyone speaks English and participates.

- Check with the groups regularly and have them self-assess and report to the class how much English they are speaking.

- Explain the task completely and make sure the students have the experience and knowledge to do it.

- Speak English yourself.

- Encourage; don't reprimand.

- Encourage more fluent students to work with less fluent ones or form groups by student level, so you can support students who need further review and explanation.

DIALOGS

The purpose of dialogs is to help students practice real life conversations. In *Stand Out,* students are given many opportunities to substitute information. To help students prepare for this practice, it is important to present the dialog in a clear manner. It is also important to find different ways for students to practice the dialogs to add variety to their experience.

Dialog Presentation:

1. Present the dialog in context in its entirety by allowing the students to hear the model, either from the recording or read aloud by you.

2. Have the students repeat each line as a class. Work on rhythm and other pronunciation features.

3. Have students take A's role while you take B. Then reverse roles.

4. Ask one student to practice the dialog with you and reverse roles with another student.

5. Ask two students to demonstrate together. Repeat the above steps with word or information substitutions.

Types of Dialog Practice:

- Practice in pairs.

- Have all the students stand and speak to a given number of students.

- Pass out note cards labeled with different substitutions. Ask the students to discover what is on other students' cards by performing the dialog and looking for matches with what is on their personal card.

- Ask students to provide personal information for substitutions.

- Have students perform a task (e.g. mime an action) as they practice the dialog.

- Ask half the class to form a circle facing outward. Ask the other half of the class to form a circle outside of the first, facing inward. Individuals from each circle pair up and perform the dialog. Next have one circle rotate and have the students perform the dialog with a new partner. **Note:** This activity is a good icebreaker in the first weeks of class and can be used for introductions. Limit introductory conversation or small talk to one minute.

DICTATION

The purpose of dictation is to help students improve their listening skills. You can dictate single words, sentences, or an entire paragraph to students. The idea is to get students to understand what you've said before they write it down.

Dictation Suggestions:

- Tell students that the most important part of dictation is to LISTEN FIRST.

- Tell students that you will only be reading the statements or words one time. (You may have to dictate more than once for lower levels.) This will encourage them to listen more carefully.

- Tell students to listen to the whole sentence before they begin writing. Remind them that if they start writing before you've finished speaking, they won't hear the end of what you say.

- Once you've finished dictating, have students check their answers with a partner or group. Encourage them to write down what they missed or fix what they think they got wrong.

- Read the dictation one more time.

- Call on volunteer students to write the dictation on the board.

- Ask the class to check and help correct what's on the board.

FOCUSED LISTENING

The purpose of focused listening is to expose students to real-life listening situations and teach them how to pick out the important information. These activities help students develop strategies they need to be successful listeners outside of the classroom. Focused listening is always accompanied by a specific task.

1. Make it clear to students that they don't need to understand everything spoken to grasp the meaning.

2. Present the context.

3. Make sure the students understand what they are listening for.

4. Help them understand that the recordings are at an authentic pace to help prepare them for real-life experiences.

5. Start with a few examples and allow students to be successful before you expect them to complete the listening in bigger chunks. Evaluate what they are learning before you move to more extensive tasks.

6. After they complete the task, ask for a report.

VOCABULARY

- **PAVE**

The PAVE vocabulary method is a unique way of making vocabulary cards that help students predict the word's meaning, verify their prediction, evaluate, and then create an associative link to help students remember the word.

Prediction	Write the original context in which the word appears. Write the word again, this time predicting its part of speech and definition.
Verification	Check the part of speech and meaning in the dictionary. Write the definition from the dictionary. Also write the sample sentence if there is one.
Evaluation	Look at the sentence written in Verification and write an original or better one if necessary.
Association	Draw an image to help remember the meaning of the word.

PAVE Presentation Suggestions:

- If possible, put up a transparency of a sample vocabulary card using the PAVE method.

- Give the class a new word and have them create a card as a class, using a template on an overhead projector or following one drawn on the board.

- Divide students into small groups and give each group a word to create a card for. Have each group present their word to the class.

- Have students create their own cards with words that are new to them.

- Schedule time each week for vocabulary review or practice.

TEAM PROJECTS

In team projects, students apply all of the objectives they learned in the unit. A project contains task-based activities that generate teamwork through work on one or more products.

Suggestions for Team Projects:

- Set the stage
  -Give an overview.
  -Show examples.
  -Don't be too specific about results.

- Form teams
  -Mix language groups and students of varying ability.

- Assign team positions (all team members are expected to assist with every task)
  Lower levels:
  -Explain leader position.
  -Immediately ask all leaders to stand for recognition.
  -Initially assign roles if class is uncertain how to proceed.
  -Repeat introductions and recognition for all positions.

  Higher levels:
  -Explain all positions.
  -Allow students to discuss and assign positions in their teams.
  -Ask teams to report names and positions.

- Go through the steps
  - Give a few steps at a time.
  - Avoid allowing teams to get too far ahead.
  - Have students keep minutes in an agenda/minutes format.
  - For two-day team projects: Collect work at end of first day with names of team members to be re-distributed on the following day. Ask teams to include names and job positions on their work.

- Work on the project
  - Have assigned students lead efforts.
  - Make sure all students participate in each task.
  - Use computers when possible.
  - Be flexible and adapt when time runs short.

- Facilitate
  - Walk from team to team, listening.
  - Ask questions.
  - Help the leader to make sure everyone is participating.

- Classroom management tips
  - Encourage English use.
  - Have contingency plans for faster teams.
  - Prepare teams for their presentations.
  - Post all or some of the projects in the classroom.

EVALUATION

The purpose of evaluation is twofold: to confirm that your students have mastered the objectives for a given lesson and to evaluate the effectiveness of your own teaching.

Methods of Evaluation:

- Tests or quizzes

  - Original

  - Quizzes created with the *Stand Out ExamView® Pro Test Bank CD-ROM.*

- Written exercises

  - Peer evaluation:
  Ask students to review each others' written work for ease of comprehension. Do not request that students review each others'

spelling, punctuation, or grammar as this is best left to the teacher.

  - Portfolio:
  Have students maintain a portfolio of their writing assignments. This folder should include copies of the written assignments from team projects as well as individual work.

- Observation

  - Dialog Demonstration:
  See Teaching Hints on Dialog Presentation.

  - Fingers: This approach to evaluation allows students to respond nonverbally as a class to questions when there are a set number of responses. The advantage to this approach is that the instructor can better identify which students understand a concept or idea. For example, an instructor may give the students a series of pictures labeled 1 through 5 and make a series of statements about one picture, without naming its number. Students identify which picture is being talked about by holding up the corresponding number of fingers.

  - Oral Reponses: You can either ask for volunteers to respond, or throw a soft ball or wadded piece of paper randomly to students and have them toss it to each other for questions and answers.

  - Cards: Students are given note cards on which to anonymously write information that will be evaluated later as a class. The teacher may use this activity to ask questions about specific activities students recently attempted or approaches the teacher is using. For example, the teacher can ask students how they feel about a previous activity, choosing from three choices: *I learned a lot from* the past activity, *I learned a little from* the past activity, *and I didn't learn anything from* the past activity. Students write their response on the card. Then have one student collect the cards and, as a class, review the responses. Encourage the students to be honest by telling them that you want to be a better instructor and that their responses will help you.

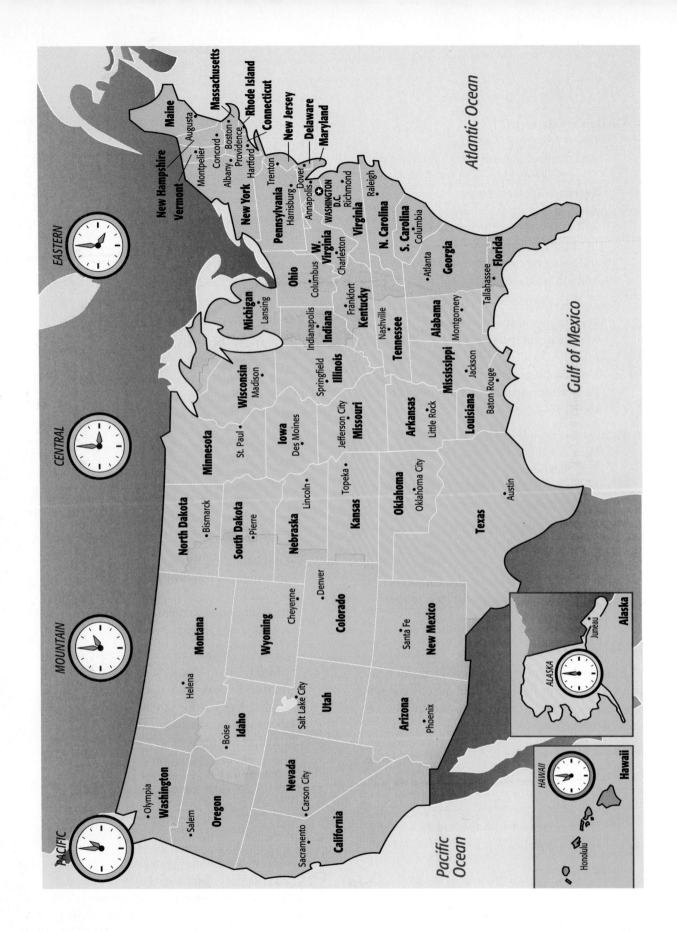